SPOKEN IRAQI ARABIC

by Merrill Y. Van Wagoner, Ph.D.

Originally prepared for publication by
THE UNITED STATES ARMED FORCES INSTITUTE

1866

HENRY HOLT AND COMPANY

This material was prepared under the direction of the Linguistic Society of America and the Intensive Language Program of the American Council of Learned Societies.

GENERAL FOREWORD

This is one of a series of self-teaching textbooks in more than thirty languages initially prepared and published for the Armed Forces and now offered to the general public. Like every other book in the series, it is a product of team-work between numerous collaborators. The authors of the various books have conformed throughout to the patterns developed by the experience of the group.

A brief review of the origin and growth of the program to produce these texts will not only be of general interest in itself but will also provide some indications of the manner in which they may be most efficiently used as well as some of the limitations of their employment.

Early in 1942, within a month of Pearl Harbor, the Joint Army and Navy Committee on Welfare and Recreation began consideration of the means whereby large numbers of troops might be instructed in the colloquial forms of the numerous languages spoken in the areas in which they were likely to be employed. A survey of materials already available for such instruction confirmed their suspected inadequacy. Many of the pertinent languages had never been taught in the United States; few of them had ever been studied or described by competent linguists. Only the unusual textbook was designed to teach the spoken forms to linguistically untrained students, and even when a book was available, it was, as often as not, written in French, German, or Dutch, or for some other reason not susceptible of general use. Consequently, the first necessity was a program of basic implementation which would provide materials, as nearly uniform throughout the various idioms as practicable, for elementary teaching of spoken language to Americans without special linguistic training or, indeed, aptitude. The form of the materials had to be such that they could be used for self-instruction in situations where no competent teachers were available.

There had been little study of most of these languages in America. But the Army and Navy fortunately did not have to start completely from scratch, for several months previously the American Council of Learned Societies had organized its Intensive Language Program for the purpose of developing teachers, teaching materials, and instruction in all languages not normally taught in the United States, yet likely to be necessary in the war effort. Most of the competent technical linguists in the country were gradually absorbed into this Intensive Language Program through their membership in the Linguistic Society of America, that constituent of the Council most concerned with this subject-matter. The Joint Army-Navy Committee drew the Intensive Language Program into its deliberations and planned a development of language instruction for the Armed Forces. Responsibility for the prosecution of this development was entrusted to the Education Branch of the Information and Education Division, A.S.F., functioning through its subsidiaries, the Language Section and the Editorial Staff of the United States Armed Forces Institute. These in turn called upon the Intensive Language Program of the Council for cooperation in the production of materials, a cooperation which became so intimate that it was impossible to tell what proportion of any single operation is the responsibility of each.

The series of more than thirty language textbooks is one result of this cooperative effort. Each textbook is designed to provide materials for approximately the first two hundred hours of language study. It is divided into thirty learning units, the first twelve of which are accompanied by twenty-four double faced recordings of the foreign language material contained in them. Mastery of the thirty units will give the student not only a sufficient general vocabulary to perform all the language operations necessary for everyday life but enough skill in the manipulation of this vocabulary to provide adequate control of it. It is with respect to this latter — manipulation of the elements known — that most language instruction is weak. While the primary emphasis is upon the spoken tongue, the student should have begun reading well before the conclusion of the thirtieth unit, normally probably at about the twelfth, excepting in those cases where the spoken and the written forms are widely divergent.

The group responsible for the creation of this series believes that ideally one learns a foreign language most efficiently when taught intensively by a bi-lingual trained technical linguist while resident in the country to which the language is native. Since this happy state of affairs hardly ever exists, in practice recourse must be had to various successive approximations to it, approximations in which one or more of the desirable elements is attenuated or entirely wanting. This present series — text and records — is designed to be useful at the very lowest level of language learning, that is to say to the single student working by himself. In this case, the text takes the place of the trained linguist, and the records double for the native-speaker. Naturally, better results are obtained when, either in individual or classroom work, a native-speaker is available and utilized as the texts direct. Here the text takes the place of the trained linguist; the records are still very valuable but not absolutely essential. These latter are the conditions under which the series has most commonly been successfully used. So on for successive approximations to the ideal, and even when this is reached, the selected materials and pedagogic devices provided by these texts will be useful.

Prosecution of the war created the need for these materials to teach spoken language. Perhaps it is not to be assumed that under peacetime conditions the demand for speaking, as against reading or writing, competence will be of the same order. Fortunately the several competences are not incompatible; indeed, a very substantial body of proof exists that the acquisition of spoken competence in a foreign language is the most efficient first step towards the others. In addition there seems reason to believe that the second-half of the twentieth century will see much increased concern for instruction in speaking foreign languages, not only as the road to reading them but because the acquisition and the possession of colloquial control of a language not one's own is a humanistic educational experience in its own right not requiring justification by other criteria, because properly taught it is the most easily acquired of the several competences, because the multitude of foreign language broadcasts will dispose of the alleged uselessness of teaching spoken language to students who will never visit the countries in question, and because many more Americans than ever before will exercise their trades and professions abroad.

The cooperative nature of this enterprise can hardly be overemphasized; not only has practically every listed author cooperated in the production of elements of the series other than his own, but also many of the most valued collaborators do not appear as authors at all. Linguistic scientists provided the descriptive analyses of the several languages; professional language teachers furnished pedagogical devices; specialists in education assisted in ordering the materials in accordance with the best principles of learning; printers, editors, and textbook designers contributed their specialized competences; technicians in the recording of sound made possible success in the exceedingly exacting operation of keying the records to the printed texts. Under such conditions it would seem almost invidious to cite the names of those collaborators, in addition to authors, whose contributions are more readily identifiable than those of others. Yet for the sake of the record, perhaps this should be done. The Intensive Language Program of the American Council of Learned Societies, without which this series would not have been possible or would have been of completely different character, owes its existence to Mortimer Graves, Administrative Secretary of the Council. Colonel Francis T. Spaulding, Chief of the Education Branch above referred to, saw the implications of teaching language to American troops and assumed the responsibility for developing a program to this end. The detailed planning and construction of the series now presented owes more to Dr. Henry Lee Smith, Jr., (then Major and Chief of the Language Section in the Education Branch) than to anyone else. Constant liaison with the Intensive Language Program was maintained through J. Milton Cowan, its director during the preparation of the series. William E. Spaulding directed the Editorial Staff of the United States Armed Forces Institute. The dean of American linguistic scientists, Leonard Bloomfield of Yale University, gave unstintingly in many ways — ways as difficult to appreciate too highly as they are to describe succinctly. Almost the same may be said of Lt. Morris Swadesh, Lt. Charles Hockett, Robert A. Hall, Jr., Norman A. McQuown, Doris Goss, José Padín, and others who served from time to time on a special advisory and editorial board.

The series is offered in the hope that it may modestly conduce to the improvement of teaching the speaking of foreign languages to Americans. The authors make no claim to perfection, indeed they are rather appalled at the task which they set themselves, and their pride in completing it under the existent conditions is tinctured with humility at the thought of the imperfections which must sooner or later come to light. But through the discovery of these imperfections will come progress, and nobody will be more greatly pleased than the collaborators on this enterprise if, a decade from now, the teaching of spoken foreign languages in America shall have reached such a developed stage that their first efforts will seem obsolete.

AUTHOR'S PREFACE

This book has been written to help you learn *spoken Iraqi Arabic*. The whole emphasis is on the kind of Arabic spoken currently by the man-in-the-street, not the type of speech known only to those who have had formal education.

Iraqi Arabic is the colloquial speech of the kingdom of Iraq, which has a population of nearly 6 million people. The dialect presented in this course is that of Baghdad, the capital city. It will be understood throughout Iraq.

The Arabic Language today is spoken by more than 25 million people. Beginning in the 7th century A.D., it was spread by conquest from Arabia westward to North Africa (and even into Spain), northward to present-day Turkey, and eastward as far as India. It spread even farther as a language of commerce. And the Arabic alphabet was borrowed by several other language areas (Persian, Turkish and Malay, for example) and adapted to their needs.

This book was begun in 1943 as one of more than 30 *spoken* language courses prepared for the U. S. Armed Forces. The rapidly changing course of events, however, made it unnecessary to publish it immediately. The wartime situation remains reflected in the contents, hence the principle characters are two American soldiers in Baghdad.

The desired end in such a course is development of a "feel" for the language. To this end, grammatical presentation has been kept on a simple, direct and informal level. The result may appear oversimplification, but this is a deliberate part of the method.

Previous work in the field is meager, only that of John Van Ess having didactic value. My preliminary work in spoken Iraqi was with Mr. Nouri Khangar el-Menahi. The present text, however, represents the dialect of Mr. Abdul Rahman Taha el-Salman, to whom special thanks are due. Mr. Noury Michael Mansy aided with the final work.

The language content alone is original; the underlying theory and form of the course were developed by the group mentioned in the General Foreword.

M. Y. V. W.

New York City, 1948

CONTENTS

PART ONE

PART TWO

PART THREE

ADDITIONAL AIDS

UNIT 1

Getting Around

BASIC SENTENCES

Beginning RECORD 1A

ENGLISH EQUIVALENTS	AIDS TO LISTENING	ARABIC SPELLING
peace	sa'laam	سلام
upon you	9a'laykum	عليكم
Greetings to you.	sa'laam 9a'laykum.	سلام عليكم ٠
the peace	issa'laam	السلام
And to you greetings.	wu9a'laykum issa'laam.	وعليكم السلام ٠
How are you?	'šloonak? *or* 'šloon 'kayfak?	شلونك ؟ (ايضا) شلون كيفك ؟
good, well	'zayn	زين
I thank you	'ʔaškurak	اشكرك
Well, thanks.	'zayn, 'ʔaškurak.	زين ، اشكرك ٠
you	'ʔinta *or* 'ʔanta*	انت
and you	wu'ʔinta	وانت
And how are you?	'winta 'šloonak?	وانت ، شلونك ؟
I	'ʔana *or* 'ʔaanii	انا (ايضا) آني
also, too	'hamm	هم
praise be to God	'ḥamdillaa	الحمد لله
I'm well too, praise God.	'ʔana 'hamm 'zayn, 'ḥamdillaa.	انا هم زين ، الحمد لله ٠
Not well.	'muu 'zayn.	مو زين ٠
you speak	'tiḥčii *or* 'tiḥkii	تحكي
Arabic	'9arabii	عربي
Do you speak Arabic?	'ʔinta 'tiḥčii '9arabii?	انت تحكي عربي ؟
only	'bass	بس
a little, some	'šwayya	شويه
Only a little.	'bass 'šwayya.	بس شويه ٠

* Not on record.

ENGLISH EQUIVALENTS	AIDS TO LISTENING	ARABIC SPELLING
Do you understand me?	tifti'himnii?	تفهمني ؟
Yes.	'na9am. *or* 'balii. *or* '?ii.	نعم • (ايضا) بلي • (ايضا) اي •
I understand you.	'?ana '?afhamak.	انا افهمك •
No.	'laa.	لا •
not	'maa	ما
I understand	'?afham	افهم
I don't understand.	'maa '?afham.	ما افهم •
please	?ar'juuk	ارجوك
speak!	'?iḥkii *or* '?iḥčii	احكي
slowly, gently	ya'waaš	يواش
Please speak slowly.	?ar'juuk '?iḥčii ya'waaš.	ارجوك احكي يواش •
what	'šinuu	شنو
this (masculine)	'haaδa	هذا
this (feminine)	'haaδii *and* 'haay	هذي (ايضا) هاي
What ['s] this?	'šinuu 'haaδii?	شنو هذي ؟

Beginning RECORD 1B

ENGLISH EQUIVALENTS	AIDS TO LISTENING	ARABIC SPELLING
cigarette	ji'gaara	جكارة
This [is] a cigarette.	'haaδii ji'gaara.	هذي جكارة •
these (plural)	haa'δool *or* haa'δoolii	هاذول (ايضا) هاذولي
What [are] these?	'šinuu haa'δoolii?	شنو هاذولي ؟
cigarettes	ji'gaayir	جكاير
These [are] cigarettes.	haa'δool ji'gaayir.	هاذول جكاير •
you want	'triid	تريد
Do you want a cigarette?	'triid ji'gaara?	تريد جكارة ؟
[I'm much] obliged.	mam'nuun.	ممنون •
with you, you have	'9indak *or* '9iddak	عندك
match	ši'xaaṭa	شخاطة
Do you have a match?	'9indak ši'xaaṭa?	عندك شخاطة ؟
tell to me!	'gullii	قل لي
where	'wayn	وين
there is *or* there are	'?akuu	اكو
hotel	?uu'tayl	اوتيل
Tell me, where's there a hotel?	'gullii, 'wayn '?akuu ?uu'tayl?	قل لي ، وين اكو اوتيل ؟
restaurant	'maṭ9am	مطعم
coffee shop	'gahwa	قهوة
Where's the railroad station?	'wayn ilma'ḥaṭṭa?	وين المحطة ؟

ENGLISH EQUIVALENTS	AIDS TO LISTENING		ARABIC SPELLING
the movie	is'siinama		السينما
the toilet(s)	ilmaraa'ḥiiḍ	*elmaarḥaaḍ*	المراحيض
Here.	hi'naa.* or hi'naaya.	*huna honɛ*	هنا • (ايضا) هنايه •
There.	hi'naak.		هناك •
on or upon	'9ala		على
your right	ya'miinak		يمينك
On your right.	'9ala ya'miinak.		على يمينك •
your† left	ya'saarak		يسارك
On your left.	'9ala ya'saarak.		على يسارك •
Ahead of you.	gid'daamak.	*a'amaamak*	قدّامك •
Straight ahead.	'gubaḷ.	*(Bedum)*	قبل •
walk!	'?imšii		امشي
Walk straight ahead.	'?imšii 'gubaḷ.		امشي قبل •
Show me!	raa'wiinii.		راويني •
See!	'šuuf.	*ašuuf*	شوف •
the postoffice	il'booṣṭa	*il barud*	البوسطة
(particle for introducing a question)	'hal		هل
Is this the postoffice?	'hal 'haaδii l'booṣṭa?	*haaḍa lbarud*	هل هذي البوسطة ؟
Good evening.	ma'saaʔ il'xayr.		مساء الخير •

Beginning RECORD 2A

What do you want?	'šitriid?		شتريد ؟
I want	?a'riid		اريد
I eat	'?aakul		آكل
I want to eat.	?a'riid '?aakul.		اريد آكل •
food	'?akil		اكل
I want food.	?a'riid '?akil.		اريد اكل •
rice	'timman	*raz*	تمّن
bread	'xubuz		خبز
meat or fish	'laḥam '?aw 'simač	*šimak*	لحم او سمك
I don't want	'maa 'riid		ما اريد
I don't want potatoes.	'maa 'riid puu'tayta.		ما اريد بتيتة •
you drink	'tišrab		تشرب
What do you want to drink?	'šitriid 'tišrab?		شتريد تشرب ؟

* The first pronunciation on the record 'huna is classical, the second pronunciation hi'naa is colloquial.
† Not on record.

ENGLISH EQUIVALENTS	AIDS TO LISTENING	ARABIC SPELLING
what is there	'šakuu	شكو
What do you have?	'šakuu '9indak?	شكو عندك ؟
There's tea, milk, and beer.	'ʔakuu 'čaay, ḥa'liib, wu'biira.	اكو شاي ، حليب ، وبيرا ٠
[I'm] sorry.	mit'ʔassif. *or* 'ma9a l'ʔasaf.	متأسف ٠ (ايضا) مع الاسف ٠
there isn't *or* there aren't	'maakuu	ماكو
with us, we have	'9idna	عندنا
coffee	'gahwa	قهوة
We haven't [any] coffee.	'maakuu '9idna 'gahwa.	ماكو عندنا قهوة ٠
bring to me!	'jiiblii	جيب لي
water	'maay	ماء
Bring me a glass of water!	'jiiblii 'glaaṣ-'maay.	جيب لي كلاص ماء ٠
how much	'bayš	بيش
package of cigarettes	paa'kayt-ji'gaayir	باكيت جكاير
I want a package of cigarettes.	ʔa'riid paa'kayt-ji'gaayir.	اريد باكيت جكاير ٠
How much [are] these?	'bayš haa'ðool?	بيش هاذول ؟
two	θi'nayn	ثنين
in; for	'bii*	بي
a hundred fils†	'miit-'fils	مية فلس
Two for a hundred fils.	θi'nayn 'bii 'miit-'fils.	ثنين بي مية فلس ٠
Goodbye.	fiimaani'laa. *or* 'ma9a ssa'laama.	في امان الله ٠ (ايضا) مع السلامة ٠

Numbers

one	'waaḥid	١ واحد
two	θi'nayn	٢ ثنين
three	θi'laaθa	٣ ثلاثة
four	'ʔarba9a	٤ اربعة
five	'xamsa	٥ خمسة
six	'sitta	٦ ستة
seven	'sab9a	٧ سبعة
eight	θi'maanya	٨ ثمانية
nine	'tis9a	٩ تسعة
ten	'9ašra	١٠ عشرة

* On the record, *by* is an error, *bii* is correct.

† About forty cents. Of course, prices and the rate of exchange vary from time to time. All prices and figures given in this book are primarily for practice, and do not necessarily coincide with actual prices.

PRONUNCIATION

Comment On The Aids To Listening

The best way to learn any language is to listen to a native speaker and then imitate exactly what he says. That is why we ask you to listen carefully to your Guide (or the speaker on the records) and imitate him as exactly as you can. It would be ideal if you could remember everything he says simply by listening and repeating. However, most of us need to have something on paper to remind us of what we have heard. This is the purpose of the *Aids To Listening*. They are simply an attempt to put down systematically on paper the sounds that your Guide will probably say, or that you will hear on the records. Remember, however, that they are only *aids* to listening. The listening itself is still the most important thing; the printed material is just a reminder.

In the *Aids To Listening, each letter is used to represent only one sound.* That means that every letter stands for a sound that must be pronounced. This is much simpler than English spelling where we have the *k*-sound spelled differently in *kid, cat* and *chord*, or the *f*-sound in *half, bluff* and *enough*, and so on. Notice that a mark (ʹ) is placed before the part of a word which is spoken the loudest. For example, using this system we would write for English *ʹrecords, reʹcordings, preʹpare, prepaʹrations*, and so on.

In the first Units, the *Aids To Listening* follow the records in every detail. You will most likely hear different pronunciations from your Guide and from other speakers. If your Guide pronounces the words differently, always follow him. If you don't understand the Guide, ask him to *repeat.*

Two or more forms are often written in the *Aids To Listening*, as ʔiḥčii *or* ʔiḥkii. The Guide will probably speak only one or the other, since there is only one spelling in the Arabic from which he is reading. Eventually you will hear the other forms. Where more than one form is given, it is best for you at this stage to adopt one, and always use it rather than hesitate between two possibilities. Note that words which do not appear on the record are followed by an asterisk (*as* your* left).

Each sound and the symbol used to represent it will be given special attention in the *Pronunciation* sections in Units 1 to 10. New words are marked with an asterisk, as dukʹkaana **his shop.* You are not expected to learn these words until they are introduced in *Basic Sentences.*

For ready reference, at the back of the book you will find the *symbols* collected together in the *Key To Aids To Listening* (Page **iii**) and the *sounds* arranged in the *Index To Pronunciation Practices* (Page **v**).

The Arabic spelling given in the third column should *not* be studied at this time. It is almost a complete waste of time to try to learn the written language until *after* you have a fair grasp of the spoken language. Then it is a comparatively simple matter to learn to read. The Arabic spelling is given (1) primarily for the Guide, and (2) secondarily for your benefit after you have acquired the spoken forms. Do not concern yourself with the written Arabic until you have completed the first Units at least. Then you can consult the section READING ARABIC at the back of the book (Page **vi**).

Hints On Pronunciation

The pronunciation of Iraqi is a fifty-fifty proposition. About half of the sounds are similar to English sounds, and about half involve something new. However, it is good to know that there are few if any sounds in Iraqi that you haven't all made at some time or other, from clearing your throat to visiting the dentist. The difference is that the people of Iraq use these sounds all the time in speaking. None of these sounds is so hard that you won't be able to make and control it after earnest practice.

It is important for you to speak so well that they will pay attention only to the things you are telling them and not to the way you talk. You can learn to make the sounds correctly by imitating your Guide carefully and by studying the sections on *Pronunciation*, which will tell you what to listen for and give you pointers on how to improve your imitation of the Iraqi sounds.

The written form of the words given in the *Aids To Listening* serves as an aid by 'showing' what to listen for. It also helps you recall the pronunciation as you heard it from your Guide. The sounds can be explained to you in a general way, but you will have to listen to your Guide, or the records, carefully and imitate carefully to get them just right. Remember to imitate your Guide always, even when he says something different from the way it is written here or the way it is on the records.

Beginning RECORD 2B

PRACTICE 1

The vowel-sounds which are written with one letter are very short, that is, it takes little time to say them. On the other hand, you should hold the sounds that are written with two letters about twice as long. One of the reasons they are written double is to remind you of this.

’ʔilii	**to me, for me*	الي
’jiiblii	**bring me!*	جيب لي
’ʔuxut	**sister*	اخت
’šuuf	*see!*	شوف
’šakuu	*what is there?*	شكو
’maakuu	*there isn't*	ماكو
’ʔakil	*food*	اكل
’ʔaakul	*I eat*	آكل
’ʔana	*I*	انا
’ʔaanii	*I*	آني

PRACTICE 2

Each consonant-letter stands for a single sound, therefore you must pronounce just one consonant where one is written, but two where two are written.

’simač	*fish*	سمك
’timman	*rice*	تمّن
’ʔana	*I*	انا
’minnii	**from me*	منّي
’balii	*yes*	بلي
’gullii	*tell me!*	قل لي
’ʔila	**to; for*	الى
’ʔilla	**except*	الاّ

'šita	*winter	شتاء
'sitta	six	ستة
duk'kaana	*his shop	دكانه
duk'kaanna	*our shop	دكاننا

PRACTICE 3

ʔ: The sign ʔ stands for a sound often made in English, but not written. It is similar to a slight cough. It is heard in English as a break between two vowel sounds, as in *oh-oh*. We say it also before words beginning with vowels, especially when we are excited. Linguists call it a *glottal stop*.

'ʔana	I	انا
'ʔimšii	walk!	امشي
'ʔisʔal	*ask!	اسأل
mit'ʔassif	sorry	متأسف
ra'ʔiis	*chief, head	رئيس
'siʔala	*he asked him	سأله
ma'saaʔ il'xayr	Good evening.	مساء الخير
'muʔmin	*faithful	مؤمن
'tisʔala	*you ask him	تسأله
wuza'raaʔ	*ministers	وزراء

ANALYSIS

In the sections entitled ANALYSIS you are given more information concerning the words and sentences you have already learned. This will help you get a better understanding of the things which go to make up Iraqi Arabic. The discussion is simple and direct. Once you understand a principle discussed and are able to apply it yourself, then you can forget the discussion that lead up to it.

1. *And* is expressed by wu– (sometimes also pronounced w– or uu–) before a word. For example:

wu9a'laykum	and upon you	وعليكم
ḥa'liib wu'biira	milk and beer	حليب وبيرا
'xubuz wupuu'tayta	bread and potatoes	خبز وبتيتة

Notice that 'winta *and you* is shortened from wu'ʔinta.

2. Absence of *am, is, are.*

'ʔana 'zayn.	I [am] well.	انا زين .
'šinuu 'haaδa?	What [is] this?	شنو هذا ؟
'šinuu haa'δool?	What [are] these?	شنو هاذول ؟
'wayn is'siinama?	Where [is] the movie?	وين السينما ؟

You see that Iraqi doesn't use words meaning *am, is, are* in sentences such as the above. Later you will learn words for *was, were* and *will be*. The brackets [ ] are used in the Basic Sentences to remind you that the enclosed words are not expressed by separate Iraqi words.

3.

'ʔakuu 'čaay.	*There's tea.*	اكو شاي •
'ʔakuu 'šwayya 'xubuz.	*There's a little bread.*	اكو شوية خبز •
'ʔakuu ji'gaayir.	*There are cigarettes.*	اكو جكاير •
'ʔakuu ʔuu'tayl hi'naak.	*There's a hotel there.*	اكو اوتيل هناك •

The word 'ʔakuu means *there exists, there is, there are.* On the other hand, note that location *there* is expressed by hi'naak. The negative is 'maakuu ('maa 'ʔakuu), which means *there doesn't exist, there isn't, there aren't.*

'maakuu 'gahwa.	*There isn't [any] coffee.*	ماكو قهوة •
'9indak 'čaay? 'maakuu.	*Have you [any] tea? There isn't [any].*	عندك شاي ؟ ـ ماكو •
'maakuu ʔuu'tayl hi'naak.	*There isn't a hotel there.*	ماكو اوتيل هناك •

4.

The words you have learned in this Unit, such as 'ʔinta *you*, ʔaš'kurak *I thank you*, 'šloonak? *How are you?*, ʔar'juuk *please*, gid'daamak *ahead of you*, and so on, are used when you are talking to a man or a boy. We can call them *masculine* forms for that reason. Later you will learn forms for talking to a woman or a girl (*feminine* forms), and to more than one person (*plural* forms).

Note that 'haaδa *this* is used with masculine nouns, while 'haaδii and 'haay *this* are used with feminine nouns. The plural forms haa'δool or haa'δoolii *these* are interchangeable and are used with any plural noun.

5.

You will note that some meanings are attached to several words. For example, 'huna, 'hina, hi'naa and hi'naaya all mean *here.* 'ʔana and 'ʔaanii both mean *I*, but 'ʔaanii is found chiefly in Baghdad. Of course there are often several expressions with about the same meaning, as 'šloonak? and 'šloon 'kayfak? *How are you?*

6. Greetings.

In Iraq the usual greeting when you meet a friend or acquaintance is 'šloonak? or 'šloon 'kayfak? *How are you?*. The reply is either 'zayn, ʔaš'kurak *Well, thanks* or simply 'ḥamdillaa *Praise be to God.*, which implies that you are well and that you thank God for it.

The greeting sa'laam 9a'laykum *Peace be upon you* is more dignified and formal than the greetings above, but it is almost as commonly used. It is used only for men, and always has the same form whether you are talking to one or more than one person. Note that it is the person who enters a room or a house who first says sa'laam 9a'laykum, and then the person who is already there (that is, the host) arises and replies wu9a'laykum issa'laam.

The usual expressions for saying *goodbye* are fiimaani'laa, which means *In the care of God*, and 'ma9a ssa'laama, which means *with a good condition* or *good health to you!*

7. Coffee and Tea.

As to coffee and tea: 'gahwa is what we call Turkish or Arabic coffee. It is dark brown with a thick residue, and is served in a small cup. The regular coffee we know, with cream or milk, is called 'gahwa ʔamriikaa'niiya *American coffee.* Similarly, 'čaay is black tea. If you want cream in it, you order 'čaay ḥa'liib or 'čaay ibḥa'liib.

8. NUMBERS.

The numbers given in this Unit are used only for plain counting, as *one, two, three.* Later you will learn the slightly different forms used in counting things, as *three boys, four boys.*

WHAT WOULD YOU SAY?

1. *You ask someone where the railroad station is.*
   a. 'triid 'gahwa? — ١ ـ تريد قهوة ؟
   b. 'wayn ilma'ḥaṭṭa? — ٢ ـ وين المحطة ؟
   c. tifti'himnii? — ٣ ـ تفتهمني ؟

2. *He answers.*
   a. 'zayn, 'ḥamdillaa. — ١ ـ زين ، الحمد لله •
   b. ʔa'riid 'ʔaakul. — ٢ ـ اريد آكل •
   c. 'ʔimšii 'gubaḷ. — ٣ ـ امشي قبل •

3. *You are not sure what he said.*
   a. ilʔuu'tayl '9ala ya'miinak. — ١ ـ الاوتيل على يمينك •
   b. 'maa ʔa'riid 'simač. — ٢ ـ ما اريد سمك •
   c. 'maa 'ʔafham; ʔar'juuk 'ʔiḥkii ya'waaš. — ٣ ـ ما افهم ، ارجوك احكي يواش •

4. *You thank him and walk on.*
   a. 'maakuu 'gahwa. — ١ ـ ماكو قهوة •
   b. 'ʔaškurak. — ٢ ـ اشكرك •
   c. 'na9am, 'ʔafhamak. — ٣ ـ نعم افهمك •

5. *In a restaurant the waiter asks what you want.*
   a. 'šinuu 'haaδa? — ١ ـ شنو هذا ؟
   b. 'šitriid? — ٢ ـ شتريد ؟
   c. 'bayš haa'δool? — ٣ ـ بيش هاذول ؟

6. *You order.*
   a. 'maa ʔa'riid 'ʔaakul. — ١ ـ ما ريد آكل •
   b. 'jiiblii 'čaay, 'xubuz, wu'laḥam 'ʔaw 'simač. — ٢ ـ جيبلي شاي خبز ولحم اوسمك •
   c. mit'ʔassif, 'maakuu '9idna 'ʔakil. — ٣ ـ متأسف ماكو عندنا اكل •

7. *You eat and then ask how much it is.*
   a. 'bayš 'haaδa? — ١ ـ بيش هذا ؟
   b. 'šloonak? — ٢ ـ شلونك ؟
   c. 'šitriid? — ٣ ـ شتريد ؟

8. *The cost is moderate.*
   a. 'ʔana 'hamm 'zayn, 'ʔaškurak. — ١ ـ انا هم زين اشكرك •
   b. 'na9am, 'ʔakuu 'šwayya 'gahwa. — ٢ ـ نعم ، اكو شوّية قهوة •
   c. 'miit-'filis. — ٣ ـ مية فلس •

9. *A friend greets you.*

a. 'šloonak? — ١ ـ شلونك ؟
b. 'šitriid 'tišrab? — ٢ ـ شتريد تشرب ؟
c. ʔa'riid ji'gaara. — ٣ ـ اريد جكارة •

10. *You are well.*

a. ʔar'juuk 'ʔiḥčii ya'waaš. — ١ ـ ارجوك احكي يواش •
b. il'maṭ9am hi'naak. — ٢ ـ المطعم هناك •
c. 'ḥamdillaa. 'winta 'šloonak? — ٣ ـ الحمد لله ، وانت شلونك ؟

11. *You ask where the movie is.*

a. 'wayn is'siinama? — ١ ـ وين السينما ؟
b. 'wayn ilma'ḥaṭṭa? — ٢ ـ وين المحطة ؟
c. 'wayn ilmaraa'ḥiiḍ? — ٣ ـ وين المراحيض ؟

12. *It is on your left.*

a. gid'daamak. — ١ ـ قدامك •
b. '9ala ya'saarak. — ٢ ـ على يسارك •
c. '9ala ya'miinak. — ٣ ـ على يمينك •

13. *You are uncertain.*

a. il'booṣṭa 'muu hi'naa. — ١ ـ البوسطة مو هنا •
b. ʔar'juuk raa'wiinii. — ٢ ـ ارجوك راويني •
c. '9indak ši'xaaṭa? — ٣ ـ عندك شخاطة ؟

14. *You express your appreciation.*

a. mam'nuun ka'θiir. — ١ ـ ممنون كثير •
b. 'triid ji'gaara? — ٢ ـ تريد جكارة ؟
c. 'maa 'ʔafham. — ٣ ـ ما افهم •

15. *You ask about a hotel.*

a. 'gullii, 'wayn 'ʔakuu ʔuu'tayl? — ١ ـ قل لي وين اكو اوتيل ؟
b. 'hal 'haaδii l'booṣṭa? — ٢ ـ هل هذي بوسطة ؟
c. '9indak ši'xaaṭa? — ٣ ـ عندك شخاطة ؟

16. *It's ahead of you.*

a. 'ʔakuu ʔuu'tayl '9ala ya'miinak. — ١ ـ اكو اوتيل على يمينك •
b. 'maakuu ʔuu'tayl hi'naa. — ٢ ـ ماكو اوتيل هنا •
c. 'ʔimšii 'gubaḷ! — ٣ ـ امشي قبل •

17. *In another restaurant a waiter wants to serve you.*

a. 'ʔinta 'tiḥčii '9arabii? — ١ ـ انت تحكي عربي ؟
b. 'šitriid 'tišrab? — ٢ ـ شتريد تشرب ؟
c. 'bayš haa'δool? — ٣ ـ بيش هاذول ؟

18. *You ask what there is.*

a. 'šakuu '9indak? — ١ ـ شكو عندك ؟
b. '9indak 'čaay? — ٢ ـ عندك شاي ؟
c. '9indak ḥa'liib? — ٣ ـ عندك حليب ؟

19. *You order tea, but there isn't any.*

   a. il'gahwa hi'naaya. — ١ ـ القهوة هناية .
   b. mit'ʔassif, 'maakuu 'čaay. — ٢ ـ متأسف ماكو شاي .
   c. 'maa ʔa'riid 'čaay. — ٣ ـ ما ريد شاي .

20. *Water will do.*

   a. ʔa'riid 'biira. — ١ ـ اريد بيرا .
   b. 'jiiblii ḥa'liib. — ٢ ـ جيبلي حليب .
   c. 'jiiblii 'maay. — ٣ ـ جيبلي ماي .

21. *You meet an acquaintance one evening.*

   a. ma'saaʔ il'xayr. — ١ ـ مساء الخير .
   b. 'triid 'biira? — ٢ ـ تريد بيرا ؟
   c. ʔa'riid 'ʔakil. — ٣ ـ اريد اكل .

22. *He offers you a cigarette.*

   a. '9indak ji'gaara? — ١ ـ عنده جكارة ؟
   b. 'triid ji'gaara? — ٢ ـ تريد جكارة ؟
   c. '9indak si'xaaṭa? — ٣ ـ عندك شخاطة ؟

23. *You say goodbye.*

   a. fiimaani'laa. — ١ ـ في امان الله .
   b. mam'nuun. — ٢ ـ ممنون .
   c. mit'ʔassif. — ٣ ـ متأسف .

LISTENING IN

CONVERSATION ONE

John Carter has just arrived in Baghdad, the capital of Iraq. He strikes up a conversation with Hassan.

Continuing RECORD 2B

JOHN sa'laam 9a'laykum.	جان ـ سلام عليكم .
HASSAN wu9a'laykum issa'laam. 'šloonak?	حسن ـ وعليكم السلام . شلونك ؟
JOHN 'zayn, 'ḥamdillaa. 'winta 'šloon 'kayfak?	جان ـ زين ، الحمد لله . وانت شلون كيفك ؟
HASSAN 'ʔana 'hamm 'zayn, 'ʔaškurak. 'tiḥčii '9arabii?	حسن ـ انا هم زين ، اشكرك . تحكي عربي ؟
JOHN 'šwayya, 'bass 'muu 'zayn.	جان ـ شوية ، بس مو زين .
HASSAN 'laa, 'ʔanta 'tiḥčii '9arabii 'zayn.	حسن ـ لا ، انت تحكي عربي زين .
JOHN 'ʔaškurak. ʔar'juuk 'gullii 'wayn 'ʔakuu ʔuu'tayl?	جان ـ اشكرك . ارجوك قل لي وين اكو اوتيل ؟

HASSAN 'ʔimšii 'gubaḷ.	حسن ـ امشي قبل •
'ʔakuu ʔuu'tayl '9ala ya'miinak.	اكو اوتيل على يمينك •
JOHN ʔar'juuk 'ʔiḥčii ya'waaš.	جان ـ ارجوك احكي يواش •
'maa 'ʔafhamak.	ما افهمك •
HASSAN 'ʔakuu ʔuu'tayl '9ala ya'miinak.	حسن ـ اكو اوتيل على يمينك •
tif'hamnii?	تفهمني ؟
JOHN 'na9am.	جان ـ نعم •
'gullii 'wayn 'ʔakuu 'maṭ9am 'ʔaw 'gahwa?	قل لي وين اكو مطعم او قهوة ؟
ʔa'riid 'ʔaakul.	اريد آكل •
HASSAN 'ʔakuu 'maṭ9am 'hamm '9ala ya'miinak.	حسن ـ اكو مطعم هم على يمينك •
'bass il'gahwa '9ala ya'saarak.	بس القهوة على يسارك •
JOHN 'ʔaškurak.	جان ـ اشكرك •
fiimaani'laa.	في امان الله •
HASSAN 'ma9a ssa'laama.	حسن ـ مع السلامة •

CONVERSATION TWO

John goes into a restaurant. A 'boy' comes up to him. Waiters are called 'boys' in Iraq.

BOY ma'saaʔ il'xayr.	بوي ـ مساء الخير •
JOHN ma'saaʔ il'xayr.	جان ـ مساء الخير •
'šakuu '9indak?	شكو عندك ؟

The waiter gives John a menu written in Arabic. John points to some of the items.

'šinuu 'haaδa?	شنو هذا ؟
BOY 'haaδa 'laḥam.	بوي ـ هذا لحم •
JOHN wu'šinuu 'haaδa?	جان ـ وشنو هذا ؟
BOY 'haaδa 'simač.	بوي ـ هذا سمك •
'triid 'laḥam 'ʔaw 'simač?	تريد لحم او سمك ؟
JOHN ʔa'riid 'simač.	جان ـ اريد سمك •
BOY 'triid 'timman?	بوي ـ تريد تمن ؟
JOHN* 'laa, 'maa 'riid 'timman.	جان ـ لا ، ما اريد تمن •
'ʔakuu '9indak puu'tayta?	اكو عندك بتيتة ؟
BOY 'na9am.	بوي ـ نعم •
JOHN 'zayn 'jiiblii puu'tayta.	جان ـ زين جيب لي بتيتة •
BOY 'šitriid 'tišrab?	بوي ـ شتريد تشرب ؟
JOHN ʔa'riid 'ʔašrab 'gahwa ʔamriikaa'niiya.*	جان ـ اريد اشرب قهوة امريكانية •

Beginning RECORD 3A

BOY mit'ʔassif, 'maakuu '9idna 'gahwa ʔamriikaa'niiya.	بوي ـ متأسف ، ماكو عندنا قهوة امريكانية •

* Not on record.

JOHN	'jiiblii 'čaay ḥa'liib.	جان ـ جيب لي شاي حليب .
BOY	(*In summary.*) 'triid 'simač, puu'tayta, wu'čaay ḥa'liib?	بوي ـ تريد سمك ، بتيتة ، وشاي حليب ؟
JOHN	'balii.	جان ـ بلي .

The waiter goes out and gives the order. Then he brings a small basket with flat pieces of bread and puts it on the table.

JOHN	'boy, 'šinuu haa'ðool?	جان ـ «بوي» ، شنو هاذول ؟
BOY	'xubuz.	بوي ـ خبز .
JOHN	?ar'juuk 'jiiblii 'glaaṣ-'maay.	جان ـ ارجوك جيب لي كلاص ماء .

(*John eats and then asks how much he owes.*)

	'bayš 'haaða?	بيش هذا ؟
BOY	'miit-'filis.	بوي ـ مية فلس .

(*John pays.*)

	'?aškurak.	اشكرك .
JOHN	'?akuu '9indak ji'gaayir wuši'xaaṭ?*	جان ـ اكو عندك جكاير وشخاطة ؟
BOY	mit'?assif, 'maakuu ji'gaayir hi'naa.	بوي ـ متأسف ، ماكو جكاير هنا .
JOHN	?ar'juuk 'gullii 'wayn ilmaraa'ḥiiḍ?	جان ـ ارجوك قل لي وين المراحيض ؟
BOY	'?imšii '9ala ya'saarak.	بوي ـ امشي على يسارك .
JOHN	'?aškurak.	جان ـ اشكرك .
	fiimaani'laa.	في امان الله .
BOY	'ma9a ssa'laama.	بوي ـ مع السلامة .

CONVERSATION THREE

John stops at a cigarette stand and talks to the bay'yaa9 clerk.

JOHN	?a'riid paa'kayt-ji'gaayir.	جان ـ اريد باكيت جكاير .
	'bayš 'haaða?	بيش هذا ؟
CLERK	θi'nayn ib'miit-'filis.	البياع ـ ثنين بمية فلس
JOHN	?a'riid θi'nayn.	جان ـ اريد ثنين
	?ar'juuk raa'wiinii 'wayn is'siinama.	ارجوك راويني وين السينما .
CLERK	'?imšii 'gubaḷ. is'siinama gid'daamak.	البيّاع ـ امشي قبل . السينما قدّامك

CONVERSATION FOUR

John walks on until he comes to a large building. He asks a stranger† about it.

JOHN	sa'laam 9a'laykum.	جان ـ سلام عليكم .
STRANGER	wu9a'laykum issa'laam.	الغريب ـ وعليكم السلام .
JOHN	'hal 'haaðii s'siinama?	جان ـ هل هذي السينما ؟
STRANGER	'laa, 'haay il'boosṭa.	الغريب ـ لا ، هاي البوسطة .
	is'siinama hi'naak, '9ala ya'saarak.	السينما هناك ، على يسارك .
JOHN	'?aškurak.	جان ـ اشكرك .

* *matches.*

† ga'riib.

CONVERSATION FIVE

After the movie, John asks about another restaurant.

JOHN ma'saa? il'xayr.	جان ـ مساء الخير •
STRANGER ma'saa? il'xayr.	الغريب ـ مساء الخير •
JOHN ?a'riid '?aakul.	جان ـ اريد آكل •
'?akuu 'gahwa '?aw 'maṭ9am hi'naa?	اكو قهوة او مطعم هنا ؟
STRANGER 'maakuu 'maṭ9am hi'naaya.	الغريب ـ ماكو مطعم هنايه •
'bass '?akuu 'gahwa '9ala ya'saarak.	بس اكو قهوة على يسارك •
JOHN ?ar'juuk raa'wiinii 'wayn il'gahwa.	جان ـ ارجوك راويني وين القهوة ؟
'triid ji'gaayir ?amriikaa'niiya?	تريد جكارة امريكانية ؟
STRANGER '?aškurak.	الغريب ـ اشكرك •
JOHN '?akuu '9indak ši'xaaṭa?	جان ـ اكو عندك شخاطة ؟
STRANGER 'na9am.	الغريب ـ نعم •
'šuuf, il'gahwa hi'naak.	شوف ، القهوة هناك •
JOHN '?aškurak.	جان ـ اشكرك •

CONVERSATIONS

A. Asking Directions.

You are in Baghdad. You go up to a Baghdadi, Hassan, and ask your way around.

1. You greet Hassan, who returns the greeting.
2. You then ask where there is (a) a hotel (b) a restaurant (c) the railroad station (d) the toilet (e) the movie.
3. Hassan gives directions (a) on your right (b) on your left (c) straight ahead (d) here (e) there.
4. You say you don't understand and ask Hassan to please speak slowly.
5. Hassan repeats slowly and clearly, and then asks you if you understand him.
6. You say you understand well, and then ask where the postoffice is.
7. Hassan tells you (a) on your right (b) on your left.
8. You thank Hassan, and walk on. You see a building and ask another Baghdadi if this is the postoffice.
9. The man answers that it isn't; it's the movie. The postoffice is not here.
10. You ask him to show you where the postoffice is. The Baghdadi points it out to you. You thank him and say goodbye.

B. At A Restaurant.

1. You go into a restaurant and sit down. A waiter comes up to you. The waiter says good evening, and asks what you want.
2. You ask what there is, and the waiter gives a list of food including rice, fish, meat, potatoes, bread. You order a full meal of whatever you want.

3. The waiter asks you what you want to drink. You order tea. The waiter says he is sorry, but there isn't any. You then ask for coffee, American style, and also tell the waiter to bring you water.

4. You eat, then ask how much it is. The waiter says about forty cents. You pay and the waiter thanks you.

5. You remember you need cigarettes and matches. You see some and ask how much they are. Two packs for about forty cents, the waiter replies. You take two.

6. Before leaving, you ask where the toilet is. The waiter directs you to it.

C. *Meeting A Friend.*

You meet a friend and talk with him.

1. You greet him and ask how he is. He replies and asks about you. You're well too, thank goodness.

2. He asks if you want a cigarette. You accept, then have to ask for a match too. You thank him and as you leave you say goodbye to each other.

D. *Free Conversation.*

VOCABULARY

Words are listed in the usual alphabetical order of English. Words beginning with g will be after g, ḥ will be after h, ṣ and š will be after s, and so on. Words beginning with the new symbols ʔ, 9, δ, θ, will be placed in that order at the *end* of the list.

'balii	yes
'bass	only, but
'bayš	how much?
'bii	in; for
'biira	beer
'booṣṭa	postoffice
il'booṣṭa	the postoffice
'čaay	tea
fiimaani'laa.	goodbye.
'gahwa	coffee; coffee shop
gid'daamak	ahead of you
'glaaṣ	glass tumbler
'glaaṣ-ḥa'liib	a glass of milk
'glaaṣ-'maay	a glass of water
'gubaḷ	straight ahead
'gullii	tell me!
'haaδa; 'haaδii, 'haay	this (m; f)
haa'δool, haa'δoolii	these (pl)
'hal	(*introduces a question*)
'hamm	also, too
hi'naa, hi'naaya, 'hina	here
hi'naak	there
ḥa'liib	milk
'ḥamdillaa	praise be to God; thank God
ji'gaara	cigarette
ji'gaayir	cigarettes
'jiiblii	bring me!
'laa	no
'laḥam	meat
'maa	not
'maa 'riid	I don't want
'maakuu	there isn't, there aren't
'maay	water
mam'nuun	much obliged, thanks
ma'ḥaṭṭa	railroad station
ilma'ḥaṭṭa	the railroad station
maraa'ḥiiḍ	toilets
ma'saaʔ il'xayr.	Good evening.
'maṭ9am	restaurant
il'maṭ9am	the restaurant
'ma9a l'ʔasaf	with regret *or* I'm sorry
'ma9a ssa'laama.	Goodbye.
'miit-'filis	a hundred fils (about 40 cents)
mit'ʔassif	sorry
'muu	not
'na9am	yes
paa'kayt	package
paa'kayt-ji'gaayir	package of cigarettes
puu'tayta	potatoes
raa'wiinii	show me!
'sab9a	seven
sa'laam	peace
sa'laam 9a'laykum.	Greetings to you. (*lit.*, Peace be upon you.)
wu9a'laykum issa-laam.	And to you greetings.
'siinama	movie
is'siinama	the movie
'simač	fish
'sitta	six
'šakuu	what is there
'šakuu '9indak?	What do you have? (*lit.*, What is there with you?)
'šinuu	what
'šitriid?	What do you want?
ši'xaaṭa	match
ši'xaaṭ	matches
'šloonak?	How are you?
'šloon 'kayfak?	How are you?

'šuuf	see!
'šwayya	a little, some
tif'himnii?	Do you understand me?
tifti'himnii?	Do you understand me?
'tiḥkii *or* 'tiḥčii	you speak
'timman	rice
'tis9a	nine
'tišrab	you drink
'triid	you want
'waaḥid	one
'wayn	where
wu–	and
'xamsa	five
'xubuz	bread
ya'waaš	slowly, gently
'zayn	well, good
'ʔaakul	I eat
'ʔaanii	I
'ʔafham	I understand
'ʔafhamak	I understand you
'ʔakil	food
'ʔakuu	there is, there are
'ʔana	I
'ʔarba9a	four
ʔa'riid	I want
ʔar'juuk	please
'ʔaškurak	I thank you; thanks
'ʔaw	or
'ʔiḥkii *or* 'ʔiḥčii	speak!
'ʔii	yes
'ʔimšii	walk!
'ʔinta *or* 'ʔanta	you
'winta	and you
ʔuu'tayl	hotel
ilʔuu'tayl	the hotel
'9ala	on, upon
'9ala ya'miinak	on your right
'9ala ya'saarak	on your left
'9arabii	Arabic
'9ašra	ten
'9idna	with us; we have
'9indak	with you; you have
'šakuu '9indak?	What do you have?
θi'laaθa	three
θi'maanya	eight
θi'nayn	two

UNIT 2

Meeting People

BASIC SENTENCES

Bill Reed and John Carter make some acquaintances in Baghdad.

Continuing RECORD 3A

ENGLISH EQUIVALENTS	AIDS TO LISTENING	ARABIC SPELLING
Bill	*Bill*	بل
we	'ʔiḥna	احنا
now	'hassa	هسّه
in	'fii	في
Baghdad	baġ'daad	بغداد
Now we ['re] in Baghdad.	'ʔiḥna 'hassa 'fii baġ'daad.	احنا هسّه في بغداد .
John	*John*	جان
the Baghdadi	ilbaġ'daadii	البغدادي
Look at that Baghdadi.	'šuuf ilbaġ'daadii.	شوف البغدادي.
I talk *or* I speak	'ʔaḥčii	احكي
with him	wii'yaa	ويّاه
I want to talk with him.	ʔa'riid 'ʔaḥčii wii'yaa.	اريد احكي ويّاه .
you come	'tijii	تجي
with me	wii'yaaya *or* wii'yaay*	ويّاي
Do you want to come with me?	'triid 'tijii wii'yaaya?	تريد تجي ويّاي ؟

Beginning RECORD 3B

(*John talks to Said.*)		
Good day.	ʔaḷ'ḷaa bil'xayr.	الله بالخير .
my name	'ʔismii	اسمي
My name ['s] John.	'ʔismii John.	اسمي جان .

* Not on the record.

ENGLISH EQUIVALENTS	AIDS TO LISTENING	ARABIC SPELLING
Said	*Said*	سعيد
I'm glad to know you. (*Literally*, I am honored, *and* You honor us.)	ʔat'šarraf. *or* tšar'rafna.	اتشرّف (ايضا) تشرّفنا •
John	*John*	جان
please	minn 'faḍlak	من فضلك
What ['s] your name, please?	'šismak, minn 'faḍlak?	شسمك ، من فضلك ؟
Said	*Said*	سعيد
Said.	sa'9iid.	سعيد •
John	*John*	جان
my friend	ṣa'diiḳii	صديقي
This [is] my friend.	'haaδa ṣa'diiḳii.	هذا صديقي •
his name	'ʔisma	اسمه
His name ['s] Bill.	'ʔisma Bill.	اسمه بل•
Said	*Said*	سعيد
from where	mi'nayn	منين
you came (*more than one*)	'jiitum *or* 'jaytum*	جيتم
Where are you from?	mi'nayn 'jiitum?	منين جيتم ؟
John	*John*	جان
we came	'jiina	جينا
from	'minn	من
We come from America.	'jiina 'minn* ʔam'riika.	جينا من امريكا•
I came	'jiit *or* 'jayt*	جيت
I come from (the) New York.	'ʔana 'jiit 'minn inNew York.	انا جيت من نيويورك •
he came	'ʔija	اجا
Bill comes from Texas.	Bill 'ʔija 'minn Texas.	بل اجا من تكسس•
Said	*Said*	سعيد
my brother	ʔa'xuuya *or* 'ʔaxii	اخوي (ايضا) اخي •
in America	'bii ʔam'riika *or* bam'riika*	بامريكا
My brother [is] in America.	ʔa'xuuya bam'riika.	اخوي بامريكا •
please (*more than one*)	ʔar'juukum	ارجوكم
come! (*more than one*)	ta'9aaluu	تعالوا
Please come with me.	ʔar'juukum ta'9aaluu wii'yaaya.	ارجوكم تعالوا وياي •
see! (*more than one*)	'šuufuu	شوفوا
my father	ʔa'buuya *or* 'ʔabii	ابوي (ايضا) ابي
Look [there's] my father.	'šuufuu ʔa'buuya.	شوفوا ابوي•

* Not on the record.

ENGLISH EQUIVALENTS	AIDS TO LISTENING	ARABIC SPELLING
he	'huuwa	هو
standing	'waaguf	واقف
by *or* near	'yamm	يم
our shop	duk'kaanna	دكّانا
He ['s] standing by our shop.	'huuwa 'waaguf 'yamm duk'kaanna.	هو واقف يم دكّانا .
Bill	*Bill*	بل
we see	n'šuuf	نشوف
your father	ʔa'buuk	ابوك
the door	il'baab	الباب
Yes, we see your father near the door.	'na9am, in'šuuf ʔa'buuk 'yamm il'baab.	نعم ، نشوف ابوك يم الباب .
Said	*Said*	سعيد
my mother	'ʔummii	امّي
in the house	bil'bayt	بالبيت
My mother ['s] at home.	'ʔummii bil'bayt.	امّي بالبيت .
(*They walk up to Said's father.*)		
I introduce you	ʔa'9arfak	اعرفك
I want to introduce you	ʔa'riid ʔa'9arfak	اريد اعرفك
on *or* upon *or* concerning	'9ala	على
these Americans	haa'ðool ilʔamrii'kaan	هاذول الامريكان
Beginning RECORD 4A		
(My) father, I want to introduce these Americans to you.	ʔa'buuya, ʔa'riid ʔa'9arfak '9ala haa'ðool ilʔamrii'kaan.	ابوي ، اريد اعرفك على هاذول الامريكان .
his friend	ṣa'diiḳa	صديقه
This [is] John, and this [is] his friend Bill.	'haaða John, wu'haaða ṣa'diiḳa Bill.	هذا جان وهذا صديقه بل .
Said's Father	*Said's Father*	ابو سعيد
Welcome!	'ʔahlan wu'sahlan.	اهلا وسهلا !
Said	*Said*	سعيد
but	'laakin *or* wu'laakin	لكن (ايضا) ولكن .
John ['s] from New York, but Bill ['s] from Texas.	John 'minn New York, wu'laakin Bill 'minn Texas.	جان من نيويورك ولكن بل من تكسس .
Said's Father	*Said's Father*	ابو سعيد
my son	'ʔibnii	ابني
big *or* old (*of people*)	ča'biir *or* ka'biir*	كبير
he went	'raaḥ	راح
to *or* for	'ʔila	الى
My oldest son went to America.	'ʔibnii čča'biir 'raaḥ 'ʔila ʔam'riika.	ابني الكبير راح الى امريكا .

ENGLISH EQUIVALENTS	AIDS TO LISTENING	ARABIC SPELLING
American	ʔamrii'kaanii	امريكاني
He ['s] an American now.	'hassa 'huuwa ʔamrii'kaanii.	هسّه هو امريكاني •
Said	*Said*	سعيد
you (*more than one*)	'ʔintum	انتم
you speak (*more than one*)	tiḥ'čuun *or* tiḥ'kuun*	تحكون
You speak Arabic well.	'ʔintum tiḥ'čuun '9arabii 'zayn.	انتم تحكون عربي زين •
John	*John*	جان
we studied	di'rasna	درسنا
I studied	di'rasit	درست
much *or* many	ka'θiir	كثير
We studied Arabic in America, only I didn't study much.	di'rasna '9arabii 'bii ʔam'riika, 'bass 'maa di'rasit ka'θiir.	درسنا عربي بامريكا بس ما درست كثير •
you speak	'tiḥčii *or* 'tiḥkii*	تحكي
English	ʔin'gliizii	انكليزي
sir	'sayyidii	سيّدي
Do you speak English, sir?	'tiḥčii ʔin'gliizii, 'sayyidii?	تحكي انكليزي ، سيّدي ؟
Said's Father	*Said's Father*	ابو سعيد
French	fran'saawii	فرنساوي
more	'ʔakθar	اكثر
I speak more French.	'ʔaḥčii fran'saawii 'ʔakθar.	احكي فرنساوي اكثر •
John	*John*	جان
Excuse us!	ʔisma'ḥuulna.	اسمحوا لنا •
necessary	'laazim	لازم
we go	n'ruuḥ	نروح
We have to go now.	'laazim in'ruuḥ 'hassa.	لازم نروح هسّه •
we want	n'riid	نريد
we see	n'šuuf	نشوف
our friend	ṣa'diiḳna	صديقنا
We want to see our friend.	n'riid in'šuuf ṣa'diiḳna.	نريد نشوف صديقنا •
He ['s] in the postoffice.	'huuwa bil'boosṭa.	هو بالبوسطة •
Said	*Said*	سعيد
visit us! (*more than one*)	zuu'ruuna	زورونا
always *or* often	'daayman	دائما

Beginning Record 4B

Come see us often.	zuu'ruuna 'daayman.	زورونا دائما •
found	moo'juud *or* maw'juud*	موجود
I ['m] always (found) here.	'ʔana 'daayman maw'juud hi'naa.	انا دائما موجود هنا •

* Not on the record.

ENGLISH EQUIVALENTS	AIDS TO LISTENING	ARABIC SPELLING
Bill	*Bill*	بل
[We're much] obliged.	mamnuu'niin.	ممنونين •
(*On their way to the postoffice, a man directs them to the King Ghazi Bridge. They don't find it and come back to ask about it again.*)		
John	*John*	جان
we saw	'šifna	شفنا
[the] King Ghazi Bridge	'jisir-'malik-'ğaazii	جسر الملك غازي
We didn't see [the] King Ghazi Bridge.	'maa 'šifna 'jisir-'malik-'ğaazii.	ما شفنا جسر الملك غازي •
show us	raa'wiina*	راوينا
him *or* it (m)	ʔi'yaa	اياه
Please show it to us.	ʔar'juuk raa'wiina 'yaa.	ارجوك راوينا ايّاه •
(*Later Said asks John if he saw his friend.*)		
Said	*Said*	سعيـد
you saw	'šifit	شفت
Did you see your friend?	'šifit ṣa'diiḳak?	شفت صديقك ؟
John	*John*	جان
we saw him	šif'naa	شفناه
he was	'čaan *or* 'kaan	كان
No, we didn't see him; he wasn't there.	'laa, 'maa šif'naa; 'maa 'čaan hi'naak.	لا ، ما شفناه • ما كان هناك •

PRONUNCIATION

Continuing RECORD 4B

PRACTICE 1

x: The sign x stands for a sound you have often made when clearing your throat or when trying to loosen something in the back of your mouth. You can make the sound as hard as you want.

'xamsa	*five*	خمسة
'ʔaxii	*my brother*	اخي
baḳ'šiiš†	**tip, to porter*	
'xubuz	*bread*	خبز
'ʔuxut	**sister*	اخت
ʔa'xuu	*his brother*	اخوه
mit'ʔaxxir	**late*	متأخّر

* The record adds 'yaa *him, it.*

† This word does not belong here.

PRACTICE 2

9: The sign 9 stands for a sound made by tightening the muscles of the throat. You will notice that it gives vowels touching it a special 'color'. Give this sound care and effort.

′9arabii	*Arabic*	عربي
′9ala	*on, upon*	على
′na9am	*yes*	نعم
′sab9a	*seven*	سبعة
′9indak	*you have*	عندك
′li9ib	**playing*	لعب
′šaari9	**street*	شارع
′9ašra	*ten*	عشرة
9iš′riin	**twenty*	عشرين
′9umrii	**my life*	عمري
saa′9aat	**hours; clocks*	ساعات
?arba′9iin	**forty*	اربعين
maa′9uun	**dish*	ماعون
′baa9	**he sold*	باع
yi′bii9	**he sells*	يبيع
mam′nuu9	**forbidden*	ممنوع

ANALYSIS

1. QUESTIONS.

′minuu ′haaδa?	*Who [is] this?*	منو هذا ؟
′wayn ilma′ḥaṭṭa?	*Where [is] the railroad station?*	وين المحطة ؟
′šinuu ′triid? *or* ′šitriid?	*What do you want?*	شنو تريد ؟ شتريد ؟
′šakuu ′biik?	*What's the matter (with you)?*	شكوبيك ؟

Notice from the above that sentences containing question-asking words (such as ′minuu *who?*, *whom?*, ′wayn *where?*, ′šinuu *what?*, š(i)– *what?*, ′bayš *how much?*, and so on) follow the very same pattern in Iraqi and English. But, there is a difference in sentences which have no question-asking words, such as the following:

tifti′himnii.	*You understand me.*	تفتهمني
tifti′himnii?	*Do you understand me?*	تفتهمني ؟
′triid ′maay.	*You want [some] water.*	تريد ماي
′triid ′maay?	*Do you want [some] water?*	تريد ماي ؟
′?inta ′zayn.	*You [are] well.*	انت زين
′?inta ′zayn?	*Are you well?*	انت زين ؟

'haaδii l'boosṭa.	*This [is] the postoffice.*	هذي البوسطة
'hal 'haaδii l'boosṭa?	*Is this the postoffice?*	هل هذي البوسطة ؟

In English, if we want to turn a statement like *You are well.* into a question, we change the words around, as *Are you well?* Less often we keep the words as they were and then raise our voice at the end of the statement, as *You are well?* In Iraqi you follow the latter pattern; that is, you keep the words as they were and then raise your voice at the end of the statement to indicate it is a question. You NEVER change the words around in order to ask a question. The word 'hal is sometimes used just to introduce such questions, but most often it is omitted. Question-asking intonation can only be learned by carefully listening to people who speak Iraqi, then imitating them exactly.

2. Stress.

In English we say one part of a word harder or louder than the remainder. We say that this part is STRESSED. We could write a mark (') before the stressed part, as in *po'tato, can'teen, 'parcel.*

Iraqi words are also stressed. Usually the stress follows a regular mechanical pattern. Starting from the end of the word, the stressed part is

(1) the nearest double vowel followed by a consonant:

?a'riid	*I want*	اريد
'šuufuu	*see!*	شوفوا
raa'wiinii	*show me!*	راويني
'siinama	*movie*	سينما

or (2) the nearest single vowel followed by two consonants:

mu'himm	**important*	مهم
'gahwa	*coffee; coffee shop*	قهوة
tifti'himnii	*you understand me*	تفتهمني
ma'ḥaṭṭa	*railroad station*	محطة

or (3) lacking these conditions, the stress falls on the first vowel of the word:

'xubuz	*bread*	خبز
'laḥam	*meat*	لحم
'9arabii	*Arabic*	عربي

Some words, however, do not follow the regular mechanical pattern given above. They are certain verb forms alone, or verb forms and prepositions with pronoun endings (see Note 4, below). For example,

di'rasit	*I studied*	درست
tif'tikir	**you think*	تفتكر
?aš'kurak	*I thank you*	اشكرك
wii'yaa	*with him*	ويّاه

Even then, the mechanical pattern is often followed by verb forms which have two consonants after the first vowel, giving such couplets as

tif'tikir *and* 'tiftikir	**you think*	تفتكر
?aš'kurak *and* '?aškurak	*I thank you*	اشكرك

There is no difference in meaning. In the first five Units of this book the stress is written on all Iraqi words. Afterwards it is written only on words which do not follow the regular mechanical pattern.

3. š(i)– *what?* Compare the following:

'triid	*you want*	تريد
'ʔismak	*your name*	اسمك
'ʔakuu	*there is, there are*	اكو
'šitriid?	*What do you want?*	شتريد ؟
'šismak?	*What is your name?*	شسمك ؟
'šakuu?	*What is there?*	شكو ؟

Note that š(i)– added to the front of a word means *what?*. It has the same meaning and is interchangeable with šinuu *what?*. Note that the sound written ʔ drops out when š(i)– is added. Note also that 'šitriid has the stress at the beginning, hence it is an exception to the mechanical pattern of stress.

4. Pronoun Endings — Equivalents of *my, me, your, you, our, us.*

'ʔismii	*my name*	اسمي
'ʔismak	*your name*	اسمك
duk'kaanna	*our shop*	دكّاننا
raa'wiinii	*show me!*	راويني
ʔaš'kurak	*I thank you*	اشكرك
zuu'ruuna	*visit us!*	زورونا
9a'laykum	*upon you*	عليكم

From the words above, you see that Iraqi doesn't have separate words meaning *my, your, our,* and so on after nouns. Likewise there are no special words (with one exception to be explained later) for *me, you, us* and so on after verbs and prepositions. Instead, certain endings are added to the word to give these meanings. These are the PRONOUN ENDINGS. The frequent use of these endings is one of the chief characteristics of Iraqi and all other Arabic dialects. Three of the pronoun endings are given below.

(I)

'ʔismii	*my name*	اسمي
'ʔibnii	*my son*	ابني
ʔa'buuya	*my father*	ابوي
wii'yaaya	*with me*	ويّاي

BUT WITH VERBS:

tifti'himnii	*you understand me*	تفتهمني
raa'wiinii	*show me!*	راويني

These words show that the endings –ii (after consonants) and –ya (after vowels) both express *my* and *me.* Often just –y is used, as wii'yaay *with me* and ʔa'buuy *my father.* Note especially, however, that with VERBS the ending –nii is used for *me.* In fact, this is the only instance where there is a special pronoun ending which is used only with verbs. Elsewhere the same pronoun ending is used with nouns, prepositions and verbs.

(II)

'ʔismak	*your name*	اسمك
ʔa'buuk	*your father*	ابوك
'ʔummak	*your mother*	امّك
ʔaš'kurak	*I thank you*	اشكرك
wii'yaak	*with you*	ويّاك

The ending –ak (just –k after vowels) means *your* and *you.* This is used when you are speaking to a boy or man (masculine singular).

(III)

duk'kaanna	*our shop*	دكّانّا
wii'yaana	*with us*	ويّانا
zuu'ruuna	*visit us!*	زورونا

The ending –na means *our* and *us*.

You will note that some words have two slightly different forms when these endings are added. One form is found with endings beginning with a vowel (as –ii and –ak); the other form with endings beginning with a consonant (as –na). Some examples are:

'yamm	*beside*	يم
'ʔisim	*name*	اسم
'yammii	*beside me*	يمّي
'ʔismii	*my name*	اسمي
'yamna	*beside us*	يمنا
ʔi'simna	*our name*	اسمنا

5. Commands.

If you hear someone speaking English say 'See!', you can't tell whether he is speaking to one person or to more than one, or whether to a male or a female. But if you hear an Iraqi speak, you know from the form of the word he uses just whom he is addressing. In Iraqi, COMMANDS have three forms: one spoken to a man (masculine), one spoken to a girl (feminine), and one spoken to more than one person (plural). Some examples are:

'šuuf (m)	*see!*	شوف
'šuufii (f)		شوفي
'šuufuu (pl)		شوفوا
'jiib (m)	*bring!*	جيب
'jiibii (f)		جيبي
'jiibuu (pl)		جيبوا
ta'9aal (m)	*come!*	تعال
ta'9aalii (f)		تعالي
ta'9aaluu (pl)		تعالوا

In contrast to the above examples, verbs which end in a vowel, as 'yimšii *he walks* and yi'raawii *he shows*, have identical forms for the masculine and feminine commands, both ending in –ii:

'?imšii (m)	*walk!*	امشي
'?imšii (f)		امشي
'?imšuu (pl)		امشوا
'?iḥčii (m)	*speak!*	احكي
'?iḥčii (f)		احكي
'?iḥčuu (pl)		احكوا
'raawii (m)	*show!*	راوي
'raawii (f)		راوي
'raawuu (pl)		راووا

6. SUFFIXED –l–, EQUIVALENT TO *to, for*. Compare the commands below.

'jiib	*bring!*	جيب
'jiibii		جيبي
'jiibuu		جيبوا
'jiiblii	*bring (to) me!*	جيب لي
jii'biilii		جيبي لي
jii'buulii		جيبوا لي

The commands beneath have a suffixed –l– meaning *to, for* placed before the pronoun ending. Together they indicate *to whom* or *for whom* the action named is done. Note that it is always –ii for *me* after this –l– and never –nii. The other pronoun endings are also found here, as jii'bilna *bring (to) us*, and so on. Other examples are:

'gull	*tell!*	قل
'gullii		قولي
'gulluu		قولوا
'gullii	*tell (to) me!*	قلّي
gul'liilii		قولي لي
gul'luulii		قولوا لي
'?ismaḥ	*excuse!*	اسمح
'?ismaḥii		اسمحي
'?ismaḥuu		اسمحوا
?is'maḥlii	*excuse (to) me!*	اسمح لي
?isma'ḥiilii		اسمحي لي
?isma'ḥuulii		اسمحوا لي

EXERCISES

A. Practice on the pronoun endings (–ii, –ya *my, me,* –nii *me* (with verb); –ak, –k *you;* –na *our, us*). Select the correct word.

1.	(My friend) 'ʔija 'minn bag'daad.	ṣa'diiḳii, ṣa'diiḳna, ṣa'diiḳak
2.	(Your shop) 'muu ka'biir.	duk'kaanna, duk'kaanak, duk'kaanii
3.	(Our father) 'muu maw'juud bil'bayt.	ʔa'buuya, ʔa'buuk, ʔa'buuna
4.	ʔar'juuk (show us) 'wayn 'baytak.	raa'wiinii, raa'wiina, raa'wuuna
5.	il'boosṭa '9ala (our right).	ya'saarna, ya'miinak, ya'miinna
6.	(Our house) 'yamm idduk'kaan.	'baytak, 'baytii, 'baytna
7.	ʔa'buuya 'waaguf (beside me).	'yammak, 'yammii, 'yamna
8.	'wayn (your mother)?	'ʔummii, 'ʔummak, 'ʔumna
9.	ʔar'juuk (visit me) 'daayman.	'zuurnii, 'zuurna, zuu'ruunii
10.	(We have) 'ṣadiiḳ 'fii New York.	'9idna, '9indii, '9indak
11.	'triid 'tijii (with me)?	wii'yaay, wii'yaana
12.	'wayn 'raaḥ (your brother)?	ʔa'xuuya, ʔa'xuuk, ʔa'xuuna
13.	(Our friend) 'maa 'ʔija wii'yaana.	ṣa'diiḳii, ṣa'diiḳna, ṣa'diiḳak
14.	'hal (your son) bil'bayt?	'ʔibnii, 'ʔibnak, ʔi'binna
15.	(Your hotel) 'yamm 'baytna.	ʔuu'taylii, ʔuu'taylak, ʔuu'taylna

B. These commands are spoken to a man. What would you say to a girl? To more than one person?

1. ta'9aal hi'naa!
2. 'šuuf ilbag'daadii!
3. 'ʔimšii 'gubaḷ!
4. 'zuurna bil'bayt!
5. 'šuufnii!
6. raa'wiinii yaa!
7. 'jiiblii 'glaaṣ-'maay!
8. ʔis'maḥlii!

WHAT WOULD YOU SAY?

1. *A Baghdadi speaks to you and your friend.*
   - *a.* 'šloonak? — ١ ـ شلونك ؟
   - *b.* 'šloonkum? — ٢ ـ شلونكم ؟
   - *c.* 'šloon 'kayfkum? — ٣ ـ شلون كيفكم ؟

2. *You ask what his name is.*
   - *a.* 'šakuu 'biik? — ١ ـ شكوبيك ؟
   - *b.* 'šitriid? — ٢ ـ شتريد ؟
   - *c.* 'šismak? — ٣ ـ شسمك ؟

3. *He asks where you are from.*
   - *a.* mi'nayn 'jiitum? — ١ ـ منين اتتم ؟
   - *b.* 'ʔintum ʔamrii'kaan? — ٢ ـ اتتم امريكان ؟
   - *c.* mi'nayn 'jiit? — ٣ ـ منين جيت ؟

4. *You tell him.*

a. duk'kaana binNew York. — ١ ـ دكانه بنيويورك •

b. '?ana 'muu 'zayn, wuṣa'diiḳii 'muu 'zayn. — ٢ ـ انا مو زين وصديقي مو زين •

c. '?ana 'minn New York, wuṣa'diiḳii 'minn Texas. — ٣ ـ انا من نيويورك وصديقي من تكسس •

5. *He introduces you to his father.*

a. ?a'buuya, 'šuuf 'ðool il?amrii'kaan! — ١ ـ ابوي شوف ذول الامريكان •

b. ?a'buuya, 'haaða ?amrii'kaanii. — ٢ ـ ابوي هذا امريكاني •

c. ?a'buuya, ?a'riid ?a'9arfak ib'ðool il?amrii'kaan. — ٣ ـ ابوي اريد اعرفك بذول الامريكان •

6. *You acknowledge the introduction.*

a. 'wayn '?ibnak? — ١ ـ وين ابنك ؟

b. tšar'rafna. — ٢ ـ تشرفنا •

c. 'hassa ?a'riid '?aakul. — ٣ ـ هسّه اريد آكل •

7. *His father compliments you.*

a. '?intum tiḥ'kuun '9arabii 'zayn. — ١ ـ انتم تحكون عربي زين •

b. '?inta 'tiḥkii '9arabii 'zayn. — ٢ ـ انت تحكي عربي زين •

c. ?ar'juukum '?iḥkuu '9arabii! — ٣ ـ ارجوكم احكوا عربي •

8. *You have to leave.*

a. 'laazim in'ruuḥ 'hassa. — ١ ـ لازم نروح هسّه •

b. ?isma'ḥuulna! — ٢ ـ اسمحوا لنا •

c. maa n'riid in'ruuḥ. — ٣ ـ ما نريد نروح •

9. *You are asked to come again.*

a. 'šuufuu duk'kaana! — ١ ـ شوفوا دكّانه •

b. 'baytna '9ala lya'miin. — ٢ ـ بيتنا على اليمين •

c. zuu'ruuna 'daayman! — ٣ ـ زورونا دائما •

10. *You say goodbye.*

a. 'ḥamdillaa. — ١ ـ الحمد لله •

b. fiimaani'laa. — ٢ ـ في امان الله •

c. 'ma9a ssa'laama. — ٣ ـ مع السلامة •

11. *You knock on a door and a boy opens it. You ask for his father.*

a. ?a'riid ?a'šuuf ?a'buuk. — ١ ـ اريد اشوف ابوك •

b. ?a'riid ?a'šuuf '?ummak. — ٢ ـ اريد اشوف امك •

c. 'wayn ?a'xuuk? — ٣ ـ وين اخوك ؟

12. *His father isn't at home.*

a. ?a'buuya 'muu 'zayn. — ١ ـ ابوي مو زين •

b. ?a'xuuya bil'bayt. — ٢ ـ اخوي بالبيت •

c. ?a'buuya 'muu maw'juud bil'bayt. — ٣ ـ ابوي موجود بالبيت •

13. *You ask a boy what's the matter with him.*

a. 'šakuu 'biik? — ١ ـ شكو بيك ؟
b. 'šitriid? — ٢ ـ شتريد ؟
c. š'tišrab? — ٣ ـ شتشرب ؟

14. *You ask where his parents are.*

a. 'wayn 'ʔummak wuʔa'buuk? — ١ ـ وين امك وابوك ؟
b. 'šloon 'ʔummak wuʔa'buuk? — ٢ ـ شلون امك وابوك ؟
c. 'ʔana 'muu ʔa'buuk. — ٣ ـ انا مو ابوك ٠

15. *A Baghdadi says he has an older brother in America.*

a. 'ʔaxii maw'juud bil'bayt. — ١ ـ اخي موجود بالبيت ٠
b. 'ʔaxii l'kabiir 'fii New York. — ٢ ـ اخي الكبير في نيويورك ٠
c. 'ʔaxii 'waaguf 'yamm duk'kaana. — ٣ ـ اخي واقف يم دكانه ٠

16. *You ask if he speaks English.*

a. 'ʔana 'maa 'ʔaḥčii ʔin'gliizii. — ١ ـ انا ما احكي انكليزي ٠
b. 'tiḥkii ʔin'gliizii? — ٢ ـ تحكي انكليزي ؟
c. 'ʔana 'ʔaḥkii ʔin'gliizii 'ʔakθar. — ٣ ـ انا احكي انكليزي اكثر ٠

17. *His French is better.*

a. 'ʔana 'ʔaḥkii 'šwayya fran'saawii. — ١ ـ انا احكي شوية فرنساوي ٠
b. 'ʔaḥkii fran'saawii 'ʔakθar minn ʔin'gliizii. — ٢ ـ احكي فرنساوي اكثر من انكليزي ٠
c. 'ʔaḥkii '9arabii 'ʔakθar 'minn fran'saawii wuʔin'gliizii. — ٣ ـ احكي عربي اكثر من فرنساوي وانكليزي ٠

18. *You studied Arabic.*

a. di'rasna '9arabii bam'riika. — ١ ـ درسنا عربي بامريكا ٠
b. 'laa, 'maa di'rasna '9arabii 'fii bag'daad. — ٢ ـ لا ، ما درسنا عربي في بغداد ٠
c. di'rasna ʔin'gliizii 'ʔakθar 'minn '9arabii. — ٣ ـ درسنا انكليزي اكثر من عربي ٠

LISTENING IN

CONVERSATION ONE

John and Bill are walking around Baghdad.

Continuing RECORD 4B

BILL 'hassa 'ʔiḥna 'fii bag'daad. — بل ـ هسه نحن في بغداد ٠
JOHN 'šuuf ilbag'daadii; ʔa'riid 'ʔaḥčii wii'yaa. ʔar'juuk ta'9aal wii'yaaya. — جان ـ شوف البغدادي ، اريد احكي وياه ٠ ارجوك تعال وياي ٠

(*They walk over to the Baghdadi.*)

JOHN ʔaḷ'ḷaa bil'xayr. — جان ـ الله بالخير٠
SAID ʔaḷ'ḷaa bil'xayr. — سعيد ـ الله بالخير٠

JOHN '?ana ?amrii'kaanii; '?ismii John.	جان - انا امريكاني ، اسمي جان •
SAID ?at'šarraf.	سعيد - اتشرّف
JOHN 'šismak, 'minn 'faḍlak?	جان - شسمك ، من فضلك ؟
SAID '?ismii sa'9iid.	سعيد - اسمي سعيد •
JOHN 'haaδa ṣa'diiḳii Bill.	جان - هذا صديقي بل •
SAID ?at'šarraf.	سعيد - اتشرّف •
'tiḥčii '9arabii?	تحكي عربي ؟
BILL '?aḥčii 'šwayya '9arabii; '?aḥčii ?in'gliizii '?akθar.	بل - احكي شويّه عربي ، احكي انكليزي اكثر •

Beginning RECORD 5A

SAID mi'nayn 'jiitum?	سعيد - منين جيتم ؟
BILL '?aanii 'jayt 'minn Texas.	بل - انا جيت من تكسس •
JOHN '?aanii 'minn New York.	جان - انا من نيويورك •
SAID ?a'xuuya čča'biir hi'naak; '?isma 'šaakir.*	سعيد - اخوي الكبير هناك ، اسمه شاكر •
BILL 'wayn ?a'buuk? 'huuwa 'hamm binNew York?	بل - وين ابوك ؟ هو هم بالنيويورك ؟
SAID 'laa.	سعيد - لا •
'šuufuu, ?a'buuya 'waaguf 'yamm duk'kaanna.	شوفوا ابوي واقف يم دكّاننا •
?ar'juukum ta'9aaluu wii'yaaya.	ارجوكم تعالوا ويّاي •

CONVERSATION TWO

They walk over to Said's father.

SAID ?a'buuya, ?a'riid ?a'9arfak '9ala haa'δool il?amrii'kaan. 'haaδa John, wu'haaδa ṣa'diika Bill.	سعيد - ابوي ، اريد اعرفك على هاذول الامريكان • هذا جان ، وهذا صديقه بل •
FATHER† '?ahlan wu'sahlan!	الاب - اهلا وسهلا !
'?ibnii čča'biir 'fii ?am'riika; 'hassa 'huuwa ?amrii'kaanii.	ابني الكبير في امريكا ، هسّه هو امريكاني •
JOHN 'wayn 'huuwa?	جان - وين هو ؟
FATHER 'binNew York.	الاب - بنيويورك •
JOHN '?aanii 'jayt 'minn New York.	جان - انا جيت من نيويورك •
FATHER (*surprised*) tiḥ'čuun '9arabii?	الاب - تحكون عربي ؟
BILL 'na9am, di'rasna '9arabii bam'riika.	بل - نعم ، درسنا عربي في امريكا •
SAID '?antum tiḥ'čuun 'zayn.	سعيد - انتم تحكون زين •
JOHN '?aškurak.	جان - اشكرك •
(*To Said's father:*) 'tiḥčii ?in'gliizii, 'sayyidii?	(الى الاب) تحكي انكليزي ، سيّدي ؟
FATHER 'laa, 'laakin '?aḥčii 'šwayya fran'saawii.	الاب - لا ، لكن احكي شويّه فرنساوي •

* Shakir, a man's name.

† The record has il'?ab *the father*.

JOHN ʔisma'ḥuulna, 'hassa 'laazim in'ruuḥ. n'riid in'šuuf ṣa'diiḳna; 'huuwa bil'boosṭa.	جان ـ اسمحوا لنا ، هسّه لازم نروح • نريد نشوف صديقنا ، هو بالبوسطة •
FATHER ʔar'juukum zuu'ruuna 'daayman. 'ʔaanii 'daayman maw'juud hi'naaya.	الاب ـ ارجوكم زورونا دائما • انا دائما موجود هنا •
JOHN ʔaš'kurak, 'sayyidii.	جان ـ اشكرك ، سيّدي •
BILL fiimaani'laa.	بل ـ في امان الله •

CONVERSATION THREE

John and Bill stop to ask a stranger the way to the postoffice.

JOHN ʔar'juuk 'gullii 'wayn il'boosṭa.	جان ـ ارجوك قل لي وين البوسطة ؟
STRANGER* 'ʔimšii 'gubaḷ; il'boosṭa 'yamm 'jisir-'malik-'gaazii.	غريب ـ امشي قبل ، البوسطة يم جسر الملك غازي •
JOHN 'ʔaškurak.	جان ـ اشكرك •
(*They walk a little way, and then come back.*)	
JOHN 'maa 'šifna 'jisir-'malik-'gaazii; ʔar'juuk raa'wiina 'yaa.	جان ـ ما شفنا جسر الملك غازي ، ارجوك راوينا اياه •
STRANGER ta'9aaluu wii'yaaya. 'šuufuu,† 'haaδa 'jisir-il'malik'-gaazii wil'-boosṭa hi'naak.	غريب ـ تعالوا ويّاي • شوفوا ، هذا جسر الملك غازي والبوسطة هناك •
JOHN mamnuu'niin ka'θiir.	جان ـ ممنونين كثير •

CONVERSATION FOUR

Later John and Bill meet Said and his friend Hassan. John already knows Hassan.

JOHN 'ḥasan, ʔa'riid ʔa'9arfak '9ala ṣa'diiḳii Bill.	جان ـ حسن ، اريد اعرفك على صديقي بل •
HASSAN ʔat'šarraf.	حسن ـ اتشرف •
SAID 'šifit ṣa'diiḳak?	سعيد ـ شفت صديقك ؟
JOHN 'laa, 'maa šif'naa; 'maa 'čaan bil'boosṭa.	جان ـ لا ، ما شفناه ، ما كان بالبوسطة •
HASSAN 'ʔaanii wusa'9iid in'riid in'ruuḥ lis'siinama. John, 'triid 'tijii wii'yaana?	حسن ـ آني وسعيد نريد نروح للسينما • جان ، تريد تجي ويّانا ؟
JOHN 'laa, 'ʔaanii 'laazim ʔa'ruuḥ lilʔuu'tayl.	جان ـ آنا لازم اروح للأوتيل •
SAID 'winta, Bill?	سعيد ـ وانت ، بل ؟
BILL ʔaš'kurak, ʔa'riid ʔa'ruuḥ 'wiiya John.	بل ـ اشكرك ، اريد اروح ويّا جان •
JOHN fiimaani'laa.	جان ـ في امان الله •
SAID fiimaani'laa.	سعيد ـ في امان الله •

* The record has ilga'riib *the stranger*.

† On the record twice.

CONVERSATIONS

A. Making Yourself Acquainted.

1. You decide to strike up an acquaintance with an Iraqi you happen to meet. You say 'Good day' to him, and he replies.
2. You introduce yourself by telling him your name.
3. He says he is glad to know you, and then he tells you his name.
4. He asks you where you came from, and you tell him.
5. He says he has a friend in America; he is an American, he adds.
6. You offer him a cigarette; he thanks you for it.
7. He invites you to visit him at his home.
8. You excuse yourself, saying you have to go to the hotel.
9. You say goodbye to each other.

B. Introducing Someone.

1. You and your friend meet the same Iraqi later. You call him by name and ask him how he is, to which he replies.
2. You introduce your friend to the Iraqi, and tell him where he is from.
3. The Iraqi says he is glad to know him, then he asks your friend if he speaks Arabic too.
4. Your friend answers yes, saying you studied some in America.
5. The Iraqi compliments him on his Arabic.
6. You ask the Iraqi if he speaks English, and he replies not English, but French.
7. A friend of the Iraqi comes along. The Iraqi introduces you both to his friend, and tells him that you are Americans.
8. Later you excuse yourselves and say goodbye.

VOCABULARY

'baab	door
baġ'daad	Baghdad
ilbaġ'daadii	the Baghdadi
'bayt	house
bil'bayt	in the house, at home
'bii	in
čaan	he was
ča'biir	big; old (of people)
'daayman	always, often
di'rasit	I studied
di'rasna	we studied
duk'kaan	shop
duk'kaanna	our shop
'fii	in
fran'saawii	French
'hassa	now
'huuwa	he
'jayna *or* 'jiina	we came
'jayt *or* 'jiit	I came
'jaytum *or* 'jiitum	you came (pl)
'jisir	bridge
'jisir-il'malik-'ġaazii	[the] King Ghazi Bridge
'kaan	he was
ka'biir	big; old (of people)
ka'θiir	many, much, a lot
'laakin, wu'laakin	but
'laazim	necessary
'laazim ʔa'ruuḥ.	I have to go.
lilboosṭa	to the postoffice
mamnuu'niin	much obliged, thanks (pl)
maw'juud *or* 'moojuud	found, present
mi'nayn	from where
'minn	from
'minn 'faḍlak	if you please
n'riid	we want
n'šuuf	we see
'raaḥ	he went
raa'wiina	show us!
sa'9iid	Said (man's name)
'sayyidii	sir
ṣa'diiḳ	friend
ṣa'diiḳii	my friend
ṣa'diiḳa	his friend
ṣa'diiḳna	our friend
ṣa'diiḳak	your friend
'šaakir	Shakir (*man's name*)
šifit	you saw
'šifna	we saw
šif'naa	we saw him, we saw it
'šismak?	What is your name?
'šuufuu	see! (pl)
ta'9aaluu	come! (pl)
tiḥ'kuun *or* tiḥčuun	you speak (pl)
'tijii	you come (m)
tšar'rafna.	How do you do.
'waaguf	standing
'wiiya	with
wii'yaaya	with me
wii'yaa	with him
'yamm	beside, by
'zuuruu	visit! (pl)
zuu'ruuna	visit us!
'ʔab	father
'ʔabii, ʔa'buuya	my father
ʔa'buuk	your father
'ʔahlan wu'sahlan!	Welcome!
'ʔaḥkii, 'ʔaḥčii	I speak
'ʔakθar	more
'ʔakθar 'minn	more than
ʔaḷ'ḷaa bil'xayr.	Good day.
ʔam'riika	America
bam'riika	in America

ʔamrii'kaanii	American; an American (m)
ʔamrii'kaan	Americans
ʔar'juukum	please (pl)
ʔat'šarraf.	I'm glad to know you.
'ʔaxii, ʔa'xuuya	my brother
ʔa'9arfak '9ala	I introduce you to
'ʔibnii	my son
'ʔiḥna	we
'ʔija	he came
ʔin'gliizii	English
'ʔila	to; for
'ʔintum	you (pl)
'ʔisma	his name
'ʔismii	my name
ʔisma'ḥuulna	Excuse us!
'ʔummii	my mother
ʔi'yaa	him, it
raa'niinii 'yaa	show it to me!
'9ala	on, upon; concerning

UNIT 3

What's Your Job?

BASIC SENTENCES

Continuing RECORD 5A

ENGLISH EQUIVALENTS	AIDS TO LISTENING	ARABIC SPELLING
Bill	*Bill*	بل
Ali	'9alii	علي
good morning	ṣa'baaḥ il'xayr	صباح الخير
Good morning, Ali.	ṣa'baaḥ il'xayr, '9alii.	صباح الخير ، علي •
This is my friend John.	'haaδa ṣa'diiḳii John.	هذا صديقي جان •
Ali	*Ali*	علي
I'm glad to know you.	ʔat'šarraf.	اتشرّف •
Bill	*Bill*	بل
I like *or* I love	ʔa'ḥibb	احب
I know	'ʔa9ruf	اعرف
I would like to know	ʔa'ḥibb 'ʔa9ruf	احب اعرف
your work	'šuglak	شغلك
I'd like to know what your work [is].	ʔa'ḥibb 'ʔa9ruf 'šinuu 'šuglak.	احب اعرف شنو شغلك •

Beginning RECORD 5B

ENGLISH EQUIVALENTS	AIDS TO LISTENING	ARABIC SPELLING
Ali	*Ali*	علي
contractor	mu'ḳaawil	مقاول
I'm a contractor.	'ʔana mu'ḳaawil.	انا مقاول •
you were	'činit *or* 'kunit *or* 'kinit	كنت
you do *or* you make	'tsawwii	تسوّي
you were doing	'činit it'sawwii	كنت تسوّي
what were you doing	'ščinit it'sawwii	شكنت تسوّي
before	'gabul	قبل
the war	il'ḥarb	الحرب
John, what were you doing before the war?	John, 'ščint it'sawwii 'gabl il'ḥarb?	جان ، شكنت تسوّي قبل الحرب ؟

ENGLISH EQUIVALENTS	AIDS TO LISTENING	ARABIC SPELLING
John	*John*	جان
I was	'činit *or* 'kinit	كنت
I work	'?aštugul	اشتغل
I was working	'činit '?aštugul	كنت اشتغل
factory	'ma9mal	معمل
automobiles	siiyaa'raat	سيّارات
automobile factory	'ma9mal-siiyaa'raat	معمل سيّارات
I was working in an automobile factory.	'kunit '?aštugul bi'ma9mal-siiyaa'raat.	كنت اشتغل بمعمل سيّارات •
laborer	'9aamil	عامل
[the] Ford factory	'ma9mal-Ford	معمل فورد
I was a workman in the Ford factory.	'činit '9aamil 'fii 'ma9mal-Ford.	كنت عامل في معمل فورد •
Ali	*Ali*	علي
how	'šloon	شلون
How was the work?	'šloon 'čaan iš'šugul?	شلون كان الشغل ؟
John	*John*	جان
very	'kulliš	كلّش
Very good.	'kulliš 'zayn.	كلّش زين •
head *or* chief *or* boss	ra'?iis *or* 'rayyis*	رئيس
My brother was the head of the factory.	?a'xuuya 'čaan ra'?iis-il'ma9mal.	اخي كان رئيس المعمل •
Ali	*Ali*	علي
Ford automobiles	siiyaa'raat-Ford	سيّارات فورد
Ford cars [are] good.	siiyaa'raat-Ford zayna.	سيّارات فورد زينة •
we have	'9idna	عندنا
a Ford automobile	sii'yaarat-Ford†	سيّارة فورد
We have a Ford.	'9idna sii'yaarat-Ford.	عندنا سيّارة فورد •
she	'hiiya	هي
she walks *or* she goes	'timšii	تمشي
It runs very well.	'hiiya 'timšii 'kulliš 'zayn.	هي تمشي كلّش زين •
you work	'tištugul	تشتغل
What do you do, Bill?	wu'?inta Bill, 'štištugul?‡	وانت بل ، شتشتغل ؟
Bill	*Bill*	بل
engineer	mu'handis	مهندس
I'm an engineer.	'?ana mu'handis.	انا مهندس •

* Not on record. † The record has siiyaa'raat-Ford *Ford automobiles.* ‡ The record has tiš'tugul.

ENGLISH EQUIVALENTS	AIDS TO LISTENING	ARABIC SPELLING
he has	′9inda	عنده

Beginning RECORD 6A

ENGLISH EQUIVALENTS	AIDS TO LISTENING	ARABIC SPELLING
farm	′mazra9a	مزرعة
My father has a farm.	?a′buuya ′9inda ′mazra9a.	ابوي عنده مزرعة .
John	*John*	جان
let's	′xallii	خلّي
we take a walk	nit′mašša	نتمشّى
to the market	lis′suug	للسوق
Let's take a walk to the market.	′xallii nit′mašša lis′suug.	خلّي نتمشّى للسوق .
Ali	*Ali*	علي
good *or* okay	′ṭayyib	طيّب
I take a walk	?at′mašša	اتمشّى
with you	wii′yaakum	ويّاكم
Okay, I'd like to take a walk with you.	′ṭayyib, ?a′ḥibb ?at′mašša wii′yaakum.	طيّب ، احب اتمشّى ويّاكم .

(*In the market.*)

ENGLISH EQUIVALENTS	AIDS TO LISTENING	ARABIC SPELLING
John	*John*	جان
that	′δaaka *or* δaak*	ذاك
man	raj′jaal	الرجّال
that man	′δaaka rraj′jaal	ذاك الرجّال
Look at that man.	′šuufuu ′δaaka rraj′jaal.	شوفوا ذاك الرجّال .
Ali	*Ali*	علي
porter	ḥam′maal	حمّال
He ['s] a porter.	′huuwa ḥam′maal.	هو حمّال .
he carries	′yiḥmil	يحمل
load	′ḥimil	حمل
heavy	θi′giil	ثقيل
his back	′ḍaḥra	ظهره
He's carrying a heavy load on his back.	′yiḥmil ′ḥimil θi′giil ′9ala ′ḍaḥra.	يحمل حمل ثقيل على ظهره .
he works	′yištugul	يشتغل
for a merchant	li′taajir	لتاجر
He works for a merchant.	′yištugul li′taajir.	يشتغل لتاجر .
the merchant	it′taajir	التاجر
master *or* owner *or* friend	′ṣaaḥib	صاحب
The merchant ['s] the owner of that shop.	it′taajir ′ṣaaḥib-′δaak idduk′kaan.	التاجر صاحب ذاك الدكّان .

* Not on record.

ENGLISH EQUIVALENTS	AIDS TO LISTENING	ARABIC SPELLING
John	*John*	جان
you know him	ti'9urfa	تعرفه
Do you know him?	'?inta ti'9urfa?	انت تعرفه ؟
Ali	*Ali*	علي
his son	'?ibna	ابنه
No, but I know his son.	'laa, 'laakin '?a9ruf '?ibna.	لا ، لكن اعرف ابنه •
I saw him	'šifta	شفته
he takes a walk	yit'mašša	يتمشّى
I saw him taking a walk	'šifta yit'mašša	شفته يتمشّى
yesterday	il'baarḥa	البارحة
I saw him on the street yesterday.	'šifta yit'mašša l'baarḥa.	شفته يتمشى البارحة •
Bill	*Bill*	بل
tobacco	'titin	تتن
I don't have [any] tobacco.	'maakuu '9indii 'titin.	ماكو عندي تتن •
Ali	*Ali*	علي
I smoke	?a'daxxin	ادخّن
[And] I don't smoke.	'?ana 'maa ?a'daxxin.	انا ما ادخّن •
Bill	*Bill*	بل
father of cigarettes	'?abuu-ji'gaayir	ابو جكاير
Where's somebody who sells cigarettes?	'wayn '?akuu '?abuu-ji'gaayir?	وين اكو ابو جكاير ؟

Beginning RECORD 6B

Ali	*Ali*	علي
his shop	duk'kaana	دكّانه
the baker	ilxab'baaz*	الخبّاز
The shop ['s] near the baker['s].	duk'kaana 'yamm ilxab'baaz.	دكّانه يم الخبّاز •
John	*John*	جان
the hour	is'saa9a	الساعة
What time [is] it?	is'saa9a 'bayš?	الساعة بيش ؟
Bill	*Bill*	بل
in the five	bil'xamsa	بالخمسة
It's five o'clock.	is'saa9a bil'xamsa.	الساعة بالخمسة •
John	*John*	جان
we go back *or* we come back	'nirja9	نرجع
We have to go back to the hotel.	'laazim 'nirja9 lil?uu'tayl.	لازم نرجع للاوتيل •

* Not on record.

Ali	*Ali*	علي
I see you	ʔa'šuufkum	اشوفكم
tomorrow	'baačir	باكر
I'll see you tomorrow.	ʔa'šuufkum 'baačir.	اشوفكم باكر .

PRONUNCIATION

Continuing RECORD 6B

PRACTICE 1

r: This sound is not the r-sound found in English. To pronounce it correctly, the tip of the tongue touches rapidly just back of the teeth, making a short trill. It corresponds roughly to the Scottish burr. Give it special attention at the end of a word.

'raas	**head*	راس
'rijil	**leg*	رجل
'wara	**behind*	وراء
ʔa'riid	*I want*	اريد
'jisir	*bridge*	جسر
'tamur	**dates*	تمر
'kisara	**he broke it*	كسره
'ʔaaxar	**other*	آخر
'ʔaaxir	**last*	آخِر

PRACTICE 2

rr: This is the above sound said longer. The tip of the tongue touches behind the teeth several times making a longer trill. Put plenty of force into making this trill.

'marra	**a single time, once*	مرّة
ʔat'šarraf	*I'm honored*	اتشرّف
yi'jarrub	**he tries*	يجرّب
irrij'jaal	*the man*	الرجّال
'jarra	**he pulled him*	جرّه
'ḥaarra	**hot* (f)	حارّة

PRACTICE 3

l: For this l-sound, place the tip of your tongue just behind your upper front teeth and hold it there. It is like the l in **leaf** rather than the l in **feel**.

'laa	*no*	لا
'walad	**boy*	ولد
'jabal	**mountain*	جبل

'filfil	**pepper*	فلفل
lil?uu'tayl	*to the hotel*	للاوتيل
bil'layl	**in the night*	بالليل
'?ila	*to, for*	الى
'?illa	**except*	الا

PRACTICE 4

ḷ: This sound occurs in few words. The tip of the tongue is just behind the teeth the same as for l above. Now, however, the back of the tongue is also raised somewhat toward the roof of the mouth.

?aḷ'ḷaa	**Allah*	الله
'gubaḷ	*straight ahead*	قبل
'xaḷḷ	**vinegar*	خل
'xaaḷii	**my uncle (maternal)*	خالي

ANALYSIS

1. The Article Prefix.

?uu'tayl	*hotel*	اوتيل
il?uu'tayl	*the hotel*	الاوتيل
mu'handis	*engineer*	مهندس
ilmu'handis	*the engineer*	المهندس
'baab	*door*	باب
il'baab	*the door*	الباب

Iraqi has no separate word for *a*, *an*, hence 'baab means *door, a door*. On the other hand, THE is expressed by il– (an older form is al–) added to the front of the word. This is the *article prefix*. Note that the stress never occurs on this prefix itself, but only on the word to which it is added. This accords with the patterns explained in Unit 2.

The –l of the article prefix is assimilated to certain consonants at the beginning of words, and the result is a double consonant. Therefore you can say either of two forms:

il'siinama *or* is'siinama	*the movie*	السينما
il'taajir *or* it'taajir	*the merchant*	التاجر
ilrij'jaal *or* irrij'jaal	*the man*	الرجّال
il'čaay *or* ič'čaay	*the tea*	الشاي

Throughout this book the doubled consonants are used, but both forms are possible. You will observe as you go along that it is the t-sounds (t ṭ θ), the d-sounds (d δ ḍ), the s-sounds (s ṣ š z), and č j n r which double in this way. The –l remains unchanged before all other consonants. Also observe that after a word ending in a vowel, the i– drops out freely and only the l (or doubling) remains. Thus, 'hal 'haaδii l'boosṭa? *Is this the postoffice ?*, and 'šifta l'baarḥa *I saw him yesterday.*

Iraqi uses the article prefix in places unexpected from the point of view of English. Compare the following:

'ðaak rij'jaal.	*That [is] a man.*	ذاك رجّال •
'ðaak irrij'jaal	*that man*	ذاك الرجّال
'haaða duk'kaan.	*This [is] a shop.*	هذا دكّان •
'haaða dduk'kaan	*this shop*	هذا الدكّان
'haaðii 'bint.	*This [is] a girl.*	هذي بنت •
'haaðii l'bint	*this girl*	هذي البنت
'haaðii 'booṣṭa.	*This [is] a postoffice.*	هذي بوسطة •
'haaðii l'booṣṭa	*this postoffice*	هذي البوسطة

Note that nouns in *equivalent sentences* (that is, sentences saying that 'something *is* something') do not have the article prefix. On the other hand, nouns after 'ðaak *that*, 'haaða *this* and related words always have the prefix il– (or doubling) when they go together as a phrase, as in ðaak irrij'jaal *that man.*

Another use quite different from the English pattern is as follows:

'ʔibnii lka'biir	*my oldest son* (lit., *my son the old*)	ابني الكبير
il'ʔibin ilka'biir	*the oldest son* (lit., *the son the old*)	الابن الكبير
'ʔibin ka'biir	*an old son*	ابن كبير

Note that the article prefix is spoken with an adjective which follows a noun having (1) a pronoun ending, or (2) its own article prefix (first two examples). But if the noun has neither, then the adjective doesn't have il– (last example).

2. Equivalents of in, to, for, on.

Here are examples of three common *prepositions* (words meaning *in, to, for, from, with,* and so on). Read through them carefully so that you will be able to recognize them and see somewhat the way they work, but you don't have to try to memorize each word.

I

'bii bag'daad	*in Baghdad*	بي بغداد
'biiya	*in me*	بيّ
bil'bayt	*in the house, at home*	بالبيت
bis'suug	*in the market*	بالسوق
ibbag'daad	*in Baghdad* (same as first example)	ببغداد
ib'baytii	*in my house*	ببيتي
bam'riika	*in America*	بامريكا

From these words you see that 'in' is expressed by 'bii (which can have the pronoun endings, as second example) and by its shorter form b–, which is added before words. The short form appears with the article prefix as bil– (or with doubling, as in bis–) *in the.* When the short form is added to a word beginning with a consonant, an i is added (as in ibbag'daad *in Baghdad*). Another word with the very same meaning and use is 'fii, short form fi–. A special usage of 'bii is in counting, where we have *for* or *per*, as in θi'nayn 'bii 'miit-'filis *two for a hundred fils* and bil'yoom *per day* (lit., *in the day*).

II

'ʔila bag'daad	*to Baghdad*	الى بغداد

'ʔilii	*to me, for me*	الي
'ʔilak	*to you, for you*	الك
li'taajir	*for a merchant*	لتاجر
li'ford	*for Ford*	لفورد
lilʔuu'tayl	*to the hotel*	للاوتيل
lis'suug	*to the market*	للسوق

Thus you see that *to, for, for the benefit of* is expressed by 'ʔila and its shorter forms 'ʔil– (with pronoun endings) and li– (added to words). With the article prefix, the latter appears as lil– (or with doubling, as in lis–).

III

'9ala ya'miinak	*on your right*	على يمينك
'9ala 'ḍahra	*on his back*	على ظهره
9al'bayt	*on the house*	على البيت
9assii'yaara	*on the automobile*	على السيّارة
9a'layya	*on me*	عليّ
9a'layk	*on you*	عليك

Finally you see that *on, upon* is expressed by '9ala and its related forms. With the article prefix, the form is 9al– (or with doubling, as in 9as–) *on the.* Note that the form with pronoun endings is 9alay– (9a'layya *on me*, 9a'layk *on you*).

There is just one other thing to note about the short forms of these prepositions, and that is that they are never stressed; instead, the stress always comes on the word to which they are added. So we have lis'suug *to the market*, but never 'lissuug. You will remember that the stress never comes on the article prefix either.

The other prepositions, such as 'wiiya *with*, minn *from*, 'yamm *near*, and so on, do not have shorter forms which are added to the front of words, hence we do not include them in this discussion.

3. Pronoun Endings — Equivalents of his, him

In Unit 2, three of the pronoun endings were presented. They were

–ii, –ya	*my, me*
–nii	*me* (with verbs only)
–ak, –k	*your, you* (m)
–na	*our, us*

The pronoun ending, meaning HIS, HIM is expressed in the following ways, depending on the structure of the underlying word.

I

'ʔisma	*his name*	اسمه
'šugla	*his work*	شغله
'ḍaḥra	*his back*	ظهره
'ʔila	*to him; for him*	اله
'šifta	*I saw him*	شفته
ti'9arfa	*you know him*	تعرفه

After a word ending in a CONSONANT, *his, him* is expressed by the pronoun ending –a, as you see from the above.

II		
'wiiya	*with*	ويّا
wii'yaa	*with him*	ويّاه
'šifna	*we saw*	شفنا
šif'naa	*we saw him*	شفناه

If the word already ends in –a, the pronoun ending –a is added, and now the stress falls on the resulting double –aa.

III		
'šuufuu	*see!* (pl)	شوفوا
'šuufii	*see!* (f)	شوفي
'bii	*in*	بي
'xallii	*put!* (m, f)	خلّي
šuu'fuu	*see him!*	شوفوه
šuu'fii	*see him!*	شوفيه
'bii	*in him*	بيه
xal'lii	*put him!*	خلّيه

Finally, you see that if the underlying word already ends in a DOUBLE VOWEL (*uu* or *ii*), then nothing is added, but the stress now falls on this double vowel. Because the position of the stress is now not according to the regular pattern, it will always be marked in this book.

4. 9ind.

'9ind '?abii 'mazra9a.	*My father has a farm.*	عند ابي مزرعة •
'?abii '9inda 'mazra9a.	*My father has a farm.*	ابي عنده مزرعة •
'9indii sii'yaara.	*I have an automobile.*	عندي سيّارة •
'kaan '9indii sii'yaara.	*I had an automobile.*	كان عندي سيّارة •
'maa '9indii sii'yaara.	*I don't have an automobile.*	ما عندي سيّارة •
'maa 'kaan '9indii sii'yaara.	*I didn't have an automobile.*	ما كان عندي سيّارة •
'9indak 'titin?	*Do you have [any] tobacco?*	عندك تتن ؟
'maakuu '9indii.	*I haven't [any].*	ماكو عندي •

The word '9ind has the primary meaning *with.* It is equivalent to *have, has* in showing possession. It can stand alone *before* the owner (first example) or with a pronoun ending *after* the owner (remaining examples). Past time, *I had,* is expressed by 'kaan '9indii. The negative is 'maa '9indii *I don't have,* and 'maa 'kaan '9indii *I didn't have.*

There are two other uses.

'?ijaw '9indii.	*They came to me.*	اجوا عندي •
'yištugul '9indii.	*He works for me.*	يشتغل عندي •

With verbs of *coming* or *going,* '9ind serves as *goal.* With 'yištugul *he works,* '9ind indicates *for whom.*

5. Agent Affixes of Verbs.

?a'riid	*I want*	اريد
'triid	*you want*	تريد
n'riid	*we want*	نريد

In these verb forms you will notice that there is a part which is the same in all (–riid) and a part which is different (?a–, t–, n–). The part that doesn't change tells what the action is (–riid means *want*), while the part that does change shows who is doing the action (*I*, *you*, *we*). We shall call these latter parts agent affixes because they indicate who the *agent* or *doer* of the action is.

The agent affix itself shows who is doing the action, so it is not necessary to use the separate words '?ana, '?inta, '?iḥna and so on. When these words are used together with verbs, it is usually for emphasis or contrast. For example

'triid 'maay?	*Do you want (some) water?*	تريد ماء ؟
'?inta 'triid 'maay?	*Do* you *want (some) water?*	انت تريد ماء ؟

Remember, every verb form includes an agent affix. You cannot say a verb form without an affix.

There are three *different groups of agent affixes*. (1) One occurs with *commands*. (2) A second group occurs with verb forms indicating *completed action*. (3) A third group is with verb forms indicating *action which has not been completed*. Following are four of the latter group.

I

yi'riid	*he wants*	يريد
yi'jiib	*he brings*	يجيب
yi'šuuf	*he sees*	يشوف
yi'ruuḥ	*he goes*	يروح
'yijii	*he comes*	يجي
'yiḥčii	*he speaks*	يحكي
'yimšii	*he walks*	يمشي
'yišrab	*he drinks*	يشرب
'yifham	*he understands*	يفهم
'yiḥmil	*he carries*	يحمل
'ya9ruf	*he knows*	يعرف
'yaakul	*he eats*	يا كل
yi'sawwii	*he does, makes*	يسوّي
yit'mašša	*he takes a walk*	يتمشّى
'yištugul	*he works*	يشتغل

You will note that the agent affix meaning he is yi– (ya– before 9 and in 'yaakul). Note that the stress follows the mechanical pattern.

II

'triid	*you want*	تريد
'tjiib	*you bring*	تجيب
'tšuuf	*you see*	تشوف
'truuḥ	*you go*	تروح

'tijii	*you come*	تجي
'tiḥčii	*you speak*	تحكي
'timšii	*you walk*	تمشي
'tišrab	*you drink*	تشرب
'tifham	*you understand*	تفهم
'tiḥmil	*you carry*	تحمل
'ta9ruf	*you know*	تعرف
'taakul	*you eat*	تاكل
'tsawwii	*you do, you make*	تسوّي
tit'mašša	*you take a walk*	تتمشّى
'tištuġul	*you work*	تشتغل

The agent affix meaning YOU (masculine) is t– (ti– before two consonants and ta– before 9 and in taakul. Remember that this refers to a *man or boy.*

III

ʔa'riid	*I want*	اريد
ʔa'jiib	*I bring*	اجيب
ʔa'šuuf	*I see*	اشوف
ʔa'ruuḥ	*I go*	اروح
ʔa'ḥibb	*I love, I like*	احب
'ʔajii	*I come*	اجي
'ʔaḥčii	*I speak*	احكي
'ʔamšii	*I walk*	امشي
'ʔašrab	*I drink*	اشرب
'ʔafham	*I understand*	افهم
'ʔaḥmil	*I carry*	احمل
'ʔa9ruf	*I know*	اعرف
'ʔaškurak	*I thank you*	اشكرك
'ʔaakul	*I eat*	آكل
ʔa'sawwii	*I do, I make*	اسوّي
ʔat'mašša	*I take a walk*	اتمشّى
'ʔaštuġul	*I work*	اشتغل
ʔat'šarraf	*I'm honored*	اتشرّف

The agent affix ʔa– means I. In ordinary conversation, this affix often drops after 'maa *not,* as in 'maa 'riid *I don't want* for ('maa ʔa'riid), and in 'maa 'šuuf *I don't see* for 'maa ʔa'šuuf.

IV

n'riid	*we want*	نريد
n'jiib	*we bring*	نجيب
n'šuuf	*we see*	نشوف
n'ruuḥ	*we go*	نروح
n'ḥibb	*we love, like*	نحب

′nijii	*we come*	نجي
′niḥčii	*we speak*	نحكي
′nimšii	*we walk*	نمشي
′nišrab	*we drink*	نشرب
′nifham	*we understand*	نفهم
′niḥmil	*we carry*	نحمل
′na9ruf	*we know*	نعرف
′naakul	*we eat*	ناكل
n′sawwii	*we do, make*	نسوّي
nit′mašša	*we take a walk*	نتمشّى
′ništuġul	*we work*	نشتغل

The agent affix meaning WE is n– (ni– before two consonants and na– before 9 and in ′naakul).

In Iraqi, in general three consonants aren't spoken together. Or, putting it another way, no more than two vowels or consonants are spoken in sequence. In keeping with this, an i is spoken before two consonants at the beginning of a word if the preceding word ends in a consonant. Of course if the preceding word ends in a vowel, the i is not necessary. Thus we have

After a consonant

n′ruuh	*we go*	نروح
′laazim in′ruuḥ	*we have to go*	لازم نروح
′tsawwii	*you do*	تسوّي
′kunit it′sawwii	*you were doing*	كنت تسوّي

After a vowel

n′šuuf	*we see*	نشوف
′maa n′šuuf	*we don't see*	ما نشوف
′tsawwii	*you do*	تسوّي
′maa t′sawwii	*you don't do*	ما تسوّي

This added i doesn't affect the meaning in any way.

6. VERB FORMS IN SEQUENCE.

I

ʔa′riid ′ʔaakul.	*I want to eat.*	اريد اكل •
ʔa′riid ′ʔaštuġul.	*I want to work.*	اريد اشتغل •
ʔa′riid ʔa′ruuḥ	*I want to go.*	اريد اروح •
ʔa′riid ′ʔajii.	*I want to come.*	اريد اجي •
ʔa′ḥibb ʔat′mašša.	*I would like to take a walk.*	احب اتمشّى •
n′riid in′šuuf.	*We want to see.*	نريد نشوف
n′riid nit′mašša.	*We want to take a walk.*	نريد نتمشّى •
n′riid ′nijii.	*We want to come.*	نريد نجي •

'šitriid 'tišrab?	*What do you want to drink?*	شتريد تشرب ؟
'šitriid 'taakul?	*What do you want to eat?*	شتريد تاكل ؟
'šitriid it'sawwii?	*What do you want to do?*	شتريد تسوّي ؟

From the above you see that verbs can be used together. What you really say is *I want I eat* for *I want to eat*, and *we want we see* for *we want to see*, and so on.

II

The first verb can indicate action in the past, as in the words below:

'kaan 'yištugul.	*He was working.* or *He used to work.*	كان يشتغل .
'kunit 'timšii.	*You were walking.*	كنت تمشي .
'kunit '?amšii.	*I was walking.*	كنت امشي .
'kunit ?a'zuura.	*I used to visit him.*	كنت ازوره .
'škunit it'sawwii?	*What were you doing?*	شكنت تسوّي ؟
'šifta yit'mašša.	*I saw him taking a walk.*	شفته يتمشى .

From the above you see that 'kaan *he was* and its related forms is used with an incompleted action verb form to indicate action which *was taking place* or which *used to take place* at some past time.

Remember, every verb form has to have an agent affix, and the agent affix always refers to the person who performs the action. Thus the last example is literally *I saw him he takes a walk* for *I saw him taking a walk.*

7. Two Equivalents of not.

'maa di'rasit.	*I didn't study.*	ما درست
'maa 'šifta.	*I didn't see him.*	ما شفته
'maa 'kunit hi'naak.	*I wasn't there.*	ما كنت هناك
'maa '9indii 'titin.	*I haven't [any] tobacco.*	ما عندي تتن
'muu 'zayn.	*Not well.* or *Not good.*	مو زين
'muu ka'θiir.	*Not much.*	مو كثير
'muu 'hassa.	*Not now.*	مو هستّه
'muu 'laazim.	*Not necessary.*	مو لازم

You will note that 'maa and 'muu both mean *not.* Now note that 'maa is used with *verbs* and '9ind, while 'muu is used elsewhere.

EXERCISES

A. *Supply the agent affix corresponding to* ?ana *I, then* 'huuwa *he,* '?inta *you* (m), and '?iḥna *we.*

1. __štugul 'fii bag'daad.
2. 'maa __9ruf 'wayn '9alii 'yištugul.
3. __daxxin ji'gaara ?amriikaa'niiya.
4. 'maa __šuuf ?a'buuk.
5. __mšii ya'waaš.
6. __riid __šrab 'biira.

B. VERBS IN SEQUENCE. *Read aloud, supplying the agent affix called for.*

1. n'riid __jii wii'yaak.
2. 'triid __tmašša wii'yaay?
3. n'ḥibb __9ruf '?ismak.
4. '?akuu rij'jaal yi'riid __šuufak.
5. 'šuufnii __mšii!
6. n'riid __šrab 'čaay-ḥa'liib.
7. '9alii, 'šinuu __sawwii?
8. ta'9aal 'šuufnii __sawwii 'haaδa!
9. 'šitriid __aakul?
10. sa'9iid 'maa __daxxin ka'θiir.

C. kaan *with incompleted action verb form. Supply the agent affixes.*

1. '?axii 'kaan __štugul '9ind mu'ḳaawil.
2. '?ana 'kunit __tmašša bis'suug.
3. 'maa 'kunit ?a'ḥibb __aakul 'simač.
4. ilḥam'maal 'kaan __ḥmil 'ḥimil '9ala 'ḍahra.
5. 'gullii, š'kunit __sawwii hi'naa?
6. '?iḥna 'kunna __ḥčii 'wiiya ?a'xuuk.

D. PRONOUN ENDINGS. Express *I have*, then *you have, we have*, and *he has.*

1. '9ind__ sii'yaarat-Ford.
2. 'maakuu 9ind__ ji'gaara.
3. il'baarḥa 'kaan 9ind__ 'miit-'filis, 'hassa 'maa 9ind__.

E. Supply 'maa or 'muu *not*.

1. ?a'xuuya __ 'kaan'yištugul 'fii bag'daad.
2. __ 'laazim ?a'ruuḥ lil'booṣṭa.
3. '?abii __'9inda 'mazra9a, 'bass '9inda duk'kaan.
4. '9alii, 'tḥibb 'tijii wii'yaay? __ 'hassa.
5. __ n'riid 'naakul.
6. __ ?a'ḥibb '?amšii ka'θiir.

F. Change these sentences to express 'Where is *a* hotel?' and so on, instead of 'Where is *the* hotel?'

Example: 'wayn il'?uutayl? becomes 'wayn '?akuu ?uu'tayl?

1. 'wayn is'siinama?
2. 'wayn is'suug?
3. 'wayn il'maṭ9am?
4. il'gahwa '9ala ya'miinak.
5. il'booṣṭa '9ala ya'saarak.
6. idduk'kaan gid'daamak.

WHAT WOULD YOU SAY?

1. *You ask a Baghdadi what his work is.*
   a. ʔa'ḥibb 'ʔa9ruf 'šinuu 'šuglak. ١ ـ احب اعرف شنو شغلك ٠
   b. 'šinuu 'hassa tiš'tugul? ٢ ـ شتشتغل هسه ؟
   c. 'šitsawwii hi'naak? ٣ ـ شتسوّي هناك ؟

2. *He's a contractor.*
   a. 'ʔana 'kunit mu'ḳaawil. ١ ـ انا كنت مقاول ٠
   b. 'ʔana 'muu ḥam'maal. ٢ ـ انا مو حمّال ٠
   c. 'ʔana mu'ḳaawil. ٣ ـ انا مقاول ٠

3. *He asks you what you used to do.*
   a. 'gullii, 'šitsawwii? ١ ـ قل لي شتسوّي ؟
   b. 'ščinit it'sawwii? ٢ ـ شكنت تسوّي ؟
   c. 'ščinit 'triid it'sawwii? ٣ ـ شكنت تريد تسوي ؟

4. *You used to work in a factory.*
   a. 'kunit 'ʔaštugul bil'ma9mal. ١ ـ كنت اشتغل بالمعمل ٠
   b. 'kunit 'ʔamšii lis'suug. ٢ ـ كنت امشي للسوق ٠
   c. 'kunit '9aamil, 'laakin 'hassa 'ʔana 'rayyis-il'ma9mal. ٣ ـ كنت عامل لكن هسّه انا رئيس المعمل ٠

5. *Your brother was foreman there.*
   a. ʔa'xuuya 'kaan 'rayyis 'bii. ١ ـ اخوي كان رئيس بيه ٠
   b. ʔa'xuuya 'kaan 'yiš'tugul wii'yaay. ٢ ـ اخوي كان يشتغل ويّاي ٠
   c. ʔa'xuuya ir'rayyis 'bii. ٣ ـ اخوي الرئيس بيه ٠

6. *How was the work?*
   a. 'maa ʔa'riid 'ʔaštugul bil'ma9mal. ١ ـ ما اريد اشتغل بالمعمل ٠
   b. 'šloon 'kaan iš'šugul? ٢ ـ شلون كان الشغل ؟
   c. 'ta9ruf 'šloon 'šuglii? ٣ ـ تعرف شلون شغلي ؟

7. *You liked it.*
   a. 'šuglii 'čaan 'zayn. ١ ـ شغلي كان زين ٠
   b. 'ma9mal-'Ford 'kulliš ka'biir. ٢ ـ معمل فورد كلش كبير
   c. ʔa'ḥibb iš'šugul bil'ma9mal. ٣ ـ احب الشغل بالمعمل

8. *You ask if there are many cars in Baghdad.*
   a. siiyaa'raat-Ford 'timšii 'zayn? ١ ـ سيارات فورد تمشي زين ٠
   b. 'ʔakuu siiyaa'raat ka'θiira 'fii bag'daad? ٢ ـ اكو سيّارات كثيرة في بغداد ؟
   c. 'ʔana 'daayman ʔa'šuuf siiya'raat-Ford. ٣ ـ انا دائما اشوف سيارات فورد ٠

9. *He suggests a walk.*
   a. 'laazim nit'mašša bis'suug. ١ ـ لازم تتمشى بالسوق ٠
   b. 'xallii nit'mašša bis'suug. ٢ ـ خلّي نتمشّى بالسوق ٠
   c. 'xallii 'nimšii lis'suug. ٣ ـ خلّي نمشي للسوق ٠

10. *You agree.*

a. ʹṭayyib, ˀaʹḥibb ˀatʹmašša wiiʹyaak. — ١ ـ طيّب ، احب اتمشّى ويّاك ٠

b. ʹˀana ʹmaa ʹˀa9ruf ʹwayn isʹsuug. — ٢ ـ انا ما اعرف وين السوق ٠

c. ˀarʹjuuk raaʹwiinii ʹwayn isʹsuug. — ٣ ـ ارجوك راويني وين السوق ٠

11. *You ask if his father is a contractor too.*

a. ˀaʹbuuk ʹhamm ʹkaan muʹḳaawil? — ١ ـ ابوك هم كان مقاول ؟

b. ˀaʹbuuk ʹhamm muʹḳaawil? — ٢ ـ ابوك هم مقاول ؟

c. ˀaʹbuuk ʹkaan muʹhandis ˀaw muʹḳaawil? — ٣ ـ ابوك كان مهندس او مقاول ؟

12. *Your father has a farm.*

a. ˀaʹbuuya ʹkaan yišʹtuġul wiiʹyaay bilʹma9mal. — ١ ـ ابوي كان يشتغل ويّاي بالمعمل ٠

b. ʹˀabii ʹ9inda ʹmazra9a čaʹbiira. — ٢ ـ ابي عنده مزرعة كبيرة ٠

c. ʹhuuwa ʹṣaaḥib-ʹδaak iddukʹkaan. — ٣ ـ هو صاحب ذاك الدكّان ٠

13. *You are out of cigarettes.*

a. ʹmaa ʹkaan ʹ9indii ʹjiʹgaayir. — ١ ـ ما كان عندي جكاير ٠

b. ʹmaakuu ʹ9indii jiʹgaayir. — ٢ ـ ماكو عندي جكاير ٠

c. ʹwayn ʹˀakuu ʹˀabuu-jiʹgaayir? — ٣ ـ وين اكو ابو الجكاير ؟

14. *There's a cigarette seller near the baker's.*

a. ʹˀakuu ʹˀabuu-jiʹgaayir ʹyamm ilxabʹbaaz. — ١ ـ اكو ابو الجيكاير يم الخبّاز ٠

b. ilʹbaarḥa ʹšifit dukʹkaana. — ٢ ـ البارحة شفت دكانه ٠

c. ʹˀa9ruf ʹδaak itʹtaajir. — ٣ ـ اعرف ذاك التاجر ٠

15. *You ask the time.*

a. isʹsaa9a bilʹxamsa. — ١ ـ الساعة بالخمسة ٠

b. ʹbayš isʹsaa9a? — ٢ ـ بيش الساعة ؟

16. *You have to leave.*

a. ṣaʹdiiḳii ʹmaa ʹˀija wiiʹyaay. — ١ ـ صديقي ما اجي وياي ٠

b. ˀisʹmaḥlii, ʹhassa ʹlaazim ˀaʹruuḥ. — ٢ ـ اسمح لي ، هسّه لازم اروح ٠

c. ʹšitriid ʹminnii? — ٣ ـ شتريد مني ؟

LISTENING IN

Bill and John meet Ali one morning. Bill is already acquainted with Ali.

Concluding RECORD 6B

BILL ṣaʹbaaḥ ilʹxayr. — بل ـ صباح الخير ٠

ˀaʹriid ˀaʹ9arfak ʹ9ala ṣaʹdiiḳii John. — اريد اعرفك على صديقي جان ٠

ALI ?at'šarraf, John.	علي ـ اتشرّف ، جان •
'?anta 'hamm 'minn ?am'riika?	انت هم من امريكا ؟
JOHN 'na9am, 'minn New York.	جان ـ نعم ، من نيويورك •
BILL '9alii, ?a'ḥibb '?a9ruf 'šinuu 'šug̱lak.	بل ـ علي ، احب اعرف شنو شغلك •
ALI '?ana mu'ḳaawil.	علي ـ انا مقاول •
BILL 'wayn 'tištug̱ul?	بل ـ وين تشتغل ؟
ALI '?aštug̱ul hi'naa 'fii bag̱'daad.	علي ـ اشتغل هنا في بغداد •
BILL 'šloon 'šug̱lak?	بل ـ شلون شغلك ؟
ALI 'hassa 'kulliš 'zayn, bass 'gabul il'ḥarb 'maa 'čaan 'zayn.	علي ـ هسّه كلّش زين ، بس قبل الحرب ما كان زين •
BILL 'xallii nit'mašša lis'suug.	بل ـ خلّي نتمشّى للسوق •
ALI 'ṭayyib, ?a'ḥibb ?at'mašša wii'yaakum.	علي ـ طيّب ، احب اتمشّى وياكم •
Bill, 'ščint it'sawwii bam'riika?	بل ، شكنت تسوّي بامريكا ؟
BILL '?ana mu'handis.	بل ـ انا مهندس •
'laakin ?a'buuya '9inda 'mazra9a ka'biira 'fii Texas.	لكن ابوي عنده مزرعة كبيرة في تكسس •
ALI 'winta John, 'ščint it'sawwii?	علي ـ وانت جان ، شكنت تشتغل ؟
JOHN '?ana 'čint '?aštug̱ul 'fii 'ma9mal-siiyaa'raat.	جان ـ انا كنت اشتغل في معمل سيّارات •
ALI 'wayn? 'fii Detroit?	علي ـ وين ؟ في ديترويت ؟
JOHN 'na9am, 'fii 'ma9mal-Ford.	جان ـ نعم ، في معمل فورد •

(Remaining Conversation not RECORDED.)

'?axii 'hamm 'yištug̱ul 'wiiya Ford.	اخوي هم يشتغل ويّا فورد •
'?ana 'činit '9aamil, wu'laakin 'huuwa 'čaan ra'?iis-il'ma9mal.	انا كنت عامل ولكن هو كان رئيس المعمل •
ALI siiyaa'raat-Ford 'kulliš 'zayna.	علي ـ سيّارات فورد كلّش زينة •
JOHN '?akuu ka'θiira 'fii bag̱'daad?	جان ـ اكو كثيرة في بغداد ؟
ALI 'balii.	علي ـ بلي •
'?akuu '9idna sii'yaarat-Ford, wu'hiiya 'timšii 'daayman 'zayn.	اكو عندنا سيّارة فورد ، وهي تمشي دائما زين •
BILL 'wayn 'hassa sii'yaartak?	بل ـ وين هسّه سيارتك ؟
ALI bil'bayt.	علي ـ بالبيت •
'?ana 'daayman ?a'ḥibb '?amšii.	انا دائما احب امشي •
BILL 'šuufuu 'ðaaka rrij'jaal.	بل ـ شوفوا ذاك الرجّال •
'šinuu 'šug̱la?	شنو شغله ؟
ALI 'huuwa ḥam'maal.	علي ـ هو حمّال •
BILL 'šinuu ḥam'maal?	بل ـ شنو حمّال ؟
ALI 'huuwa rij'jaal 'yiḥmil 'ḥimil '9ala 'ḍahra.	علي ـ هو رجّال يحمل حمل على ظهره •
'ðaaka lḥam'maal 'yištug̱ul li'taajir.	ذاك الحمّال يشتغل لتاجر •
it'taajir 'ṣaaḥib-'ðaaka dduk'kaan.	التاجر صاحب ذاك الدكّان •
JOHN '?inta ti'9urfa?	جان ـ انت تعرفه ؟
ALI 'laa, 'laakin '?a9ruf '?ibna.	علي ـ لا ، لكن اعرف ابنه •
'huuwa 'maa 'yištug̱ul ka'θiir.	هو ما يشتغل كثير •
il'baarḥa 'šifta yit'maašša bis'suug.	البارحة شفته يتمشّى بالسوق •

Bill takes his pipe out of his pocket, but finds that he hasn't any tobacco.

BILL	John, 'ʔakuu '9indak 'titin?	بل ـ جان ، اكو عندك تتن ؟
JOHN	'laa, 'maakuu '9indii.	جان ـ لا ، ماكو عندي ●
ALI	'ma9a l'ʔasaf, 'ʔana 'maa ʔa'daxxin.	علي ـ مع الاسف ، انا ما ادخّن ●
BILL	'9alii, 'ta9ruf 'wayn 'ʔakuu 'ʔabuu-ji'gaayir?	بل ـ علي ، تعرف وين اكو ابو جكاير ؟
ALI	'ʔa9ruf 'waaḥid 'yamm ilxab'baaz.	علي ـ اعرف واحد يم الخبّاز ●
BILL	'xallii nit'mašša 'ʔila duk'kaana.	بل ـ خلّي نتمشّى الى دكّانه ●

They walk to the shop and buy some tobacco.

JOHN	is'saa9a 'ʔbayš?	جان ـ الساعة بيش ؟
ALI	is'saa9a bil'xamsa.	علي ـ الساعة بالخمسة ●
JOHN	'laazim 'nirja9 lilʔuu'tayl.	جان ـ لازم نرجع للاوتيل ●
BILL	n'šuufak 'baačir, '9alii.	بل ـ نشوفك باكر ، علي ●
ALI	'ṭayyib.	علي ـ طيّب ●

CONVERSATIONS

A. You have been introduced to an Iraqi named Ali. He asks you where you are from. You say you are an American, and tell him what part you came from. He asks you what kind of work you do. You are an engineer, you say. He asks what you did in America. You say that you were working in a factory, then you explain that it was an automobile factory. You ask him if he knows Ford cars. Yes, he says, Ford cars are good, in fact he has one. He says there is a Ford factory in Baghdad. You ask him if he worked in it, and he replies no, but his friend used to work there. His friend was an engineer, too.

You ask him what he does, and he replies he's a contractor. You ask how work is, and he says it's very good. You ask if he works in Baghdad, and he says yes. He adds that his father was a contractor too.

He asks you if you would like to drink some coffee with him. You accept, and he suggests you go to a coffee shop a little way ahead.

B. At the coffee shop, the waiter asks you what you want to eat. You say you don't want to eat anything, you only want some coffee. The waiter says there isn't any coffee, but there's tea. You tell him to bring you tea. Ali says he wants tea, too, but with cream in it. You tell Ali that you don't drink tea much; you like coffee most of the time.

C. Later you are walking around with Ali. He finds he is out of cigarettes, so he suggests you walk to the market. He knows where there's a cigarette seller; he saw his shop yesterday. You see a man carrying a heavy load on his back and tell Ali to look; Ali tells you that the man is a porter. Ali calls your attention to another man. What is his work, you ask. Ali says that he doesn't work; he is a merchant and has a big shop in the market. You ask Ali if he knows him. Ali says yes, and he also knows his son. His son doesn't work much either, he likes to walk around all the time.

At the cigarette dealer's, Ali points to some cigarettes and asks how much they are. The dealer says they are two packages for a hundred fils. Ali says he wants two packages, then he asks you if you will have a cigarette. You thank him, but say no, you don't want to smoke now.

D. Free conversation.

VOCABULARY

'baačir	tomorrow
'ḍahar	back
'ḍahra	his back
'gabul	before
'hiiya	she
ḥam'maal	porter
'ḥarb	war
'ḥimil	load
'kulliš	very; too
'kunit	I was; you were (m)
'ma9mal	factory
'ma9mal-siiyaa'raat	automobile factory
'ma9mal-Ford	[the] Ford factory
'mazra9a (f)	farm
mu'handis	engineer
mu'ḳaawil	contractor
'nirja9	we go back, we come back
nit'mašša	we take a walk
'rayyis *or* ra'?iis	head, chief, boss
'rayyis-il'ma9mal	[the] head of the factory
rij'jaal	man
'saa9a (f)	hour; clock
'bayš is'saa9a?	What time is it?
is'saa9a bil'xamsa.	It's five o'clock.
sii'yaara (f)	automobile
siiyaa'raat	automobiles
sii'yaarat-Ford	a Ford automobile
siiyaa'raat-Ford	Ford automobiles
'suug	market
lis'suug	to the market
ṣa'baaḥ il'xayr.	Good morning.
'ṣaaḥib	master, owner; friend
'šifit	I saw; you saw (m)
'šifta	I saw him; you saw him
'šloon	how
'šugul	work
'šuglak	your work
'taajir	merchant
it'taajir	the merchant
li'taajir	for a merchant
'timšii	she walks; goes, runs (of things)
'titin	tobacco
'tsawwii	you do, you make
'ta9ruf	you know
ti'9urfa	you know him
'ṭayyib	good; okay
xab'baaz	baker
'xallii	let's!
'xallii nit'mašša.	Let's take a walk!
'xallii n'ruuḥ.	Let's go!
'yiḥmil	he carries
'yištugul	he works
yit'mašša	he takes a walk
'?abuu-ji'gaayir	cigarette dealer
?a'daxxin	I smoke
?a'ḥibb	I like, I love
?a'ḥibbak	I like you
?a'ḥibb ?a9ruf	I would like to know
'?aštugul	I work
?a'šuuf	I see
?a'šuufkum	I see you (pl)
?at'mašša	I take a walk
'?a9ruf	I know
'?ibin	son
?ibna	his son
il'baarḥa	yesterday
'9aamil	laborer, workman
'9alii	Ali (*man's name*)
'9ind	with; has, have (takes *pronoun endings*)
'δaaka, 'δaak	that (m)
'δaak irrij'jaal	that man
θi'giil	heavy

UNIT 4

Family and Friends

BASIC SENTENCES

Beginning RECORD 7A

ENGLISH EQUIVALENTS	AIDS TO LISTENING	ARABIC SPELLING
Mustafa	*Mustafa*	مصطفى
you live	'tiskin	تسكن
Where were you living?	'wayn 'činit 'tiskin?	وين كنت تسكن ؟
Bill	*Bill*	بل
my family	'ʔahlii	اهلي
With my family in Texas.	'wiiya 'ʔahlii 'fii Texas.	ويّا اهلي في تكسس •
Mustafa	*Mustafa*	مصطفى
staying *or* living	'saakin	ساكن
Where [are] you staying here?	'wayn 'ʔinta 'saakin hi'naaya?	وين انت ساكن هنايه ؟
Bill	*Bill*	بل
We ['re] staying at the Regent Hotel.	'ʔiḥna saak'niin 'fii ʔuu'tayl-Regent.	احنا ساكنين في اوتيل ريجنت •
married	mit'zawwij	متزوّج
Are you married or not?	'ʔinta mit'zawwij 'ʔaw 'laa?	انت متزوّج او لا ؟
Mustafa	*Mustafa*	مصطفى
Yes, I'm married.	'na9am, 'ʔana mit'zawwij.	نعم ، انا متزوّج •
two boys	wala'dayn	ولدين
daughter *or* girl	'bint	بنت
I have two boys and a girl.	'9indii wala'dayn wu'bint.	عندي ولدين وبنت •
small *or* young	ṣa'ġiir(f. ṣa'ġiira *or* ṣa'ġayra*)	صغير
I have a young daughter.	'bintii ṣa'ġayra.	بنتي صغيرة •

* Not on record.

ENGLISH EQUIVALENTS	AIDS TO LISTENING	ARABIC SPELLING
Bill	*Bill*	بل
brother	'ʔax	اخ
some *or* several *or* how many	'kam	كم
how many brothers	'kam 'ʔax	كم اخ
How many brothers do you have?	'kam 'ʔax '9indak?	كم اخ عندك ؟
Mustafa	*Mustafa*	مصطفى
brothers	'ʔuxwa *or* ʔux'waan	اخوة (ايضا) اخوان
Three brothers.	θi'laaθ-'ʔuxwa.	ثلاث اخوة •
my brothers	ʔu'xuutii	اخوتي
in the army	bij'jayš	بالجيش
Two of my brothers [are] in the army.	θi'nayn 'minn ʔu'xuutii bij'jayš.	ثنين من اخوتي بالجيش •
one of them	'waaḥid 'minhum	واحد منهم
aviator	ṭay'yaar	طيّار
One of them ['s] an aviator.	'waaḥid 'minhum ṭay'yaar.	واحد منهم طيّار •
the second	iθ'θaanii	الثاني
officer	'ḍaabuṭ	ضابط
The second ['s] an officer.	iθ'θaanii 'ḍaabut.	الثاني ضابط •
the third	iθ'θaaliθ	الثالث
in the school	bil'madrasa	بالمدرسة
The third ['s] in school.	iθ'θaaliθ bil'madrasa.	الثالث بالمدرسة •
Bill	*Bill*	بل
he studies	'yidris	يدرس
he wants to study	yi'riid 'yidris	يريد يدرس
What does he want to study?	'šinuu yi'riid 'yidris?	شنو يريد يدرس ؟
Mustafa	*Mustafa*	مصطفى
he told (to) me	'gaallii	قال لي
he becomes	yi'ṣiir	يصير
he wants to become	yi'riid yi'ṣiir	يريد يصير
doctor	ṭa'biib	طبيب
He told me he wants to be a doctor.	'gaallii yi'riid yi'ṣiir ṭa'biib.	قال لي يريد يصير طبيب •
Bill	*Bill*	بل
sister	'ʔuxut	اخت
how many sisters	'kam 'ʔuxut	كم اخت
How many sisters do you have?	'kam 'ʔuxut '9indak?	كم اخت عندك ؟

Beginning RECORD 7B

ENGLISH EQUIVALENTS	AIDS TO LISTENING	ARABIC SPELLING
Mustafa	*Mustafa*	مصطفى
One. (f)*	'wiḥda. *or* waaḥda.*	واحدة •
She ['s] married.	'hiiya mit'zawja.	هي متزوّجة •
she lives	'tiskin	تسكن
her husband	'rajilha	رجلها
(the) Basra	il'baṣra	البصرة
She lives with her husband in Basra.	'tiskin 'wiiya 'rajilha bil'baṣra.	تسكن ويّا رجلها بالبصرة •
they came	'ʔijaw	اجوا
in the night	bil'layl	بالليل
last night	il'baarḥa bil'layl	البارحة بالليل
They came here last night. (lit., *with us*)	'ʔijaw '9idna il'baarḥa bil'layl.	اجوا عندنا البارحة بالليل •
they brought	'jaabaw* *or* 'jaabuu	جابوا
their daughter	'binthum *or* 'binithum*	بنتهم
with them	wii'yaahum	ويّاهم
They brought their daughter with them.	'jaabaw 'binithum wii'yaahum.	جابوا بنتهم ويّاهم •
she was	čaanat *or* 'kaanat	كانت
sick	ma'riiḍ	مريض
She was sick.	'kaanat ma'riiḍa.	كانت مريضة •
Bill	*Bill*	بل
what was	'škaan *or* 'ščaan*	شكان
in her	'biiha	بيها
What was the matter with her?	'škaan 'biiha?	شكان بيها ؟
Mustafa	*Mustafa*	مصطفى
I don't know.	'maa 'ʔa9ruf.	ما اعرف •
he told (to) us	gaa'linna	قال لنا
The doctor didn't tell us.	iṭṭa'biib 'maa gaa'linna.	الطبيب ما قال لنا •
Bill	*Bill*	بل
how is she	'šloonha	شلونها
today	il'yoom *or* hal'yoom	اليوم (ايضا) هليوم
How [is] she today?	'šloonha l'yoom?	شلونها اليوم ؟

* Not on record.

ENGLISH EQUIVALENTS	AIDS TO LISTENING	ARABIC SPELLING
Mustafa	*Mustafa*	مصطفى
better	'ʔaḥsan (m *and* f)	احسن
weak	ḍa'9iif	ضعيف
Better but weak.	'ʔaḥsan 'laakin ḍa'9iifa.	احسن لكن ضعيفة .

(*Mustafa calls to some children who are going by.*)

Bill	*Bill*	بل
who	'minuu	منو
they	'humma	همّا
Who [are] they?	'minuu 'humma?	منو همّا ؟
Mustafa	*Mustafa*	مصطفى
this boy	'haaδa l'walad	هذا الولد
[the] son of my brother	'ʔibin-ʔa'xuuy *or* 'ʔibin-ʔa'xuuya	ابن اخوي
This boy ['s] my brother's son.	'haaδa l'walad 'ʔibin-ʔa'xuuy.	هذا الولد ابن اخوي .
good	'xooš	خوش
He ['s] a good boy.	'huuwa 'xooš 'walad.	هو خوش ولد .
his father	ʔa'buu*	ابوه
His father ['s] the aviator.	ʔa'buu ṭṭay'yaar.	ابوه الطيّار .
this girl	'haay il'bint	هاي البنت
his sister	'ʔuxta	اخته
This girl [is] his sister.	'haay il'bint 'ʔuxta.	هاي البنت اخته .
Bill	*Bill*	بل
that girl	'δiič il'bint	ذيك البنت

Beginning RECORD 8A

standing (f)	il'waagfa	الواقفة
behind them	wa'raahum	وراهم
Who ['s] that girl standing behind them?	'minuu 'δiič il'bint il'waagfa wa'raahum?	منو ذيك البنت الواقفة وراهم ؟
Mustafa	*Mustafa*	مصطفى
She['s] the daughter of my second brother.	'hiiya 'bint-ʔa'xuuya θ'θaanii.	هي بنت اخوي الثاني .

(*Bill talks to the little girl.*)

Bill	*Bill*	بل
you (f)	'ʔintii	انتي
pretty *or* handsome	ja'miil	جميل
You ['re] a pretty girl.	'ʔintii 'bint ja'miila.	انتي بنت جميلة .

* On the record, ʔa'buuhu is classical, ʔa'buu is colloquial.

ENGLISH EQUIVALENTS	AIDS TO LISTENING	ARABIC SPELLING
What ['s] your name?	'šinuu 'ʔismič?	شنو اسمك ؟
Pearl	*Pearl*	لولو
My name [is] Pearl	'ʔismii 'luuluu.	اسمي لولو
Bill	*Bill*	بل
with you (f)	wii'yaač	ويّاك
Who [are] these [children] with you?	'minuu haa'δool wii'yaač?	منو هاذول ويّاك ؟
Pearl	*Pearl*	لولو
my uncle (father's brother)	'9ammii	عمي
[the] son of my uncle	'ʔibin-'9ammii	ابن عمي
My cousin and his sister.	'ʔibin-'9ammii 'wuxta.	ابن عمي واخته •
sisters	xa'waat	خوات
I don't have [any] sisters.	'maakuu '9indii xa'waat.	ماكو عندي خوات •
Bill	*Bill*	بل
you talk (f)	tiḥ'čiin	تحكين
You talk well.	'ʔintii tiḥ'čiin 'zayn.	انتي تحكين زين •
how much *or* how far	'šgad	شقد
your age	'9amrič	عمرك
How old are you?	'šgad '9amrič?	شقد عمرك ؟
Pearl	*Pearl*	لولو
my age	'9amrii	عمري
years	si'niin	سنين
eight years	θi'maan-si'niin	ثمان سنين
I'm eight years old.	'9amrii θi'maan-si'niin.	عمري ثمان سنين •
(*Pearl speaks to Mustafa.*)		
going	'raayiḥ	رايح
We ['re] going to a movie.	'ʔiḥna raay'ḥiin lis'siinama.	احنا رايحين للسينما •
Mustafa	*Mustafa*	مصطفى
to which	li'ʔay	لاي
What movie?	li'ʔay 'siinama?	لاي سينما ؟
Said	*Said*	سعيد
king	'malik	ملك
The King Ghazi (movie).	'siinamat-il'malik 'g̣aazii.	سينمة الملك غازي •
(*The children leave.*)		
Mustafa	*Mustafa*	مصطفى
Excuse me, Bill.	ʔi9'ḍirnii, Bill.	اعذرني ، بل •

ENGLISH EQUIVALENTS	AIDS TO LISTENING	ARABIC SPELLING
I visit	ʔa'zuur	ازور
his wife	'marta	مرته
I have to go visit my uncle and aunt. (literally, his wife)	'laazim ʔa'ruuḥ ʔa'zuur '9ammii wu'marta.	لازم اروح ازور عمي ومرته •
distant *or* far	ba'9iid	بعيد
Their house [is] pretty far from here.	'baythum ba'9iid 'minn hi'naa.	بيتهم بعيد من هنا •
Bill	*Bill*	بل
I return	'ʔarja9	ارجع
I have to go back to the hotel.	'laazim 'ʔarja9 lilʔuu'tayl.	لازم ارجع للاوتيل •

PRONUNCIATION

Continuing RECORD 8A

PRACTICE 1

g: This sign stands for a sound which has no equivalent in English. To make it, raise the back of the tongue toward the roof of the mouth, but not close enough to touch it. The front of the tongue is kept tight against the lower front teeth. It is like a French or German r-sound; it is a gargling sound, not a trill.

'gaalii	**expensive*	غالي
bag'daad	*Baghdad*	بغداد
'faarug	**empty*	فارغ
'nigsil	**we wash*	نغسل
'šugul	*work*	شغل
'gurfa	**room*	غرفة
'gayr	**different, other*	غير
ṣa'giir	*small; young*	صغير

PRACTICE 2

Beginning RECORD 8B

aw: This sound is similar to ow in cow, except that it is much shorter. Round your lips as you say it. Note that w– *and* can be spoken together with the final –a of a preceding word to make aw.

'ʔaw	*or*	او
'ʔijaw	*they came*	اجوا
'miiya w'xamsa	**hundred and five*	مية وخمسة

Note carefully the difference between aw, aww, and aaw.

'hawa	**air, wind*	هوى
'hawwa	**he brought air*	هوّى

'raawa	**he showed*	راوى
maw'juud	*found, present*	موجود
'xaawlii	*towel*	خاولي

ANALYSIS

1. 'kam *several; how many?*

'kunit hi'naak 'kam 'yoom.	*I was there several days.*	كنت هناك كم يوم .
'kam '?ax '9indak?	*How many brothers do you have?*	كم اخ عندك ؟
'kam '?uxut '9indak?	*How many sisters do you have?*	كم اخت عندك ؟

Above you see that 'kam *several* or *how many?* is always followed by a *singular* noun. So you really say *how many brother?* and *how many sister?* where in English we say *brothers* and *sisters.*

2. Agent Affix for you (f).

In this Unit, the following sentence was spoken to a girl:

'?intii tiḥ'čiin 'zayn.	*You speak well.*	انتي تحكين زين .

Taking some of the other verbs you have had, you would also say the following forms to her:

trii'diin	*you want*	تريدين
tjii'biin	*you bring*	تجيبين
truu'ḥiin	*you go*	تروحين
tšuu'fiin	*you see*	تشوفين
tim'šiin	*you walk*	تمشين
ti'jiin	*you come*	تجين
titmaš'šiin	*you take a walk*	تتمشين
tsaw'wiin	*you do, you make*	تسوّين
tḥib'biin	*you love, you like*	تحبين
tisik'niin	*you live*	تسكنين
tišir'biin	*you drink*	تشربين
ti9ar'fiin	*you know*	تعرفين
taak'liin	*you eat*	تاكلين

Thus you see that the agent affix meaning you when speaking to a girl consists of two parts, namely t. . .iin (or ti. . .iin). The part of the verb coming between these is changed somewhat in some of the forms so you will have to learn each form. Thanks to the agent affix, you will have no difficulty in recognizing these forms. Note that the stress falls on the last syllable according to the regular pattern.

3. Pronoun Endings, concluded.

Most of the pronoun endings were presented in Units 2 and 3. The remaining ones are as follows:

I

'?ismič	*your name*	اسمك
'9amrič	*your age*	عمرك

'šloonič?	*How are you?*	شلونك ؟
'?aškurič	*I thank you*	اشكرك
?ar'juuč	*please*	ارجوك
wii'yaač	*with you*	ويّاك

The ending –ič (–č after a vowel) means YOUR, YOU. It refers to a girl or woman (that is, *feminine*)

II

?i'simha	*her name*	اسمها
ra'jilha	*her husband*	رجلها
wii'yaaha	*with her*	ويّاها
'šloonha?	*How is she?*	شلونها ؟
'waynha?	*Where is she?*	وينها ؟

The ending –ha means HER. Note that the ending of the last two examples above is –ha like the others even though the English equivalent requires *she*.

III

'baytkum	*your house*	بيتكم
wii'yaakum	*with you*	ويّاكم
?aš'kurkum	*I thank you*	اشكركم
?ar'juukum	*please*	ارجوكم

The ending –kum means YOUR, YOU. It is used when you are speaking to more than one person (plural), whether men or women.

IV

'binthum	*their daughter*	بنتهم
'baythum	*their house*	بيتهم
wii'yaahum	*with them*	ويّاهم

The ending –hum means THEIR, THEM.

Finally, note that a verb form (which *always* has an agent affix) can also carry a pronoun ending. For example,

yi'riid	*he wants*	يريد
yi'riidnii	*he wants me*	يريدني
yi'riidak	*he wants you* (m)	يريدك
yi'riidič	*he wants you* (f)	يريدك
yi'riida	*he wants him*	يريده
yi'riidha	*he wants her*	يريدها
yi'riidna	*he wants us*	يريدنا
yi'riidkum	*he wants you* (pl)	يريدكم
yi'riidhum	*he wants them*	يريدهم

4. COMBINING FORMS OF NOUNS AND PREPOSITIONS.

The form of the word which is found with the pronoun endings is conveniently called the *combining form* (abbreviated *cf*). There are *three* general patterns followed by *nouns* and *prepositions*. (Combining forms of verbs, similar to the above, will be explained in a later Unit.)

I The combining form is the *same* as the free form:

'bayt *cf*	bayt–	*house*	'baytii, 'baytna
ya'miin	yamiin–	*right*	ya'miinii, ya'miinna
ya'saar	yasaar–	*left*	ya'saarii, ya'saarna

II The combining form is different from the free form and *ends in a vowel-sound:*

'ʔab *cf*	ʔabuu–	*father*	ʔa'buuya, ʔa'buuna
'ʔax	ʔaxuu–	*brother*	ʔa'xuuya, ʔa'xuuna
'9ala	9alay–	*on, upon*	9a'layya, 9a'layna
'wiiya	wiiyaa–	*with*	wii'yaay, wii'yaana
'wara	waraa–	*behind*	wa'raay, wa'raana

III The combining form is different from the free form and *ends in a consonant.* Now these words have slightly different forms before endings which begin with a vowel (namely, –ii, –ak, –ič, –a) and before endings which begin with a consonant (–ha, –na, –kum, –hum).

(*a*) Two exceptions are given first. They are ʔila and ʔuxwa, which have only one combining form with all endings.

'ʔila *cf*	ʔil–	*to; for*	'ʔilii, 'ʔilna
'ʔuxwa	ʔuxuut–	*brothers*	ʔu'xuutii, ʔu'xuutna

(*b*) Words *ending in a double consonant* in the free form lose one of the consonants before the consonant-endings. (Three consonants can't come together.)

'ʔumm	*mother*	'ʔummii	'ʔumha
'minn	*from*	'minnii	'minha
'yamm	*beside*	'yammii	'yamha

(*c*) Words having *a single vowel before a final single consonant* in the free form appear as follows before the endings:

'ʔibin	*son*	'ʔibnii	'ʔibinha
'ʔisim	*name*	'ʔismii	'ʔisimha
'ʔuxut	*sister*	'ʔuxtii	'ʔuxutha
'gabul	*before*	'gablii	'gabulha
'ḍahar	*back*	'ḍahrii	'ḍaharha
'ʔahil	*family*	'ʔahlii	'ʔahilha

Note loss of the single vowel when vowel-initial endings are added. You will learn later that not all words having an a before the final consonant lose it before vowel-endings. On the other hand, i and u in this position always drop before vowel-endings.

(*d*) Another large group of words comes under this heading. They are nouns ending in –a in the free form. Most nouns with final –a are feminine. They have –at– in the combining form before consonant-endings. Before vowel-endings, the a drops in the combining form.

'madrasa	*school*	madra'satna	mad'rastii
'mazra9a	*farm*	mazra'9athum	maz'ra9tii
sii'yaara	*automobile*	siiyaa'ratna	sii'yaartii
'saa9a	*clock, watch*	saa'9atna	'saa9tii
'mara	*wife*	ma'ratna	'martii
'badla	*suit*	bad'latna	ba'diltii

Notice the last word especially. Note that there are two consonants before the –a; hence when the –a drops before the vowel-endings, an i comes in to prevent three consonants coming together (hence ba'diltii *my suit*).

In summary, here are sample words of the patterns discussed above, with complete pronoun endings.

I 'bayt	*house*	بيت
'baytii	my house	بيتي
'baytak	your house (m)	بيتك
'baytič	your house (f)	بيتِك
'bayta	his house	بيته
'baytha	her house	بيتها
'baytna	our house	بيتنا
'baytkum	your house (pl)	بيتكم
'baythum	their house	بيتهم
II '?ab *cf* ?abuu–	*father*	اب
?a'buuya *or* '?abii		ابي
?a'buuk		ابوك
?a'buuč		ابوكِ
?a'buu		ابوه
?a'buuha		ابوها
?a'buuna		ابو نا
?a'buukum		ابوكم
?a'buuhum		ابوهم
III*b* 'minn	*from*	من
'minnii		مني
'minnak		منك
'minnič		منكِ
'minna		منا
'minha		منها
'minna		مننا
'minkum		منكم
'minhum		منهم
III*c* '?ibin	*son*	ابن
'?ibnii		ابني
'?ibnak		ابنك
'?ibnič		ابنكِ
'?ibna		ابنه
'?ibinha *or* ?i'binha		ابنها
'?ibinna *or* ?i'binna		ابننا
'?ibinkum *or* ?i'binkum		ابنكم
'?ibinhum *or* ?i'binhum		ابنهم

III*d* 'madrasa	*school*	مدرسة
mad'rastii		مدرستي
mad'rastak		مدرستك
mad'rastič		مدرستكِ
mad'rasta		مدرسته
madra'satna		مدرستنا

III*e* 'badla	*suit*	بدلة
ba'diltii		بدلتي
ba'diltak		بدلتك
ba'dilta		بدلته
bad'latna		بدلتنا
bad'latkum		بدلتكم
bad'lathum		بدلتهم

5. Noun Compounds.

Nouns can be put together to form a compound.

''ʔibin-ʔa'xuuya	*son of my brother*	ابن اخوي
'bint-'ʔuxtii	*daughter of my sister*	بنت اختي
'ma9mal-siiyaa'raat	*factory of automobiles*	معمل السيّارات

In English we can say either *my brother's son* or else *the son of my brother*. But in Iraqi the only way to express this idea is by saying ''ʔibin-ʔa'xuuya. Likewise in English we usually say *automobile factory*, but we could say *factory of automobiles*. In Iraqi, however, there is only the one way to express it, by 'ma9mal-siiyaa'raat. The meaning of the compound usually can best be understood by adding *of* between the nouns, as we have done above. This is the only type of compound in Iraqi, but it is an important feature of the language.

There are three points to notice especially. (1) First, the *first* member of the compound is always a *combining form*. For this reason we write a hyphen (-) between the two parts. It is the form which appears before pronoun endings which begin with a consonant. (2) Second, the first member *never* has the article prefix il– *the*, while the second member can have it. Note that 'ma9mal-siiyaa'raat means *an automobile factory*, while 'ma9mal-issiiyaa'raat means *the automobile factory*. (3) Third, each member retains its individual stress, as if it were standing alone. For example:

'siinama *cf* 'siinamat-		سينما
sii'yaara *cf* sii'yaarat-		سيّارة
'ʔab *cf* 'ʔabuu-		اب

'siinamat-il'malik-'gaazii	سينما الملك غازي
sii'yaarat-Ford	سيّارة فورد
'ʔabuu-l'bint	ابو البنت

Now note that *names* are always in second place.

'ʔabuu-sa'9iid	*Said's father*	ابو سعيد
sii'yaarat-Ford	*a Ford automobile*	سيّارة فورد
'ma9mal-Ford	*a Ford factory*	معمل فورد
jisir-'mood	[*the*] *Maude Bridge*	جسر مود

'siinamat-il'malik-'gaazii	*the King Ghazi Theatre*	سينما الملك غازي
ʔuu'tayl-Tigris Palace	*[the] Hotel Tigris Palace*	اوتيل تايكرس بالس

Note that compounds are used to name *containers* and *contents*.

'glaaṣ-'maay	*a glass of water*	كلاص ماء
paa'kayt-ji'gaayir	*a package of cigarettes*	باكيت جكاير
maa'9uun-'timman	*a dish of rice*	ماعون تمن

Finally, note that when numbers are used in *counting things*, they form compounds with the things counted.

'miiya *cf* miit-	*hundred*	مية
'miit-'filis	*a hundred fils*	مية فلس
θi'laaθa *cf* θilaaθ-		ثلاثة
θi'laaθ-'ʔuxwa	*three brothers*	ثلاث اخوة
θi'maanya *cf* θimaan-		ثمانية
θi'maan-is'niin	*eight years*	ثمان سنين
'ʔarba9a *cf* ʔarba9-		اربعة
'ʔarba9-xa'waat	*four sisters*	اربع خوات

6. Family Relationships.

In Iraqi there are not always single words to name the different family relationships. There is a word for *mother* and *daughter*, for example, but there is no single word for *cousin* or *niece*. There is, however, a simple system using noun compounds for naming relatives. Read through the following discussion to see what the system is, but you don't have to memorize it.

First, you have learned most of the following words:

ʔa'buuya *or* 'ʔabii	*my father*	ابوي - ابي
'ʔummii	*my mother*	امي
ʔa'xuuya *or* 'ʔaxii	*my brother*	اخوي - اخي
'ʔuxtii	*my sister*	اختي
'ʔibnii	*my son*	ابني
'bintii	*my daughter*	بنتي
'rajlii	*my husband*	رجلي
'martii	*my wife*	مرتي
'9ammii	*my uncle (father's brother)*	عمي
'9amtii	*my aunt (father's sister)*	عمتي
'xaaḷii	*my uncle (mother's brother)*	خالي
'xaaḷtii	*my aunt (mother's sister)*	خالتي

These words are put together as noun compounds to give other family relationships.

grandchildren

'ʔibin-'ʔibnii	*the son of my son*	ابن ابني
'ʔibin-'bintii	*the son of my daughter*	ابن بنتي

'bint-'ʔibnii — *the daughter of my son* — بنت ابني
'bint-'bintii — *the daughter of my daughter* — بنت بنتي

nephews and nieces

'ʔibin-ʔa'xuuya — *the son of my brother* — ابن اخوي
'ʔibin-'ʔuxtii — *the son of my sister* — ابن اختي

'bint-ʔa'xuuya — *the daughter of my brother* — بنت اخوي
'bint-'ʔuxtii — *the daughter of my sister* — بنت اختي

cousins

'ʔibin-9ammii — *the son of my father's brother* — ابن عمي
'ʔibin-'9amtii — *the son of my father's sister* — ابن عمتي
'ʔibin-'xaaḷii — *the son of my mother's brother* — ابن خالي
'ʔibin-'xaaḷtii — *the son of my mother's sister* — ابن خالتي

'bint-'9ammii — *the daughter of my father's brother* — بنت عمي
'bint-'9amtii — *the daughter of my father's sister* — بنت عمتي
'bint-'xaaḷii — *the daughter of my mother's brother* — بنت خالي
'bint-'xaaḷtii — *the daughter of my mother's sister* — بنت خالتي

Only blood relatives are aunts and uncles. If they are not related by blood, then they are called the 'husband of my aunt' or the 'wife of my uncle'.

'marat-'9ammii — *the wife of my father's brother* — مرت عمي
'rajil-'9amtii — *the husband of my father's sister* — رجل عمتي

'marat-'xaaḷii — *the wife of my mother's brother* — مرت خالي
'rajil-'xaaḷtii — *the husband of my mother's sister* — رجل خالتي

In-laws are treated the same way.

'rajil-'ʔuxtii — *the husband of my sister* — رجل اختي
'marat-ʔa'xuuya — *the wife of my brother* — مرت اخوي

Of course, the appropriate pronoun endings will be used on the end of the compound to indicate other persons, as 'ʔibin-ʔa'xuu *the son of his brother*, and so on.

EXERCISES

A. PRONOUN ENDINGS. *Give the forms with* –na our, *then with* –hum their, –ha her, –ii my, –ak your (*m*), *and* –a his.

1. (madrasa) 'muu ka'biira.
2. (saa9a) 'maa 'timšii 'zayn.
3. (siiyaara) 'waagfa bil'baab.
4. ṣa'diiḳii 'kaan 'yištugul 'fii (mazra9a).

B. *Supply forms with* –ak your, you (*m*), *then with* –kum your, you (*pl*), *and finally with* –ič your, you (*f*).

1. (bayt) ba'9iid minn hi'naa?
2. ''ʔakuu ʔuu'tayl '9ala (yamiin).
3. il'baarḥa 'maa 'šifna (ʔab) 'yimšii lis'suug.
4. 'šifna rij'jaal 'waaguf (yamm).
5. ʔa'ḥibb ''ʔamšii (wiiya).
6. 'minuu 'ðaak il'walad (wara)?
7. 'šloon 'timšii (siiyaara)?
8. (ʔaškur).

C. *These sentences are spoken to a boy. Change them as you would if speaking to a girl. Then to more than one person.*

1. ʔar'juuk 'gullii ''ʔismak.
2. ta'9aal 'jiiblii 'maay.
3. ʔis'maḥlii, 'maa ʔa'riid ʔat'mašša wii'yaak.

D. *Give the correct form of the first member of the following compounds. Not all require change.*

1. (ʔibin)-'bintii 'maa 'raaḥ lil'madrasa.
2. (ʔab)-l'walad 'maa 'kaan mu'ḳaawil.
3. (ʔax)-ṣa'diiḳii 'hamm 'yiskin ibbag'daad.
4. (siiyaara)-ʔa'xuuya 'hiiya Ford.
5. ʔar'juuk 'jiiblii (paakayt)-ji'gaayir.
6. ta'9aaluu ''ʔila (dukkaan)-ʔa'buuya.
7. duk'kaan-''ʔabuu-'simač 'muu 'yamm
   duk'kaan-(ʔab)-ji'gaayir.
8. (rajil)-''ʔuxtii '9inda 'mazra9a ka'biira.
9. (ʔab)-sa'9iid 'maa 'ya9ruf 'wayn 'raaḥ sa'9iid.
10. (mara)-ʔa'xuuya 'bint ja'miila.
11. (mazra9a)-ʔa'xuuya 'muu ba'9iida 'minn
    mazra'9atna.
12. 'maa 'na9ruf (ʔisim)-'ðaak irrij'jaal.

WHAT WOULD YOU SAY?

1. *You ask a recent acquaintance where he lives.*

a. 'kam 'walad '9indak?	١ ـ كم ولد عندك ؟
b. mi'nayn 'jiit?	٢ ـ منين جيت ؟
c. 'wayn 'tiskin?	٣ ـ وين تسكن ؟

2. *He tells you.*

a. ʔa'buuya 'yiskin wii'yaay.	١ ـ ابوها يسكن وياي •
b. ''ʔaskin hi'naa bbag'daad.	٢ ـ اسكن هنا ببغداد •
c. ''ʔuxtii 'tiskin wii'yaana.	٣ ـ اختي تسكن ويانا •

3. *You tell him where you are staying.*

a. 'ˀana wṣa'diiḳii saak'niin fii ˀuu'tayl ṣa'giir. ١ ـ انا وصديقي ساكنين في اوتيل صغير ٠

b. ˀa'ḥibb 'ˀaskin fii 'ðaak ilˀuu'tayl. ٢ ـ احب اسكن في ذاك الاوتيل ٠

c. 'kunit 'ˀaskin 'wiiya '9ammii. ٣ ـ كنت اسكن ويّا عمي ٠

4. *You ask about his brothers.*

a. hal '9indak ˀux'waan? ١ ـ هل عندك اخوان ؟

b. 'kam 'ˀax '9indak? ٢ ـ كم اخ عندك ؟

c. 'wayn yištag'luun ˀux'waanak? ٣ ـ وين يشتغلون اخوانك ٠

5. *He has three.*

a. '9indii θi'laaθ-'ˀuxwaan. ١ ـ عندي ثلاث اخوان ٠

b. 'maa '9indii 'ˀuxwaan. ٢ ـ ما عندي اخوان ٠

c. 'waaḥid 'minhum 'yiskin wii'yaana. ٣ ـ واحد منهم يسكن ويّانا ٠

6. *One is in the army.*

a. 'waaḥid minn ˀux'waanii bij'jayš. ١ ـ واحد من اخواني بالجيش ٠

b. 'layš ˀinta muu bij'jayš? ٢ ـ ليش انت مو بالجيش ؟

c. iθ'θaanii yi'riid yi'ṣiir ṭay'yaar. ٣ ـ الثاني يريد يصير طيّار ٠

7. *And how many sisters?*

a. wayn xa'waatak? ١ ـ وين خواتك ؟

b. kam 'ˀuxut '9indak? ٢ ـ كم اخت عندك ؟

c. '9indak xa'waat? ٣ ـ عندك خوات ؟

8. *He looks at some girls down the street.*

a. ðoo'laak ilba'naat xa'waatii. ١ ـ ذولاك البنات خواتي ٠

b. 'maa '9indii 'ˀuxut. ٢ ـ ما عندي اخت ٠

c. humma yim'šuun lis'suug. ٣ ـ همّا يمشون للسوق ٠

9. *Is he married?*

a. 'ˀinta mit'zawwij? ١ ـ انت متزوّج ؟

b. 'ˀintum mitzaw'jiin? ٢ ـ انتم متزوّجين ؟

c. 'layš 'ˀinta 'muu mit'zawwij? ٣ ـ ليش انت مو متزوّج ؟

10. *Yes, he has a boy and two girls.*

a. 'na9am, '9indii 'walad wubin'tayn. ١ ـ نعم عندي ولد وبنتين ٠

b. 'na9am, '9indii wala'dayn wu'bint. ٢ ـ نعم عندي ولدين وبنت ٠

c. 'maa '9indii 'walad 'laakin '9indii 'bint. ٣ ـ ما عندي ولد لكن عندي بنت ٠

11. *He has a married sister too.*

a. 'maa '9indii 'ˀuxwa ˀaw xa'waat. ١ ـ ما عندي اخوة او خوات ٠

b. '9indii 'ˀuxut mit'zawja wu'hiiya 'tiskin 'wiiya 'rajilha fii mazra'9athum. ٢ ـ عندي اخت متزوجة وهي تسكن ويّا رجلها في مزرعتهم ٠

c. 'bint-'ˀuxtii 'kaanat ma'riiḍa. ٣ ـ بنت اختي كانت مريضة ٠

12. *His niece was sick.*

a. 'binthum 'muu ma'riiḍa. ١ ـ بنتهم مو مريضة ٠

b. ʹʔuxtii wuʹrajilha ʹjaabaw ʹbinthum 9idna; ʹbinthum ʹkaanat maʹriiḍa. — ٢ ـ اختي ورجلها جابوا بنتهم عدنا • بنتهم كانت مريضة•

c. ʹhiiya ʹhamm ʹtiskin ʹfii lʹmazra9a. — ٣ ـ هي هم تسكن في المزرعة •

13. *How is she now?*

a. ṣaʹgiira wuʹjamiila. — ١ ـ صغيرة وجميلة •

b. ʹhiiya ʹmaa ʹkaanat bilʹbayt. — ٢ ـ هي هم كانت بالبيت •

c. ilʹyoom ʹʔaḥsan ʹlaakin ḍaʹ9iifa. — ٣ ـ اليوم احسن لكن ضعيفة •

14. *His sister has a son.*

a. ðaak ilʹwalad ʹʔibin-ʹʔuxtii. — ١ ـ ذاك الولد ابن اختي •

b. ðiič ilʹbint ʹbint-ʹʔuxtii. — ٢ ـ ذيك البنت بنت اختي •

c. ðaak ilʹwalad ʹʔibin-ʹʔibnii. — ٣ ـ ذاك الولد ابن ابني •

15. *He is going to visit his uncle and aunt.*

a. ʹraaḥ ʔaʹzuur ʹ9ammii wuʹmarta. — ١ ـ راح ازور عمي ومرته •

b. ʹxallii nʹzuur ʹ9ammii wuʹmarta. — ٢ ـ خلّي نزور عمّي ومرته ؟

c. ʹta9ruf wayn yisikʹnuun ʹ9ammii wuʹmarta? — ٣ ـ تعرف وين يسكنون عمي ومرته ؟

16. *He leaves.*

a. mamʹnuun. — ١ ـ ممنون •

b. ʔi9ʹḍirnii. — ٢ ـ اعذرني •

c. ʹma9a ssaʹlaama. — ٣ ـ مع السلامة •

17. *You talk to a little girl.*

a. ʹšloonič? — ١ ـ شلونك ؟

b. ʹšinuu ʹʔismič? — ٢ ـ شنو اسمك ؟

c. gulʹliilii, ʹminuu ʹhaaða lwiiʹyaač? — ٣ ـ قليلي منو هذا الويّاك ؟

18. *You ask how old she is.*

a. šgad ʹ9amrak? — ١ ـ شقد عمرك ؟

b. šgad ʹ9amrič? — ٢ ـ شكو عمرك ؟

c. šgad ʹ9amurkum? — ٣ ـ شكو عمركم ؟

19. *She is eight.*

a. ʹʔana ʹbint ṣaʹgiira. — ١ ـ انا بنت صغيرة •

b. ʹ9amrii θiʹmaan-isʹniin. — ٢ ـ عمري ثمان سنين •

c. ʹ9amrii θiʹlaaθ-isʹniin. — ٣ ـ عمري ثلاث سنين •

LISTENING IN

Bill and Mustafa are talking.

Continuing RECORD 8B

MUSTAFA 'wayn '?inta 'raayiḥ?	مصطفى ـ وين انت رايح ؟
BILL ?a'ḥibb ?at'mašša; 'triid tit'mašša wii'yaaya?	بل ـ احب اتمشّى ، تريد تتمشّى ويّاي ؟
MUSTAFA 'ṭayyib.	مصطفى ـ طيّب •
BILL 'wayn '?inta 'činit 'tiskin 'fii ?am'riika?	بل ، وين انت كنت تسكن في امريكا ؟
BILL 'činit '?askin 'wiiya '?ahlii bil'mazra9a 'fii Texas.	بل ـ كنت اسكن ويّا اهلي بالمزرعة في تكسس •
MUSTAFA 'wayn '?inta 'saakin 'fii bag'daad?	مصطفى ـ وين انت ساكن في بغداد ؟
BILL '?ana wuṣa'diiḳii saak'niin 'fii ?uu'tayl-Regent.	بل ـ انا وصديقي ساكنين في اوتيل ريجنت •
MUSTAFA 'gullii, '?inta mit'zawwij '?aw 'laa?	مصطفى ـ قل لي ، انت متزوّج او لا ؟
BILL 'laa, '?ana 'muu mit'zawwij. wu'?inta?	بل ـ لا ، انا مو متزوّج • وانت ؟
MUSTAFA 'na9am, '9indii wala'dayn wu'bint. 'bintii ṣa'ġiira wuja'miila. '?isimha* 'luuluu.	مصطفى ـ نعم ، عندي ولدين وبنت • بنتي صغيرة وجميلة • اسمها لولو •
BILL 'čam '?ax '9indak?	بل ـ كم اخ عندك ؟
MUSTAFA '9indii θi'laaθ-'?uxwa. θi'nayn 'minn ?u'xuutii bij'jayš. 'waaḥid 'minhum ṭay'yaar, wiθ'θaanii 'ḍaabuṭ. iθ'θaaliθ bil'madrasa.	مصطفى ـ عندي ثلاث اخوة • ثنين من اخوتي بالجيش • واحد منهم طيّار والثاني ضابط • والثالث بالمدرسة •
BILL wiθ'θaaliθ, 'šinuu yi'riid 'yidris?	بل ـ والثالث ـ شنو يريد يدرس ؟
MUSTAFA 'gallii yi'riid yi'ṣiir ṭa'biib. 'hal '?inta '9indak '?uxwa?	مصطفى ـ قال لي يريد يصير طبيب • هل انت عندك اخوة ؟
BILL 'laa, 'bass '9indii '?uxut. 'hiiya mit'zawja wu'tiskin 'wiiya 'rajilha 'fii 'mazra9a. mazra'9athum 'muu ba'9iida 'minn mazra'9atna.	بل ـ لا ، بس عندي اخت • هي متزوّجة وتسكن ويّا رجلها في مزرعة • مزرعتهم مو بعيدة من مزرعتنا •
MUSTAFA '?ana 'hamm '9indii '?uxut 'waaḥda, 'hamm mit'zawja. 'hiiya wu'rajilha '?ijaw '9idna il'baarḥa bil'layl wu'jaabaw 'binthum wii'yaahum. 'binthum 'čaanat 'kulliš ma'riiḍa.	مصطفى ـ انا هم عندي اخت واحدة ، هم متزوّجة • هي ورجلها اجوا عندنا البارحة بالليل وجابوا بنتهم ويّاهم • بنتهم كانت كلّش مريضة •
BILL 'ščaan 'biiha?	بل ـ شكان بيها ؟
MUSTAFA iṭṭa'biib 'maa gaa'linna.	مصطفى ـ الطبيب ما قال لنا •
BILL 'šloonha l'yoom?	بل ـ شلونها اليوم ؟
MUSTAFA 'hiiya '?aḥsan 'laakin ḍa'9iifa.	مصطفى ـ هي احسن لكن ضعيفة •

* Record has a variant form '?ismaha.

(*Mustafa calls some children going by.*)

BILL 'minuu 'humma?	بل – منو همّا ؟
MUSTAFA 'haaδa l'walad '?aḥmad* '?ibin-?a'xuuy.	مصطفى – هذا الولد احمد ، ابن اخوي .
'huuwa 'xooš 'walad.	هو خوش ولد .
?a'buu ṭṭay'yaar.	ابوه الطيّار .
BILL 'minuu 'haay il'bint wii'yaa?	بل – منو هاي البنت ويّاه ؟
MUSTAFA 'hiiya '?uxta. '?ismaha 'zalma.†	مصطفى – هي اخته ، اسمها سلمى .
wu'δiič il'bint il'waagfa wa'raahum, 'hiiya 'bint-'?axii θ'θaanii.	وذيك البنت الواقفة وراهم ، هي بنت اخي الثاني .

(*Bill talks to the little girl.*)

BILL ta'9aalii hi'naa! 'šlooničʼ?	بل – تعالي هنا ، شلونك ؟
GIRL 'zayna, '?aškurak.	البنت – زينة ، اشكرك .
BILL 'šinuu '?ismič?	بل – شنو اسمك ؟
GIRL '?ismii ja'miila.	البنت – اسمي جميلة .
BILL wu'?intii 'bint ja'miila.	بل – وانتي بنت جميلة .
'minuu haaδool wii'yaač?	منو هاذول ويّاك ؟
GIRL '?ibin-'9ammii 'wuxta.	البنت – ابن عمّي واخته .
'maakuu '9indii xa'waat '?aw '?uxwa.	ماكو عندي خوات او اخوة .
BILL gul'liilii, šgad '9amrič?	بل – قولي لي شقد عمرك ؟
GIRL θi'maan-is'niin.	البنت – ثمان سنين .
BILL '?antii tiḥ'čiin 'zayn.	بل – انتي تحكين زين .
MUSTAFA 'wayn '?intum raay'ḥiin?	مصطفى – وين انتم رايحين ؟
AHMAD lis'siinama.	احمد – للسينما .
MUSTAFA li'?ay 'siinama?	مصطفى – لاي سينما ؟
AHMAD 'siinamat-il'malik 'gaazii.	احمد – سينمة الملك غازي .

(*The children go.*)

MUSTAFA ?i9'ḍirnii, Bill, 'laazim ?a'ruuḥ ?a'zuur '9ammii wu'marta.	مصطفى – اعذرني ، بل ، لازم اروح ازور عمّي ومرته .
'triid 'tijii wii'yaaya?	تريد تجي ويّاي ؟
BILL 'wayn 'baythum?	بل – وين بيتهم ؟
MUSTAFA ba'9iid‡ 'minn hi'naa.	مصطفى – بعيد من هنا .

CONVERSATIONS

A. The Group Leader will ask two of you at a time to stand up and tell about your families and friends. Answer with correct answers as much as possible. You will ask each other such questions as the following, and add others of your own.

1. Where are you living?
2. Where did you used to live?
3. How many brothers do you have? Sisters? Where are they, and what do they do?

* Ahmad.
† Zelma.
‡ Record has ba9ii'diin *they* [*are*] *far*.

4. Are you married or not? If so, where is your wife?
5. Do you have any children? If so, how old are they?
6. Other questions?

B. You are talking to a little girl. You tell her to come over where you are. She comes and you ask her her name. She tells you. You ask how old she is, she replies that she is eight. You ask where she lives, and she replies that she lives with her family. Their house is nearby, she says. You ask if she has brothers or sisters. She hasn't any brothers, but she has one sister. You ask where her sister is. She is in school today, but yesterday she was sick. What was the matter with her? The little girl says she doesn't know. She thanks you and says goodbye.

VOCABULARY

il'baṣra (f)	Basra
ba'9iid	distant, far
'bii	in
'biiha	in her
'škaan 'biiha?	What was the matter with her?
'bint	daughter, girl
'binthum	their daughter
'ḍaabuṭ	officer
ḍa'9iif	weak
'gaal	he said, told
gaa'linna	he told us
'gaallii	he told me
'humma	they
'jaabaw	they brought
ja'miil	pretty, handsome
ja'miila	Jamila (*girl's name*)
'jayš	army
'kaanat, čaanat	she was
'kam *or* čam	several; how many
'kam 'ʔax '9indak?	How many brothers do you have?
'kam 'ʔuxut '9indak?	How many sisters do you have?
'layl	night
bil'layl	in the night, at night
il'baarḥa bil'layl	last night
'luuluu	Pearl (*girl's name*)
'madrasa	school
bil'madrasa	in school, at school
'malik	king
il'malik-'gaazii	King Ghazi
'siinamat-il'malik-'gaazii	The King Ghazi Movie
ma'riiḍ	sick
'mara	woman; wife
'marta	his wife
'marat-'9ammii	my uncle's wife
'minn	from
θi'nayn 'minhum	two of them
'minuu	who?
mit'zawwij	married
'nimšii	we walk
'raayiḥ, raay'ḥiin (pl)	going
'rajil	man, husband
'rajilha	her husband
'saakin, saak'niin (pl)	staying, living
'salma	Zelma (*girl's name*)
'siinama	movie
'siinamat-il'malik-'gaazii	the King Ghazi movie
si'niin	years
ṣa'giir, ṣa'giira *and* z'gayra (f)	small; young (of people)
'šgad	how much, how far
'tiskin	she lives; you live (m)
ṭa'biib	doctor
ṭay'yaar	aviator
'waaḥid, 'waaḥda *and* 'wiḥda (f)	one
'walad	boy
wala'dayn	two boys
'wara	behind, in back of
wa'raahum	behind them
wa'raa	behind him
xa'waat	sisters
'xooš	good
'xooš 'walad	a good boy
'yidris	he studies
yi'riid	he wants
yi'ṣiir	he becomes
'yoom	day
il'yoom *or* hal'yoom	today
'ʔab	father
'ʔahal	family
'ʔahlii	my family
'ʔaḥmad	Ahmad (*man's name*)
'ʔaḥsan	better (m *and* f)

'ʔajii	I come
'ʔarja9	I go back, I come back
'ʔay	what, which
'ʔay 'siinama?	Which movie?
'ʔax	brother
ʔa'zuur	I visit
'ʔibin	son
'ʔibin-ʔa'xuuya	my brother's son (my nephew
'ʔibin-'9ammii	my uncle's son (my cousin)
'ʔiḥna	we
'ʔijaw	they came
'ʔintii	you (f)
ʔi9'ḍirnii.	Excuse me!
'ʔuxut	sister
'ʔuxtii	my sister
'ʔuxta	his sister
'ʔuxwa, ʔux'waan	brothers
ʔux'waanii *or* ʔu'xuutii	my brothers
'9amm	uncle (father's brother)
'9ammii	my uncle (on father's side)
'9amur	age
'šgad '9amrak?	How old are you?
'9amrii θi'maan-is'niin.	I'm eight years old.
'δiič	that (f)
'δiič il'bint	that girl
'θaaliθ	third
iθ'θaaliθ	the third, the third one
'θaanii	second; other
iθ'θaanii	the second, the other
θi'maanya	eight
θi'maan-is'niin	eight years

UNIT 5

Let's Talk About the Weather

BASIC SENTENCES

In an Arabic Restaurant in New York.

Beginning RECORD 9A

ENGLISH EQUIVALENTS	AIDS TO LISTENING	ARABIC SPELLING
Tom	*Tom*	توم
I see you aren't an American.	ʔa'šuuf 'ʔanta 'muu ʔamrii'kaanii.	اشوف انت مو امريكاني •
Nouri	*Nouri*	نوري
No, I'm an Iraqi.	'laa, 'ʔana 9i'raaḳii.	لا ، انا عراقي •
Tom	*Tom*	توم
I can *or* I may	'ʔagdar	اقدر
I ask you	'ʔasʔalak	اسائلك
May I ask (you) what you're doing here?	'ʔagdar 'ʔasʔalak 'šitsawwii hi'naa?	اقدر اسائلك شتسوّي هنا ؟
Nouri	*Nouri*	نوري
(the) Iraq	il9i'raaḳ	العراق
in order to	li'kay	لكي
I study	'ʔadris	ادرس
I came from Iraq to study.	'ʔana 'jayt 'minn il9i'raaḳ li'kay 'ʔadris.	انا جيت من العراق لكي ادرس •
Tom	*Tom*	توم
In what school?	'fii 'ʔay 'madrasa?	في اي مدرسة ؟
Nouri	*Nouri*	نوري
university	'jaami9a	جامعة
Columbia University.	'jaami9at-Columbia.	جامعة كولومبيا •
Tom	*Tom*	توم
student	til'miiδ	تلميذ
I was a student too.	'ʔana 'hamm 'činit til'miiδ.	انا هم كنت تلميذ •

ENGLISH EQUIVALENTS	AIDS TO LISTENING	ARABIC SPELLING
Nouri	*Nouri*	نوري
why	'layš *or* '?ilwayš	ليش (ايضا) الويش
Why not now?	'layš 'muu 'hassa?	ليش مو هسّة ؟
Tom	*Tom*	توم
I go in *or* I enter	'?adxul	ادخل
I'm going to enter	'raaḥ '?adxul*	راح ادخل
month	'šahar	شهر
coming	'jaay	جاي
next month	iš'šahar ij'jaay	الشهر الجاي
Next month I'm going to go into the army.	iš'šahar ij'jaay 'raaḥ '?adxul bij'jayš.	الشهر الجاي راح ادخل بالجيش •
Nouri	*Nouri*	نوري
you think	'tiftikir	تفتكر
you are going to go	'raaḥ it'ruuḥ	راح تروح
Do you think you are going to go to Iraq?	'tiftikir 'raaḥ it'ruuḥ lil9i'raaḳ?	تفتكر راح تروح للعراق ؟
Tom	*Tom*	توم
Only the army knows.	'bass ij'jayš 'ya9ruf.	بس الجيش يعرف •
to wherever	'?ila 'wayn 'maa	الى وين ما
they send me	yirsi'luunii	يرسلوني
I have to go wherever they send me.	'laazim ?a'ruuḥ '?ila 'wayn 'maa yirsi'luunii.	لازم اروح الى وين ما يرسلوني •
the weather	ilma'naax	المناخ
How's the weather in Iraq?	'šloon ilma'naax bil'9iraaḳ?	شلون المناخ بالعراق ؟
thing *or* anything*	'šii	شيء
about him *or* it	'9anna	عنه
I don't know a thing about it.	'?ana 'maa '?a9ruf 'šii '9anna.	انا ما اعرف شيء عنه •
Nouri	*Nouri*	نوري
like	'miθil	مثل
Not like in New York.	'muu 'miθil ibNew York.†	مو مثل بي نيويورك •
rain	'muṭar *or* maṭar*	مطر
the winter	iš'šita	الشتاء
the summer	iṣ'ṣayf	الصيف
There's lots of rain in the winter, but not in the summer.	'?akuu 'muṭar ka'θiir biš'šita, 'bass 'muu biṣ'ṣayf.	اكو مطر كثير بالشتاء بس مو بالصيف •

* Not on record.
† The second repetition is without ib– *in*.

Beginning RECORD 9B

ENGLISH EQUIVALENTS	AIDS TO LISTENING	ARABIC SPELLING
it snows	'tiθlij	تثلج
in the north	biššiʹmaal	بالشمال
(the) Mosul	ilʹmooṣul	الموصل
It snows in the north near Mosul.	'tiθlij biššiʹmaal 'yamm ilʹmooṣul.	تثلج بالشمال يم الموصل .
self	'nafis	نفس
the south	ijjiʹnuub	الجنوب
I myself am from the south, from Basra.	'ʔana 'nafsii minn ijjiʹnuub, minn ilʹbaṣra.	انا نفسي من الجنوب ، من البصرة .
all *or* every	'kull	كل
the people	inʹnaas	الناس
they sleep	yinaaʹmuun	ينامون
the roofs	iṣṣuʹṭuuḥ	الصطوح
Do you know all the people sleep on the roofs?	'ta9ruf 'kull inʹnaas yinaaʹmuun '9ala ṣṣuʹṭuuḥ?	تعرف كل الناس ينامون على الصطوح ؟
Tom	*Tom*	توم
No, I didn't know (this).	'laa, 'maa 'ʔa9ruf 'haaδa.	لا ، ما اعرف هذا .
the cause *or* the reason	isʹsabab	السبب
What's the reason?	'šinuu sʹsabab?	شنو السبب ؟
Nouri	*Nouri*	نوري
because	'minn 'sabab	من سبب
the wind *or* air (m)	ilʹhawa	الهواء
cold *or* cool (of things)	'baarid	بارد
Because the air ['s] cool there.	'minn 'sabab ilʹhawa 'baarid hiʹnaak.	من سبب الهواء بارد هناك .
also *or* moreover	'ʔayḍan	ايضا
it rains	'tumṭur	تمطر
And besides it doesn't rain.	wuʹʔayḍan 'maa 'tumṭur.	وايضا ما تمطر .
Tom	*Tom*	توم
How ['s] Baghdad?	'šloon bagʹdaad?	شلون بغداد ؟
Nouri	*Nouri*	نوري
hot	'ḥaarr	حار
in the day	binnaʹhaar	بالنهار
in the night	bilʹlayl	بالليل
It's hot during the day and cold at night.	'hiiya 'ḥaarra binnaʹhaar wuʹbaarda bilʹlayl.	هي حارّة بالنهار وباردة بالليل .

ENGLISH EQUIVALENTS	AIDS TO LISTENING	ARABIC SPELLING
I lived	si'kanit	سكنت
while *or* when	'lamma	لما
I lived in Baghdad three years when I was young.	si'kanit 'fii bag'daad θi'laaθ-si'niin 'lamma 'činit ṣa'ġiir.	سكنت في بغداد ثلاث سنين لما كنت صغير •
afterwards	ba9'dayn	بعدين
I used to visit	'čint ʔa'zuur	كنت ازور
uncle (mother's brother)	'xaaḷ	خال
Afterwards, I often visited my uncle there.	ba9'dayn, 'čint ʔa'zuur 'xaaḷii ka'θiir hi'naak.	بعدين كنت ازور خالي كثير هناك •

(*They leave the restaurant together.*)

Nouri	*Nouri*	نوري
bad	'duunii	دو ني
What a nasty day!	'šloon 'yoom 'duunii!	شلون يوم دو ني !
strong	'ḳawii *or* 'guwii	قوي
sun (f)	'šamis	شمس
The wind's strong and there's no sun.	il'hawa 'guwii wu'maakuu 'šamis.	الهواء قوي وماكو شمس •

Beginning RECORD 10A

it is going to rain	'raaḥ 'tumṭur	راح تمطر
Do you think it's going to rain?	tif'tikir 'raaḥ 'tumṭur?	تفتكر راح تمطر ؟
Tom	*Tom*	توم
this morning	haṣ'ṣubuḥ	هالصبح
it rained (f)	'muṭrat	مطرت
much *or* a lot	ha'waaya	هوايه
This morning it rained a lot.	haṣ'ṣubuḥ 'muṭrat ha'waaya.	هالصبح مطرت هوايه •
I think	'ʔaftikir	افتكر
yet *or* more	'ba9ad	بعد
although	'waḷaw	ولو
the world	id'dinya	الدنيا
cloudy (f)	m'ġayma	مغيمة
I don't think it's going to rain any more, even though it's cloudy.	'maa 'ʔaftikir 'ba9ad 'raaḥ 'tumṭur, 'waḷaw id'dinya m'ġayma.	ما افتكر بعد راح تمطر ولو الدنيا مغيمة •
Nouri	*Nouri*	نوري
It doesn't matter; let'er rain!	maa yi'xaalif; xal'liiha 'tumṭur!	ما يخالف ، خلّيها تمطر !
Tom	*Tom*	توم
she rose *or* came out	'ṭiḷ9at	طلعت
Look, the sun's just come out.	'šuuf, 'hassa 'ṭiḷ9at iš'šamis.	شوف ، هسة طلعت الشمس •

ENGLISH EQUIVALENTS	AIDS TO LISTENING	ARABIC SPELLING
he is going to be	ʼraaḥ yiʼkuun	راح يكون
Tomorrow's going to be a good day.	ʼbaačir ʼraaḥ yiʼkuun naʼhaar ʼṭayyib.	باكر راح يكون نهار طيّب •
Nouri	*Nouri*	نوري
it is possible *or* perhaps	ʼyumkin *or* ʼyimkin	يمكن
some *or* a certain	ʼfadd	فرد
Goodbye, perhaps I'll see you in Iraq some day.	fiimaaniʼlaa, ʼyimkin ʼfadd ʼyoom ʔaʼšuufak bil9iʼraaķ.	في امان الله ، يمكن فرد يوم اشوفك بالعراق •

PRONUNCIATION

Continuing RECORD 10A

PRACTICE 1

ḥ: This sign stands for a 'heavy' h-sound. If you try panting you will come close to it, but you must keep your tongue tight on the bottom of your mouth, especially the back part of the tongue. Also tighten your throat muscles. Constant practice is necessary. For contrast we give some words with h, then words with ḥ.

ʼhamm	*also*	هم
ʼʔahil	*family*	اهل
ʔiʼlaah	**God*	الإ
ʼḥarb	*war*	حرب
ʼlaḥam	*meat*	لحم
ʼʔiftaḥ	**open!*	افتح
ʼḥimil	*load*	حمِل
ʼḥumur	**red* (pl)	حُمُر
ʔaʼḥibb	*I like, I love*	احب
ʔaʼḥuṭṭ	*I put, I place*	احط
ʼʔiḥna	*we*	احنا
ʼṣubuḥ	*morning*	سُبُح
ʼraaḥ	*he went*	راح
ʼruuḥ	*go!*	روح
ṣaʼḥiiḥ	**true*	صحيح

PRACTICE 2

oo: This stands for a sound like the vowel-sound of *more.* Note that it doesn't have the final -u sound heard at the end of *go* or *slow.* Round your lips as you say it.

ʼyoom	*day*	يوم
ʼšloon	*how*	شلون

'foog	**above*	فوق
šaa'foo	*they saw him*	شافوه

PRACTICE 3

ay: This stands for a sound like the first part of the vowel-sound in *fake.* It doesn't have the final ee-sound heard at the end of *day* or *say.*

'bayš	*how much*	بيش
wayn	*where*	وين
'niišan	**he aimed*	نيشان
'sayyidii	*sir*	سيّدي
ni'sayt	**I forgot*	نسيت
xal'layt	**I put*	خلّيت

PRACTICE 4

Note the difference between ay and aay. aay is similar to ai in *aisle*, but the first part is longer.

ji'gaayir	*cigarettes*	جكاير
jaa'yiin	*coming* (pl)	جايين
'maay	*water*	ماء
'ʔay	*which*	اي
'haay	*this* (f)	هاي
'zayn	*good, well*	زين
'zayyan	**he shaved*	زيّن
'daayman	*always*	دايما

ANALYSIS

1. Place Names.

The article prefix il– regularly occurs with the names of certain lands and cities, but not with others. Among those you've learned are il9i'raaḳ (*the*) *Iraq*, il'mooṣul (*the*) *Mosul*, and il'baṣra (*the*) *Basra*, but bag'daad without it. This is similar to The Bronx, The Hague, The Netherlands, but New York, Iraq, and so on.

The names of cities and lands take *feminine* verbs, adjectives, and pronoun endings: bag'daad ka'biira. *Baghdad is big.*

2. Agent Affixes of Incompleted Action Verb Forms, concluded.

There are three other incompleted action agent affixes in addition to those you have learned.

I

'tumṭur	*it rains*	تمطر
'tiθlij	*it snows*	تثلج
'tiskin	*she lives*	تسكن
'tigdar	*she can*	تقدر
'tisʔal	*she asks*	تسائل

'timšii	*she walks*	تمشي
'tijii	*she comes*	تجي
'taakul	*she eats*	تاكل
'ta9ruf	*she knows*	تعرف
'triid	*she wants*	تريد
'tjiib	*she brings*	تجيب
'tšuuf	*she sees*	تشوف
'truuḥ	*she goes*	تروح
'tguul	*she says*	تقول
'tnaam	*she sleeps*	تنام
tit'mašša	*she takes a walk*	تتمشى
'tištugul	*she works*	تشتغل
'tiftikir	*she thinks*	تفتكر

The agent affix for SHE is t– (ti– before two consonants and in 'tijii, and ta– before 9 and in 'taakul. This is exactly the same as the agent affix for *you* (m). Note that processes of nature ('timṭur, 'tiθlij) take their place with these feminine verb forms.

II

yirii'duun	*they want*	يريدون
yijii'buun	*they bring*	يجيبون
yišuu'fuun	*they see*	يشوفون
yiruu'ḥuun	*they go*	يروحون
yiguu'luun *or* yig'luun	*they say*	يقولون
yinaa'muun	*they sleep*	ينامون
yi'juun	*they come*	يجون
yim'šuun	*they walk*	يمشون
yaak'luun	*they eat*	ياكلون
yiḥ'kuun	*they speak*	يحكون
yisaw'wuun	*they do, make*	يسوّون
yitmaš'šuun	*they take a walk*	يتمشّون
yiftik'ruun	*they think*	يفتكرون
yisik'nuun	*they live*	يسكنون
yidix'luun	*they go in*	يدخلون
yidir'suun	*they study*	يدرسون
yisiʔ'luun	*they ask*	يسائلون
yigid'ruun	*they can, are able to*	يقدرون
yi9ar'fuun	*they know*	يعرفون
yištag'luun	*they work*	يشتغلون

The agent affix meaning THEY consists of two parts, yi . . . uun. Note the above forms very carefully, especially those in the second column; and note the a vowel in th last two words (before g, and after 9) where the preceding verbs of similar pattern have i.

III

trii'duun	*you want*	تريدون
tšuu'fuun	*you see*	تشوفون

tnaa'muun	*you sleep*	تنامون
tim'šuun	*you walk*	تمشون
ti'juun	*you come*	تجون
tiḥ'kuun	*you speak*	تحكون
titmaš'šuun	*you take a walk*	تتمشّون
tisik'nuun	*you live*	تسكنون
tišir'buun	*you drink*	تشربون
ti9ar'fuun	*you know*	تعرفون
tištag'luun	*you work*	تشتغلون
taak'luun	*you eat*	تاكلون

The agent affix meaning YOU, when speaking to more than one person (plural), regardless of sex, also consists of two parts, t . . . uun (ti . . . uun). Note the similarity to the verb forms in (II) above.

SUMMARY OF AGENT AFFIXES, INCOMPLETED ACTION.

We present now a summary of verbs with the agent affixes you have learned so far. You will note that these verbs all indicate *action which has not been completed.* Verbs follow *three* general patterns. For convenience, we quote verbs in the *he* form.

I Verbs of the shape of yi'riid with a *double vowel before the final consonant*, and yiḥibb, with *two final consonants*, follow this pattern:

yi'riid	*he wants*	يريد
'triid	*she wants*	تريد
'triid	*you want* (m)	تريد
trii'diin	*you want* (f)	تريدين
ʔa'riid	*I want*	اريد
yirii'duun	*they want*	يريدون
trii'duun	*you want* (pl)	تريدون
n'riid	*we want*	نريد

Such verbs are: yi'jiib *he brings*, yi'šuuf *he sees*, yi'guul *he says*, yi'naam *he sleeps*, yi'ruuḥ *he goes.*

yi'ḥibb	*he loves*	يحب
'tḥibb	*she loves*	تحب
'tḥibb	*you love* (m)	تحب
tḥib'biin	*you love* (f)	تحبين
ʔa'ḥibb	*I love*	احب
yiḥib'buun	*they love*	يحبون
tḥib'buun	*you love*	تحبون
n'ḥibb	*we love*	نحب

II Verbs whose *he* form ends in a *vowel* follow this pattern:

'yimšii	*he walks*	يمشي
'timšii	*she walks*	تمشي
'timšii	*you walk* (m)	تمشي
tim'šiin	*you walk* (f)	تمشين
'ʔamšii	*I walk*	امشي

yim'šuun	*they walk*	يمشون
tim'šuun	*you walk* (pl)	تمشون
'nimšii	*we walk*	نمشي

Such verbs are: 'yimšii *he walks*, 'yijii *he comes*, yit'mašša *he takes a walk*, 'yiḥkii *he speaks, he talks*, yi'sawwii *he does, he makes*.

III Verbs whose *he* form ends in a *consonant preceded by a single vowel* follow two general patterns. The first is for verbs like 'yiskin, which has *three* consonants; the second, for verbs like yif'tikir, which has *more than three* consonants.

'yiskin	*he lives*	يسكن
'tiskin	*she lives*	تسكن
'tiskin	*you live* (m)	تسكن
tisik'niin	*you live* (f)	تسكنين
'ʔaskin	*I live*	اسكن
yisik'nuun	*they live*	يسكنون
tisik'nuun	*you live* (pl)	تسكنون
'niskin	*we live*	نسكن

Other three-consonant verbs are: 'yidris *he studies*, 'yisʔal *he asks*, 'yigdar *he can, he is able to*, 'ya9ruf *he knows*, 'yišrab *he drinks*, 'yidxul *he enters, goes in, comes in*, 'yirsil *he sends*.

Note the *a* in the forms:

yi9ar'fuun	*they know*
ti9ar'fuun	*you know* (pl)
ti9ar'fiin	*you know* (f)

'yiftikir	*he thinks*	يفتكر
'tiftikir	*she thinks*	تفتكر
'tiftikir	*you think* (m)	تفتكر
tiftik'riin	*you think* (f)	تفتكرين
'ʔaftikir	*I think*	افتكر
yiftik'ruun	*they think*	يفتكرون
tiftik'ruun	*you think* (pl)	تفتكرون
'niftikir	*we think*	نفتكر

Another four-consonant verb you have had is 'yištugul, *he works*. Note the a-vowel in:

yištag'luun	*they work*
tištag'luun	*you work* (pl)
tištag'liin	*you work* (f)

3. 'raaḥ IN IMPENDING ACTION.

'ʔiḥna 'raaḥ 'nimšii.	*We are going to walk.*	احنا راح نمشي .
'raaḥ ʔa'zuur '9ammii.	*I'm going to visit my uncle.*	راح ازور عمي .
'raaḥ it'ruuḥ wii'yaay?	*Are you going to go with me?*	راح تروح ويّاي ؟
'ʔaftikir 'raaḥ 'tumṭur.	*I think it is going to rain.*	افتكر راح تمطر .
raaḥ yi'kuun na'haar 'ṭayyib.	*It's going to be a good day.*	راح يكون نهار طيّب .

You will observe that raaḥ plus any incompleted action verb form means *going to, will.* Note that raaḥ is *invariable*, regardless of the verb accompanying it. This combination shows intended or impending action. Do not confuse it with *going in order to do so-and-so.* Contrast these two sentences:

′ʔana ′raaḥ ′ʔadris.	*I'm going to study* (that is, *I intend to study*)	انا راح ادرس •
′ʔana ʔa′ruuḥ li′kay ′ʔadris.	*I'm going in order to study.*	انا اروح لكي ادرس •

Action which *was going to take place* in the past or was intended in the past is expressed as follows:

′kaan ′raaḥ yi′ruuḥ.	*He was going to go.*	كان راح يروح •
′kaanat ′raaḥ it′ruuḥ.	*She was going to go.*	كانت راح تروح •
′kunit ′raaḥ ʔa′ruuḥ.	*I was going to go.*	كنت راح اروح •
′kunit ′raaḥ ʔaš′tuġul.	*I was going to work.*	كنت راح اشتغل •

Thus you simply add a form of ′kaan to the combination of raaḥ plus incompleted action verb to indicate *was going to do so-and-so, intended to do so-and-so.* Note that these sentences contrast with the following:

′kaan ′raayiḥ lis′siinama.	*He was going to the movie.*	كان رايح للسينما •
′kaanat ′raayḥa lil′bayt.	*She was going home.*	كانت رايحة للبيت •
′kunit ′raayiḥ liš′šuġul.	*I was going to work.*	كنت رايح للشغل •

These latter sentences indicate that the person *was in the process of going, was on the way.*

4. Masculine and Feminine Nouns.

ʔa′buuya ′zayn.	*My father* [*is*] *well.*	ابوي زين •
ič′čaay ′zayn.	*The tea* [*is*] *good.*	الشاي زين •
′ʔummii ′zayna.	*My mother* [*is*] *well.*	امي زينة •
il′gahwa ′zayna.	*The coffee* [*is*] *good.*	القهوة زينة •

All nouns in Iraqi are divided into *two* groups. One group takes the short form of adjectives, as ʔa′buuya and ′čaay are with ′zayn. Because most nouns naming males are in this group, we call it *masculine.*

The second group takes the longer form of adjectives, having –a, as ′ʔummii and ′gahwa are with ′zayna. We call all words of this group *feminine*, because practically all nouns naming females are in it.

Notice, however, that many nouns occur arbitrarily in one group or the other, even though they refer to sexless objects, as ′čaay and ′gahwa. And remember that *all* nouns belong to either one or the other of these two groups. There is no sure way of telling which group each noun belongs in. Practice and observation will have to show you that. In general, included in the masculine group are nouns referring to men and male animals. And included in the feminine group are (1) nouns referring to women and female animals, (2) almost all nouns ending in –a (but not all, for ′šita *winter*, ′hawa *air*, and some others are masculine), (3) names of cities and lands, (4) and natural objects such as the sun, rivers, etc. In both groups there are many words that are not easily classified.

Now this *arrangement into a masculine and feminine group is one of the fundamental divisions in Iraqi.* It runs throughout nouns, adjectives, agent affixes, and pronoun endings. Masculine nouns take masculine forms, while feminine nouns take feminine forms. There is no word for *it*, only 'huuwa *he* and 'hiiya *she*. For example

ič'čaay 'zayn; 'huuwa 'muu 'baarid.	*The tea [is] good; it isn't cold.*	الشاي زين ، هو مو بارد •
il'gahwa 'zayna; 'hiiya 'ḥaarra.	*The coffee [is] good; it's hot.*	القهوة زينة ، هي حارّة •
il'hawa 'raaḥ 'yibrad.	*The wind is going to get cold.*	الهواء راح يبرد •
id'dinya 'raaḥ 'tibrad.	*It* (lit., *the world*, f) *is going to get cold.*	الدنيا راح تبرد •

5. ADJECTIVES WITH PLURAL NOUNS.

ʔu'xuutii zay'niin.	*My brothers [are] well.*	اخوتي زينين •
xa'waatii zay'naat.	*My sisters [are] well.*	خواتي زينات •
ijji'gaayir duu'niiya.	*The cigarettes [are] bad.*	الجكاير دونية •
'ʔakuu siiyaa'raat ka'θiira hi'naa.	*There are many automobiles here.*	اكو سيّارات كثيرة هنا •

Nouns which refer to more than one person or thing are termed *plural*. From the above sentences you see that –iin is added to adjectives going with plural nouns which refer to *men*, and –aat is added to adjectives going with plural nouns which refer to *women*. This is the general rule, but often –iin is used indiscriminately for both.

On the other hand, –a is added to adjectives going with *plural nouns* which refer to *all other things than persons*. This is the same form of the adjective, you will note, that goes with singular feminine nouns.

6. WORDS WITH PLURAL NOUNS.

It is very important to note that only plural nouns referring to *persons* take plural adjectives, plural agent affixes on verbs, plural pronouns, and plural pronoun endings. All other plural nouns, the *non-person plurals*, are treated as if they were feminine singulars. They take feminine singular verb forms, pronouns, pronoun endings, and adjectives.

7. ADJECTIVE FORMS, SINGULAR AND PLURAL.

Here are most of the adjectives you have met. They are grouped according to how they vary, if any, when the feminine and plural endings are added. They are listed in the masculine singular, feminine singular, and personal plurals. Remember that non-person plurals are identical with the feminine singular forms.

I. Adjectives *with no changes* before the adjective endings:

m. s.	*f. s.; non-person pl.*	*m. pl.*	*f. pl.*		
'zayn	'zayna	zay'niin	zay'naat	*good; well*	زين – زينة – زينين – زينات
'ḥaarr	'ḥaarra	ḥaar'riin	ḥaar'raat	*hot*	حر – حارة – حارين – حارات
ja'miil	etc	etc	etc	*pretty, handsome*	جميل – جميلة – جميلين – جميلات
bar'daan				*cold (of people)*	بردان – بردانة – بردانين – بردانات
mam'nuun				*grateful, obliged*	ممنون – ممنونة – ممنونين – ممنونات
maw'juud				*found; present*	موجود – موجودة – موجودين – موجودات
jaay				*coming*	جايي – جاية – جايين – جايات

II. Adjectives *with shortening* before the adjective endings:

'waaḥid	'waaḥda *or* wiḥda			*one*	واحد ـ واحدة ـ وحدة
'baarid	'baarda			*cold* (*of things*)	بارد ـ باردة
'saakin	'saakna	saak'niin	saak'naat	*living, staying*	ساكن ـ ساكنة ـ ساكنين ـ ساكنات
'raayiḥ	'raayḥa	raay'ḥiin	raay'haat	*going*	رايح ـ رايحة ـ رايحين ـ رايحات
'waaguf	'waagfa	waag'fiin	waag'faat	*standing*	واقف ـ واقفة ـ واقفين ـ واقفات
'ṭayyib	'ṭayba	ṭay'biin	ṭay'baat	*good*	طيّب ـ طيبة ـ طيبين ـ طيبات
mit'zawwij	mit'zawja	mitzaw'jiin	mitzaw'jaat	*married*	متزوّج ـ متزوّجة ـ متزوّجين ـ متزوّجات
mit'ʔassif	mit'ʔasfa	mitʔas'fiin	mitʔas'faat	*sorry*	متأسّف ـ متأسّفة ـ متأسّفين ـ مأسّفات

In adjectives of the above pattern, a single vowel before a final consonant (usually *i*, less often *u*) drops before the adjective endings. This results in loss of one of the doubled consonants in adjectives of the second group ('ṭayyib: 'ṭayba). Of course, full forms (as 'saakina or mit'zawwija) are sometimes heard.

III. Adjectives *ending in* –ii.

m. s.	*f. s., non-person pl.*	*m. pl.*	*f. pl.*		
'duunii	duu'niiya	duunii'yiin	duunii'yaat	*bad*	دوني ـ دونية ـ دونيين ـ دونيات
'ḳawii	ḳa'wiiya	ḳawii'yiin	ḳawii'yaat	*strong*	قوي ـ قوية ـ قويين ـ قويات
'θaanii	'θaaniya	θaani'yiin	θaani'yaat	*second; other*	ثاني ـ ثانية ـ ثانيين ـ ثانيات
9i'raaḳii	9iraa'ḳiiya	etc	etc	*Iraqi; an Iraqi*	عراقي ـ عراقية ـ عراقيين ـ عراقيات
bag'daadii	bagdaa'diiya			*Baghdadi; a Baghdadi*	بغدادي ـ بغدادية ـ بغداديين ـ بغداديات
fran'saawii	fransaa'wiiya			*French; a Frenchman*	فرنساوي ـ فرنساوية ـ فرنساويين ـ فرنساويات
9arabii	9ara'biiya	'9arab		*Arabic; an Arab*	عربي ـ عربية ـ عرب
ʔamrii'kaanii	ʔamriikaa'niiya	ʔamrii'kaan		*American; an American*	امريكاني ـ امريكانية ـ امريكان
ʔin'gliizii	ʔinglii'ziiya	ʔin'gliiz		*English; an Englishman*	انكليزي ـ انكليزية ـ انكليز

Adjectives in –ii take the endings –ya, –yiin, –yaat. Note, however, that the last three plurals have no endings at all, and are shorter than the corresponding singulars. Adjectives in –ii commonly occur alongside nouns, thus beside 'ṣayf *summer* is 'ṣayfii *pertaining to summer, summerish.*

IV. Adjectives with '*broken*' *plurals:*

m. s.	*f. s.*	*pl.*		
ka'biir	ka'biira	k'baar	*big; old* (of people)	كبير ـ كبيرة ـ كبار
ṣa'giir	ṣa'giira	ṣ'gaar	*small; young* (of people)	صغير ـ صغيرة ـ صغار
ḍa'9iif	ḍa'9iifa	ḍ'9aaf	*weak*	ضعيف ـ ضعيفة ـ ضعاف

Adjectives and nouns form plurals in two ways. First, some have plurals with endings, such as –iin, –aat. Others, however, have plurals which differ from the singular in all but the consonants (as ka'biir and the plural k'baar have only the consonants k b r). Such plurals are traditionally called 'broken' plurals. Few adjectives have broken plurals. Three you have had are given above. The plural is used for both men and women. Of course the feminine singular is used with non-person plurals (ji'gaayir ka'biira *big cigarettes*).

V. Adjectives which are *invariable*.

'ʔaḥsan	*better*	احسن
'ʔakθar	*more*	اكثر
'ʔakbar	*bigger*	اكبر
'ʔabrad	*colder*	ابرد

Adjectives of the above pattern, which indicates comparison *more so-and-so*, have only one form at all times, for masculine, feminine or plural. Note that 'minn is used in comparisons: hiiya ʔaḥsan 'minn 'ʔintii *She is better than you are.;* ma'naax-bagdaad ʔaḥsan minn ma'naax-ilbaṣra *The weather in Baghdad is better than that of Basra.*

8. Position of Adjectives.

Almost all adjectives *follow* the nouns they are with. Three exceptions are given below; a fourth one gayr *other, different* will be met later.

I

'fadd 'yoom	*a certain day, one day, some day*	فرد يوم
'fadd 'walad	*a certain boy, some boy*	فرد ولد
'fadd 'bint	*a certain girl, some girl*	فرد بنت

Another form of fadd is farid, used in the very same way.

II

'kull in'naas	*all the people*	كل الناس
'kull il'ʔakil	*all the food*	كل الاكل
'kull il'yoom	*all the day, the whole day*	كل اليوم
'kull 'yoom	*every day, each day*	كل يوم
'kull 'waaḥid	*everyone, each one*	كل واحد
'kulšii	*everything*	كل شيء
'kulhum	*all of them*	كلهم
'kulna	*all of us*	كلنا

Note that kull il– is equivalent to *all the,* while kull with a noun not having the prefix il– means *each, every.* A variant form is kill.

III

'xooš 'walad	*a good boy*	خوش ولد
'xooš 'bint	*a good girl*	خوش بنت
'xooš 'wulid	*good boys*	خوش ولد
'xooš ba'naat	*good girls*	خوش بنات

'xooš siiyaa'raat	*good automobiles*	خوش سيّارات
'xooš ji'gaayir	*good cigarettes*	خوش جكاير

These three adjectives have two features in common: first, they occur *before* their nouns, and second, they have only the *one form*, regardless of whether they are with masculine, feminine, singular, or plural nouns.

9. 'THIS', 'THESE', 'THAT', 'THOSE'.

I *This, these.*

'haaδa l'walad	*this boy*	هذا الولد
'haaδii l'bint	*this girl*	هذي البنت
'haay il'bint	*this girl*	هاي البنت
haa'δool il'wulid	*these boys*	هاذول الولد
haa'δool ilba'naat	*these girls*	هاذول البنات

II *That, those.*

'δaak il'walad	*that boy*	ذاك الولد
'δiič il'bint	*that girl*	ذيك البنت
δoo'laak il'wulid	*those boys*	دولاك الولد
δoo'laak ilba'naat	*those girls*	دولاك البنات

III *These* (non-person).

'haay ijji'gaayir	*these cigarettes*	هاي الجكاير
'haay issiiyaa'raat	*these autos*	هاي السيّارات

From the above, you will observe that there is a masculine form ('haaδa) and feminine forms ('haaδii and haay) for THIS. Likewise, there is a masculine form ('δaak) and a feminine form ('δiič) for *that.* On the other hand, there is no gender distinction in the words for *these* and *those,* where you have only one form for *these* (haa'δool) and one for *those* (δoo'laak). (You will also hear shorter forms for the latter, namely 'δool *these* and 'δook *those.*) Many variants occur.

Note that haay is used with non-person plural nouns (III). This follows the point which you learned earlier, that all non-person plurals take feminine singular pronouns, pronoun endings, adjectives, and verbs. Of course, in the singular, the words for 'this' and 'that' are used with non-person nouns (haaδa l'bayt *this house*, and so on).

Finally, in addition to the words given above, there is a shorter form hal–.

hal'yoom	*this day, today*
hal'walad	*this boy*
haṣ'ṣubuḥ	*this morning*
hat'taajir	*this merchant*
hal'wulid	*these boys*
halba'naat	*these girls*
hajji'gaayir	*these cigarettes*

The prefix hal– *this, these* is used with any noun, masculine or feminine, singular or plural. The l is replaced by doubling the same way as it was with the article prefix il– *the.* The stress never falls on it.

EXERCISES

A. Give the form corresponding to humma *they*, then the forms for ʔintum *you* (pl), and ʔintii *you* (f).

1. (yi'riid yi'šuuf) 'wayn 'baytii?
2. 'wayn ('yiskin)?
3. 'maa (yi'naam) 'kulliš.
4. 'ʔay 'siinama (yi'ḥibb yi'šuuf)?

B. Complete the following sentences with the necessary agent affixes.

1. 'maa 'ʔaftikir 'raaḥ __mṭur 'baačir biṣ'ṣubuḥ.
2. 'ʔuxtii __9ruf 'bintak.
3. sa'9iid 'maa __9ruf 'wayn 'ḥasan __štugul.
4. 'hal __θlij 'bii ji'nuub-il'9iraaḳ?
5. 'haay il'bint 'laazim __štugul ha'waaya.
6. 'laazim __sawwii 'šuglak.
7. ('ʔana) 'kunit 'raaḥ __tmašša 'wiiya 'ḥasan.

C. Replace the verb forms in parentheses by the forms called for by the sentence. The forms given are *he* forms.

1. halba'naat 'maa (yi'riid 'yaakul).
2. šitrii'duun ('yišrab)?
3. ilʔamrii'kaan (yi'riid yi'šuuf) 'kulšii.
4. 'maa 'ʔa9ruf 'wayn 'ʔintum ('yiskin).
5. 'raaḥ (yi'jiib) ʔa'buuhum wii'yaahum.
6. hal'wulid (yi'guul) 'maa 'šaafaw 'ʔibnak.
7. haa'ðoolii ('ya9ruf) 'wayn ilʔamrii'kaan.

D. Give the forms of ya9ruf *he knows* called for by the sentence.

1. ('ʔana) 'maa __ 'ʔismak.
2. 'ðiič il'bint __ 'kull bag'daad.
3. 'ðook il'wulid 'maa __ 'wayn raay'ḥiin.
4. ja'miila, __ 'wayn 'ʔuxtič?
5. __ 'niḥkii '9arabii.
6. sa'9iid, __ 'šinuu ʔa'riid ʔa'sawwii?
7. ʔaf'tikir 'ʔaxii 'maa 'kaan __ 'šinuu yi'sawwii.

E. Supply the form of the adjectives called for by the sentence. Some need no change; others will require one of the endings –a, –iin, –aat.

1. 'ʔumm-sa'9iid 'muu ('zayn).
2. hajji'gaara 'kulliš ('zayn).
3. ʔa'ḥibb ʔa'daxxin ji'gaayir (ʔamrii'kaanii).
4. 'wayn 'ʔinta wuṣa'diiḳak ('raayiḥ)?
5. hal'gahwa 'muu ('ḥaarr).
6. 'ʔaftikir 'ðook ilba'naat (ja'miil).
7. 'ʔiḥna ('saakin) 'fii ʔuu'tayl.
8. θi'nayn 'minn xa'waatii (mit'zawwij).

9. il'yoom '?akuu 'hawa ('ḳawii).
10. haa'δoolii 'muu (?in'gliizii) 'laakin (fran'saawii).
11. '?uxtii t'guul 'hiiya (mit'?assif).
12. '?iḥna (mam'nuun) 9alji'gaayir.
13. ?a'šuuf 'bintak ('jaay) 'minn il'madrasa.
14. 'wayn '?intii ('raayiḥ)?

F. The following call for a form of *this* or *that*, or their plurals *these* and *those*. You will remember these forms are haaδa (m), haaδii and haay (f) *this;* δaak (m), δiič (f) *that;* haaδool (or δool) *these;* and δoolaak (or δook) *those.*

1. (*This*) ijji'gaara duu'niiya.
2. (*That*) issii'yaara 'timšii ya'waaš.
3. (*These*) issiiyaa'raat ja'miila.
4. (*Those*) ilba'naat 'muu ?amriikaanii'yaat.
5. (*This*) il'gahwa 'zayna.
6. (*These*) il'wulid yirii'duun yištag'luun '9indak.

G. Read the above sentences, using hal– 'this, these' in place of the words in parentheses.

WHAT WOULD YOU SAY?

1. *You talk to someone in an Arabic restaurant in New York.*
   a. mi'nayn '?inta 'jiit? — ١ ـ منين انت جيت ؟
   b. 'tḥibb 'taakul wii'yaay? — ٢ ـ تحب تاكل ويّاي ؟
   c. '?inta 9i'raaḳii? — ٣ ـ انت عراقي ؟
2. *He came here to study.*
   a. 'jiit 'minn il9i'raaḳ li'kay '?adris hi'naa. — ١ ـ جيت من العراق لكي ادرس هنا •
   b. '?ana 9i'raaḳii; '?ismii 'nuurii. — ٢ ـ انا عراقي ، اسمي نوري •
   c. 'hassa '?ana 'muu til'miiδ. — ٣ ـ هسه انا مو تلميذ •
3. *You ask what school he is going to.*
   a. 'jaami9at-Columbia 'kulliš ka'biira? — ١ ـ جامعة كولوميا كلّش كبيرة ؟
   b. 'layš 'maa 'truuḥ '?ila 'jaami9a 'θaaniya? — ٢ ـ ليش ما تروح الى جامعة ثانية ؟
   c. 'fii '?ay 'jaami9a 'raaḥ 'tidxul? — ٣ ـ في اي جامعة راح تدخل ؟
4. *He asks why you aren't in school.*
   a. 'laazim '?adxul bil'jaami9a. — ١ ـ لازم ادخل بالجامعة •
   b. 'layš 'hassa '?inta 'muu til'miiδ? — ٢ ـ ليش هسّه انت مو تلميذ ؟
   c. 'tigdar it'ruuḥ wii'yaay lil'jaami9a? — ٣ ـ تقدر تروح ويّاي للجامعة ؟
5. *You tell him why not.*
   a. '?akuu 'jaami9a bij'jayš. — ١ ـ اكو جامعة بالجيش •
   b. ij'jayš il?amrii'kaanii 'kulliš ka'biir. — ٢ ـ الجيش الامريكاني كلّش كبير •
   c. 'šahar ij'jaay 'raaḥ '?adxul bij'jayš. — ٣ ـ الشهر الجاي راح ادخل بالجيش •

6. *You have no choice.*

a. 'tiftikir 'raaḥ it'ruuḥ lil'9iraak?
١ ـ تفتكر راح تروح للعراق ؟

b. bij'jayš 'laazim ʔa'ruuḥ 'ʔila 'wayn 'maa yirsi'luunii.
٢ ـ بالجيش لازم اروح الى وين ما يرسلوني •

c. 'hassa 'wayn 'ʔahlak?
٣ ـ هسة وين اهلك ؟

7. *What about the weather in Iraq.*

a. 'šloon il'manaax fii ši'maal-il9i'raaḳ?
١ ـ شلون المناخ في شمال العراق ؟

b. 'hal ilma'naax bišši'maal 'ʔaḥsan 'minn ijji'nuub?
٢ ـ هل المناخ بالشمال احسن من الجنوب ؟

c. 'šloon ilma'naax fil'9iraaḳ?
٣ ـ شلون المناخ في العراق ؟

8. *He contrasts winter and summer.*

a. biš'šita 'ʔakuu 'maṭar ha'waaya.
١ ـ بالشتا اكو مطر هوايه •

b. 'timṭur biš'šita, 'bass 'muu biṣ'ṣayf.
٢ ـ تمطر بالشتاء بس مو بالصيف •

c. 'hiiya 'baarda biš'šita wu'ḥaarra biṣ'ṣayf.
٣ ـ هي باردة بالشتاء وحارّة بالصيف •

9. *Does it snow there?*

a. 'timṭur hi'naak?
١ ـ تمطر هناك ؟

b. 'tiθlij hi'naak?
٢ ـ تثلج هناك ؟

c. ma'naax-New York 'ʔaḥsan 'minn bag'daad?
٣ ـ مناخ نيويورك احسن من بغداد ؟

10. *Yes, in the north.*

a. 'maa 'tiθlij bil9i'raaḳ.
١ ـ ما تثلج بالعراق •

b. 'na9am, bišši'maal 'yamm il'mooṣul.
٢ ـ نعم بالشمال يم الموصل •

c. 'bass bijji'nuub.
٣ ـ بس بالجنوب •

11. *He adds information on sleeping.*

a. biṣ'ṣayf 'kull in'naas yinaa'muun '9ala ṣṣu'ṭuuḥ.
١ ـ بالصيف كل الناس ينامون على السطوح •

b. ilma' naax'kulliš 'baarid biṣ'ṣayf.
٢ ـ المناخ كلّش بارد بالصيف •

c. 'laa, 'maa 'ʔa9ruf 'wayn yinaa'muun.
٣ ـ لا ، ما اعرف وين ينامون •

12. *You ask why.*

a. 'šinuu s'sabab?
١ ـ شنو السبب ؟

b. 'layš 'haaδa?
٢ ـ ليش هذا ؟

c. 'šloon 'haaδa?
٣ ـ شلون هذا ؟

13. *He gives two reasons.*

a. 'minn 'sabab ilma'naax 'baarid.
١ ـ من سبب المناخ بارد •

b. 'minn 'sabab il'maay 'baarid.
٢ ـ من سبب الماء بارد •

c. 'minn 'sabab il'hawa 'baarid 'wayḍan 'maa 'timṭur.
٣ ـ من سبب الهواء بارد ودائما تمطر •

14. *You ask how long he lived in Baghdad.*

a. 'šgad si'kanit 'fii bag'daad?
١ ـ اشقد سكنت في بغداد ؟

b. 'minuu 'kaan wii'yaak 'fii bag'daad?
٢ ـ منو كان وياك في بغداد ؟

c. 'ta9ruf 'šii '9ann bag'daad?
٣ ـ تعرف شيء عن بغداد ؟

15. *Several years.*
   a. 'kunit ?a'ruuḥ lij'jaami9a 'wiiya '?axii. — ١ ـ كنت اروح للجامعة ويّا اخي ٠
   b. si'kanit 'biiha θi'laaθ-is'niin 'lamma 'kunit ṣa'giir, wuba9'dayn 'kunit ?a'zuur 'xaaḷii hi'naak. — ٢ ـ سكنت بيها ثلاث سنين لما كنت صغير ، وبعدين كنت ازور خالي هناك ٠
   c. 'kunit ?a'šuuf 'xaaḷii 'lamma 'kaan 'fii bag'daad. — ٣ ـ كنت اشوف خالي لما كان في بغداد ٠

16. *He tells of the weather in Baghdad.*
   a. bag'daad 'ḥaarra binna'haar wu'baarda bil'layl, 'bass biš'šita 'hiiya 'daayman 'baarda. — ١ ـ بغداد حارّة بالنهار وباردة بالليل ، بس بالشتاء هي دائما باردة ٠
   b. ilma'naax 'fii bag'daad 'muu 'kulliš 'ḥaarr. — ٢ ـ المناخ في بغداد مو كلّش حار ٠
   c. ma'naax-bag'daad '?aḥsan 'minn ma'naax-il'baṣra. — ٣ ـ مناخ بغداد احسن من مناخ البصرة ٠

17. *You leave the restaurant. Your friend asks if it's going to rain.*
   a. xal'liiha timṭur! — ١ ـ خليها تمطر ٠
   b. 'layš 'triidha 'timṭur? — ٢ ـ ليش تريدها تمطر ؟
   c. 'tiftikir 'raaḥ 'timṭur? — ٣ ـ تفتكر راح تمطر ؟

18. *He doesn't want it to rain.*
   a. ?a'ḥibb yi'kuun na'haar 'ṭayyib. — ١ ـ احب يكون نهار طيّب ٠
   b. 'šuuf, 'hassa 'ṭil9at iš'šamis. — ٢ ـ شوف هسة طلعت الشمس ٠
   c. 'maa ?a'riidha 'timṭur. — ٣ ـ ما اريدها تمطر ٠

19. *You say it doesn't matter.*
   a. may'xaalif. — ١ ـ ما يخالف ٠
   b. 'maa '?a9ruf 'šii '9anna. — ٢ ـ ما اعرف شيء عنّه ٠
   c. '?ana ?a'ḥibha 'timṭur. — ٣ ـ انا احبها تمطر ٠

LISTENING IN

CONVERSATION ONE

Tom has gone to an Arabic restaurant in New York. He talks to one of the other guests.

Concluding RECORD 10A

TOM ?is'maḥlii, ?a'šuuf '?anta 'muu ?amrii'kaanii. — توم ـ اسمح لي ، اشوف انت مو امريكاني ٠

NOURI 'laa, '?ana 9i'raaḳii. '?ismii 'nuurii. — نوري ـ لا ، انا عراقي ٠ اسمي نوري ٠

TOM ?at'šarraf, '?ismii Tom. '?agdar '?as'alak 'šitsawwii hi'naa? — توم ـ اتشرّف ، اسمي توم ٠ اقدر اسائلك شتسوّي هنا ؟

NOURI 'jayt 'minn il9i'raaḳ li'kay '?adris.

نوري ـ جيت من العراق لكي ادرس •

TOM 'fii '?ay 'madrasa?

توم ـ في اي مدرسة ؟

Beginning RECORD 10B

NOURI 'fii 'jaami9at-Columbia.

نوري ـ في جامعة كولومبيا •

TOM '?ana 'hamm 'činit til'miiδ 'fii 'jaami9at-Columbia.

توم ـ انا هم كنت تلميذ في جامعة كولومبيا •

NOURI 'layš '?anta 'muu til'miiδ 'hassa?

نوري ـ ليش انت مو تلميذ هسّة ؟

TOM 'šahar ij'jaay 'raaḥ '?adxul bij'jayš.

توم ـ الشهر الجاي راح ادخل بالجيش •

NOURI 'tiftikir 'raaḥ it'ruuḥ lil9i'raaḳ?

نوري ـ تفتكر راح تروح للعراق ؟

TOM '?ana 'maa '?a9ruf; 'bass ij'jayš 'ya9ruf.
'laazim ?a'ruuḥ '?ila 'wayn 'maa yirsi'luunii.
?a'ḥibb ?a'ruuḥ lil9i'raaḳ, 'laakin 'maa '?a9ruf 'šii '9anna.
'gullii, 'šloon ilma'naax hi'naak?

توم ـ انا ما اعرف ، بس الجيش يعرف •
لازم اروح الى وين ما يرسلوني •
احب اروح للعراق لكن ما اعرف شيء عنه •
قل لي شلون المناخ هناك ؟

NOURI 'muu 'miθil New York.

نوري ـ مو مثل نيويورك •

TOM '?akuu 'muṭar ha'waaya?

توم ـ اكو مطر هواية ؟

NOURI 'balii*, biš'šita 'bass 'muu biṣ'ṣayf.

نوري ـ بلي ، بالشتاء بس مو بالصيف •

TOM 'hal 'tiθlij hi'naak?

توم ـ هل تثلج هناك ؟

NOURI 'bass 'yamm il'mooṣul.
'ta9ruf 'wayn il'mooṣul?

نوري ـ بس يم الموصل •
تعرف وين الموصل ؟

TOM '?aftikir 'hiiya biššii'maal.
'hal '?inta 'minn hi'naak?

توم ـ افتكر هي بالشمال •
هل انت من هناك ؟

NOURI 'laa, 'jayt 'minn ijji'nuub, 'minn il'baṣra.

نوري ـ لا ، جيت من الجنوب ، من البصرة •

TOM 'šloon ilma'naax bijji'nuub?

توم ـ شلون المناخ بالجنوب ؟

NOURI 'kulliš 'ḥaarr biṣ'ṣayf wu'baarid biš'šita.
ta9ruf bil9i'raaḳ 'kull in'naas yinaa'muun '9ala ṣṣu'ṭuuḥ biṣ'ṣayf?

نوري ـ كلش حار بالصيف وبارد بالشتاء •
تعرف بالعراق كل الناس ينامون على الصطوح بالصيف ؟

TOM 'laa, 'maa '?a9ruf 'haaδa. 'šinuu s'sabab?

توم ـ لا ، ما اعرف هذا • شنو السبب ؟

NOURI 'minn 'sabab il'hawa 'baarid hi'naak,
wu'?ayḍan 'maa 'tumṭur biṣ'ṣayf.

نوري ـ من سبب الهواء بارد هناك •
وايضا ما تمطر بالصيف •

TOM wubag'daad, 'ta9ruf ka'θiir '9anha?

توم ـ وبغداد ، تعرف كثير عنها ؟

NOURI 'na9am, si'kanit 'biiha θi'laaθ-is'niin 'lamma 'činit ṣa'giir.
wuba9'dayn 'činit ?a'zuur 'xaaḷii ka'θiir hi'naak.
bag'daad 'ḥaarra binna'haar wu'baarda bil'layl.
'haaδa 'bass biṣ'ṣayf; biš'šita 'hiiya 'daayman 'baarda.

نوري ـ نعم ، سكنت بيها ثلاث سنين لما كنت صغير •
وبعدين كنت ازور خالي كثير هناك •
بغداد حارّة بالنهار وباردة بالليل
هذا بس بالصيف ـ بالشتاء هي دائما باردة •

TOM ?i9'ḍirnii, 'nuurii, 'laazim ?a'ruuḥ.
'yimkin 'fadd 'yoom ?a'šuufak bil'9iraaḳ.

توم ـ اعذرني ، نوري ، لازم اروح •
يمكن فرد يوم اشوفك بالعراق •

NOURI '?aw 'yimkin bil'madrasa. fiimaani'laa, Tom.

نوري ـ او يمكن بالمدرسة • في امان الله ، توم •

* Not complete on record.

CONVERSATION TWO

Hassan meets Said.

HASSAN ʹšloon ʹyoom ʹduunii! ilʹhawa ʹkulliš ʹgawii wuʹmaakuu ʹšamis.	حسن ـ شلون يوم دوني ! الهواء كلّش قوي وماكو شمس •
SAID ʹtiftikir ʹraaḥ ʹtumṭur halʹyoom?	سعيد ـ تفتكر راح تمطر هاليوم ؟
HASSAN ʹmaa ʹʔaftikir, ʹwalaw idʹdinya mʹgayma.	حسن ـ ما افتكر ، ولو الدنيا مغيمة •
haṣʹṣubuḥ ʹmuṭrat haʹwaaya, wuʹmaa ʹʔaftikir ʹba9ad ʹraaḥ ʹtumṭur.	هالصبح مطرت هواية وما افتكر بعد راح تمطر •
SAID ʹmaa yiʹxaalif, ilʹmuṭar ʹzayn. xalʹliiha ʹtumṭur!	سعيد ـ ما يخالف ، المطر زين ، خلّيها تمطر !
HASSAN ʹʔana ʹmaa ʔaʹriidha ʹtumṭur.	حسن ـ انا ما اريدها تمطر •
ʹlaazim ʹbaačir ʔaʹruuḥ lilʹmooṣul.	لازم باكر اروح للموصل •
SAID ʹʔaftikir ʹbaačir ʹraaḥ yiʹkuun naʹhaar ʹṭayyib.	سعيد ـ افتكر باكر راح يكون نهار طيّب •
ʹšuuf, ʹhassa ʹṭil9at išʹšamis.	شوف هسّه طلعت الشمس •

CONVERSATIONS

A. Two at a time, discuss the weather of your home areas. Ask your partner all the questions you can, and when you are answering give all the facts you can. Some suggestions are as follows:

1. Where do you come from?
2. Is that in the north or the south?
3. How long did you live there?
4. How is the weather there compared with the weather here?
5. Do you have snow, or only rain?
6. Is the summer better than the winter?
7. Is there much wind?
8. Other questions.

B. Two of you will discuss the weather as it is today. Some suggestions are:

1. How is the weather today?
2. What a beautiful day it is, or what a bad day!
3. Do you think it is going to rain?
4. Is it windy or cloudy, or is it hot today?
5. How was the weather yesterday?
6. What about the weather tomorrow?
7. You want it to rain, or else you don't want it to rain.

VOCABULARY

Hereafter, nouns whose form doesn't show whether they are masculine or feminine are marked (m) or (f). For example 'hawa (m) *air*.

'baarid, 'baarda (f)	cold (of things)
baar'daan, –a (f)	cold (of people)
ba'naat	girls, daughters
'ba9ad	yet, more
ba9'dayn	afterwards, then
'dinya	world
'duunii, duu'niiya (f)	bad
'fadd	some, a certain
'fadd 'yoom	some day
'guwii, gu'wiiya (f)	strong
'hassa	now; just now
'hawa (m)	air
ha'waaya	much, a lot
'ḥaarr, –a (f)	hot
'jaami9a	university
'jaami9at-Columbia	Columbia University
'jaay, 'jaaya (f)	coming
'šahar ij'jaay	the coming month
ji'nuub	south
ji'nuub-il9i'raaḳ	the south of Iraq
ka'θiir	much; often
'kull *or* 'kill	all; every, each
'ḳawii, ḳa'wiiya (f)	strong
'lamma	while, when
'layš	why
li'kay	in order to
ma'naax	weather
'maṭar *or* muṭar	rain
may'xaalif ('maa yi'xaalif)	it doesn't matter
m'gayma (f)	cloudy
'muṭrat (f)	it rained
'miθil	like, as
il'mooṣul (f)	Mosul
'naas (f *or* pl)	people
in'naas	the people

'nafis	self
'nafsii	myself
'raaḥ	he went; going to
'raaḥ 'timṭur	it is going to rain
'raaḥ yi'kuun	he is going to be
'sabab	cause, reason
'šinuu s'sabab?	What's the reason?
'minn 'sabab	because
si'kanit	I lived, I stayed; you lived, you stayed
'ṣayf	summer
ṣu'ṭuuḥ (pl)	roofs
'ṣubuḥ	morning
biṣ'ṣubuḥ	during the morning
'šahar	month
'šahar ij'jaay	the coming month
'šamis (f)	sun
'šii *or* 'šay	thing, a thing, anything
ši'maal	north
bišši'maal	in the north
'šita (m)	summer
'šloon	how; what a!
til'miiδ	student
'tiftikir	you think
'tiθlij (f)	it snows
'tumṭur (f)	it rains
'ṭil9at (f)	she rose; it came out (of the sun)
'wulid	boys
'waḷaw	although, even though
'xaaḷ	uncle (mother's brother)
'ya9ruf	he knows
'yibrad	he gets cold

'yimkin	perhaps, possibly
yinaa'muun	they sleep
yirsi'luun	they send
'ʔadris	I study
'ʔadxul bii	I go in, I enter
'ʔaftikir	I think
'ʔagdar	I can
'činit 'ʔagdar	I could, I was able to
'ʔasʔal	I ask
'ʔasʔalak *or* ʔa'siʔlak	I ask you
'ʔayḍan	also, moreover, besides
'ʔila 'wayn 'maa	(to) wherever
'ʔilwayš	why
'ʔisʔal	ask!
ʔis'maḥ 'ʔila	pardon!
ʔis'maḥlii	pardon me!
ʔišmaḥuulna	pardon us!
'9ann	about, concerning
'9anna	about him, it
'9anha	about her
il'9iraaḳ (f)	Iraq
9i'raaḳii	Iraqi

UNIT 6

First Review

This review Unit contains a number of exercises which will help you make sure that you thoroughly covered the work of the first five Units. They will show what you need to restudy or review.

A. *True-False Test.*

Concluding RECORD 10B and Beginning RECORD 11A.

Here are 36 statements. Decide whether they are *true* or *false*. Repeat as often as necessary for comprehension. The Arabic is to be read twice by the guide, or until you understand.

١ ـ تثلج كثير بالجنوب •
٢ ـ ماكو خبّازين بالعراق •
٣ ـ مطرت هوايه لما طلعت الشمس •
٤ ـ كل واحد يفهمك لما تحكي عربي •
٥ ـ بنات جميلات يمشون يواش وما يحكون شيء •
٦ ـ الامريكان يحبّون يروحون للسينما •

٧ ـ ماكو مراحيض في كل سينما •
٨ ـ بالصبح انا آكل شاي واشرب خبز •
٩ ـ اكو جسر في بغداد اسمه جسر الملك غازي •
١٠ ـ كل واحد يحب شغله •
١١ ـ يسوّون سيّارات فورد بامريكا •
١٢ ـ بالعراق موكل الناس يسكنون في اوتيلات •

١٣ ـ جكاير امريكانية ماكو بيهم تتن •
١٤ ـ الجنود لازم يرجعون الى البيت كل ليلة •
١٥ ـ دائما تقول باكر راح يكون نهار طيّب •
١٦ ـ كل طبيب يعمل جسر •
١٧ ـ كل بنت اسمها لولو •
١٨ ـ ندرس عربي لكي نحكي عربي •

١٩ ـ كل واحد يفتكر قهوة احسن من شاي •
٢٠ ـ كل الامريكان يدرسون عربي •
٢١ ـ مناخ بغداد مو مثل مناخ نيويورك •
٢٢ ـ كل يوم بالصيف اكو هواء قوي •
٢٣ ـ في نيويورك لازم تنام على الصطوح •
٢٤ ـ احنا نسوّي قهوة ويّا ماء حار •

٢٥ ـ كل البنات متزوّجات •
٢٦ ـ هو كان بنت زينة لما كان بالمدرسة •
٢٧ ـ في العراق الناس ياكلون تمّن •
٢٨ ـ الجيش يرسلك الى وين ما يريد •
٢٩ ـ خوات مو مثل اخوة •
٣٠ ـ رجّال قوي يقدر يحمل حمل كبير •

٣١ ـ اخي مو متزوّج ومرته مو متزوّجة •
٣٢ ـ نشوف ناس هواية بالسينمات •
٣٣ ـ اليوم انا كلّش زين ولو مريض •
٣٤ ـ سيّارة زينة ما تمشي زين •
٣٥ ـ كل الامريكان يسكنون بالشمال •
٣٦ ـ لما الدنيا مغيمة ، نفتكر راح تمطر •

B. *Conversations and Questions.*

RECORDS 11B and 12A.

Here are 8 conversations. Answer in Arabic the questions following each conversation. The Arabic text is for the guide. Have him repeat as necessary.

Conversation 1. Hassan goes to Nouri's house to see him.

الاب ـ اهلا وسهلا ، حسن .
حسن ـ احب اشوف نوري .
الاب ـ هو مو موجود بالبيت .
حسن ـ تعرف وين اقدر اشوفه ؟
الاب ـ ها الصبح راح الى مزرعتنا .
قال لي باكر راح يرجع .
حسن ـ لما يجي ، ارجوك قل له انا كنت هنا واريد اشوفه .
الاب ـ مع السلامة .

(الاسئلة)

١ ـ منو اجا للباب ؟
٢ ـ وين كان نوري ؟
٣ ـ شنو راح ابو نوري يقول الى ابنه ؟

Conversation 2. Ali tries to find work.

علي ـ افتكر انت مهندس .
مقاول ـ لا ، انا مقاول .
علي ـ احب اشتغل ويّاك .
مقاول ـ عندي شغل هوايه ، شتقدر تسوّي ؟
علي ـ اقدر اسوّي كل شيء .
مقاول ـ زين ، وين كنت تشتغل قبل هسّة ؟
علي ـ ما كنت اشتغل من سبب كنت بالمدرسة .
مقاول ـ تعال عندي باكر الصبح لكي اراويك شنيو شغلك .

(الاسئلة)

١ ـ ويّا منو علي كان يحكي ؟
٢ ـ اكو عنده شغل ؟
٣ ـ شنو المقاول يسائل علي ؟
٤ ـ شقال علي يقدر يسوّي ؟
٥ ـ ليش علي ما كان يشتغل قبل هسّة ؟

Conversation 3. Going to a movie.

احمد ـ شلونك ، سعيد ؟
سعيد ـ الحمد لله ، شلونكم ؟ وين تتمشّون ؟
احمد ـ انا ومصطفى رايحين للسينما .
تقدر تروح تشوفها ويّانا ؟
سعيد ـ زين ، ما عندي شغل .
اي سينما راح تشوفون ؟
مصطفى ـ ها الشهر ما شفنا سينمة الملك غازي .
ممكن هي تكون زينة .
احمد ـ ما يخالف ، تعرف انا احب كل سينما بيها بنت جميلة .

(الاسئلة)

١ ـ من اي سبب سعيد يقدر يروح ويّاهم ؟
٢ ـ اي سينما همّا ما شافوا ؟
٣ ـ اي شيء احمد يحب يشوف في كل سينما ؟

Conversation 4. Ali's father is sick.

علي ـ سلام عليكم .
نوري ـ وعليكم السلام .
صديقنا حسن قال لي ابوك مو زين .
علي ـ نعم ، هو كلّش مريض .
نوري ـ شكو بيه ؟
علي ـ ما نعرف ، ما يقدر ياكل شيء وايضا هو ضعيف .
نوري ـ شقال الطبيب عنه ؟
علي ـ ما قال لنا شكو بيه ، بس لما راح قال هو راح يصير زين .
افتكر اليوم هو احسن من البارحة .
نوري ـ هذا زين . ارجوك قل له انا كنت هنا .
علي ـ اشكرك ، ارجوك زورنا دائما .

(الاسئلة)

١ ـ منو قال الى علي عن ابو نوري ؟
٢ ـ يقدر ابو نوري ياكل شيء ؟
٣ ـ هل اجا الطبيب ؟
٤ ـ شلون ابو نوري اليوم ؟
٥ ـ هل هو راح يصير زين او لا ؟

Conversation 5. Mustafa talks to his daughter.

مصطفى ـ وين رايحة ؟
لولو ـ الى الدكّان •
مصطفى ـ ارجوك جيبي لي باكيت جكاير •
تعرفين وين دكّان ابو جكاير ؟
لولو ـ نعم ، اعرفه •
مصطفى ـ وين صديقتك جميلة ؟ هي دائما ويّاك •
لولو ـ هي مريضة وما تقدر تجي عندي• ما اعرف شكو بيها •
اليوم راح تروح ويّا امها للطبيب •

(الاسئلة)

١ ـ وين رايحة لولو ؟
٢ ـ شنو ابوها يريدها تجيب له ؟
٣ ـ هل هي تعرف وين دكّان ابو جكاير ؟
٤ ـ منو جميلة ؟
٥ ـ وين لازم تروح جميلة ؟

Conversation 6. Ali wants Said to go with him.

علي ـ سعيد ، تعال ويّاي •
سعيد ـ وين تريد تروح ؟
علي ـ خلّي نتمشّى الى السوق •
سعيد ـ الويش للسوق ؟
علي ـ اريد جكاير واريد اتمشّى شويّه •
سعيد ـ اكو ابو جكاير هناك ؟
علي ـ بلي ، البارحة شفت دكّانه لمّا كنّا نتمشّى •
قل لي ، تريد تتمشّى ويّاي او لا ؟
سعيد ـ احب أروح ويّاك ، لكن لازم ادرس •

(الاسئلة)

١ ـ وين علي يريد يروح ؟
٢ ـ شلون علي يعرف اكو ابو جكاير هناك ؟
٣ ـ ليش سعيد ما يقدر يروح ويّاه ؟

Conversation 7. Bill introduces John to Said.

بل ـ الله بالخير ، سعيد •
شلون كيفك اليوم ؟
سعيد ـ كلّش زين ، الحمد لله •
بل ـ سعيد ، اريد اعرفك على جان •
سعيد ـ اتشرّف ، جان •
جان ـ اتشرّف ، سعيد •
بل ـ جان اجا من امريكا لكي يشتغل وايضا يريد يدرس عربي بالعراق •
سعيد ـ افتكر هسّة انت تقدر تحكي عربي •
جان ـ مو كثير • درست بامريكا ، بس اريد ادرس اكثر •
سعيد ـ انا احب ادرس انكليزي •
جان ـ زين ، انا احكي انكليزي ويّاك وانت تقدر تحكي عربي ويّاي •

(الاسئلة)

١ ـ ليش جان اجا للعراق ؟
٢ ـ هل سعيد يقدر يحكي انكليزي ؟
٣ ـ شنو جان وسعيد راح يسوّون ؟

Conversation 8. Said borrows Ali's automobile.

سعيد ـ صباح الخير ، علي •
علي ـ صباح الخير ، سعيد •
وين سيّارتك ؟ اشوفك تمشي •
سعيد ـ خليتها بالبيت ، البارحة ما مشت زين •
هسّة ما اعرف شنو اسوّي •

(الاسئلة)

١ ـ وين سعيد خلّى سيّارته ؟
٢ ـ ليش ؟
٣ ـ منو سعيد يريد يزور ؟
٤ ـ منين سعيد راح ياخذ سيّارة ؟

٥ - يقدر علي يروح ويّاه ؟

علي - ليش ؟
سعيد - اليوم اريد اروح ازور ابن عمّي في شمال بغداد •
علي - تقدر تاخذ سيّارتي بس لازم تجيبها قبل الليل•
سعيد - تقدر تجي ويّاي اذا تحب •
علي - اشكرك ، لازم اروح ويّا اهلي الى بيت صديقنا •

C. Supply the article prefix il– *the*, with doubling when possible.

1. 'ʔuxtii __ka'biira 'kaanat ma'riiḍa. — ١ - اختي الكبيرة كانت مريضة •
2. __taajir '9inda sii'yaarat-Ford. — ٢ - التاجر عنده سيّارة فورد •
3. 'haay __'siinama 'ʔaḥsan 'minn 'ðiič. — ٣ - هاي السينما احسن من ذيك •
4. il'walad __ṣa'ġiir 'ʔibin-ʔa'xuuya. — ٤ - الولد الصغير ابن اخوي •
5. 'haaða __'bayt 'bayt-ṣa'diiḳii. — ٥ - هذا البيت بيت صديقي •
6. 'šloon __ma'naax bil9i'raaḳ? — ٦ - شلون المناخ بالعراق ؟
7. 'haaða __rij'jaal mu'ḳaawil. — ٧ - هذا الرجّال مقاول •
8. 'ʔaxii __'θaanii 'kaan 'ḍaabuṭ bij'jayš. — ٨ - اخي الثاني كان ضابط بالجيش •
9. 'šahar __'jaay 'raaḥ 'ʔadxul bij'jaami9a. — ٩ - الشهر الجاي راح ادخل بالجامعة •
10. 'šloon __'šita 'fii baġ'daad? — ١٠ - شلون الشتاء في بغداد ؟

D. Read these sentences adding the pronoun ending –ii *me, my* to the appropriate form of the words in parentheses. Repeat, adding the pronoun endings –a *him, his*, –na *us, our*, and –ha *her*.

1. (xawaat) yisik'nuun 'wiiya 'ʔabii 'wummii. — ١ - خواتي يسكنون ويّا ابي وامي •
2. 'ʔaftikir 'kull 'waaḥid 'ya9ruf (ʔisim). — ٢ - افتكر كل واحد يعرف اسمي •
3. (9amm) 'yiskin 'fii 'bayt ka'biir 'yamm 'jisir-'mood. — ٣ - عمي يسكن في بيت كبير يم جسر مود •
4. yig'luun 'ʔakuu maṭ9am 'zayn (giddaam). — ٤ - يقلون اكو مطعم زين قدّامي •
5. 'ʔakuu 'wulid wu'ʔayḍan ba'naat 'fii (madrasa). — ٥ - اكو ولد وايضا بنات في مدرستي •
6. iṭ'ṭabiib 'kaan 'ya9ruf (ʔuxut) bam'riika. — ٦ - الطبيب كان يعرف اختي بامريكا •
7. (ʔahal) yisik'nuun ba'9iid 'minn (dukkaan). — ٧ - اهلي يسكنون بعيد من دكّاني •
8. 'minuu 'ðool ilba'naat ilwaag'faat '9ala (yamiin)? — ٨ - منو هاذول البنات الواقفات على يميني ؟
9. 'layš 'maa 'tisʔal '(ʔibin) '9aan ṣa'diiḳak? — ٩ - ليش ما تسائل ابني عن صديقك ؟
10. ʔa'ḥibb 'ʔa9ruf 'šii '9ann (ʔax). — ١٠ - احب اعرف شي عن اخي •
11. harrij'jaal yi'riid 'yijii (wiiya). — ١١ - هالرجّال يريد يجي ويّاي •

E. Complete the following sentences with pronoun endings.

1. sa'9iid, ʔar'juuk 'jiib (ʔax) wii'yaak. — ١ - سعيد ، ارجوك جيب اخوك ويّاك •
2. 'ʔagdar ʔa'šuuf 'ʔaḥmad, 'laakin 'maa 'ʔagdar ʔa'šuuf il'walad il'waaguf (wara). — ٢ - اقدر اشوف احمد ولكن ما اقدر اشوف الولد الواقف وراه •
3. 'lamma 'ʔajii 'raaḥ ʔa'jiib (siiyaara). — ٣ - لمّا اجي راح اجيب سيّارتي •
4. 'maa 'ʔaftikir haa'ðool yiḥib'buun (šugul). — ٤ - ما افتكر هذول يحبون شغلهم •
5. 'ʔisʔal 'ʔabuu-'ḥassan 'wayn (ʔibin). — ٥ - اسائل ابو حسن وين ابنه ••

6. hal'walad '?ija yi'šuuf (?ab). — ٦ ـ هالولد اجا يشوف ابوه •
7. yig'luun (dukkaan) '?akbar 'minn duk'kaanii. — ٧ ـ يقلون دكانه اكبر من دكاني •
8. 'layš 'maa '?agdar '?aḥkii 'wiiya 'waaḥid 'minn (?uxwa)? — ٨ ـ ليش ما اقدر احكي ويّا واحد من اخوتي ؟
9. '?aḥmad, 'šgad (9amur), wu'šgad '9amur-'?uxtak? — ٩ ـ احمد شقد عمرك وشقد عمر اختك ؟
10. 'maa šif'naak bil'madrasa; 'škaan (bii)? — ١٠ ـ ما شفناك بالمدرسة ، شكان بيك ؟

F. Add pronoun endings to 9ind.

1. sa'9iid, '?akuu 9ind__ 'titin? — ١ ـ سعيد ، اكو عندك تتن ؟
2. mit'?assif, 'maakuu 9ind__. — ٢ ـ متأسف ماكو عندي •
3. John 'kaan 9ind__ sii'yaarat-Ford. — ٣ ـ جان كان عنده سيارة فورد •
4. 'haay il'bint 9ind__ θi'laaθ-xa'waat. — ٤ ـ هاي البنت عندها ثلاث خوات •
5. 'gaallii 'maa 'kaan 9ind__ 'šugul ka'θiir 'gabul il'ḥarb. — ٥ ـ قال لي ما كان عنده شغل كثير قبل الحرب •
6. ṣa'diiḳna '?ija 9id__, 'bass 'maa šifn'aa. — ٦ ـ صديقنا اجا عدنا بس ما شفناه •
7. '?akuu 'fadd rij'jaal yi'riid 'yištuġul 9id__ 'fii duk'kaankum. — ٧ ـ اكو فرد رجّال يريد يشتغل عندكم في دكانكم •
8. 'ḥasan, 'kam 'walad 9ind__? — ٨ ـ حسن ، كم ولد عندك ؟
9. 'bintii lmit'zawja 9ind__ wala'dayn. — ٩ ـ بنتي المتزوجة عندها ولدين •
10. sa'9iid, 'minuu 'yištuġul 9ind__? — ١٠ ـ سعيد ، منو يشتغل عندك •

G. Give the correct form of the adjectives in parentheses, with –a, –iin, or –aat where necessary. Not all require change.

1. il?amrii'kaan (waaguf) 'yamm siiyaa'rathum. — ١ ـ الامريكان واقفين يم سيّاراتهم •
2. '?iḥna (saakin) 'fii ?uu'tayl ṣa'ġiir. — ٢ ـ احنا مساكنين في اوتيل صغير •
3. il'baarḥa 'šifna θi'laaθ-ba'naat (jamiil). — ٣ ـ البارحة شفنا ثلاث بنات جميلات •
4. '?aḥmad 'wuxta (ṣaġiir). — ٤ ـ احمد وخته صغار •
5. il'hawa 'maa 'kaan (baarid). — ٥ ـ الهواء ما كان بارد •
6. il'yoom id'dinya (baarid). — ٦ ـ اليوم الدنيا باردة •
7. 'jaami9at-Columbia 'hiiya 'madrasa (kabiir). — ٧ ـ جامعة كولومبيا هي مدرسة كبيرة •
8. 'tigdar it'šuuf il'bint (ijjaay) 'minn il'madrasa? — ٨ ـ تقدر تشوف البنت الجاية من المدرسة ؟
9. 'ðaak il'walad 'kulliš (ḳawii), 'laakin ?u'xuuta 'muu (ḳawii); 'humma (ḍa9iif). — ٩ ـ ذاك الولد كلّش قوي لكن اخوته مو قويين ، همّا ضعاف •
10. '?ila '?ay 'siinama '?intum (raayiḥ)? — ١٠ ـ الى اي سينما انتم رايحين ؟

H. Supply haaða *this* (m), haaðii or haay *this* (f), ðaak *that* (m), ðiič *that* (f), haaðool or ðool *these* (pl), ðoolaak or ðook *those* (pl) as needed.

1. (This) sii'yaarat-'?axii. — ١ ـ هذي سيارة اخي •
2. 'šinuu (this)? il'boosṭa. — ٢ ـ شنو هذي ؟ البوسطة •

3. 'minuu (that) il'walad? — ٣ ـ منو ذاك الولد ؟
4. (These) ijji'gaayir 'zayna. — ٤ ـ هذي الجكاير زينة •
5. (Those) ilba'naat 'muu ʔamriikaanii'yaat, 'humma fransaawii'yaat. — ٥ ـ هاذول البنات مو امريكانيات ، هما فرنساويات •
6. 'šuuf (those) il'wulid yidux'luun bil'bayt. — ٦ ـ شوف هدول الولد يدخلون بالبيت •
7. 'ʔa9ruf (this) il'bint, 'bass 'maa (that) [one]. — ٧ ـ اعرف هالبنت بس ما ذيك •
8. (This) rrij'jaal 'ḍaabuṭ bij'jayš, wu (that one) ṭay'yaar. — ٨ ـ هالرجال ضابط بالجيش وذاك طيّار •
9. 'maa 'riid (this), ʔa'riid (that). — ٩ ـ ما ريد هذا ، اريد ذاك •
10. 'ʔaxii 'huuwa 'ṣaaḥib-(that) issii'yaara. — ١٠ ـ اخي هو صاحب ذيك السيّارة •

I. Give the correct form of the first members of the compounds. Note that not all have to be changed.

1. 'maa 'ʔa9ruf 'šgad (9amur)-'ðaak il'walad. — ١ ـ ما اعرف شقد عمر ذاك الولد •
2. si'kanit 'fii bag'daad (θilaaθa)-is'niin. — ٢ ـ سكنت في بغداد ثلاث سنين •
3. n'riid in 'šuuf (ʔax)-'nuurii. — ٣ ـ نريد نشوف اخو نوري •
4. 'wayn (mazra9a)-ʔa'buuk? — ٤ ـ وين مزرعة ابوك ؟
5. 'ʔakuu (siiyyaaraat)-Ford ka'θiira 'fii bagdaad. — ٥ ـ اكو سيارات فورد كثيرة في بغداد •
6. (mara)-ʔa'xuuya 'kulliš ja'miila. — ٦ ـ مرت اخوي كلّش جميلة •
7. (ʔibin)-'9ammii 'ʔisma 'ʔaḥmad. — ٧ ـ ابن عمّي اسمه احمد •
8. (rajil)-'ʔuxtii 'yištugul 9ind mu'ḳaawil. — ٨ ـ رجل اخته يشتغل عند مقاول •

J. The following commands are spoken to a man. What would you say to a girl? To more than one person?

1. 'ʔimšii '9ala ya'miinak! — ١ ـ امشي على يمينك •
2. 'zuurnii 'daayman! — ٢ ـ زورني دائما •
3. 'jiiblii ssii'yaara! — ٣ ـ جيبلي السيّارة •
4. ʔis'maḥlii, 'laazim ʔa'ruuḥ lil'bayt! — ٤ ـ اسمحلي ، لازم اروح للبيت •
5. raa'wiina 'wayn 'ʔakuu 'ʔuutayl! — ٥ ـ راوينا وين اكو اوتيل •

K. The verbs in the following sentences have the agent affix yi– *he*. Make the necessary changes in the agent affixes first for *she*, then *I*, *they*, and *we*.

1. 'šraaḥ yi'sawwii 'fii bag'daad? — ١ ـ شراح يسوّي في بغداد ؟
2. 'maa 'raaḥ 'yimšii, 'raaḥ 'yijii bissii'yaara. — ٢ ـ ما راح يمشي ، راح يجي بالسيّارة •
3. yi'riid 'yidris '9arabii. — ٣ ـ يريد يدرس عربي •
4. 'daayman 'yaakul ka'θiir. — ٤ ـ دائما ياكل كثير •
5. yi'guul 'ya9ruf 'fadd ṭay'yaar ʔamrii'kaanii. — ٥ ـ يقول يعرف فرد طيّار امريكاني •

L. Add raaḥ to the following sentences to express *going to*. Then add kaan raaḥ, kaanat raaḥ, or kunit raaḥ to express *was going to*.

1. 'ʔana 'ʔadris ʔing'liizii. — ١ ـ انا ادرس انكليزي •
2. 'ʔuxtii it'zuur 'xaaltii. — ٢ ـ اختي تزور خالتي •
3. sa'9iid 'yištugul '9ind mu'ḳaawil. — ٣ ـ سعيد يشتغل عند مقاول •

M. The following sentences are spoken to a boy. Make the necessary changes to say them to a girl, then to more than one person.

1. 'triid it'ruuḥ wii'yaay?	١ ـ تريد تروح ويّاي ؟
2. ta'9aal hi'naa!	٢ ـ تعال هنا •
3. 'wayn 'raayiḥ?	٣ ـ وين رايح ؟
4. 'jiiblii paa'kayt-ji'gaayir!	٤ ـ جيبلي باكيت جكاير •
5. 'kam '?ax '9indak?	٥ ـ كم اخ عندك ؟
6. ?ar'juuk 'zuurnii 'daayman!	٦ ـ ارجوك زورني دائما •
7. š'kaan 'biik?	٧ ـ شكان بيك ؟
8. il'yoom 'šitriid it'sawii?	٨ ـ اليوم شتريد تسوّي ؟
9. 'ta9ruf 'wayn 'bayt-'ðaak irrij'jaal?	٩ ـ تعرف وين بيت ذاك الرجّال ؟
10. 'tigdar it'šuuf 'minn hi'naa?	١٠ ـ تقدر تشوف من هنا ؟
11. 'layš '?inta 'waaguf hi'naak?	١١ ـ ليش انت واقف هناك ؟
12. 'layš 'maa tit'mašša wii'yaay?	١٢ ـ ليش ما تتمشى ويّاي ؟
13. 'šifna ?a'buuk 'yimšii.	١٣ ـ شفنا ابوك يمشي
14. ?is'maḥlii, 'laazim ?a'ruuḥ ?a'šuuf sa'9iid.	١٤ ـ اسمحلي ، لازم اروح اشوف سعيد •
15. 'triid 'tidxul 'bii hal'maṭ9am?	١٥ ـ تريد تدخل بهذا المطعم ؟
16. 'šitḥibb 'taakul?	١٦ ـ شتحب تاكل ؟
17. '?akuu ?uu'tayl 'zayn gid'daamak.	١٧ ـ اكو اوتيل زين قدّامك •
18. ?ar'juuk '?iḥkii ya'waaš!	١٨ ـ ارجوك احكي يواش •
19. 'ruuḥ 'šuuf 'wayn sa'9iid!	١٩ ـ روح شوف وين سعيد •
20. 'gullii, 'wayn 'tištugul?	٢٠ ـ قل لي وين تشتغل ؟
21. 'wayn '?inta 'saakin?	٢١ ـ وين انت ساكن ؟
22. 'triidnii '?ajii wii'yaak?	٢٢ ـ تريدني اجي وياك ؟
23. 'šloon 'ta9ruf 'haaða?	٢٣ ـ شلون تعرف هذا ؟
24. 'šinuu 'raaḥ it'jiib 'minn bag'daad?	٢٤ ـ شنو راح تجيب من بغداد ؟
25. 'kaan '9indak sii'yaara?	٢٥ ـ كان عندك سيّارة ؟

N. Conversation Outlines.

1. *Arriving in Baghdad.*

You and your friend have just arrived in Baghdad. You say 'Here we are in Baghdad'. He asks 'Why are you talking Arabic with me? Don't you know English?' You reply 'Yes, I speak English, but when we are in Baghdad, we have to speak Arabic like the people here'. He says, 'Okay, let's talk to that Baghdadi; I want to eat, and perhaps he knows where there's a good restaurant'.

You walk up to the Baghdadi and your friend asks him where there's a restaurant. The man replies that he doesn't know. He just came from Mosul, he continues, and he doesn't know much about Baghdad.

You ask another man the same thing. He says that there is a big restaurant ahead of you. You ask him to please show you where the restaurant is. He tells you to come with him.

As you are walking, he asks you where you are from. You tell him that you are Americans and that that you just came from America. He says that he would like to go to America some day;

one of his brothers is in New York. He also says that you speak Arabic well. You reply that you studied Arabic in America and that you want to study it more in Iraq.

Finally he points and says 'See, the restaurant is on your right'. You thank him, and all say goodbye.

2. *At a restaurant.*

You and your friend go into the restaurant. A waiter comes up and tells you 'good day'. You reply, then he asks you what you want to eat. You ask him what he has. He names several items, such as meat, fish, rice, potatoes. You make your choice. He then asks your friend what he wants to eat, and he tells him what he wants.

Next the waiter asks what you wish to drink. You ask for a glass of milk. The waiter says he's sorry, but there isn't any milk today. But there is tea, coffee, and beer. You tell him to bring you coffee. Your friend says that he wants tea with milk.

The waiter brings the food. You remind him to bring water. You also tell him that you want a package of cigarettes. He says that they don't have any, but there is a cigarette seller near the restaurant.

You ask him how much you owe. He says it's a hundred fils. He thanks you as you pay.

3. *Getting acquainted.*

You are walking alone. You want to talk to someone, so you talk to a young Baghdadi. You tell him 'good evening', and he replies. Then you say that you are an American and tell him your name. He is glad to know you, and tells you his name is Said. You say that you have just come to Iraq. You add that your friend came with you. He asks where you are staying. You reply that you are staying at the Regent Hotel, and that your friend is there now. The Baghdadi comments that the Regent Hotel is a good hotel.

He asks you what kind of work you do. You reply that you are an engineer. He asks if you like your work. You say that you like it very much. You ask him what he does, and he says he is a contractor. He adds that his oldest brother is an engineer and works in Basra. You ask where Basra is, and he replies that Basra is in the south of Iraq.

He asks if your father was an engineer too. No, you say, he has a farm near New York. Were you working on (in) the farm, he asks. Yes, when you were young, you say, but you were working in a factory before the war. You add that it was a big automobile factory. He asks how the work was in the factory. You say it was good. And you want to work in the factory when you go back to America.

While you are talking, Said's friend, Hassan, comes up to you. They ask each other how they are, then Said introduces you to Hassan. Hassan says he is glad to know you, and you say the same. Said tells Hassan that you are an American, and adds that you are an engineer. He tells you that Hassan wants to become a doctor, and studies a lot.

You offer them cigarettes, and they thank you.

Said asks Hassan where he is going. Hassan says to the King Ghazi movie. He asks you both if you want to go with him. It's a good movie, he says. Said wants to go, he says. You thank him, but say that you have to go back to the hotel. You say goodbye and leave.

4. *An invitation from Said.*

You and Said are talking. You comment on the fine day. Said says yes, it isn't like it was yesterday. Yesterday morning it was cloudy, and in the afternoon it rained a lot. Said says he doesn't want it to rain today. You ask why. He answers that he has to visit his uncle (on his father's side) and aunt. You ask where they live. He says they live here in Baghdad, but their house is a long way from here. You ask if he is going to go by automobile; but he says no, he is going to walk. His automobile isn't running well; he doesn't know what's wrong with it.

You ask Said if his uncle has any sons. He says yes, he has three sons. All of them are in Baghdad. One of them is an officer in the army; two are in school. One of them wants to go to study in America. His friend is at Columbia University and he wants to go there. You ask what he wants to study; Said replies he wants to become a doctor.

Said asks you if you would like to come with him to their house. You say yes.

5. *What about your family?*

Two at a time, discuss your families as much as you can. Ask each other all the questions you can, and answer them according to the facts. Make the conversation real. Ask about mothers, fathers, sisters, and brothers, and about being married and the in-laws. Find out what their names are, where they are living, what work they are doing. Bring in other relatives, too, such as aunts and uncles.

6. *Try other conversations of your own devising.*

UNIT 7

Getting a Room

BASIC SENTENCES

Concluding RECORD 12B

ENGLISH EQUIVALENTS	AIDS TO LISTENING	ARABIC SPELLING
Manager	*Manager*	المدير
the manager*	ilmudiir	المدير
I'm the manager.	ʔaanii lmudiir.*	آني المدير •
I do for you	ʔasawwiilkum	اسوّي لكم
What can I do for you?	šagdar ʔasawwiilkum?	شاقدر اسوّي لكم ؟
you want (pl)	triiduun	تريدون
room	gurfa	غرفة
for	lišaan	لشان
person	nafar	نفر
two persons	nafarayn	نفرين
Do you want a room for one or for two?	triiduun gurfa lišaan nafar waaḥid ʔaw nafarayn?	تريدون غرفة لشان نفر واحد او نفرين ؟
John	*John*	جـــان
we can	nigdar	نقدر
we see her	nšuufha	نشوفها

Beginning RECORD 13A

ENGLISH EQUIVALENTS	AIDS TO LISTENING	ARABIC SPELLING
Can we see it?	nigdar inšuufha?	نقدر نشوفها ؟
Manager	*Manager*	المدير
if you please (pl)	tfaḍluu	تفضّلوا
Please [come] with me.	tfaḍluu wiiyaaya.	تفضّلوا ، ويّاي •
Bill	*Bill*	بل
in her	biiha	بيها
bath	ḥammaam	حمّام
special	xuṣuuṣii	خصوصي
Has it got a private bath?	ʔakuu biiha ḥammaam xuṣuuṣii?	اكو بيها حمّام خصوصي ؟

* Not on the record.

ENGLISH EQUIVALENTS	AIDS TO LISTENING	ARABIC SPELLING
price (rental)	ʔujra	اجرة
How much is it?	šgad ilʔujra?	شقد الاجرة ؟
Manager	*Manager*	المدير
we take *or* receive	naaxuδ	ناخذ
two dinars	diinaarayn	دينارين
per day	bilyoom	باليوم
in advance	ligiddaam	لقدّام
We charge two dinars per day, in advance.	naaxuδ diinaarayn bilyoom, ligiddaam.	ناخذ دينارين باليوم لقدّام •
That's with meals. (*lit.*, food)	haay wiiya lʔakil.	هاي ويّا الاكل •
John	*John*	جان
What do you think of it?	štiftikir biiha?	شتفتكر بيها ؟
Bill	*Bill*	بل
she seems *or* looks	tbayyin	تبيّن
It seems good.	hiiya tbayyin zayna.	هي تبيّن زينة •
Monday	yoom iliθnayn	يوم الاثنين
we take her	naaxuδha	ناخذها
Thursday	yoom ilxamiis	يوم الخميس
to *or* for *or* until	ʔila	الى
Today's Monday; let's take it until Thursday.	halyoom iliθnayn; xallii naaxuδha ʔila yoom ilxamiis.	هاليوم الاثنين ، خلّي ناخذها الى يوم الخميس •
(*They go downstairs to the desk.*)		
Manager	*Manager*	المدير
register!	sajjiluu	سجّلوا
notebook	daftar	دفتر
Please register your names in the book.	ʔarjuukum sajjiluu ʔisimkum biddaftar.	ارجوكم سجّلوا اسمكم بالدفتر •
bags	jinaṭ	جنط
Do you have [any] bags?	ʔakuu 9idkum jinaṭ?	اكو عندكم جنط ؟
John	*John*	جـان
These are our bags.	haaδool jinaṭna.	هاذول جنطنا •
he brings out *or* up	yiṭaḷḷi9	يطلّع
above *or* up *or* upstairs	foog	فوق
Tell the waiter to bring them upstairs.	gull lilboy yiṭaḷḷi9hum foog.	قل للبوي يطلّعهم فوق •
Manager	*Manager*	المدير
here's *or* take	haak	هاك
key	miftaaḥ	مفتاح
Here's the key.	haak ilmiftaaḥ.	هاك المفتاح •

ENGLISH EQUIVALENTS	AIDS TO LISTENING	ARABIC SPELLING
John	*John*	جـان
to when	liyamta	ليمتى
he stays *or* remains	yibḳa	يبقى
open	maftuuḥ	مفتوح
How long does the restaurant stay open?	liyamta lmaṭ9am yibḳa maftuuḥ?	ليمتى المطعم يبقى مفتوح ؟
Manager	*Manager*	المدير
we close him	nsidda	نسدّه
about *or* almost*	ḥawaalii *or* taḳriiban	حوالي (ايضا) تقريبا
ten o'clock	issaa9a bil9ašra	الساعة بالعشرة
We close it about ten.	nsidda ḥawaalii ssaa9a bil9ašra.	نسدّه حوالي الساعة بالعشرة .

Beginning RECORD 13B

There's a phone in the lobby.	ʔakuu talafoon biṣṣaaloon.	اكو تلفون بالصالون .
if	ʔiδa	اذا
ring *or* knock!	digg	دق
bell	jaras	جرس
If you want anything, ring the bell.	ʔiδa triid šii, digg ijjaras.	اذا تريد شيء ، دق الجرس .

(*John and Bill go upstairs to their room.*)

John	*John*	جـان
open!	ʔiftaḥ	افتح
Open the door!	ʔiftaḥ ilbaab.	افتح الباب .
you took	ʔa'xaδit* *or* ʔaxatta	اخذت
You took the key.	ʔinta ʔa'xaδit ilmiftaaḥ.*	انت اخذت المفتاح .
Bill	*Bill*	بل
I think *or* suppose	ʔaḍinn	اظن
I forgot him	nisayta	نسيته
down *or* below *or* downstairs	jawwa	جوّى
I think I left it downstairs.	ʔaḍinn nisayta jawwa.	اظن نسيته جوّى .

(*Bill comes back with the key, and they go into the room. The waiter brings the bags into the room.*)

John	*John*	جـان
put them!	xalliihum	خلّيهم
Put them [over] there!	xalliihum hinaak.	خلّيهم هناك !
close!	sidd	سد
you go out	tuṭla9	تطلع
Please close the door when you go out.	ʔarjuuk sidd ilbaab lamma tuṭla9.	ارجوك سد الباب لمّا تطلع .

* Not on record.

ENGLISH EQUIVALENTS	AIDS TO LISTENING	ARABIC SPELLING
Bill	*Bill*	بل
you gave him	nṭayta	انطيته
tip	baḳšiiš	بقشيش
Did you give him a tip?	nṭayta baḳšiiš?	انطيته بقشيش ؟
John	*John*	جـان
I gave him	nṭayta	انطيته
twenty	9išriin	عشرين
I gave him twenty fils.	nṭayta 9išriin-filis.	انطيته عشرين فلس •
What's the matter (with you)?	šakuu biik?	شكو بيك ؟
you seem *or* look	tbayyin	تبين
tired	ti9baan	تعبان
You look tired.	ˀinta tbayyin ti9baan.	انت تبين تعبان •
Bill	*Bill*	بل
I slept	nimit	نمت
enough	kaafii	كافي
I didn't sleep enough last night.	maa nimit kaafii lbaarḥa billayl.	ما نمت كافي البارحة بالليل •
I sleep *or* I go to sleep	ˀanaam	انام
time	wakit *or* waḳit	وقت
early	minn wakit	من وقت
I want to go to bed early.	ˀariid ˀanaam minn wakit.	اريد انام من وقت •
John	*John*	جـان
sleepy	ni9saan	نعسان
I write	ˀaktib	اكتب
letter	maktuub	مكتوب
I'm sleepy too, but I have to write a letter.	ˀana hamm ni9saan, laakin laazim ˀaktib maktuub.	انا هم نعسان ، لكن لازم اكتب مكتوب •
I received	sti'lamit	ستلمت
my sweetheart (f)	ḥabiibtii	حبيبتي
this week	halˀisbuu9	هالاسبوع
I haven't gotten a letter from my girl this week.	maa sti'lamit maktuub minn ḥabiibtii halˀisbuu9.	ما ستلمت مكتوب من حبيبتي هالاسبوع •
I should have written	kinit laazim ˀaktib	كنت لازم اكتب
I should have written before now.	kinit laazim ˀaktib gabul hassa.	كنت لازم اكتب قبل هسه •

Beginning RECORD 14A

pen *or* pencil	ḳalam	قلم
ink	ḥibir	حبر
Where's the pen and the ink?	wayn ilḳalam wilḥibir?	وين القلم والحبر ؟

ENGLISH EQUIVALENTS	AIDS TO LISTENING	ARABIC SPELLING
Bill	*Bill*	بل
you find them	tuujidhum	توجدهم
table *or* desk	mayz	ميز
You'll find them on the table.	tuujidhum 9almayz.	توجدهم على الميز •
paper	warak̦	ورق
Paper, too.	ʔayd̦an warak̦.	ايضا ورق •
I put them	xallaythum	خليتهم
I just put them there.	hassa xallaythum hinaak.	هسه خليتهم هناك •
John	*John*	جـان
late	mitʔaxxir	متاٰخر
Do you want to sleep late?	triid itnaam mitʔaxxir?	تريد تنام متاٰخر ؟
Bill	*Bill*	بل
If I can.	ʔiδa ʔagdar.	اذا اقدر
you wake me	tga99idnii	تقعدني
you get up *or* wake up	tig9ud	تقعد
Don't wake me when you get up.	laa tga99idnii lamma tig9ud.	لا تقعدني لمّا تقعد •

PRONUNCIATION

Continuing RECORD 14A

PRACTICE 1

t: Iraqi has two t-sounds which must be kept apart at all times. First t, which is the usual t of English *tea* and *tag*.

tiin	**figs*	تين
tuujad	*you find*	توجد
taajir	*merchant*	تاجر
titin	*tobacco*	تتن
banaat	*daughters, girls*	بنات
sitta	*six*	ستة

PRACTICE 2

ṭ: Place the tip of your tongue farther back in your mouth than you do for the usual English t, raise the back of your tongue somewhat toward the roof of your mouth, and make your tongue stiffer. Finally, tighten your throat muscles. Note the vowel 'color.'

muṭar	*rain*	مطر
jinaṭ	*bags, baggage*	جنط

ṭifil	**child*	طفل
tumṭur	*it rains* (f)	تمطر
?axayyuṭ	**I sew*	اخيّط
nṭaanii	*he gave me*	انطاني
nṭiinii	*give me!*	انطيني
nṭayt	*I gave; you gave*	انطيت
ṭayyib	*good*	طيّب
ṭayyaar	*aviator*	طيّار

PRACTICE 3

Note that vowel-sounds touching ṭ have a slightly different sound from those with t.

tiin	**figs*	تين
ṭiin	**mud*	طين
jiit	*I came; you came*	جيت
basiiṭ	**simple, easy*	بسيط
tuujad	*you find*	توجد
ṭuul	**length*	طول
maktuub	*written*	مكتوب
maḥṭuuṭ	**placed*	محطوط
taajir	*merchant*	تاجر
ṭaar	**he flew*	طار
banaat	*daughters, girls*	بنات
šixaaṭ	*matches*	شخاط
titin	*tobacco*	تتن
ṭirit	**I flew, you flew*	طرت
tayl	**wire*	تيل
ṭayr	**bird*	طير
ittaajir	*the merchant*	التاجر
iṭṭabiib	*the doctor*	الطبيب

ANALYSIS

1. An Expression of Politeness.

One of the commonest expressions of politeness is tfaḍḍal, plural tfaḍḍaluu. As in all polite expressions, the plural is often used even when you are speaking to one person only, especially to show respect to an older person. The general meaning of tfaḍḍal is *If you please.* The following examples will best show how it is used. A person opens a door and says tfaḍḍal, when he means *Please go first.* Or he walks ahead to show you the way and says tfaḍḍal, now meaning *Please follow me.* He also says tfaḍḍal, meaning *Please sit down,* and points to a chair. You will hear this word in many similar situations; it always shows politeness. A related expression with a similar range is minn faḍlak.

2. yamta AND lamma.

yamta raaḥ itruuḥ ʔila bagdaad?	*When are you going to go to Baghdad?*	يمتى راح تروح الى بغداد ؟
yamta txaḷḷuṣhum?	*When will you finish them?*	يمتى تخلّصوهم ؟
lamma taaxuδ ḥammaam, ʔana raaḥ ʔazayyin.	*While you take a bath, I'm going to shave.*	لمّا تاخذ حمّام انا راح ازيّن .
šifta lamma činit ibbagdaad.	*I saw him when I was in Baghdad.*	شفته لما كنت في بغداد .

It is clear that yamta *when?* is a question-asking word. It is always used in asking when something happened or is going to happen. In contrast, lamma means *while*, or *during the time when* and is not used to ask questions.

3. –ayn *two, a couple of.*

walad	*boy*	ولد
waladayn	*two boys*	ولدين
nafar	*person*	نفر
nafarayn	*two persons*	نفرين
diinaar	*dinar*	دينار
diinaarayn	*two dinars*	دينارين
saa9a	*hour*	ساعة
saa9atayn	*two hours*	ساعتين

The ending –ayn means *a couple of, two.* It is added to the combining form of nouns. It is especially common with parts of the body which occur in pairs. You will note that the singular of these parts of the body is feminine, taking feminine adjectives and verbs. Two examples are:

ʔiid (f)	*hand*	ايد
ʔiidayn	*two hands*	ايدين
rijil (f)	*leg*	رجل
rijlayn	*two legs*	رجلين

With pronoun endings the final –n drops:

ʔiidayya	*my hands*	ايديّ
ʔiidayk	*your hands*	ايديك
ʔiidayč	*your hands*	ايديكِ
ʔii'day	*his hands*	ايده
ʔiidayha	*her hands*	ايديها
ʔiidayna	*our hands*	ايدينا
ʔiidaykum	*your hands*	ايديكم
ʔiidayhum	*their hands*	ايديهم

Words with this ending are plural and take the appropriate plural adjectives as explained in Unit Five. Contrast the following:

ilwaladayn zayniin.	*The two boys are well.*	الولدين زينين .
ilbintayn zaynaat.	*The two girls are well.*	البنتين زينات .
ʔii'day kabiira.	*His hands are big.*	ايده كبيرة .

4. The Article Prefix il– in Phrases and Sentences.

I

ʔibin kabiir	*a big son*	ابن كبير
bint ṣagiira	*a little daughter*	بنت صغيرة
hawa baarid	*cold air*	هواء بارد

II

ilʔibin ilkabiir	*the big son*	الابن الكبير
ilbint iṣṣagiira	*the little daughter*	البنت الصغيرة
ilhawa lbaarid	*the cold wind*	الهواء البارد

III

ʔibnii lkabiir	*my big son*	ابني الكبير
bintii ṣṣagiira	*my little daughter*	بنتي الصغيرة

As you learned earlier, almost all adjectives follow nouns. In I above, the noun and adjective don't refer to any definite person or thing. In II, both the noun and the adjective have the prefix il– and refer to definite persons or things. In III, the noun has a pronoun ending and the adjective has the prefix il–, and refer also to definite persons, namely *my son* or *my daughter*. In all three groups, the noun and the adjective are together, forming a phrase. In contrast to these phrases, we have the sentences below:

IV

ilʔibin kabiir.	*The son [is] big.*	الابن كبير •
ilbint ṣagiira.	*The daughter [is] small.*	البنت صغيرة •
ilhawa baarid.	*The air [is] cold.*	الهواء بارد •

V

ʔibnii kabiir.	*My son [is] big.*	ابني كبير •
bintii ṣagiira.	*My daughter [is] little.*	بنتي صغيرة •

In IV and V, the noun is separated from the adjective by *is* or *are*, forming a sentence *of equivalence.* Note that the adjective in these sentences *doesn't* have the prefix il– even though the noun does have il– or a pronoun ending.

Here is a summary of the various possibilities:

ʔibin kabiir	*a big son*	ابن كبير
ilʔibin ilkabiir	*the big son*	الابن الكبير
ʔibnii lkabiir	*my big son*	ابني الكبير
ilʔibin kabiir.	*The son [is] big.*	الابن كبير •
ʔibnii kabiir.	*My son [is] big.*	ابني كبير •

5. Agent Affixes — Completed Action.

ʔašuuf	*I see*	اشوف
ʔajiib	*I bring*	اجيب
ʔadris	*I study*	ادرس

šifit	*I saw*	شفت
jibit	*I brought*	جبت
di'rasit	*I studied*	درست

From the above you will observe again that Iraqi verbs indicate whether action has been completed or not. The verb forms at the top show action which has *not been completed,* that is, it has not been brought to an end yet (*I see, I bring, I study*). These are INCOMPLETED ACTION forms. On the other hand, the verb forms beneath show action which definitely *has been completed* (*I saw; I brought, I studied*). These are COMPLETED ACTION forms. Verbs have different forms for the two kinds of action, but you will observe that the forms are closely related. And again, remember that every verb form includes an agent affix. Our chief interest at this time, is in the agent affixes.

In the first five units, you learned the set of agent affixes which are found as part of the *incompleted action* verb forms. To review, this set is seen in the forms yišuuf *he sees,* tšuuf *she sees,* tšuuf *you see* (m), tšuufiin *you see* (f), ʔašuuf *I see,* yišuufuun *they see,* tšuufuun *you see* (pl), nšuuf *we see.*

The *completed action* verb forms also have their own set of agent affixes. They are presented below.

I

šaaf	*he saw*	شاف
jaab	*he brought*	جاب
raaḥ	*he went*	راح
naam	*he slept*	نام
ʔija	*he came*	اجا
nisa	*he forgot*	نسى
miša	*he walked*	مشى
'nṭa	*he gave*	نطى
sawwa	*he made, he did*	سوّى
tmašša	*he took a walk*	تمشّى
diras	*he studied*	درس
sikan	*he lived*	سكن
ʔakal	*he ate*	اكل
ʔaxaδ	*he took, he received*	اخذ

In the completed action verbs, you see from the above, there is really no special agent affix indicating HE. It is the *absence* of an affix that marks this form. Note, however, that the last vowel in this form is always an a.

II

ʔijat	*she came*		اجت
šaafat	*she saw*		شافت
nisat	*she forgot*		نست
'nṭat	*she gave*		نطت
dirsat	*she studied*		درست
miṭrat	*it rained*	–at indicates SHE	مطرت

III			
ʔijaw	*they came*		اجوا
jaabaw	*they brought*		جابوا
'nṭaw	*they gave*		نطوا
nisaw	*they forgot*		نسوا
dirsaw	*they studied*	–aw indicates THEY	درسوا
IV			
jiit	*you came*		جيت
šifit	*you saw*		شفت
nisayt	*you forgot*		نسيت
di'rasit	*you studied*	–t (–it) indicates YOU (m)	درست
V			
jiitii	*you came*		جيتي
šiftii	*you saw*		شفتي
nisaytii	*you forgot*		نسيتي
dirastii	*you studied*	–tii indicates YOU (f)	درستي
VI			
jiit	*I came*		جيت
šifit	*I saw*		شفت
n'ṭayt	*I gave*		نطيت
nisayt	*I forgot*		نسيت
di'rasit	*I studied*	–t (–it) also indicates I	درست
VII			
jiitum	*you came*		جيتم
šiftum	*you saw*		شفتم
nisaytum	*you forgot*		نسيتم
dirastum	*you studied*	–tum indicates YOU (pl)	درستم
VIII			
jiina	*we came*		جينا
sifna	*we saw*		شفنا
nisayna	*we forgot*		نسينا
dirasna	*we studied*	–na indicates WE	درسنا

There are two variations to be noted: (1) –uu often replaces –aw *they*, as jaabuu *they brought;* (2) –tuu is often found in place of –tum *you* (pl), as šiftuu *you saw.*

In summary, here is šaaf with all the completed action agent affixes:

šaaf	*he saw*	شاف
šaafat	*she saw*	شافت
šifit	*you saw* (m)	شفت
šiftii	*you saw* (f)	شفتي
šifit	*I saw*	شفت
šaafaw	*they saw*	شافوا
šiftum	*you saw* (pl)	شفتم
šifna	*we saw*	شفنا

EXERCISES

A. *Read these sentences with* yamta WHEN? *or* lamma WHEN, WHILE *as needed.*

1. __ šifit ʔaxuuk?
2. ʔana šifta __ kunit bilbayt.
3. maa ʔagdar ʔaruuḥ wiiyaak __ tirja9 lil9iraaḳ.
4. __ laazim itruuḥ liššugul?
5. __ kunit ṣagiir, kunit ʔazuur 9ammii wumarta.
6. ʔisʔal ðaak irrajjaal __ raaḥ yijiib issiiyaara.
7. __ ʔinta fiʼtaḥit ilbaab?
8. __ nṭaytlii lmiftaaḥ?
9. John, __ raaḥ tig9ud?
10. šifna sa9iid __ kunna nitmašša.

B. *Change the following phrases to sentences by adding or removing* il– THE. *The first two are examples.*

1.	hawa baarid	*a cold wind*
	ilhawa baarid.	*The wind is cold.*
2.	ilʔibin ilkabiir	*the big son*
	ilʔibin kabiir.	*The son is big.*
3.	ilgurfa lzayna	*the good room*
4.	ḥammaam xuṣuuṣii	*a private bath*
5.	baab maftuuḥ	*an open door*
6.	šita baarid	*a cold winter*
7.	iḷmaay ilḥaarr	*the hot water*
8.	bintii ṣṣagiira	*my little daughter*
9.	bintayn jaamiilaat	*two pretty girls*
10.	ṣadiiḳii lmariiḍ	*my sick friend*
11.	ʔaxuuya lkabiir	*my big brother*
12.	ʔuxuutii likbaar	*my big brothers*

C. Completed Action Verb Forms *Select the correct form of the verb from the three possibilities at the right.*

1. saˀ9iid (*studied*) ʔingliizii.	diras, dirsaw, dirsat
2. ʔana maa (*studied*) kaθiir.	di'rasit, dirastii, dirasna
3. humma (*lived*) bamriika.	sikan, siknaw, sikanna
4. ilbaarḥa ʔabuuya (*walked*) liddukkaan.	miša, mišat, mišaw
5. ilwulid (*brought*) ṣadiiḳhum	jaab, jaabat, jaabaw
lamma (*they came*).	ʔija, ʔijat, ʔijaw
6. nuurii, (*did you bring*) ilmiftaaḥ?	jibit, jibtum, jibna
7. (*I visited*) ʔahlii.	zirit, zirtii, zirna
8. (*We went*) naaxuδ ḥammaam.	riḥit, riḥtii, riḥna
9. (*He made*) miftaaḥ lilbaab.	sawwa, sawwat, sawwaw
10. ilboy (*put*) ijjinaṭ jawwa lmayz.	xalla, xallat, xallaw
11. wayn (*did you put*) ilḥibir?	xallayt, xallaytum, xallayna
12. (*We forgot*) jinaṭna jawwa.	nisayt, nisaytum, nisayna
13. (*He slept*) mitʔaxxir.	naam, naamat, naamaw
14. (*He wanted*) yiruuḥ wiiyaay.	raad, raadat, raadaw
15. ilbint (*forgot*) tijii.	nisa, nisat, nisaw
16. (*I gave*) lilboy baḳšiiš.	nṭayt, nṭaytum, nṭayna
17. jamiila, (*did you see*) luuluu?	šifit, šiftii, šifna
18. (*We were*) nitmašša.	kunit, kuntum, kunna
19. ilbaarḥa billayl (*we slept*) zayn.	nimit, nimtum, nimna
20. (*She came*) minn ilbaṣra.	ʔija, ʔijat, ʔijaw

D. *These sentences have verbs of the* šaaf *type. Read them aloud, changing them from* HE *to* SHE, *then* THEY, YOU (m), YOU (f), YOU (pl), I, *and* WE.

1. (raaḥ) lilbooṣṭa.
2. (jaab) issiiyaara.
3. (zaar) ṣadiiḳa.
4. lamma (kaan) hinaak, (šaaf) sa9iid.
5. (raad yiruuḥ) wiiyaahum.
6. lamma (kaan) bil9iraaḳ, (naam) 9aṣṣuṭuuḥ.

E. More Incompleted Action Verb Forms. *Supply the correct form of the verb in parentheses with the appropriate agent affixes.*

1. šbiik? ʔinta (yibayyin) mariiḍ? (*you*, m)
2. gulluulii, šgad raaḥ (yibḳa) hinaa? (*you*, pl)
3. ʔiḥna raaḥ (yibḳa) taḳriiban šaharayn. (*we*)
4. humma (yisidd) ilmaṭ9am ḥawaalii saa9a bil9ašra. (*they*)
5. yamta raaḥ (yiktib) ʔila ḥabiibtak? (*you*, m)
6. kunit (yiktib) ʔila ṣadiiḳtii lamma sti'lamit halmaktuub minha. (*I*)
7. maa ʔaḥibb (yig9ud) minn waḳit. (*I*)
8. John, xalliina (yig9ud) minn waḳit. (*we*)
9. maa ʔariidak (yiga99idnii) lamma tig9ud. (*you*, m)
10. yibayyin maa tigdar (yisidd) ilbaab. (*you*, m)
11. ʔana kunit (yiftaḥ) ilbaab lamma lboy jaab jinaṭna. (*I*)
12. humma (yibayyin) ti9baaniin. (*they*)

WHAT WOULD YOU SAY?

1. *You wonder where you are going to stay in Baghdad.*
   a. maakuu ʔuutayl zayn hinaa. — ١ ـ ماكو اوتيل زين هنا ٠
   b. wayn raaḥ niskin? — ٢ ـ وين راح نسكن ؟
   c. ta9aal, laazim inšuuf ġurfatna. — ٣ ـ تعال ، لازم نشوف غرفتنا ٠

2. *You ask about a hotel.*
   a. ʔiḥna ʔamriikaan; maa na9ruf wayn raaḥ niskin. — ١ ـ احنا امريكان ، ما نعرف وين راح نسكن ٠
   b. raawiina wayn ilmaḥaṭṭa. — ٢ ـ راوينا وين المحطة ٠
   c. ʔarjuuk raawiina wayn ʔakuu ʔuutayl. — ٣ ـ ارجوك راوينا وين اكو اوتيل ٠

3. *At the hotel you want service.*
   a. digg ijjaraṣ. — ١ ـ دق الجرس ٠
   b. sidd ilbaab. — ٢ ـ سد الباب ٠
   c. ʔiftaḥ ilbaab. — ٣ ـ افتح الباب ٠

4. *Someone walks up to you.*
   a. ʔana lmudiir; šagdar ʔasawwiilkum? — ١ ـ انا المدير ، شقدر اسوّي لكم ؟
   b. ʔahlan wusahlan! — ٢ ـ اهلا وسهلا !
   c. ʔakuu 9indkum fluus? — ٣ ـ اكو عندكم فلوس ؟

5. *You want a double room.*
   a. raaḥ timṭur ilyoom? — ١ ـ راح تمطر اليوم ؟
   b. jiibinna maay ḥaarr. — ٢ ـ جيب لنا ماء حار ٠
   c. nriid ġurfa lišaan nafarayn. — ٣ ـ نريد غرفة لشان نفرين ٠

6. *You ask to see the room.*
   a. nigdar inšuuf ilġurfa? — ١ ـ نقدر نشوف الغرفة ؟
   b. gull lilboy minayn jiina. — ٢ ـ قل للبوي منين جينا ٠
   c. šloon haay ilġurfa? — ٣ ـ شلون هاي الغرفة ؟

7. *What about the bath?*
   a. ʔakuu hawa ḳawii? — ١ ـ اكو هواء قوي ؟
   b. wayn ilmaraaḥiiḍ? — ٢ ـ وين المراحيض ؟
   c. biiha ḥammaam xuṣuuṣii? — ٣ ـ بيها حمّام خصوصي ؟

8. *It isn't private.*
   a. maa šifit ḥammaam hinaa. — ١ ـ ما شفت حمّام هنا ٠
   b. ʔakuu ḥammaam hinaak, wara lbaab. — ٢ ـ اكو حمّام هناك ، ورا الباب ٠
   c. tigdar taaxuδ ḥammaam hassa. — ٣ ـ تقدر تاخذ حمّام هسّة ٠

9. *What is the charge?*
   a. šgad taaxδuun? — ١ ـ شقد تاخذون ؟
   b. šgad ilʔujra? — ٢ ـ شقد الاجرة ؟
   c. triid baḳšiiš? — ٣ ـ تريد بقشيش ؟

10. *A couple of dinars a day.*
   a. naaxuδ diinaarayn bilyoom.
   b. naaxuδ šwayya fluus.
   c. maa ʔa9ruf šgad yaaxδuun bilyoom.

١ - ناخذ دينارين باليوم •
٢ - ناخذ شويّة فلوس •
٣ - ما اعرف شقد ياخذون باليوم •

11. *Where's the key?*
   a. laazim ʔadigg talafoon.
   b. ʔaḍinn nisayt ilmiftaaḥ bilʔoofiis.
   c. ʔana maa ʔaʼxaδit miftaaḥ-ilgurfa.

١ - لازم ادق تلفون •
٢ - اظن نسيت المفتاح بالاوفيس •
٣ - انا ما اخذت مفتاح الغرفة ؟

12. *You are sleepy.*
   a. ʔana ti9baan.
   b. ʔana mamnuun minnak.
   c. ʔana ni9saan.

١ - انا تعبان •
٢ - انا ممنون منك •
٣ - انا نعسان •

13. *You didn't get enough sleep last night.*
   a. maa nimit kaafii ilbaarḥa billayl.
   b. maa nimit zayn ilbaarḥa billayl.

١ - ما نمت كافي البارحة بالليل •
٢ - ما نمت زين البارحة بالليل •

14. *Your friend has a letter to write.*
   a. laazim ʔaktib ʔila ṣadiiḳtii.
   b. maa kiʼtabit ʔila ṣadiiḳtii halisbuu9.
   c. maa stiʼlamit maktuub minn ṣadiiḳtii.

١ - لازم اكتب الى صديقتي •
٢ - ما كتبت الى صديقتي هذا الاسبوع •
٣ - ما ستلمت مكتوب من صديقتي •

15. *He should have written before now.*
   a. ʔana hamm laazim ʔaktib.
   b. laa tiktib maktuub ilyoom; xalʼlii ʔila baačir.
   c. kunit laazim tiktib gabul hassa.

١ - انا هم لازم اكتب •
٢ - لا تكتب مكتوب اليوم ، خلّيه الى باكر •
٣ - كنت لازم تكتب قبل هسّه •

16. *He wants the pen and ink.*
   a. wayn xallayt ilwaraḳ?
   b. wayn ilḳalam wilḥibir?
   c. ʔarjuuk jiiblii lḥibir.

١ - وين خلّيت الورق؟
٢ - وين القلم والحبر ؟
٣ - ارجوك جيب لي الحبر

17. *You tell him where they are.*
   a. tuujadhum 9almayz; hassa xallaythum hinaak.
   b. tuujadhum bilʔoofiis.
   c. nisayt wayn xallaythum.

١ - توجدهم على الميز ، هسّة خلّيتهم هناك •
٢ - توجدهم بالاوفيس •
٣ - نسيت وين خلّيتهم

18. *You don't want to be waked up.*
   a. ʔariid ʔanaam mitʔaxxir; ʔarjuuk laa tga99idnii lamma tig9ud.
   b. raaḥ ʔanaam kull illayl.
   c. maa raaḥ ʔag9ud minn waḳit.

١ - اريد انام متأخر ، ارجوك لا تقعّدني لما تقعد •
٢ - راح انام كل الليل •
٣ - ما راح اقعد من وقت •

LISTENING IN

John and Bill are at a hotel looking for a room.

Continuing RECORD 14A

MANAGER masaaʔ ilxayr.	المدير ـ مساء الخير •
ʔaanii lmudiir; šagdar ʔasawwiilkum?	آني المدير ، شاقدر اسوّي لكم ؟
JOHN nriid gurfa.	جان ـ نريد غرفة •
MANAGER triiduun gurfa lišaan nafar waaḥid ʔaw nafarayn?	المدير ـ تريدون غرفة لشان نفر واحد او نفرين ؟
JOHN lišaan nafarayn.	جان ـ لشان نفرين •
nigdar inšuufha?	نقدر نشوفها ؟
MANAGER tfaḍluu wiiyaay; ilgurfa foog.	المدير ـ تفضّلوا ويّاي ، الغرفة فوق •

(*They go upstairs to one of the rooms.*)

MANAGER haay ilgurfa.	المدير ـ هاي الغرفة •
BILL gullii, halgurfa baarda billayl?	بل ـ قل لي ، هالغرفة باردة بالليل ؟
MANAGER hiiya daayman baarda.	المدير ـ هي دائما باردة •
BILL ʔakuu biiha ḥammaam xuṣuuṣii?	بل ـ اكو بيها حمّام خصوصي ؟
MANAGER laa, laakin ʔakuu ḥammaam hinaak.	المدير ـ لا ، لكن اكو حمّام هناك •
BILL šgad ilʔujra?	بل ـ شقد الاجرة ؟
MANAGER naaxuδ diinaarayn bilyoom; haay wiiya lʔakil.	المدير ـ ناخذ دينارين باليوم ، هاي ويّا الاكل •
BILL ligiddaam?	بل ـ لقدّام ؟
MANAGER balii.	المدير ـ بلي •
BILL John, šitiftikir biiha?	بل ـ جان ، شتفتكر بيها ؟

Beginning RECORD 14B

JOHN ʔaftikir hiiya tbayyin zayna.	جان ـ افتكر هي تبيّن زينة •
BILL halyoom yoom iliθnayn; xallii naaxuδha ʔila yoom ilxamiis.	بل ـ هاليوم يوم الاثنين ، خلّي ناخذها الى يوم الخميس •

(*They go downstairs to the desk.*)

MANAGER ʔarjuukum sajjiluu ʔisimkum biddaftar.	المدير ـ ارجوكم سجّلوا اسمكم بالدفتر •
ʔakuu 9idkum jinaṭ?	اكو عندكم جنط ؟
BILL haaδool jinaṭna.	بل ـ هاذول جنطنا •
guul lilboy yiṭalli9hum foog.	قل للبوي يطلّعهم فوق •
MANAGER haak ilmiftaaḥ.	المدير ـ هاك المفتاح •
JOHN wayn ʔakuu talafoon?	جان ـ وين اكو تلفون ؟
MANAGER biṣṣaaloon.	المدير ـ بالصالون •
BILL liyamta lmaṭ9am yibka maftuuḥ?	بل ـ ليمتى المطعم يبقى مفتوح ؟
MANAGER nsidda ḥawaalii ssaa9a bil9ašra.	المدير ـ نسدّه حوالي الساعة بالعشرة •
huuwa 9ala yamiin-issaaloon.	هو على يمين الصالون •

(*John and Bill go up to their room.*)

JOHN ʔiftaḥ ilbaab, Bill.	جان ـ افتح الباب ، بل •
ʔaḍinn ʔinta ʔaʼxaδit ilmiftaaḥ.	اظن انت اخذت المفتاح •
BILL laa, maa 9indii. yimkin nisayta jawwa bilʔoofiis.	بل ـ لا ، ما عندي • يمكن نسيته جوّى بالاوفيس •

(*Bill comes back with the key, opens the door and goes in.*)

ʔahlan wusahlan, John! haaδa baytna fii bagdaad.	اهلا وسهلا ، جان ، هذا بيتنا في بغداد •
JOHN šakuu biik, Bill? tbayyin ti9baan.	جان ـ شكو بيك ، بل ؟ تبيّن تعبان •
BILL na9am, ʔana kulliš ni9saan; maa nimit kaafii lbaarḥa billayl.	بل ـ نعم ، انا كلّش نعسان ، ما نمت كافي البارحة بالليل •
ʔariid ʔanạam minn waḳit wuʔanaam kull illayl.	اريد انام من وقت وانام كل الليل •
JOHN ʔana hamm ni9saan, laakin laazim ʔaktib maktuub ʔila ḥabiibtii.	جان ـ انا هم نعسان ، لكن لازم اكتب مكتوب الى حبيبتي •
maa stiʼlamit waaḥid minha halisbuu9.	ما ستلمت واحد منها هالاسبوع •
BILL kinit laazim tiktib gabul hassa.	بل ـ كنت لازم تكتب قبل هسه •
maa tistilim maktuub ʔiδa maa tiktib.	ما تستلم مكتوب اذا ما تكتب •
ʔana kiʼtabit maktuub ʔila ʔahlii gabul iḍḍuhur.	انا كتبت مكتوب الى اهلي قبل الظهر •
JOHN wayn ilḳalam wilḥibir?	جان ـ وين القلم والحبر ؟
BILL tuujadhum 9almayz, ʔayḍan waraḳ.	بل ـ توجدهم على الميز ، ايضا الورق •
hassa xallaythum hinaak.	هسّه خليتهم هناك •
JOHN balii, ʔašuufhum.	جان ـ بلي ، اشوفهم •

(*The waiter brings the baggage to the room.*)

WAITER haay jinaṭkum?	بوي ـ هاي جنطتكم ؟
JOHN na9am. xalliihum hinaak.	جان ـ نعم • خلّيهم هناك •
ʔarjuuk sidd ilbaab lamma tuṭla9.	ارجوك سد الباب لمّا تطلع •
WAITER ʔiδa triiduun šii, digguu jjaras.	بوي ـ اذا تريدون شيء دقوا الجرس •
JOHN zayn, ʔaškurak.	جان ـ زين ، اشكرك •

(*The waiter leaves.*)

BILL nṭayta baḳšiiš?	بل ـ انطيته بقشيش ؟
JOHN na9am, nṭayta 9išriin-filis.	جان ـ نعم ، انطيته عشرين فلس •
ʔana raaḥ ʔanaam.	انا راح انام •
ʔašuufak baačir, Bill.	اشوفك باكر ، بل •
BILL zayn, bass laa tga99idnii lamma tig9ud.	بل ـ زين ، بس لا تقعّدني لمّا تقعد •
ʔariid ʔanaam mitʔaxxir.	اريد انام متاخّر •
JOHN laa txaaf, maa raaḥ ʔag9ud minn waḳit.	جان ـ لا تخاف ، ما راح اقعد من وقت •

VOCABULARY

From now on verb forms will be listed under the incompleted action *he* form, with the corresponding completed action form in parentheses. The agent affix yi– is disregarded in the alphabetical arrangement.

baķšiiš	tip (money)
yibayyin (bayyan)	he seems, he appears
tbayyin	you seem (m)
yibķa (buķa)	he remains, he stays
daftar (difaatir)	notebook, copybook (pl)
yidigg (dagg)	he knocks, he rings
digg	ring!, knock!
diinaar	dinar (1000 fils; about $4)
diinaarayn	two dinars
θilaaθ-dinaaniir	three dinars
fluus	fils (pl); money
ilifluus	the money
foog	over, above, up; upstairs
yiftaḥ (fitaḥ)	he opens
?iftaḥ	open!
yiga99id (ga99ad)	he wakes (someone) up
yiga99idnii	he wakes me up
yigdar (gidar)	he can (he could, he was able to)
nigdar	we can
šagdar	what can I . . . ?
yig9ud (gi9ad)	he wakes up, he gets up; he sits down
tig9ud	you (m) wake up; you sit down
gurfa (f)	room
gurfatna	our room
guruftii	my room
guraf	rooms
gurafna	our rooms
haak	here's . . . , take . . .
ḥabiib, ḥabiiba (f)	sweetheart
ḥabiibii, ḥabiibtii (f)	my sweetheart
ḥammaam	bath; bathroom

ḥawaalii	about, almost
ḥibir	ink
jaras	bell
jawwa	under, below, down; downstairs
jinṭa (f)	bag, suitcase
jinṭatha	her bag, her suitcase
jiniṭṭii	my bag, my suitcase
jinaṭ	bags, suitcases
jinaṭna	our bags
jinaṭii	my bags
kaafii, kaafiya (f)	enough
yiktib (kitab)	he writes
ķalam	pen, pencil
ķalam-ḥibir	fountainpen
ķalam-riṣaaṣ	lead pencil
ligiddaam	in advance
lišaan	for
liyamta	until when? how long?
maftuuḥ, –a (f)	open (adjective)
maktuub, –a (f)	written (adjective)
maktuub (mikaatiib)	letter (pl)
mayz (myuuz)	table; desk (pl)
miftaaḥ (mifaatiiḥ)	key (pl)
mit?axxir, –a (f), –iin (pl)	late
mudiir	manager, director
yinaam (naam)	he sleeps; he goes to bed
?anaam	I sleep; I go to bed
nimit	I slept; you slept (m)
nafar	person (as an occupant of space)
nafarayn	two persons
θilaaθ-nafaraat	three persons

yinsa (nisa)	he forgets
nisayt	I forgot; you forgot (m)
nisayta	I forgot him
yinṭii ('nṭa)	he gives
nṭayt	I gave; you gave (m)
nṭayta	I gave him; you gave him
ni9saan, –a (f), –iin (pl)	sleepy
yiriid (raad)	he wants
triiduun	you want (pl)
saa9a (f)	hour; clock, watch
issaa9a bil9ašra.	It's ten o'clock.
saa9atayn	two hours
*θ*ilaa*θ*-saa9aat	three hours
yisajjil (sajjal)	he registers
sajjil	register!
yisidd (sadd)	he closes, he shuts
sidd	close!, shut!
nsidd	we close, we shut
yistilim (stilam)	he receives
sti'lamit	I received; you received (m)
ṣaaloon	lobby, lounge
ṣadiiḳa (f)	girl friend
ṣadiiḳtii	my girl friend
taḳriiban	about, almost
talafoon	telephone
tfaḍḍal, –uu (pl)	if you please, be good enough to
ti9baan, –a (f), –iin (pl)	tired
ʔana ti9baan minn haaδa.	I'm tired of this.
yiṭaḷḷi9 (ṭaḷḷa9)	he makes go out, he makes go up
yiṭaḷḷi9hum foog.	He brings them upstairs.
yiṭla9 (tuṭla9)	he goes out, he goes up
yuujad *or* yuujid (wujad)	he finds; it is found, there is
tuujad	you find (m)
tuujadhum	you find them
wakit *or* waḳit	time
minn waḳit	early
šwaḳit	at what time? when?
waraḳ	paper
yixallii (xalla)	he puts, he places
xallayt	I put; you put (m)
xallii	put!, place!
xalliihum	put them!
xuṣuuṣii, xuṣuuṣiiya (f)	special; private
yaaxuδ (ʔaxaδ)	he takes; he charges
yoom	day
bilyoom	per day
yoom ilxamiis	Thursday
yoom ili*θ*nayn	Monday
ʔaxaδ (yaaxuδ)	he took (he takes)
ʔa'xaδit	I took; you took (m)
naaxuδ	we take; we charge
ʔila	to; for; until
ʔisbuu9	week
halʔisbuu9	this week
ʔiδa	if
ʔujra (f)	price (rental)
9išriin	twenty
9išriin-filis	twenty fils (about 8 cents)
yiḍinn (ḍann)	he thinks, he supposes
ʔaḍinn (ʔinn)	I think (that)
ḍannayt	I thought

UNIT 8

Getting Cleaned Up

BASIC SENTENCES

Continuing RECORD 14B

ENGLISH EQUIVALENTS	AIDS TO LISTENING	ARABIC SPELLING
John	*John*	جان
we wash	nigsil	نغسل
city	balad *or* madiina	بلد (ايضا) مدينة
Let's wash up and then go see the city.	xallii nigsil wuba9dayn inruuḥ inšuuf ilbalad.	خلّي نغسل وبعـــدين نروح نشوف البلد ·
Bill	*Bill*	بل
Fine!	9aal!	عال ·
in the first	bilʔawwal	بالاوّل
barber	mzayyin *or* ḥallaaḳ*	مزيّن
First of all, where's there a barber?	bilʔawwal, wayn ʔakuu mzayyin?	بالاوّل ، وين اكو مزيّن ؟
I shave	ʔazayyin	ازيّن
I have to shave.	laazim ʔazayyin.	لازم ازيّن ·
I cut	ʔaguṣṣ	اقص
my hair	ša9arii	شعري
I want a haircut, too.	ʔariid hamm ʔaguṣṣ ša9arii.	اريد هم اقص شعري ·

Beginning RECORD 15A

ENGLISH EQUIVALENTS	AIDS TO LISTENING	ARABIC SPELLING
John	*John*	جان
ask!	ʔisʔal	اسأل
person	šaxuṣ	شخص
someone else	šaxuṣ θaanii	شخص ثاني
I don't know; ask someone else.	maa ʔa9ruf; ʔisʔal šaxuṣ θaanii.	ما اعرف ، اسأل شخص ثاني ·

ENGLISH EQUIVALENTS	AIDS TO LISTENING	ARABIC SPELLING
(*Bill first inquires about a barbershop, and then also asks*):		
can you tell me	tigdar itgullii	تقدر تقول لي
nearer *or* nearest	ʔaķrab	اقرب
clothes presser	ʔuutačii	اوتشي
Can you tell me where the nearest cleaner is?	tigdar itgullii wayn ʔakuu ʔaķrab ʔuutačii?	تقدر تقول لي وين اكو اعرب أوتشي؟
A Baghdadi	*A Baghdadi*	غريب
place	makaan	مكان
near	ķariib	قريب
I know a place near here. (*literally*, I know one his place is near here.)	ʔa9ruf waaḥid makaana ķariib minn hinaa.	اعرف واحد مكانه قريب ن ها .
(*In the pressing shop.*)		
Presser	*Presser*	اوتشي
What can I do for you?	šagdar ʔasawwiilkum?	شقدر اسوّي لكم ؟
John	*John*	جان
my suit (f)	badiltii	بدلتي
dirty	waṣux	وسخ
My suit's dirty	badiltii waṣxa.	بدلتي وسخة .
you clean her	tnaḍḍufha	تنظّفها
you strike her	tuḍrubha	تضربها
pressing iron	ʔuutii	اوتي
I want it cleaned and pressed.	ʔariidak itnaḍḍufha wutuḍrubha ʔuutii.	اريدك تنظّفها وتضربها اوتي .
Bill	*Bill*	بل
tailor	xayyaaṭ	خيّاط
Are you a tailor?	hal ʔinta xayyaaṭ?	هل انت خيّاط ؟
Presser	*Presser*	اوتشي
I sew for you	ʔaxayyuṭlak	اخيّط لك
Yes, what do you want me to sew for you?	na9am, šitriid ʔaxayyuṭlak?	نعم ، شتريد اخيّط لك ؟
Bill	*Bill*	بل
I tore	šaggayt	شقّيت
pocket	jayb	جيب
I just tore my pocket.	hassa šaggayt jaybii.	هسّه شقيت جيبي .
Presser	*Presser*	اوتشي
torn	mašguug	مشقوق
Which pocket is torn?	ʔay jayb mašguug?	اي جيب مشقوق ؟

ENGLISH EQUIVALENTS	AIDS TO LISTENING	ARABIC SPELLING
Bill	*Bill*	بل
This [one].	haaδa.	هذا •
you finish them	txaḷḷuṣhum	تخلّصهم
When will you finish them?	yamta txaḷḷuṣhum?	يمتى تخلّصهم ؟
we leave them	nxalliihum	نخلّيهم
more than	ʔakθar minn	اكثر من
two hours	saa9atayn	ساعتين
We can't leave them more than two hours.	maa nigdar nxalliihum ʔakθar minn saa9atayn.	ما نقدر نخلّيهم اكثر من ساعتين •
we wear them	nilbashum	نلبسهم
tonight	hallayla	هالليلة
We want to wear them tonight.	nriid nilbashum hallayla.	نريد نلبسهم هالليلة •
Presser	*Presser*	او تشي
I finish them	ʔaxaḷḷuṣhum	اخلّصهم
as you want (pl)	miθil maa triiduun	مثل ما تريدون
I'll have them ready for you when you want [them].	ʔaxaḷḷuṣhum miθil maa triiduun.	اخلّصهم مثل ما تريدون •
Bill	*Bill*	بل
we come	nijii	نجي
after	ba9ad	بعد
noon	ḍuhur	ظهر
afternoon	ba9ad iḍḍuhur	بعد الظهر
We'll come and get them this afternoon.	raaḥ nijii wunaaxuδhum ba9ad iḍḍuhur.	راح نجي وناخذهم بعد الظهر •

Beginning RECORD 15B

(*At the barbershop.*)

Bill	*Bill*	بل
cut!	guṣṣ	قص
shave!	zayyin	زيّن
my beard	liḥaytii	لحيتي
Please give me a haircut and a shave.	ʔarjuuk guṣṣ ša9arii wuzayyin liḥaytii.	ارجوك قص شعري وزيّن لحيتي •
Barber	*Barber*	حلاّق
Right!	9aal.	عال •
Bill	*Bill*	بل
don't cut!	laa tguṣṣ	لا تقص
Don't take off too much.	laa tguṣṣ kaθiir.	لا تقص كثير •

ENGLISH EQUIVALENTS	AIDS TO LISTENING	ARABIC SPELLING
Barber	*Barber*	حلاّق
(Word said to a person who has just had a haircut.)	na9iiman.	نعيما •
Bill	*Bill*	بل
Thank you; how much will that be?	?aškurak; šgad itriid?	اشكرك ، شقد تريد ؟
Barber	*Barber*	حلاّق
hundred	miiya	مية
fifty	xamsiin	خمسين
A hundred and fifty fils.	miiya wxamsiin-filis.	مية وخمسين فلس •
(*Back at the hotel.*)		
John	*John*	جـان
you take	taaxuð	تاخذ
bath	ḥammaam	حمّام
While you take a bath, I'm going to shave.	lamma taaxuð ḥammaam, ?ana raaḥ ?azayyin.	لما تاخذ حمّام انا راح ازيّن •
Bill	*Bill*	بل
hand me!	naawušnii	ناوشني
soap	ṣaabuun	صابون
towel	xaawlii	خاولي
Hand me the soap and the towel.	naawušnii ṣṣaabuun wilxaawlii.	ناوشني الصابون والخاولي •
bring them!	jiibhum	جيبهم
to me *or* for me	?ilii	الي
Please bring them to me now.	?arjuuk hassa jiibhum ?ilii.	ارجوك هسه جيبهم الي •
John	*John*	جان
you put	xallayt	خلّيت
razor	muus	موس
Where did you put my razor?	wayn xallayt muusii?	وين خلّيت موسي ؟
Bill	*Bill*	بل
look for!	dawwir 9ala	دوّر على
upon him	9a'lay	عليه
Look for it.	dawwir 9a'lay.	دوّر عليه •
last	?aaxir	آخر
time	marra	مرّة
Saturday	yoom issabit	يوم السبت
[The] last time I saw it was Saturday.	?aaxir marra šifta kaan yoom issabit.	آخر مرّة شفته كان يوم السبت •

ENGLISH EQUIVALENTS	AIDS TO LISTENING	ARABIC SPELLING
John	*John*	جان
my (two) hands	ʔiidayya	ايديّ
I wash	ʔagsil	اغسل
I don't like to wash my hands in cold water.	maa ʔaḥibb ʔagsil ʔiidayya bmaay baarid.	ما احب اغسل ايديّ بماء بارد .

(*John says something under his breath.*)

Bill	*Bill*	بل
What's the matter?	šbiik?	شبيك ؟
John	*John*	جان
I cut	gaṣṣayt	قصّيت
face	wajih	وجه
I cut my face.	gaṣṣayt wajhii.	قصيت وجهي .
This razor's no good	halmuus muu zayn.	هالموس مو زين .
Bill	*Bill*	بل
wrong,* at fault	giḷṭaan	غلطان
You're wrong; you don't know how to shave.	ʔanta giḷṭaan; maa ta9ruf itzayyin.	انت غلطان ، ما تعرف تزيّن .
John	*John*	جان
[That's] possible.	mumkin.	ممكن .
Bill	*Bill*	بل
shirt	θoob	ثوب
clean	naḍiif	نظيف
Do you have a clean shirt?	9indak θoob naḍiif?	عندك ثوب نظيف ؟
John	*John*	جان
you wore him	libasta	لبسته
I had one, but you wore it yesterday.	kaan 9indii waaḥid, laakin ilbaarḥa ʔanta libasta.	كان عندي واحد ، لكن البارحة انت لبسته .

Beginning RECORD 16A

Bill	*Bill*	بل
suit	badla (f)	بدلة
you wear	tilbas	تلبس
Which suit are you going to wear?	ʔay badla raaḥ tilbas?	اي بدلة راح تلبس ؟
John	*John*	جان
Why do you ask me?	layš tisʔannii?	ليش تسائلني ؟

* The record has *young*, but it's *wrong*.

ENGLISH EQUIVALENTS	AIDS TO LISTENING	ARABIC SPELLING
a single *or* a certain	fadd	فد
I only have one.	9indii fadd wiḥda.*	عندي فد واحة •

PRONUNCIATION

Continuing RECORD 16A

PRACTICE 1

s: Iraqi also has two s-sounds which must be distinguished at all times. The first is the usual s in English *seed* or *sat.*

siinama	*movie*	سينما
suud	**black* (pl)	سود
saakin	*dwelling, staying*	ساكن
saa9a	*hour; clock*	ساعة
sabab	*cause, reason*	سبب
sa9iid	*Said* (man's name)	سعيد

PRACTICE 2

ṣ: The tip of the tongue touches farther back in your mouth than for the usual s in English. In addition, raise the back of the tongue somewhat toward the roof of your mouth and make the tongue stiffer. You will notice that ṣ has a 'thick' sound compared to s.

ṣifir	**zero*	صِفر
ṣufur	**yellow* (pl)	صُفُر
ṣaff	**line, row*	صف
guṣṣ	*cut!*	قص
gaṣṣ	*he cut*	قص
ṣaaḥib	*owner; friend*	صاحب
yiṣiir	*he becomes*	يصير
ṣuuf	**wool*	صوف
biṣṣayf	*in the summer*	بالصيف
biṣṣubuḥ	*during the morning*	بالصبح

PRACTICE 3

Vowel-sounds touching ṣ have a different sound from those touching s. In pronouncing these, be sure to shift from the one sound (s) to the other (ṣ).

sidd	*close!*	سد
ṣirit	*I became*	صِرت

* The record has waaḥid (m).

salla	**basket*	سلة
ṣaff	**line, row*	صف
hassa	*now*	هسة
gaṣṣa	*he cut him*	قصه
issiinama	*the movie*	السينما
iṣṣiin	**China*	الصين
iṣṣayf	*the summer*	الصيف
suug	*market*	سوق
ṣuuf	**wool*	صوف
saalim	**safe*	سالم
ṣaaḥib	*owner, friend*	صاحب
sooda	**black* (f)	سودة
ṣooda	**soda*	صودا

ANALYSIS

1. ḳariib minn.

bagdaad muu ba9iida minn hinaa.	*Baghdad isn't far from here.*	بغداد مو بعيدة من هنا ٠
makaana ḳariib minn baytna.	*His place is near our house.*	مكانه قريب من بيتنا ٠

Note that Iraqi is consistent in saying both ba9iid minn *far from*, and ḳariib minn *near* (*from*). In English we omit *from* in the latter situation.

2. *Completed action verb form patterns.*

Completed action verb forms fall into *three* general patterns. All completed action verb forms follow one of the three.

I

First, all verbs whose *he* form has a *double vowel* (namely *aa*) between two consonants follow this pattern:

šaaf	*he saw*	شاف
šaafat	*she saw*	شافت
šifit	*you saw* (m)	شفت
šiftii	*you saw* (f)	شفتي
šifit	*I saw*	شفت
šaafaw	*they saw*	شافوا
šiftum	*you saw* (pl)	شفتم
šifna	*we saw*	شفنا

Some verbs have either *i* or *u* interchangeably, as činit, kinit and kunit *you were* (m) or *I was*, and kinna and kunna *we were.*

II

Second, all verbs whose *he* form has either *a vowel* (namely *a*) or *a double consonant* at the end follow this pattern:

miša	*he walked*	مشى
mišat	*she walked*	مشت
mišayt	*you walked* (m)	مشيت
mišaytii	*you walked* (f)	مشيتي
mišayt	*I walked*	مشيت
mišaw	*they walked*	مشوا
mišaytum	*you walked* (pl)	مشيتم
mišayna	*we walked*	مشينا

šagg	*he tore*	شق
šaggat	*she tore*	شقت
šaggayt	*you tore* (m)	شقيت
šaggaytii	*you tore* (f)	شقيتي
šaggayt	*I tore*	شقيت
šaggaw	*they tore*	شقوا
šaggaytum	*you tore* (pl)	شقيتم
šaggayna	*we tore*	شقينا

III

Third, all verbs whose *he* form ends in *a single consonant preceded by a single vowel* follow this general pattern:

kitab	*he wrote*	كتب
kitbat	*she wrote*	كتبت
ki'tabit	*you wrote* (m)	كتبت
kitabtii	*you wrote* (f)	كتبتي
ki'tabit	*I wrote*	كتبت
kitbaw	*they wrote*	كتبوا
kitabtum	*you wrote* (pl)	كتبتم
kitabna	*we wrote*	كتبنا

xaḷḷaṣ	*he finished*	خلّص
xaḷṣat	*she finished*	خلّصت
xaḷ'ḷaṣit	*you finished* (m)	خلّصت
xaḷḷaṣtii	*you finished* (f)	خلّصتي
xaḷ'ḷaṣit	*I finished*	خلّصت
xaḷṣaw	*they finished*	خلّصوا
xaḷḷaṣtum	*you finished* (pl)	خلّصتم
xaḷḷaṣna	*we finished*	خلّصنا

Note the position of the accent: it is according to the regular mechanical habit except in *two* forms, namely in the *I* form and the *you* (m) form, which are identical.

There are only these three general patterns for the completed action verb forms. To repeat, *all* completed action verb forms follow one of the three.

EXERCISES

A. The following sentences further illustrate the *completed action verb form patterns. Practice them thoroughly, just as you would Basic Sentences.* They are arranged according to the three general patterns.

I šaaf *he saw.*

1. ʔaxuuya šaaf ṣadiiḳa yimšii lilʔuutyal.
2. ʔuxtii maa šaafat siiyaartii.
3. hal ʔinta šifit maktuubii?
4. jamiila, šiftii luuluu haṣṣubuḥ?
5. ʔana šifit siinama zayna.
6. humma šaafaw ilmuḳaawil yištug̣ul.
7. wayn ʔintum šiftum kull innaas?
8. ʔiḥna maa šifna ṣadiiḳna; maa čaan bilboosṭa

IIa nisa *he forgot.*

1. ʔabuuya nisa miftaaḥ-siiyaarta.
2. ṣadiiḳtii nisat tiktiblii maktuub.
3. hal ʔinta nisayt wayn xallayt muusak?
4. jamiila, layš nisaytii tjiibiin ilmaay?
5. ilbaarḥa biṣṣubuḥ ʔana nisayt ʔaruuḥ lilmadrasa.
6. humma nisaw wayn xallaw siiyaaraathum.
7. hal ʔintum nisaytum minayn jiitum?
8. ʔiḥna maa nisayna nidris 9arabii.

IIb sadd *he closed.*

1. ṣadiiḳii maa sadd baab-siiyaarta lamma ṭila9.
2. ʔummii saddat baab-ilbayt.
3. hal ʔinta saddayt baab-ilmaṭ9am?
4. jamiila, layš maa saddaytii lbaab?
5. ʔana saddayt baab-madrastii lamma diʹxalit biiha.
6. kulhum saddaw ilbaab ilkabiir.
7. hal ʔintum saddaytum ilbaab ilmaftuuḥ?
8. ʔiḥna maa saddayna baab-ilma9mal.

IIIa kitab *he wrote.*

1. ʔaxuuya kitab maktuub ʔila ṣadiiḳta.
2. ʔuxtii maa kitbatlii maktuub lamma činit bijjayš.

3. hal ʔinta ki'tabit maktuub kabiir ʔila ṣadiiḳtak?
4. jamiila, layš kitabtii lmaktuub bilʔingliizii?
5. hassa ʔana ki'tabit maktuub, laakin nisayt wayn xallayta.
6. humma maa kitbaw.
7. hal ʔintum kitabtum mikaatiib?
8. ʔiḥna kitabna kam maktuub.

IIIb stilam *he received.*

1. iṭṭabiib maa stilam maktuub minn marta.
2. marat-ṣadiiḳii stilmat θilaaθ-mikaatiib minn rajilha.
3. maa ʔa9ruf layš ʔinta maa sti'lamit maktuub minnii lamma činit fii bag̲daad.
4. luuluu, stilamtii lmaktuub?
5. ʔana maa sti'lamit maktuub minnak minn sabab maa kitabitlak.
6. ʔuxuutii stilmaw mikaatiibhum.
7. yamta ʔintum stilamtum halmaktuub minn il9iraaḳ?
8. ʔiḥna maa stilamna mikaatiibna.

B. Completed Action Verb Forms of the Type kitab. *Select the form called for by each sentence.*

1. ilmuhandis ilʔamriikaanii (kitab, kitbat, kitbaw) maktuub ʔila ḥabiibta.
2. ʔuxtii (diras, dirsat, dirsaw) ʔingliizii bilmadrasa.
3. ʔaḥibb ʔa9ruf wayn ʔinta (sikan, si'kanit, sikantii) lamma kunit ṣag̲iir.
4. layš ʔintii (kitab, ki'tabit, kitabtii) ʔila ʔaxuuč?
5. ʔahlii (sikan, sikantum, siknaw) bilbaṣra.
6. maa (diras, di'rasit, dirasna) kaθiir lamma kunit bilmadrasa.
7. (xaḷḷaṣ, xaḷ'ḷaṣit, xaḷḷaṣna) šug̲lii gabul iḍḍuhur.
8. John (dawwar, daw'warit, dawwarna) 9ala g̲urfa kabiira.
9. (štig̲al, šti'g̲alit, štig̲alna) kaθiir, wuba9dayn riḥna lissiinama.
10. maa (sikan, si'kanit, siknaw) wiiya 9ammii.

C. Completed Action Verbs of the Type nisa and sadd. *Select the form called for by the sentence.*

1. ilbaarḥa (*we walked*) lilʔuutačii.	miša, mišayt, mišayna
2. gaallii (*he forgot*) ʔismii.	nisa, nisat, nisayna
3. (*Did you forget*) šii?	nisa, nisayt, nisaw
4. wayn (*did you put*) ilḳalam wilḥibir?	xalla, xallayt, xallaw
5. minuu (*made*) halmayz?	sawwa, sawwat, sawwaw
6. (*He closed*) ilbaab lamma ṭila9.	sadd, saddat, saddayt
7. šloon (*did you tear*) badiltak?	šagg, šaggat, šaggayt
8. (*I thought*) ʔinta tḥibb itruuḥ wiiyaana.	ḍann, ḍannayt, ḍannaw
9. (*They put*) jinaṭhum jawwa.	xalla, xallayt, xallaw
10. (*I left*) siiyaartii bilbayt.	xalla, xallayt, xallaw
11. layš (*you closed*) ilbaab?	sadd, saddayt, saddaytum
12. ʔaftikir maa (*we forgot*) šii.	nisa, nisaw, nisayna

13. (*I took a walk*) ilyoom iṣṣubuḥ. — tmašša, tmaššayt, tmaššaw
14. wayn (*did you put*) siiyaaraathum? — xalla, xallat, xallaytum
15. ʔana maa (*did*) haaδa. — sawwa, sawwayt, sawwayna

D. *Supply the incompleted action verb forms called for in the sentences.*

1. gullii, wayn nigdar (yigsil) ʔiidayna? (*we*)
2. ʔariidak (yizayyin) liḥaytii. (*you*, m)
3. hamm ʔariidak (yiguṣṣ) ša9arii (*you*, m)
4. siiyaartak waṣxa; layš maa (yinaḍḍifha)? (*you*, m)
5. triidnii (yixayyuṭlak) šii? (*I*)
6. maa ʔagdar (yixaḷḷuṣ) šuglii gabul yoomayn. (*I*)
7. ʔay badla ʔinta raaḥ (yilbas)? (*you*, m)
8. tigdar (yinaawušnii) ṣṣaabuun? (*you*, m)
9. baačir ʔana raaḥ (yidawwir) 9ala gurfa θaaniya. (*I*)
10. ʔariid (yaaxuδ) ḥammaam lamma ʔinta (yigsil) wu(yizayyin) liḥaytak. (*I; you*, m)

E. *The following sentences contain verbs whose* he *form ends in a single consonant preceded by a single vowel. Such verbs, you will remember, appear as follows, before the* –uun *and* –iin *of* INCOMPLETED *agent affixes:*

yiskin	*he lives*
yisiknuun	*they live*
tisiknuun	*you live* (pl)
tisikniin	*you live* (f)
yixaḷḷuṣ	*he finishes, he completes*
yixaḷṣuun	*they finish*
txaḷṣuun	*you finish* (pl)
txaḷṣiin	*you finish* (f)

Give the correct form, corresponding to one of the above, for the verbs in parentheses.

1. ʔintii (yibayyin) mariiḍa. (*you*, f)
2. yamta raaḥ (yixaḷḷus) šugulhum? (*they*)
3. yiriiduun (yiga99id) ṣaaḥib-δiič issiiyaara. (*they*)
4. gaalaw raaḥ (yidawwir) 9ala šugul. (*they*)
5. layš haaδoolii (yiḍrub) ilwalad? (*they*)
6. jamiila, layš maa (yiktib) ʔila luuluu? (*you*, f)
7. ʔuxuutii maa yiḥibbuun (yidris) ʔingliizii. (*they*)
8. ilʔamriikaan (yigdar) yijiibuun issiiyaara. (*they*)
9. šitriiduun taakluun, wušitriiduun (yišrab)? (*you*, pl)
10. wayn ʔuxwaanak kaanaw (yištugul) gabul ilḥarb? (*you*, m)

WHAT WOULD YOU SAY?

1. *You wonder what to do in your free time.*
   - *a.* šraaḥ insawwii hallayla?
   - *b.* šitriid naakul?
   - *c.* ʔay balda haaδii?

١ ـ شراح نسوّي ها الليلة ؟
٢ ـ شتريد ناكل ؟
٣ ـ اي بلدة هاذي ؟

2. *Your friend suggests you wash up first of all.*
   - *a.* wajhak muu naḍiif.
   - *b.* bilʔawwal xallii nigsil.
   - *c.* ʔariid ʔaaxuδ ḥammaam.

١ ـ وجهك مو نظيف •
٢ ـ بالاول خلّي نغسل •
٣ ـ اريد آخذ حمّام •

3. *You ask about the barbershop.*
   - *a.* ʔi9ḍirnii, ʔagdar ʔasiʔlak wayn ʔakuu mzayyin?
   - *b.* layš maa tzayyin hinaa?
   - *c.* gullinna wayn ʔakuu ʔuutačii.

١ ـ اعذرني ، اقدر اسائلك وين اكو مزيّن
٢ ـ ليش ما تزيّن هنا ؟
٣ ـ قل لنا وين اكو اوتشي ؟

4. *You tell the barber you want a shave.*
   - *a.* ʔariid ʔazayyin liḥaytii.
   - *b.* ʔariid ʔazuur 9ammii.
   - *c.* ʔariid ʔagsil ʔiidayya.

١ ـ اريد ازيّن لحيتي •
٢ ـ اريد ازور عمّي •
٣ ـ اريد اغسل ايديّ •

5. *A haircut, too?*
   - *a.* triid itzayyin ša9rak?
   - *b.* triid hamm ʔaguṣṣ ša9rak?
   - *c.* triid itnaam hinaa?

١ ـ تريد تزيّن شعرك ؟
٢ ـ تريد هم اقص شعرك ؟
٣ ـ تريد تنام هنا ؟

6. *You ask the barber where the cleaner's is.*
   - *a.* tigdar itgullii wayn ʔakuu ʔuutačii?
   - *b.* tigdar itnaḍḍif badiltii?
   - *c.* tigdar itxayyiṭ jaybii?

١ ـ تقدر تقول لي وين اكو اوتشي ؟
٢ ـ تقدر تنظف بدلتي ؟
٣ ـ تقدر تخيّط جيبي ؟

7. *His friend is a cleaner.*
   - *a.* maa ʔa9ruf wayn ṣadiiḳii.
   - *b.* ṣadiiḳii huuwa ʔuutačii.
   - *c.* maakuu ʔuutačii ḳariib minn hinaa.

١ ـ ما اعرف وين صديقي •
٢ ـ صديقي هو اوتشي •
٣ ـ ماكو اوتشي قريب من هنا •

8. *The barber charges only 150 fils.*
   - *a.* ʔarjuuk diinaarayn.
   - *b.* muu ʔakθar minn xamsiin-fils.
   - *c.* bass miiya wxamsiin-fils.

١ ـ ارجوك دينارين •
٢ ـ مو اكثر من خمسين فلس
٣ ـ بس مية وخمسين فلس •

9. *You tell the cleaner you want your suits cleaned and pressed.*
   - *a.* nriidak itnaḍḍifhum wutiḍrubhum ʔuutii.
   - *b.* nriid nilbashum hallayla.
   - *c.* laa txaḷḷiṣhum minn waḳit.

١ ـ نريدك تنظفهم وتضربهم اوتي •
٢ ـ نريد نلبسهم هذه الليلة •
٣ ـ لا تخلّصهم من وقت •

10. *They'll be ready Thursday.*

a. ta9aaluu xuδuuhum yoom iliθinayn. ١ ـ تعالوا اخذوهم يوم الاثنين •

b. raaḥ ʔaxaḷḷiṣhum yoom ilxamiis. ٢ ـ راح اخلصهم يوم الخميس •

c. maa ʔagdar ʔaxaḷḷiṣhum gabul yoom ilxamiis. ٣ ـ ما اقدر اخلصهم قبل يوم الخميس •

11. *Later, the razor is misplaced.*

a. wayn xallayt ilmuus? ١ ـ وين خلّيت الموس ؟

b. wayn xallayt iṣṣaabuun? ٢ ـ وين خلّيت الصابون ؟

c. wayn xallayt ilxaawlii? ٣ ـ وين خلّيت الخاولي ؟

12. *You tell your friend to go find it.*

a. dawwir 9a'lay; ʔinta tigdar tuujda. ١ ـ دوّر عليه ، انت تقدر توجده •

b. ruuḥ dawwir 9a'lay! ٢ ـ روح دوّر عليه •

c. nisayt wayn xallayta. ٣ ـ نسيت وين خليته •

13. *You don't like cold water.*

a. maakuu ḥammaam hinaa. ١ ـ ماكو حمّام هنا •

b. ilmaay baarid wuwaṣux. ٢ ـ الماء بارد ووسخ •

c. maa raaḥ ʔaaxuδ ḥammaam ibmaay baarid. ٣ ـ ما راح آخذ حمّام بي ماء بارد •

14. *Finally, you try to borrow a clean shirt.*

a. ʔariid θoob jadiid. ١ ـ اريد ثوب جديد •

b. maakuu 9indii θoob naḍiif; ilbaarḥa ʔana libasta. ٢ ـ ماكو عندي ثوب نظيف ، البارحة انا لبسته •

c. hal 9indak θoob naḍiif? ٣ ـ هل عندك ثوب نظيف ؟

LISTENING IN

John and Bill have the afternoon free.

Continuing RECORD 16A

JOHN wayn raaḥ inruuḥ ilyoom? جان ـ وين راح نروح اليوم ؟

BILL šitriid insawwii? بل ـ شتريد نسوّي ؟

JOHN xalli nigsil wuba9dayn inruuḥ inšuuf ilbalad. جان ـ خلّي نغسل وبعدين نروح نشوف البلد •

yigluun bagdaad balad jamiil. يقولون بغداد بلد جميل •

BILL ṭayyib. bilʔawwal, wayn ʔakuu mzayyin? laazim ʔazayyin. بل ـ طيب • بالاوّل ، وين اكو مزيّن ؟ لازم ازيّن •

JOHN tigdar itzayyin bilʔuutayl wiiyaaya. جان ـ تقدر تزيّن بالاوتيل ويّاي •

BILL balii, laakin ʔariid ʔaguṣṣ ša9arii. بل ـ بلي ، لكن اريد اقص شعري •

JOHN maa ʔa9ruf wayn ʔakuu mzayyin. ʔisʔal δaak ilbagdaadii ilwaaguf yamm iddukkaan. جان ـ ما اعرف وين اكو مزيّن • اسأل ذاك البغدادي الواقف يم الدكّان •

(*Bill walks over to a man standing on the corner.*)

BILL ʔismaḥlii, tigdar itgullii wayn ʔakuu mzayyin?

بل – اسمح لي ، تقدر تقول لي وين اكو مزيّن ؟

STRANGER mitʔassif, maa ʔa9ruf. laazim tisʔal šaxuṣ θaanii.

غريب – متأسف ، ما اعرف • لازم تسائل شخص ثاني •

(*Bill and John walk up to another Baghdadi, and Bill asks him the same question.*)

STRANGER ta9aaluu; ʔa9ruf waaḥid makaana ḳariib minn hinaa.

غريب – تعالوا ، اعرف واحد مكانه قريب من هنا •

JOHN wayn ʔakuu ʔaḳrab ʔuutačii? badlaatna waṣxa.

جان – وين اكو اقرب اوتشي ؟ بدلاتنا وسخة •

STRANGER šuufuu, ʔakuu mzayyin hinaak, wuyamma lʔuutačii.

غريب – شوفوا ، اكو مزيّن هناك ويمّه الاوتشي •

BILL ʔaškurak. bilʔawwal xallii nruuḥ lilʔuutačii wuba9dayn nigdar inruuḥ lilimzayyin.

بل – اشكرك • بالاوّل خلّي نروح للاوتشي وبعدين نقدر نروح للمزيّن •

JOHN 9aal.

جان – عال

(*At the cleaner's.*)

PRESSER ʔaḷḷaa bilxayr. šagdar ʔasawwiilkum?

اوتشي – الله بالخير • شقدر اسوّي لكم ؟

JOHN badlaatna waṣxa. nriidak* itnaḍḍifhum wutiḍrubhum ʔuutii.

جان – بدلاتنا وسخة • نريدك تنظفهم وتضربهم اوتي •

PRESSER zayn.

اوتشي – زين

BILL ʔakuu 9indak xayyaaṭ?

بل – اكو عندك خيّاط ؟

PRESSER ʔaanii hamm xayyaaṭ. šitriid ʔaxayyuṭlak?

اوتشي – آني هم خيّاط • شتريد اخيّط لك ؟

BILL hassa šaggayt jaybii.

بل – هسة شقّيت جيبي •

PRESSER ʔay jayb mašguug?

اوتشي – اي جيب مشقوق ؟

BILL haaδa. yamta txaḷḷuṣhum?

بل – هذا • يمتى تخلّصهم ؟

PRESSER yoom ilxamiis.

اوتشي – يوم الخميس •

BILL maa nigdar nxalliihum ʔakθar minn saa9atayn. nriid nilbashum hallayla.

بل – ما نقدر نخلّيهم اكثر من ساعتين • نريد نلبسهم هالليلة •

Beginning RECORD 16B

PRESSER zayn, raaḥ ʔaxaḷḷuṣhum miθil maa triiduun.

اوتشي – زين ، راح اخلّصهم مثل ما تريدون •

BILL raaḥ nijii wunaaxuδhum ba9ad iḍḍuhur.

بل – راح نجي و ناخذهم بعد الظهر •

(*At the barbershop.*)

BILL ʔarjuuk guṣṣ ša9arii wuzayyin liḥaytii.

بل – ارجوك قص شعري وزيّن لحيتي •

BARBER† 9aal.

الحلاق – عال •

* Not clear on the record. † ḥallaaḳ.

BILL ʔarjuuk laa tguṣṣ kaθiir.	بل – ارجوك لا تقص كثير •
BARBER šloon haaδa?	الحلاّق – شلون هذا ؟
BILL zayn. šgad* itriid?	بل – زين • شقد تريد ؟
BARBER miiya wxamsiin-filis. ʔaškurak.	الحلاّق – مية وخمسين فلس • اشكرك •
(*To John*) triid itzayyin liḥaytak?	(الى جان) تريد تزيّن لحيتك ؟
JOHN laa, ʔaškurak, maakuu 9indii wakit.	جان – لا ، اشكرك ، ماكو عندي وقت •
(*At the hotel.*)	
JOHN xallii nigsil wuba9dayn inruuḥ naakul.	جان – خلّي نغسل وبعدين نروح ناكل •
BILL zayn. bilʔawwal raaḥ ʔaaxuδ ḥammaam.	بل – زين • بالاوّل راح آخذ حمّام •
JOHN lamma taaxuδ ḥammaam, ʔana raaḥ ʔazayyin.	جان – لمّا تاخذ حمّام ، انا راح ازيّن •
BILL naawušnii ṣṣaabuun wilxaawlii.	بل – ناوشني الصابون والخاولي
ʔarjuuk hassa jiibhum ʔilii.	ارجوك هسّه جيبهم الي •
JOHN dawwir 9alayhum; ʔanta tigdar tuujadhum.	جان – دوّر عليهم ، انت تقدر توجدهم •
gullii, wayn xallayt ilmuus?	قل لي ، وين خليت الموس ؟
BILL ʔaaxir marra šifta kaan yoom issabit.	بل – آخر مرّة شفته كان يوم السبت •
maakuu maay ḥaarr.	ماكو ماء حار •
ʔana maa† raaḥ ʔaaxuδ ḥammaam ibmaay baarid.	انا ما راح آخذ حمّام بماء بارد •
JOHN laazim tigsil wajhak wuʔiidayk; hamm humma† kulliš waṣxa.	جان – لازم تغسل وجهك وايديك ، همّا كلّش وسخة •
BILL balii, miθil wajhak.	بل – بلي ، مثل وجهك •
(*John says something to himself.*)	
BILL hassa šbiik?	بل – هسّه شبيك •
JOHN halmuus muu zayn. šuuf, gaṣṣayt wajhii.	جان – ها الموس مو زين • شوف ، قصّيت وجهي •
BILL ʔanta gilṭaan; ilmuus kulliš zayn, bass ʔanta maa ta9ruf itzayyin.	بل – انت غلطان ، الموس كلّش زين ، بس انت ما تعرف تزيّن •
JOHN mumkin.	جان – ممكن •
BILL John, 9indak θoob naḍiif?	بل – جان ، عندك ثوب نظيف ؟
JOHN kaan 9indii waaḥid, laakin ilbaarḥa ʔanta libasta.	جان – كان عندي واحد ، لكن البارحة انت لبسته •
BILL ʔay badla raaḥ tilbas?	بل – اي بدلة راح تلبس ؟
JOHN layš tisʔannii?	جان – ليش تسائلني ؟
ta9ruf 9indii fadd badla naḍiifa.	تعرف عندي فد بدلة نظيفة •

* Record has an extraneous syllable.

† Not on record.

VOCABULARY

badla (f)	suit
badlatna	our suit
badiltii	my suit
badlaat	suits
balad (m), balda (f)	city
ba9ad iḍḍuhur	afternoon
yidawwir 9ala (dawwar 9ala)	he looks for
dawwir 9a'lay!	Look for it!
yiguṣṣ (gaṣṣ)	he cuts
guṣṣ	cut!
ʔaguṣṣ	I cut
gaṣṣayt	I cut; you cut (m)
gilṭaan, –a (f)	wrong, in error, at fault
yigsil (gisal)	he washes
hallayla	tonight
ḥallaaḳ	barber
jayb (jyuub)	pocket (pl)
yilbas (libas)	he wears
nilbas	we wear
li'basit	I wore; you wore (m)
libasta	I wore it; you wore it
liḥya (f)	beard
liḥaytii	my beard
makaan (makaanaat)	place (pl)
marra (f)	time, turn (repeated time)
ʔaaxir marra	the last time
marra	once, one time
marratayn	two times, twice
θilaaθ-marraat	three times
mašguug, –a	torn
miiya (f)	hundred, one hundred
miiya wxamsiin	hundred and fifty
miitayn	two hundred
miit-filis	a hundred fils
mikaatiib	letters (*pl of* maktuub)

minn	from; than
ʔakθar minn	more than
ḳariib minn	near to
ba9iid minn	far from
miθil maa	like, as
miθil maa triiduun	just as you wish
mumkin	possible
muus	razor
mzayyin	barber
yinaawuš (naawaš)	he hands over
naawušnii	hand me!
yinaḍḍuf (naḍḍaf)	he cleans, he makes clean
tnaḍḍufha	you clean her (it)
naḍiif, –a (f), nḍaaf (pl)	clean
na9iiman	(word said to person who has just had a haircut)
saa9atayn	two hours
yisʔal (siʔal)	he asks
ʔisʔal	ask!
tisʔal	you ask (m)
tisʔalnii *or* tisʔannii	you ask me
ṣaabuun	soap
yišigg (šagg)	he tears
šaggayt	I tore; you tore (m)
šaxuṣ	person
šaxuṣ θaanii	someone else
ša9ar	hair
ša9arii	my hair
wajih (wujuuh)	face (pl)
wajhii	my face
waṣux, waṣxa (f)	dirty
xaawlii	towel
xamsiin	fifty
xayyaaṭ	tailor
yixaḷḷuṣ (xaḷḷaṣ)	he finishes
txaḷḷuṣhum	you finish them
yixayyuṭ (xayyaṭ)	he sews

ʔaxayyuṭ	I sew
ʔaxayyuṭlak	I sew for you
yijii (ʔija)	he comes (he came)
nijii	we come
yoom issabit	Saturday
yizayyin (zayyan)	he shaves; he arranges, makes pretty
zayyin	shave!
ʔazayyin	I shave
ʔaaxir	last
ʔaaxir marra	[the] last time
ʔakθar minn	more than
ʔaḳrab	nearer
ʔawwal	first
bilʔawwal	at first, first of all
ʔiid (f)	hand

ʔiidayn	two hands
ʔiidayya	my hands
ʔiidayk	your hands
ʔuutačii	clothes presser, cleaner
ʔuutii	pressing iron
yiḍrub ʔuutii	he presses, he irons
9aal	fine, excellent
9ala	upon, on
9a'lay	on him (it)
dawwir 9a'lay	look for it!
θoob	shirt
yiḍrub (ḍirab)	he strikes, he hits
tiḍrub	you hit
tiḍrubha	you hit her (it)

UNIT 9

Let's Eat

BASIC SENTENCES

Continuing RECORD 16B

ENGLISH EQUIVALENTS	AIDS TO LISTENING	ARABIC SPELLING
John	*John*	جان
what time	šwaḳit	شوقت
What time are we going to eat?	šwaḳit raaḥ naakul?	شوقت راح ناكل ؟
it happened *or* it became	ṣaar	صار
time (period of time)	mudda	مدّة
from *or* since	minn	من
we ate	ʔikalna	اكلنا
hungry	joo9aan	جوعان
It's been quite a while since we ate, and I'm hungry.	ṣaar mudda minn ʔakalna, wuʔana joo9aan.	صار مدّة من اكلنا ، وانا جوعان .
Bill	*Bill*	بل
place *or* establishment	maḥall	محل
pleasant *or* nice	ḷaṭiif	لطيف
This place is nice; let's go in.	halmaḥall ḷaṭiif; xallii nidxul.	ها المحل لطيف ، خلّي ندخل .
(*To the waiter.*)		
list	ḳaayma	قائمة
the menu	ḳaaymat-ilʔakil	قائمة الاكل
let us see!	xallii nšuuf	خلّي نشوف
Let's see the menu.	xallii nšuuf ḳaaymat-ilʔakil.	خلّي نشوف قائمة الاكل .
John	*John*	جان
you read	tiḳra	تقرا
you read her	tiḳraaha	تقراها
written	maktuub	مكتوب
Can you read it if it's written in Arabic?	tigdar tiḳraaha ʔiδa maktuuba bil9arabii?	تقدر تقراها اذا مكتوبة بالعربي ؟

Beginning RECORD 17A

ENGLISH EQUIVALENTS	AIDS TO LISTENING	ARABIC SPELLING
(*To the waiter.*)		
soup	šoorba	شوربة
dish	maa9uun	ماعون
dish of rice	maa9uun-timman	ماعون تمّن
cutlet	kabaab	كباب
salad	zaḷaaṭa	زلاطة
without	biduun	بدون
olive oil	zayt	زيت
cheese	jibin	جبن
Bring me soup, and a dish of rice and a cutlet.	jiiblii šoorba wumaa9uun-timman wukabaab.	جيب لي شوربة وماعون تمّن وكباب .
Salad without oil, and cheese.	zaḷaaṭa biduun zayt, wujibin.	زلاطة بدون زيت ، وجبن .
Waiter	*Waiter*	البوي
What would you like to drink?	šitḥibb tišrab?	شتحب تشرب ؟
wine	šaraab	شراب
arak	9arag	عرق
we have milk, tea, arak and wine	9idna ḥaliib, čaay, 9arag wušaraab.	عندنا حليب ، شاي ، عرق وشراب .
John	*John*	جان
buttermilk	laban *or* liban	لبن
Do you have buttermilk?	ʔakuu 9idkum laban?	اكو عندكم لبن ؟
with regret	ma9a lʔasaf	مع الاسف
finished *or* gone	xuḷṣaan	خلصان
Waiter	*Waiter*	البوي
I'm sorry, the buttermilk's all gone.	ma9a lʔasaf, illaban xuḷṣaan.	مع الاسف ، اللبن خلصان .
John	*John*	جان
then *or* in that case	zayn	زين
Then bring me a glass of milk.	zayn jiiblii glaaṣ-ḥaliib.	زين جيب لي گلاص حليب .
Bill	*Bill*	بل
eggplant	baadinjaan	باذنجان
fried	muglii *or* maglii*	مقلي
cooked	maṭbuux	مطبوخ
chicken	dijaaj	دجاج
I want fried eggplant and rice cooked with chicken.	ʔana ʔariid baadinjaan muglii wutimman maṭbuux wiiya dijaaj.	انا اريد باذنجان مقلي وتمّن مطبوخ ويا دجاج .

ENGLISH EQUIVALENTS	AIDS TO LISTENING	ARABIC SPELLING
John	*John*	جان
I ate	ʔi'kalit	اكلت
better than	ʔaḥsan minn	احسن من
I haven't eaten better food than this.	maa ʔi'kalit ʔaḥsan minn halʔakil.	ما اكلت احسن من ها الاكل •
Bill	*Bill*	بل
sugar	šakar	شكر
Please hand me the sugar.	ʔarjuuk naawušnii ššakar.	ارجوك ناوشني الشكر •
John	*John*	جان
fruit	maywa *or* miiwa*	ميوة
Waiter, what fruit do you have?	boy, šakuu maywa 9idkum?	«بوي» شكو ميوة عندكم ؟
Waiter	*Waiter*	البوي
Grapes, figs and watermelon.	9anab, tiin wuraggii.	عنب ، تين ورقي •
John	*John*	جان
bring (to) us!	jiibilna *or* jiibinna	جيب لنا
Bring us [some] figs.	jiibilna tiin.	جيب لنا تين •
Bill	*Bill*	بل
No, I want grapes.	laa, ʔana ʔariid 9anab.	لا ، انا اريد عنب •
John	*John*	جان
I thought (*lit.*, I was thinking)	kint ʔaftikir	كنت افتكر
I thought you liked figs.	kint ʔaftikir ʔinta tḥibb tiin.	كنت افتكر انت تحب تين •
Bill	*Bill*	بل
true	ṣaḥiiḥ	صحيح
a (single) fig	tiina	تينة
That's true, but this morning I ate a bad fig.	haaδa ṣaḥiiḥ, laakin haṣṣubuḥ ʔi'kalit tiina duuniiya.	هذا صحيح ، لكن هل الصبح اكلت تينة دونية •

Beginning RECORD 17B

sour	ḥaamuḍ	حامض
It was sour.	kaanat ḥaamḍa.	كانت حامضة •
more *or* in addition	ba9ad	بعد
I don't want any more [of them].	maa ʔariid ba9ad.	ما اريد بعد •
John	*John*	جان
money	fluus	فلوس
enough	kaafii	كافي
I haven't enough money.	maa 9indii fluus kaafiya.	ما عندي فلوس كافية •

ENGLISH EQUIVALENTS	AIDS TO LISTENING	ARABIC SPELLING
lend (to) me!	daayinnii	داينني
Lend me a couple of dinars.	daayinnii diinaarayn.	داينني دينارين •
Bill	*Bill*	بل
you paid (to) me	difa9itlii	دفعت لي
who *or* what *or* which	ʔillii* *or* ʔilaδii	الّي (ايضا) الذي
you borrowed him from me*	tdaayanta minnii	تداينته مني
Sunday	yoom ilʔaḥad	يوم الاحد
You haven't paid me the dinar [which] you borrowed [it] from me Sunday.	maa difa9itlii ddiinaar ʔillii tdaayanta minnii yoom ilʔaḥad.	ما دفعت لي الدينار الّي تداينته منّي يوم الاحد •
I pay	ʔadfa9	ادفع
for both of us	liθinaynna	لثنيننا
I'll pay for both of us.	ʔana raaḥ ʔadfa9 liθinaynna.	انا راح ادفع لثنينا •
you pay [to] me	tidfa9lii	تدفع لي
the day after tomorrow	ba9ad baačir	بعد باكر
You can pay me back tomorrow or the next day.	tigdar tidfa9lii baačir ʔaw ba9ad baačir.	تقدر تدفع لي باكر او بعد باكر •
(*Later, as John and Bill are walking along.*)		
Bill	*Bill*	بل
(me) still	ba9adnii	بعدني
I'm still hungry.	ba9adnii joo9aan.	بعدني جوعان •
I buy	ʔaštirii	اشتري
apples	tiffaaḥ	تفاح
I want to buy [some] apples.	ʔariid ʔaštirii tiffaaḥ.	اريد اشتري تفّاح •
(*To the clerk.*)		
you sell them	tbii9hum	تبيعهم
How do you sell them?	šloon itbii9hum?	شلون تبيعهم ؟
Clerk	*Clerk*	البيّاع
apiece *or* each	ilwiḥda *or* ilwaaḥda*	الوحدة (ايضا) الواحدة
forty	ʔarba9iin	اربعين
Forty fils apiece.	ʔarba9iin-fils ilwiḥda.	اربعين فلس الواحدة •
pick out!	stangii	ستنقي
what you want (her)	litriidha	التريدها
Pick out what you want.	stangii litriidha.	ستنقي التريدها •
John	*John*	جان
oranges	portaḳaal	برتقال
sweet *or* pretty	ḥiluu (m) *and* ḥilwa (f)	حلو ، حلوة
Are these oranges sweet?	halportaḳaal ḥiluu?	هالبرتقال حلو ؟

ENGLISH EQUIVALENTS	AIDS TO LISTENING	ARABIC SPELLING
Clerk	*Clerk*	البيّاع
fils (pl)	fluus	فلوس
Yes. They're ten fils each.	na9am. 9ašir-ifluus ilwiḥda.	نعم ، عشر فلوس الواحدة •
John	*John*	جان
half	nuṣṣ *or* nuṣuf	نصف
dozen	dirzan	درزن
I want half a dozen.	?ariid nuṣuf-dirzan.	اريد نصف درزن •
give me!	nṭiinii	انطيني
different *or* other	gayr	غير
a (single) orange	portaḳaala	برتقالة
Give me another orange; this [one's] bad.	nṭiinii gayr portaḳaala; haaδii duuniiya.*	انطيني غير برتقالة ، هذي دونية •

PRONUNCIATION

Beginning RECORD 18A

PRACTICE 1

δ: This sign stands for a sound like *th* in *then.* Contrast it with θ, which stands for a sound like *th* in *think.*

δahab	**gold*	ذهب
haaδa	*this* (m)	هذا
kaδδaab	**liar*	كذّاب
δaak	*that* (m)	ذاك
δiič	*that* (f)	ذيك
δayl	**tail*	ذيل
haaδool	*these*	هذول

PRACTICE 2

ḍ: Place your tongue in position to say δ, but with the back of your tongue raised toward the roof of your mouth. Also make your tongue stiffer, and tighten the muscles of your throat. Note the vowel 'color'.

?aḍinn	*I think, I suppose*	اظن
ḍuhur	*noon*	ظهر
ḍahar	*back*	ظهر
yiḍrub	*he strikes, he hits*	يضرب
fuḍḍa	**silver* (f)	فضّة
?aḍrub	*I strike*	اضرب

yinaḍḍuf	*he cleans*	ينظّف
tfaḍḍal	*if you please*	تفضّل
biḍḍuhur	*at noon*	بالظهر
ʔaruḍ	**ground, earth, floor*	ارض
mariiḍ	*sick*	مريض
bayḍa	**an egg* (f)	بيضة

PRACTICE 3

The vowels touching ḍ have a somewhat different sound from those touching δ. This distinction is similar to that noted for ṭ and t, ṣ and s. It is due to (1) back position of tongue, (2) stiffness of tongue, and (3) tightening of the throat muscles.

δahab	**gold*	ذهب
ḍahar	*back*	ظهر
δiič	*that* (f)	ذيك
naḍiif	*clean*	نظيف
tilmiiδ	*student*	تلميذ
mariiḍ	*sick*	مريض
δayl	**tail*	ذيل
bayḍ	**eggs*	بيض

ANALYSIS

1. –na *and* –nii *with words ending in* –l.

ʔakalna *and* ʔakanna	*we ate*	اكلنا
jiibilna *and* jiibinna	*bring* (*to*) *us!*	جيب لنا
tisʔalnii *and* tisʔannii	*you ask me*	تسائلني
ʔisʔalnii *and* ʔisʔannii	*ask me!*	اسائلني
ʔahalna *and* ʔahanna	*our family*	اهلنا

Note that when the suffixes –nii and –na are added to words ending in –l, the l is commonly replaced by n. This is seen in the words at the right. Both forms are correct, but the latter is more common in ordinary conversation.

2.

fluus	*money*	فلوس
ilifluus	*the money*	الفلوس
halifluus	*this money*	هالفلوس

A vowel i is spoken between nouns beginning with two consonants and prefixes, for instance il– *the* and hal– *this*. This is in keeping with the habit of not speaking three consonants together.

3. Incompleted and Completed Action Verb Forms.

Compare the incompleted action forms on the left with the completed action forms on the right.

yišuuf	*he sees*	šaaf	*he saw*	يشوف ـ شاف
yiriid	*he wants*	raad	*he wanted*	يريد ـ راد
yinaam	*he sleeps*	naam	*he slept*	ينام ـ نام
yiktib	*he writes*	kitab	*he wrote*	يكتب ـ كتب
yišrab	*he drinks*	širab	*he drank*	يشرب ـ شرب
yidxul	*he goes in*	dixal	*he went in*	يدخل ـ دخل
yimšii	*he walks*	miša	*he walked*	يمشي ـ مشى

You will observe that there is a close relation between the incompleted action form of a verb and the corresponding completed action form. You will note that *both have the same consonants.* You will also note that all the completed action forms have *a* as their last vowel, while the incompleted forms have various vowels. Now, because of the regularity of the completed action forms, *if you know the incompleted action form, you can tell at once what the corresponding completed action form will be.* Thus, if you know yiruuḥ *he goes*, you can be certain the corresponding completed action form is raaḥ *he went.*

Note, however, that *the reverse is not* true. You cannot tell from the completed action form šaal *he carried* whether the incompleted action form is yišuul or yišiil or yišaal. But if you first learn yišiil *he carries*, you know automatically that *he carries* is šaal. So, to repeat, once you know the *incompleted action* form of a verb, you can make all other forms from it. For this reason we shall cite verbs in the incompleted action form in the *Vocabulary* given at the end of the book. In the *Basic Sentences*, however, we shall continue to cite the form of the verb used in the sentences.

Below are most of the verbs you have met so far. The incompleted action form is given first, followed by the completed action form. They are placed in *three* groups according to the patterns they follow. (Incompleted action patterns are explained in Unit 5; completed action patterns, in Unit 8.)

I

yinaam	*he sleeps; he goes to bed*	naam	*he slept; he went to bed*	ينام ـ نام
yixaaf minn	*he is afraid of*	xaaf minn	*he was afraid of*	يخاف من ـ خاف من
yibii9	*he sells*	baa9	*he sold*	يبيع ـ باع
yijiib	*he brings*	jaab	*he brought*	يجيب ـ جاب
yiriid	*he wants*	raad	*he wanted*	يريد ـ راد
yiṣiir	*he becomes*	ṣaar	*he became*	يصير ـ صار
yišiil	*he picks up, he carries*	šaal	*he picked up; he carried*	يشيل ـ شال
yiguul	*he says*	gaal	*he said*	يقول ـ قال
yikuun	*he will be*	kaan	*he was*	يكون ـ كان
yiruuḥ	*he goes*	raaḥ	*he went*	يروح ـ راح
yišuuf	*he sees*	šaaf	*he saw*	يشوف ـ شاف
yizuur	*he visits*	zaar	*he visited*	يزور ـ زار

II. The *he* form has either a *vowel* or else a *double consonant* at the end:

yiḥkii	*he speaks*	ḥika	*he spoke*	يحكي ـ حكى
yimšii	*he walks*	miša	*he walked*	يمشي ـ مشى

yinṭii	*he gives*	ʼnṭa	*he gave*	ينطي - نطى
yijii	*he comes*	ʔija	*he came*	يجي - اجا
yibḳa	*he remains*	buḳa	*he remained*	يبكي - بكى
yiḳra	*he reads*	ḳira	*he read*	يقرا - قراء
yinsa	*he forgets*	nisa	*he forgot*	ينسى - نسى
yiraawii	*he shows*	raawa	*he showed*	يراوي - راوى
yisawwii	*he does, he makes*	sawwa	*he did, he made*	يسوّي - سوّى
yixallii	*he puts*	xalla	*he put*	يخلّي - خلّى
yištirii	*he buys*	štira	*he bought*	يشتري - اشترى
yitmašša	*he takes a walk*	tmašša	*he took a walk*	يتمشّى - تمشّى
yidigg	*he rings, he knocks*	dagg	*he rang*	يدق - دق
yiḍinn	*he thinks, he supposes*	ḍann	*he thought*	يظن - ظن
yiḥibb	*he loves, he likes*	ḥabb	*he loved, he liked*	يحب - حب
yisidd	*he closes*	sadd	*he closed*	يسد - سد
yišigg	*he tears*	šagg	*he tore*	يشق - شق
yiguṣṣ	*he cuts*	gaṣṣ	*he cut*	يقص - قص

III. The *he* form ends in a *single consonant preceded by a single vowel:*

yidfa9	*he pays*	difa9	*he paid*	يدفع - دفع
yifham	*he understands*	fiham	*he understood*	يفهم - فهم
yiftaḥ	*he opens*	fitaḥ	*he opened*	يفتح - فتح
yig9ad	*he sits; he wakes up*	gi9ad	*he sat; he woke up*	يقعد - قعد
yilbas	*he puts on; he wears*	libas	*he put on; he wore*	يلبس - لبس
yirja9	*he goes back; he comes back*	rija9	*he went back; he came back*	يرجع - رجع
yisma9	*he hears*	sima9	*he heard*	يسمع - سمع
yisʔal	*he asks*	siʔal	*he asked*	يسائل - سئل
yišrab	*he drinks*	širab	*he drank*	يشرب - شرب
yiṭla9	*he goes out; he comes out*	ṭila9	*he went out; he came out*	يطلع - طلع
yidris	*he studies*	diras	*he studied*	يدرس - درس
yigsil	*he washes*	gisal	*he washed*	يغسل - غسل
yiḥmil	*he carries; he transports*	ḥimal	*he carried; he transported*	يحمل - حمل
yiktib	*he writes*	kitab	*he wrote*	يكتب - كتب
yirsil	*he sends*	risal	*he sent*	يرسل - رسل
yiskin	*he lives; he stays*	sikan	*he lived; he stayed*	يسكن - سكن
yidxul	*he goes in; he comes in*	dixal	*he went in; he came in*	يدخل - دخل
yiḍrub	*he strikes, hits*	ḍirab	*he struck*	يضرب - ضرب
timṭur	*it rains* (f)	miṭrat	*it rained*	تمطر - مطرت
yiškur	*he thanks*	šikar	*he thanked*	يشكر - شكر
ya9ruf	*he knows*	9iraf	*he knew*	يعرف - عرف
yaakul	*he eats*	ʔakal	*he ate*	ياكل - اكل
yaaxuδ	*he takes*	ʔaxaδ	*he took*	ياخذ - اخذ

yuujad *or* yoojad	*he finds*	wujad	*he found*	يوجد - وجد
yuugaf *or* yoogaf	*he stops; he stands*	wugaf	*he stopped; he stood*	يوقف - وقف

Notice the last four examples carefully: if the incompleted action form begins with yaa–, then the completed action form has ʔa–; similarly yuu– (or yoo–) and wu–.

yibayyin	*he seems*	bayyan	*he seemed*	يبيّن - بيّن
yidawwir 9ala	*he looks for*	dawwar 9ala	*he looked for*	يدوّر على - دوّر على
yiga99id	*he wakes (someone) up*	ga99ad	*he waked (someone) up*	يقعّد - قعّد
yinaḍḍuf	*he cleans*	naḍḍaf	*he cleaned*	ينظّف - نظّف
yixaḷḷus	*he completes; he finishes*	xaḷḷaṣ	*he completed, he finished*	يخلّص - خلّص
yixayyuṭ	*he sews*	xayyaṭ	*he sewed*	يخيّط - خيّط
yizayyin	*he shaves*	zayyan	*he shaved*	يزيّن - زيّن
yinaawuš	*he hands*	naawaš	*he handed*	يناوش - ناوش
yiftihim	*he understands*	ftaham	*he understood*	يفتهم - فهم
yiftikir	*he thinks*	ftikar	*he thought*	يفتكر - فتكر
yistilim	*he receives*	stilam	*he received*	يستلم - ستلم
yištugul	*he works*	štigal	*he worked*	يشتغل - شتغل

EXERCISES

A. *Study the following sentences which have completed action forms of* ṣaar *he became; it happened.*

1. ṣaar ḍaabuṭ biljayš.
   ṣaar yoomayn maa šifit ʔaxuuya.
2. ʔuxtii ṣaarat ʔumm-θilaaθ-walad.
3. hal ʔinta ṣirit muhandis bamriika?
4. jamiila, layš ʔintii ṣirtii mariiḍa?
5. ʔana maa ṣirit šib9aan waḷaw ʔakalit kaθiir.
6. humma ṣaaraw ti9baaniin minn iššugul.
7. hal ʔintum ṣirtum tiḥčuun 9arabii zayn?
8. ṣirna niḥčii 9arabii 9iraaḳii.

The following sentences have all forms of yiḳra *he reads.*

1. huuwa yigdar yiḳra 9arabii.
2. maa hiiya tigdar tiḳra fransaawii.
3. sa9iid, tigdar tiḳra ʔingliizii?
4. jamiila, layš maa tiḳriin maktuubič?
5. ʔana ʔagdar ʔaḳra wuʔaktib 9arabii; hassa ʔana ʔaḳra 9arabii ʔaḥsan minn ilʔawwal.
6. haaδool ilʔamriikaan yigidruun yiḳruun 9arabii.
7. ʔintum tiḳruun zayn.
8. laazim niḳra yawaaš.

1. huuwa ḳira maktuuba ʔila ṣadiiḳa.
2. hiiya ḳirat maktuub-ṣadiiḳha θilaaθ-marraat.

3. ʔinta ḳirayt ilmaaktuub kulla.
4. jamiila, layš maa ḳiraytii maktuub-9ammič?
5. ʔana ḳirayt kaθiir ḥatta ṣirit ni9saan.
6. ḳiraw kulšii ʔillii ʔana kitabta ʔilhum.
7. hal ʔintum ḳiraytum haaδa?
8. laa, maa ḳirayna.

1. ʔiḳra haaδa; laa tiḳra haaδaak!
2. ʔarjuuč ʔiḳriilii!
3. ʔiḳruu kull ilmaktuub!

B. *The following sentences have various incompleted action verb forms. Replace the forms in parentheses by the corresponding completed action forms. The first sentence is an example.*

1a. ṣadiiḳii (yiriid) yiruuḥ ʔila maṭ9am θaanii.
1b. ṣadiiḳii raad yiruuḥ ʔila maṭ9am θaanii.

2. ittilmiiδ (yidris) kaθiir.
3. ilḥammaal (yiḥmil) ḥimil 9ala ḍahra.
4. yamta (yidxul) lilbayt?
5. ilʔuutačii (yiḍrub) badiltii ʔuutii.

6. ilbagdaadii (yiškurnii) 9ala jjigaayir.
7. layš (yiftaḥ) ilbaab?
8. ilwalad (yilbas) badla jamiila.
9. il9aamil (yig9ud) mitʔaxxir.
10. kull waaḥid (yaakul) hawaaya.

11. ṣaaḥib-ilbayt (yaaxuδ) diinaarayn lilgurfa.
12. (yinaawušnii) iššakar.
13. δaak ilma9mal (yištugul) fii ma9mal kabiir.
14. iṭṭabiib (yistilim) maktuub.
15. irrijjaal (yidawwir) 9ala siiyaarta.

C. *Replace the incompleted action forms in parentheses with the corresponding completed action forms. The first is an example.*

1a. (ʔariid) ʔašuuf ʔibnak.
1b. ridit ʔašuuf ʔibnak.

2. (raaḥ injiib) issiiyaara.
3. (yiguul) huuwa minn bagdaad.
4. (yinaamuun) mitʔaxxir.
5. (ništugul) fii makaan waaḥid.
6. (yiḥkii) wiiyaay.
7. (šitsawwii)?

8. (ʔaḍinn) ʔinta minn ilbaṣra.
9. maa (yijiiblii) šii lamma (yijii) 9indii.
10. (raaḥ ʔabḳa) 9indak muddat-šahar.
11. (yuugaf) yamm ilbaab.
12. (yaakul) maa9uun-timman wudijaaj.

D. *Select the completed action form called for.*

1.	saʕiid maa (*could*) yitmašša wiiyaay.	gidar, gidraw, gidrat
2.	John (*gave*) lilboy baḳšiiš.	nṭa, nṭayt, nṭaw
3.	fadd rijjaal (*gave me*) halmaktuub.	nṭaanii, nṭaytnii
4.	(*I took*) ilbill, bass maa (*I paid*) lifluus.	ʔaxaδ, ʔixδat, ʔa'xaδit difa9, dif9at, di'fa9it
5.	(*I thought*) kaan 9indak ilmiftaaḥ.	ḍann, ḍannayt, ḍannaw
6.	gaalaw humma (*forgot*) ilmiftaaḥ foog.	nisa, nisat, nisaw
7.	(*He took*) badilta lilʔuutačii, wilʔuutačii (*cleaned it*) wu(*pressed it*) ʔuutii.	ʔaxaδ, ʔixδat, ʔixδaw naḍḍafha, naḍḍafitha ḍirabha, ḍirabitha
8.	maa (*I took*) muusak.	ʔaxaδ, ʔa'xaδit, ʔixδaw
9.	(*We got up*) mitʔaxxir.	gi9ad, gi9dat, gi9adna
10.	ilbaarḥa kunit mariiḍ wumaa (*I could*) ʔaštugul, bass (*I stayed*) bilbayt.	gidar, gi'darit, gidartii buḳa, buḳayt, buḳayna
11.	minn sabab kinna joo9aaniin (*we ate*) kull ilʔakil.	ʔakal, ʔakalna, ʔaklaw
12.	John wuBill (*they bought*) maywa ḥilwa minn issuug.	štira, štirat, štiraw
13.	(*We woke*) sa9iid lamma jiina.	ga99ad, ga9daw, ga99adna
14.	(*I loaned you*) diinaarayn.	daa'yanak, daayantak
15.	(*He asked me*) minayn jiina.	siʔalnii, siʔlatnii

E. *Verbs introduced in this Unit. Give the incompleted action forms called for by the sentence.*

1. ʔagdar (yiḳra) kulšii maktuub bil9arabii.
2. maa 9indii fluus; tigdar (yidfa9lii)?
3. minayn nigdar (yištirii) portaḳaal?
4. yigluun (yibii9) kulšii bδaak iddukkaan.
5. ʔana raaḥ (yistangii) šinuu lʔariida.
6. dirsaw 9arabii wuhassa yigidruun (yiḳra) 9arabii.
7. gullii, šinuu raaḥ (yištirii)?
8. ilʔamriikaan daayman (yidfa9) šinuu laazim.

In the following, select the completed action form called for.

9.	minuu (*paid for*) ilbill?	difa9, di'fa9it, dif9aw
10.	ʔana maa (*bought*) ittiin.	štira, štirat, štirayt
11.	minayn (*you bought*) halmaywa?	štirayt, štiraytii, štiraytum
12.	(*I lent you*) ifluus gabul yoomayn.	daa'yanak, daayantak
13.	(*I read*) ilmaktuub lamma kunna bilbooṣṭa.	ḳira, ḳirat, ḳirayt
14.	(*We paid*) ligiddaam lilgurfa.	dif9aw, difa9na, difa9tum
15.	(*Did they pay*) ilbill?	dif9aw, difa9na, difa9tum
16.	yamta (*you lent me*) iddiinaar?	daayanitlii, daayanitla

WHAT WOULD YOU SAY?

1. *When do we eat?*

a. šwaķit raaḥ ništugul? ١ ـ شوقت راح نشتغل ؟
b. šwaķit raaḥ naakul? ٢ ـ شوقت راح ناكل ؟
c. ʔinta joo9aan? ٣ ـ انت جوعان ؟

2. *Why not now?*

a. ʔana muu joo9aan. ١ ـ انا مو جوعان •
b. maa ʔariid ʔaakul wiiyaak. ٢ ـ ما اريد آكل ويّاك •
c. xallii hassa nruuḥ naakul. ٣ ـ خلّي هسّة نروح ناكل •

3. *Does he know a good place?*

a. ta9ruf wayn ʔakuu maṭ9am zayn? ١ ـ تعرف وين اكو مطعم زين ؟
b. ʔinta ʔa'kalit kulliš kaθiir? ٢ ـ انت اكلت كلّش كثير ؟

4. *You stop at a restaurant.*

a. halmaḥall laṭiif. ١ ـ هذا المحل لطيف •
b. triid nidxul wunaakil hinaa? ٢ ـ تريد ندخل و ناكل هنا ؟
c. tḥibb naakul hinaa? ٣ ـ تحب ناكل هنا ؟

5. *A table for two.*

a. maa nriid naakul; bass nriid nišrab čaay. ١ ـ ما نريد ناكل ، بس نريد نشرب شاي •
b. ʔarjuuk, mayz lišaan nafarayn. ٢ ـ ارجوك ميز لشان نفرين •
c. ʔiḥna kulliš joo9aaniin. ٣ ـ احنا كلّش جوعانين •

6. *The waiter hands you a menu.*

a. haak baķšiiš. ١ ـ هاك بقشيش •
b. haak ilmiftaaḥ. ٢ ـ هاك المفتاح
c. haay ķaaymat-ilʔakil. ٣ ـ هاي قائمة الاكل •

7. *You can't read Arabic.*

a. šakuu 9indak? ١ ـ شكو عندك ؟
b. haay ilķaayma maktuuba bil9arabii, muu bilʔingliizii. ٢ ـ هاي القائمة مكتوبة بالعربي مو بالانكليزي •
c. 9indak ķaaymat-ilʔakil bilʔingliizii? ٣ ـ عندك قائمة الاكل بالانكليزي ؟

8. *You order soup, rice and cheese.*

a. ʔarjuuk jiiblii zaḷaaṭa biduun zayt. ١ ـ ارجوك جيب لي سلاطة بدون زيت •
b. ʔariid šurba wumaa9uun-timman wujibin. ٢ ـ اريد شوربة وماعون تمّن وجبن •
c. ʔaḥibb tiin, maay wujibin. ٣ ـ احب تين وماء وجبن •

9. *Sorry, no more buttermilk.*

a. ʔakuu 9idna laban. ١ ـ اكو عندنا لبن •
b. illaban muu zayn wiiya lʔakil. ٢ ـ اللبن مو زين ويّا الاكل •
c. ma9a lʔasaf, illaban xuḷṣaan. ٣ ـ مع الاسف ، اللبن خلصان •

10. *Some Americans walk in. The waiter enquires.*

a. ti9arfuun haaδool ilʔamriikaan?
b. ti9arfuun haaδool ilʔamriikaan issaakniin fii bagdaad?
c. humma wulid ʔijaw minn ʔamriika likay yištagluun hinaa.

١ ـ تعرفون هذول الامريكان ؟
٢ ـ تعرفون هاذول الامريكان الساكنين في بغداد ؟
٣ ـ همّا ولد اجوا من امريكا لكي يشتغلون هنا .

11. *You ask the waiter for the check.*

a. minuu raaḥ yidfa9 ilbill?
b. boy, ʔarjuuk inṭiinii lbill.
c. ʔinta ʔidfa9 ilbill, wuʔana ʔanṭiik ilifluus ba9ad baačir.

١ ـ منو راح يدفع البل ؟
٢ ـ بوي ، ارجوك انطيني البل .
٣ ـ انت ادفع البل وانا أنطيك الفلوس بعد باكر .

12. *Your friend wants to borrow some money and you tell him that he hasn't paid back the money he borrowed before.*

a. šgad ifluus triid lišaan taaxuδ gurfa ʔila yoom ilʔaḥad?
b. ʔarjuuk daayinnii dinaarayn wuʔana ʔadfa9 ilbill.
c. maa difa9itlii ddiinaarayn ʔillii tdaayanitha minnii yoom ilʔaḥad.

١ ـ شقد فلوس تريد لشان تاخذ غرفة ليوم الاحد ؟
٢ ـ ارجوك داينّي دينارين وانا ادفع البل .
٣ ـ ما دفعت لي الدينارين اللي داينتها مني يوم الاحد .

13. *You'll get it tomorrow or the day after.*

a. laa txaaf, raaḥ ʔadfa9lak baačir ʔaw ba9ad baačir.
b. xalliinii ʔadfa9 liθinaynna.
c. layš maa truuḥ lilbaṣra ba9ad baačir?

١ ـ لا تخاف ، راح ادفع لك باكر او بعد باكر .
٢ ـ خلّيني ادفع لثنينا .
٣ ـ ليش ما تروح للبصرة بعد باكر ؟

14. *Still hungry, you want to buy some fruit.*

a. ba9adnii joo9aan; laazim ništirii maywa.
b. ʔaḍinn ilmaywa zayna ba9ad ilʔakil.
c. laazim ništirii maywa ḥilwa ʔila ṣadiiḳii.

١ ـ بعدني جوعان ، لازم نشتري ميوة .
٢ ـ اظن الميوة زينة بعد الاكل .
٣ ـ لازم نشتري ميوة حلوة الى صديقي .

15. *One of the oranges isn't good.*

a. haay ilportaḳaala ḥaamḍa.
b. nṭiinii gayr portaḳaala; haay duuniiya.
c. ilportaḳaal wiltiffaaḥ minn ʔaḥsan ilmaywa.

١ ـ هاي البرتقالة حامضة .
٢ ـ انطيني غير برتقالة ، هاي دونية .
٣ ـ البرتقال والتفاح من احسن الميوة .

LISTENING IN

John and Bill are walking.

Continuing RECORD 18A

JOHN šwaḳit raaḥ naakul?
BILL layš? ʔinta joo9aan?

جان ـ شوقت راح ناكل ؟
بل ـ ليش ؟ انت جوعان ؟

JOHN na9am; ṣaar mudda minn ʔakalna.	جان ـ نعم ، صار مدّة من اكلنا •
halmaḥall yibayyin ḷaṭiif.	بل ـ ها المحل يبيّن لطيف •
xallii nidxul bii.	خلّي ندخل بيه •
WAITER ʔahlan wusahlan!	البوي ـ اهلا وسهلا !
JOHN xallii nšuuf ḳaaymat-ilʔakil.	جان ـ خلّي نشوف قائمة الاكل •
BILL maa tigdar tiḳraaha maktuuba bil9arabii.	بل ـ ما تقدر تقراها مكتوبة بالعربي •
WAITER šitḥibbuun taakluun?	البوي ـ شتحبون تاكلون ؟
JOHN jiiblii šoorba, maa9uun-timman, kabaab, zaḷaaṭa biduun zayt, wujibin.	جان ـ جيب لي شوربة ، ماعون تمّن ، كباب ، زلاطة بدون زيت وجبن •
WAITER šitḥibb tišrab?	البوي ـ شتحب تشرب ؟
JOHN šakuu 9idkum?	جان ـ شكو عندكم ؟
WAITER 9idna ḥaliib, čaay, gahwa, biira, šaraab wu9arag.	البوي ـ عندنا حليب، شاي، قهوة، بيرا، شراب وعرق •
JOHN 9idkum libin?	جان ـ عندكم لبن ؟
WAITER ma9a lʔasaf, illibin xuḷṣaan.	البوي ـ مع الاسف ، اللبن خلصان •
JOHN zayn jiiblii glaaṣ-ḥaliib.	جان ـ زين جيب لي كلاص حليب •
BILL ʔariid baaδinjaan muglii, timman maṭbuux wiiya dijaaj, wugahwa ʔamriikaaniiya.	بل ـ اريد باذنجان مقلي ، تمّن مطبوخ ويّا دجاج وقهوة امريكانية •

(*The waiter brings their orders.*)

BILL halgahwa muu ḥilwa kaafii; ʔarjuuk naawušnii ššakar.	بل ـ هل قهوة مو حلوة كافي، ارجوك ناوشني الشكر •
JOHN haak iššakar.	جان ـ هاك الشكر •
boy, šakuu maywa 9idkum?	«بوي» شكو ميوة عندكم ؟
WAITER 9idna 9anab, raggii wutiin.	البوي ـ عندنا عنب ، رقّي وتين •
JOHN jiibilna tiin.	جان ـ جيب لنا تين •
BILL laa, maa ʔariid tiin; jiiblii 9anab.	بل ـ لا ، ما اريد تين ، جيب لي عنب •
JOHN layš maa taakul tiin? kint ʔaftikir ʔinta tḥibb ittiin kaθiir.	جان ـ ليش ما تاكل تين ؟ كنت افتكر انت تحب التين كثير •
BILL ṣaḥiiḥ bass haṣṣubuḥ ʔaʹkalit tiina duuniiya; kaanat ḥaamḍa.	بل ـ صحيح بس هالصبح اكلت تينة دونية، كانت حامضه•
maa ʔaḍinn ʔagdar ʔaakul ba9ad.	ما اظن اقدر آكل بعد •
JOHN ʔana kulliš šib9aan.	جان ـ انا كلّش شبعان •
maa ʔaḍinn ʔaʹkalit ʔaḥsan minn halʔakil.	ما اظن اكلت احسن من ها الاكل •
BILL boy, nṭiinii lbill.	بل ـ «بوي» ، انطيني البل •
JOHN ʔinta raaḥ tidfa9 liθinaynna?	جان ـ انت راح تدفع لتنيننا ؟
BILL balii, ʔiδa triid itdaayinnii diinaarayn.	بل ـ بلي ، اذا تريد تداينني دينارين •
JOHN bass ʔinta maa difa9itlii ddiinaar ʔillii tdaayanta minnii yoom ilʔaḥad.	جان ـ بس انت ما دفعتلي الدينار اللّي تدينته منّي يوم الاحد •
BILL laa txaaf, raaḥ ʔadfa9lak baačir ʔaw ba9ad baačir lamma tijii fluusii.	بل ـ لا تخاف ، راح ادفع لك باكر او بعد باكر لمّا تجي فلوسي •
JOHN ṭayyib, haak lifluus.	جان ـ طيّب ، هاك الفلوس •
WAITER xalliina nšuufkum daayman!	البوي ـ خلّينا نشوفكم دائما !

(*A half hour later.*)

BILL ba9adnii joo9aan; maa ʔaʼkalit kaafii.	بل – بعد ني جوعان ، ما اكلت كافي •
JOHN nigdar ništirii maywa minn haddukkaan ʔiδa triid.	جان – نقدر نشتري ميوة من ها الدكّان اذا تريد •
BILL (*To clerk*) šloon itbii9 hattiffaaḥ?	بل – شلون تبيع ها التفاح ؟
CLERK ʔarba9iin-fils ilwaaḥda.	بيّاع – اربعين فلس الواحدة •
BILL nṭiinii θinayn.	بل – انطيني ثنين •

Remaining Conversation not recorded.

CLERK stangii litriidha.	بيّاع – ستنقي التريدها •
JOHN šloon halportaḳaal?	جان – شلون هالبرتقال ؟
CLERK kulliš ḥiluu.	بيّاع – كلش حلو •
JOHN bayš ilwiḥda?	جان – بيش الوحدة ؟
CLERK 9ašir-fluus.	بيّاع – عشر فلوس •
JOHN zayn inṭiinii nuṣṣ-dirzan.	جان – زين انطيني نصن درزن •

(*The clerk gives him the oranges.*)

nṭiinii gayr portaḳaala; haay duuniiya.	انطيني غير برتقالة ، هاي دونية •

VOCABULARY

baaδinjaan	eggplant
ba9ad	yet; still
ba9adnii joo9aan.	I'm still hungry.
ba9adna maa sifnaaha.	We haven't seen her yet.
ba9ad baačir	the day after tomorrow
biduun	without
biduun zayt	without oil
biduunii	without me
yidaayin (daayan)	he lends
daayin	lend!
daayinnii	lend me!
yidfa9 (difa9)	he pays
ʔadfa9	I pay
tidfa9	you pay (m)
tidfa9lii	you pay to me
di'fa9it	you paid (m); I paid
difa9itlii	you paid to me
dijaaj	chicken
dijaaja (f)	a chicken
dirzan	dozen
fluus	fils (pl); money
9ašir-ifluus	ten fils
halifluus	this money
ġayr	different, other
ḥaamuḍ; ḥaamḍa (f)	sour
ḥiluu, ḥilwa	sweet; pretty
jibin	cheese
yijiib (jaab)	he brings
jiibilna *or* jiibinna	bring (to) us!
joo9aan, –a (f), –iin (pl)	hungry
kabaab	cutlet
ḳaayma (f)	list
ḳaaymat-ilʔakil	menu
yiḳra (ḳira)	he reads
tiḳra	you read (m)
tiḳraaha	you read her
tiḳ'raa	you read him
laban *or* liban	buttermilk (cultured)
laban xafiif	thinned buttermilk
liθinaynna	for both of us
ḷaṭiif, –a	pleasant, nice
maa9uun (mawaa9iin)	dish (pl)
maa9uun-timman	dish of rice
muglii, mugliiya (f)	fried
maḥall (maḥallaat)	place; establishment (pl)
maṭbuux, –a	cooked
maywa *or* miiwa	fruit
minn	from, since
mudda (f)	period of time, extent of time
muddat-yoom	a day's time, a whole day
muddat-ʔisbuu9	a week's time, a whole week
limuddat-šahar	for a month
nuṣuf *or* nuṣṣ	half
nuṣṣ-irraggiiya	a half of the watermelon
portaḳaal	oranges
portaḳaala (f)	an orange
raggii	watermelon
raggiiya (f)	a watermelon
yistangii (stanga)	he picks out, he selects
stangii	pick out!, select!
ṣaḥiiḥ, –a	true
yiṣiir (ṣaar)	he becomes; it happens
šib9aan, –a (f), –iin (pl)	satisfied, full (from eating)
šakar	sugar
šaraab	wine
šoorba (f)	soup
yištirii (štira)	he buys
šwaḳit	at what time?
tamur	dates
tamra (f)	a date

tiffaaḥ	apples
tiffaaḥa (f)	an apple
tiin	figs
tiina (f)	a fig
waaḥid	one
ilwaaḥid (m), ilwiḥda (f)	for one, apiece
xulṣaan, –a	finished, all gone
yoom il?aḥad	Sunday
zaḷaaṭa	salad
zayn	well; then, in that case
zayt	olive oil

?akal *or* ?ikal (yaakul)	he ate (he eats)
?a'kalit	you ate; I ate
?arba9iin	forty
?illii *or* ?i'laδii	who, whom, what, which (relative pronoun)
9anab	grapes
9arag	arak (alcoholic beverage)
θinayn	two; both
θinaynna	both of us

UNIT 10

Seeing the Sights

BASIC SENTENCES

Beginning RECORD 18B

ENGLISH EQUIVALENTS	AIDS TO LISTENING	ARABIC SPELLING
Bill	*Bill*	بل
we look around	nitfarraj 9ala	نتفرّج على
Today let's go look around Baghdad.	xallii lyoom inruuḥ nitfarraj 9ala bagdaad.	خلّي اليوم نروح نتفرّج على بغداد.
John	*John*	جــان
I'd like (us) to take Said with us.	ʔaḥibb naaxuδ sa9iid wiiyaana.	احب ناخذ سعيد ويّانا .
Bill	*Bill*	بل
office	daayra	دائرة
Perhaps he's at the office.	yimkin huuwa biddaayra.	يمكن هو بالدائرة .
talk *or* call!	kallim	كلّم
call him!	kallima *or* kalma *	كلّمه
Call him on the phone.	kallima bittalafoon.	كلّمه بالتلفون .
John	*John*	جان
That isn't necessary.	haaδa muu laazim.	هذا مو لازم .
his office	daaʔirta *or* daayirta *	دائرته
His office is near here.	daaʔirta ḳariiba minn hinaa.	دائرته قريبة من هنا .
Bill	*Bill*	بل
perfect *or* exactly	tamaam	تمام
That's right.	tamaam.	تمام .
I remember	ʔatδakkar	اتذكّر
street	šaari9	شارع
Rashid Street.	šaari9-irrašiid.	شارع الرشيد
I remember, on Rashid Street.	ʔatδakkar, fii šaari9-irrašiid.	اتذكّر، في شارع الرشيد .

* Not on record.

ENGLISH EQUIVALENTS	AIDS TO LISTENING	ARABIC SPELLING
(*At Said's office.*)		
John	*John*	جان
Do you want to come with us to look around town?	triid tijii wiiyaana nitfarraj 9albalad?	تريد تجي ويّانا نتفرّج على البلد ؟
Said	*Said*	سعيد
What do you want to see?	šinuu triiduun itšuufuun?	شنو تريدون تشوفون ؟
John	*John*	جان
The whole city, if we can.	kull ilbalad, ?iδa nigdar.	كل البلد ، اذا نقدر •
Said	*Said*	سعيد
empty *or* free	faaruģ *	فارغ
I'm free today.	?ana faaruģ ilyoom.	انا فارغ اليوم •
Bill	*Bill*	بل
parks	ḥadaayiķ	حدائق
First let's go to the parks.	bil?awwal xallii nruuḥ lilḥadaayiķ.	بالاوّل خلّي نروح للحدائق •
we saw them	šifnaahum	شفناهم
We haven't seen them yet.	ba9adna maa šifnaahum.	بعدنا ما شفناهم •
Said	*Said*	سعيد
side (of the river) *or* bank	ṣoob	صوب
that side *or* the other side	δaak iṣṣoob	ذاك الصوب
They're on the other side (of the river).	humma bδaak iṣṣoob.	هما بذاك الصوب •
Bill	*Bill*	بل
to there	lihinaak	لهناك
How do we get there?	šloon inruuḥ lihinaak?	شلون نروح لهناك ؟
Said	*Said*	سعيد
bus	baaṣṣ	باص
rowboat	balam	بلم
We can go by bus or by boat.	nigdar inruuḥ bilbaaṣṣ ?aw bilbalam.	نقدر نروح بالباص او بالبلم •
remaining *or* remainder	baagii *or* baaķii †	باقي
road *or* way	ṭariiķ	طريق
the rest of the way	baagii-ṭṭariiķ	باقي الطريق
If we take the rowboat, we'll have to walk the rest of the way.	?iδa naaxuδ ilbalam, laazim nimšii baaķii-ṭṭariiķ.	اذا ناخذ البلم ، لازم نمشي باقي الطريق •

* Record has maakuu. † Not on record.

ENGLISH EQUIVALENTS	AIDS TO LISTENING	ARABIC SPELLING
(*They walk to the river, hire a boat, and start across.*)		
Bill	*Bill*	بل
bridge	jisir	جسر
river	nahar	نهر
[the] Dijla River (Tigris)	nahar-dijla	نهر دجلة
How many bridges are there over the Dijla River?	kam jisir ʔakuu 9ala nahar-dijla?	كم جسر اكو على نهر دجلة ؟

Beginning RECORD 19A

Said	*Said*	سعيد
bridges	jisuur	جسور
Four bridges.	ʔarba9-jisuur.	اربع جسور .
Bill	*Bill*	بل
their age	9umurhum	عمرهم
How old are they?	šgad 9umurhum?	شقد عمرهم ؟
Said	*Said*	سعيد
it hasn't been long since	maa ṣaar kaθiir minn	ما صار كثير من
they built	binaw	بنوا
they built them	binoohum	بنوهم
It hasn't been long since they built them.	maa ṣaar kaθiir minn binoohum.	ما صار كثير من بنوهم .
the government	ilḥukuuma	الحكومة
she built	binat	بنت
before *or* ago	gabul	قبل
years	siniin	سنين
seven years ago	gabul sabi9-siniin	قبل سبع سنين
The government built two of them seven years ago.	ilḥukuuma binat θinayn minhum gabul sabi9-siniin.	الحكومة بنت ثنين منهم قبل سبع سنين .
Bill	*Bill*	بل
I heard about	si'ma9it 9ann	سمعت عن
I've heard a lot about the Maude Bridge.	si'ma9it kaθiir 9ann jisir-mood.	سمعت كثير عن جسر مود .
Said	*Said*	سعيد
old (of things)	9atiig	عتيق
built of	mibnii minn	مبني من
wood	xišab *or* xašab*	خشب
It was an old bridge built of wood.	kaan jisir 9atiig mibnii minn xišab.	كان جسر عتيق مبني من خشب .

* Not on record.

ENGLISH EQUIVALENTS	AIDS TO LISTENING	ARABIC SPELLING
on our right	9ala yamiinna	على يميننا
new	jadiid	جديد
before they built	gabul maa binaw	قبل ما بنوا
It used to be on our right before they built the new one.	kaan 9ala yamiinna gabul maa binaw hajjisir ijjadiid.	كان على يميننا قبل ما بنوا هذا الجسر الجديد •
they tore down	falšaw	فلّشوا
they tore him down	fal'šoo	فلّشوه
But they didn't tear it down.	laakin maa fal'šoo.	لكن ما فلّشوه •
they moved	ḥawlaw	حوّلوا
they moved him	ḥaw'loo	حوّلوه
They moved it to another place, (about) near the Karada.*	ḥaw'loo ?ila makaan θaanii, taḳriiban yamm ilkaraada.	حوّلوه الى مكان ثاني، تقريبا يم الكرادة •
John	*John*	جان
they named *or* called	sammaw	سمّوا
they named him	sam'moo	سمّوه
Why did they name it [the] Maude Bridge?	layš sam'moo jisir-mood?	ليش سمّوه جسر مود ؟
Said	*Said*	سعيد
he freed	xaḷḷaṣ	خلّص
the Turks	il?atraak	الاتراك
who *or* whom	?ilaδii *or* ?illii	الذي (ايضا) الّي
Because of General Maude; he [who] freed Baghdad from the Turks.	minn sabab General Maude, huuwa laδii xaḷḷaṣ bagdaad minn il?atraak.	من سبب جنرال مود ، هو الـذي خلّص بغداد من الاتراك •
world (noun)	9aalam	عالم
world (adjective)	9aalamii	عالمي
the World War	ilḥarb il9aalamii	الحرب العالمي
I mean	?a9nii	اعني

Beginning RECORD 19B

ENGLISH EQUIVALENTS	AIDS TO LISTENING	ARABIC SPELLING
That was in the World War, I mean the first war.	haaδa kaan filḥarb il9aalamii, ?a9nii lḥarb il?awwal.	هذا كان في الحرب العالمي، اعني الحرب الاوّل •
island (in river)	jazra	جزرة
standing *or* stopped	waaguf	واقف
Do you see the island where the boat is?	tšuufuun ijjazra ?illii lbalam waaguf yamha?	تشوفون الجزرة الّي البلم واقف يمها ؟
Bill	*Bill*	بل
Are there people on it now?	?akuu hassa naas biiha?	اكو هسّه ناس بيها ؟

* The Karada is a section of Baghdad.

ENGLISH EQUIVALENTS	AIDS TO LISTENING	ARABIC SPELLING
Said	*Said*	سعيد
she will be	tkuun	تكون
full	milyaan *or* malyaan*	مليان
because	liʔann	لأن
swimming pool	masbaḥ	مسبح
coffee shops	gahaawii	قهاوي
It's only full in summer, because there's a swimming pool and coffee shops on it.	bass biṣṣayf itkuun milyaana, liʔann ʔakuu biiha masbaḥ wugahaawii.	بس بالصيف تكون مليانة ، لأن اكو بيها مسبح وقهاوي •
Bill	*Bill*	بل
she pleases me	ti9jibnii	تعجبني
I like Baghdad.	bagdaad ti9jibnii.	بغداد تعجبني •
she pleases you	ti9ijbak	تعجبك
Do you like it, John?	ti9ijbak, John?	تعجبك ، جان ؟
John	*John*	جان
I can't say [right] now.	hassa maa ʔagdar ʔaguul.	هسه ما اقدر اقول •
old *or* ancient	ḳadiim	قديم
so far	ba9ad	بعد
It's an old city, and so far I haven't seen much.	hiiya madiina ḳadiima, wuba9ad maa šifit kaθiir.	هي مدينة قديمة وبعد ما شفت كثير •
some *or* several	kam *or* čam*	كم
I can tell you in a few days.	ʔagdar ʔagullak ba9ad kam yoom.	اقدر اقول لك بعد كم يوم •

PRONUNCIATION

Continuing RECORD 19B

PRACTICE 1

ḳ: This sign stands for a k-sound made as far back in the mouth as possible. Say *kaw-kaw* with your tongue as far back in your mouth as you can. Now — the ḳ is actually made a couple of notches farther back. In making the usual k, the middle part of your tongue touches the roof of your mouth just above it. But in making ḳ, it is the very back part of your tongue which you must raise, with the middle and front held tightly on the bottom of your mouth. Notice the vowel sounds.

ḳibal†	*he accepted*	قبل
ḳuful	*lock*	قفل
ḳalam	*pen, pencil*	قلم

* Not on record.

† Record has the variant gubal.

tiķra	*you read*	تقرأ
buķa*	*he remained*	بقى
ʔaķra	*I read*	اقرأ
ķawii	*strong*	قوي
baķar	**cattle*	بقر
waraķ	*papers*	ورق
il9iraaķ	*Iraq*	العراق
portaķaal	*oranges*	برتقال
ṣadiiķ	*friend*	صديق
ķiima	*price*	قيمة
biķayt	*I remained*	بقيت

PRACTICE 2

Vowel-sounds with ķ are somewhat different from those with k.

kitab	*he wrote*	كتب
ķibal	**he accepted*	قبَل
kutub	**books*	كُتَب
ķuful	**lock*	قفَل
kabiir	*big*	كبير
ķariib	*near*	قريب
kiis	**bag*	كيسى
ķiima	**price*	قيمة
biik	*in you*	بيك
ṭariiķ	*road*	طريق
kaan	*he was*	كان
ṣidķaan	**friends*	صدقان
bikayt	*I wept*	بكيت
biķayt	*I remained*	بقيت

ANALYSIS

1. *Two of* AND *both.*

θinayn minn ʔuxuutii	*two of my brothers*	ثنين من اخوتي
θinayn minhum	*two of them*	ثنين منهم
liθinaynna	*for both of us*	لثنينا
θinaynhum	*both of them*	ثنينهم

From the above you see that θinayn minn means *two of*, while θinayn– with pronoun endings is equivalent to *both of*.

* Record has variant buga.

2. EQUIVALENTS OF ba9ad.

The word ba9ad has several equivalents in English. Several are presented below.

1. *after.*

ba9ad ilḥarb	*after the war*	بعد الحرب
ba9ad iḍḍuhur	*afternoon*	بعد الظهر
raaḥ nibḳa hinaa ba9ad ʔakθar.	*We are going to stay here a while longer.*	راح نبقى هنا بعد اكثر •

2. *more, in addition to.*

maa ʔaftikir ba9ad raaḥ timṭur.	*I don't think it is going to rain any more.*	ما افتكر بعد راح تمطر •
triid ba9ad šii?	*Do you want something more?*	تريد بعد شي ؟

3. *so far, up til now.*

ba9ad maa šifit kaθiir.	*So far, I haven't seen much.*	بعد ما شفت كثير •

4. *still, yet.*

ba9adnii joo9aan.	*I'm still hungry.*	بعدني جوعان •
ba9adnii maa joo9aan.	*I'm not hungry yet.*	بعدني ما جوعان •
ʔakal kaθiir, bass ba9da kaan joo9aan.	*He ate a lot, but he was still hungry.*	اكل كثير بس بعده كان جوعان •
ba9adna maa šifnaahum.	*We haven't seen them yet.*	بعدنا ما شفناهم •

Note that ba9ad is used with the pronoun endings to express *still* and *yet.* With a negative, ba9ad corresponds to *yet;* without a negative, it corresponds to *still.* Note especially that ba9ad takes –nii and not –ii for *me.*

3. PRONOUN ENDINGS WITH VERB FORMS ENDING IN –a.

Compare the following verb forms:

tiḳra	*you read* (m)	تقرا
tiḳraaha	*you read her* (*it*)	تقراها
šifna	*we saw*	شفنا
šifnaahum	*we saw them*	شفناهم
šifna	*we saw*	شفنا
šif'naa	*we saw him*	شفناه

Observe that verb forms ending in –a have –aa– before the pronoun endings. This is true of *all* verb forms ending in –a. You will recall that this is like wiiya *with* and wara *behind*, which behave in the same way, as wiiyaahum, wa'raa. In this text, we mark the form with *him* because it doesn't follow the mechanical stress position.

4. PRONOUN ENDINGS WITH VERB FORM ENDING IN –aw.

The following words were met in this Unit.

binaw	*they built*	بنوا
binoohum	*they built them*	بنوهم

falšaw	*they tore down*	فلّشوا
fal'šoo	*they tore him (it) down*	فلّشوه
ḥawlaw	*they moved*	حوّلوا
ḥaw'loo	*they moved him (it)*	حوّلوه
sammaw	*they named*	سمّوا
sam'moo	*they named him (it)*	سمّوه

From the above you see that the –aw of completed action verb form is replaced by –oo– before the pronoun endings. Again we mark the stress in the form with *him*.

5. Commands, Summary

yišuuf	*he sees*	يشوف
šuuf	*see!* (m)	شوف
šuufii	*see!* (f)	شوفي
šuufuu	*see!* (pl)	شوفوا

The *command* forms of verbs are closely similar to the *incompleted action* forms. The chief difference is that the commands have their own set of agent affixes. These are, absence of affix for a man (šuuf), –ii for a girl (šuufii), and –uu for more than one person (šuufuu). In addition, there are some other modifications to be noted for various verb patterns.

First, the commands of certain verbs have ʔi– or ʔu– at the beginning:

yimšii	*he walks*	يمشي
ʔimšii	*walk!*	امشي
yisʔal	*he asks*	يسائل
ʔisʔal	*ask!*	إسائل
yidxul	*he enters*	يدخل
ʔudxul	*go in!, come in!*	ادخل
yijiib	*he brings*	يجيب
jiib	*bring!*	جيب
yizayyin	*he shaves*	يزيّن
zayyin	*shave!*	زيّن

The habit is this: ʔi– (or ʔu–, if the incompleted action form has u) is found in the command of verbs where the agent affix yi– is followed by two consonants (first three examples). Other verbs do not have ʔi– in the command forms (last two examples).

Second, there are changes in some commands when the agent affixes are added.

I

šuuf	*see!*	شوف
šuufii		شوفي
šuufuu		شوفوا
jiib	*bring!*	جيب
jiibii		جيبي
jiibuu		جيبوا

naam	*sleep; go to bed!*	نام
naamii		نامي
naamuu		ناموا

Verbs of the above pattern, having a double vowel before the last consonant, have no change before the –ii and –uu affixes.

II

yimšii	*he walks*	يمشي
ʔimšii	*walk!*	امشي
ʔimšii		امشي
ʔimšuu		امشوا
yinsa	*he forgets*	ينسى
ʔinsa	*forget!*	انسى
ʔinsii		انسي
ʔinsuu		انسوا
yiraawii	*he shows*	يراوي
raawii	*show!*	راوي
raawii		راوي
raawuu		راووا

If the incompleted action form ends in *a vowel*, the commands follow the above pattern. You will note that the vowel has dropped when –ii and –uu are added.

III

yiktib	*he writes*	يكتب
ʔiktib	*write!*	اكتب
kitbii		كتبي
kitbuu		كتبوا
yisʔal	*he asks*	يسائل
ʔisʔal	*ask!*	اسائل
siʔlii		اسائلي
siʔluu		اسائلوا

If there are three unlike consonants in the incompleted action form, the commands follow the pattern of yiktib and yisʔal. Note that ʔi– has dropped in the forms before –ii and –uu.

IV

yisidd	*he closes*	يسد
sidd	*close!*	سد
siddii		سدي
sidduu		سدوا

yiguṣṣ — he cuts — يقص

guṣṣ — cut! — قص
guṣṣii — قصي
guṣṣuu — قصوا

If there is a double consonant at the end of the incompleted action form, the above pattern is followed by the commands. You will note that both consonants remain.

V

yikallim — *he speaks with; he calls* — يكلم

kallim — *call! speak with!* — كلم
kalmii — كلمي
kalmuu — كلموا

yištugul — *he works* — يشتغل

štugul — *work!* — اشتغل
štuglii — اشتغلي
štugluu — اشتغلوا

If the incompleted action forms are of the pattern of yikallim or yištugul, then the command forms will follow the above. You will note the shortening of the form (by loss of a vowel) before the –ii and –uu endings; of course, full forms will also be heard.

VI Certain verbs have somewhat irregular commands. They are listed at the end of the following summary.

Summary of Commands

Following are the commands of the various verb types. The incompleted action form precedes the command form.

I

yišuuf			*he sees*	يشوف
šuuf	šuufii	šuufuu	*see!*	شوف ـ شوفي ـ شوفوا
yinaam			*he sleeps*	ينام
naam	naamii	naamuu	*go to sleep!*	نام ـ نامي ـ ناموا
yijiib			*he brings*	يجيب
jiib	jiibii	jiibuu	*bring!*	جيب ـ جيبي ـ جيبوا

II

yisidd			*he closes*	يسد
sidd	siddii	sidduu	*close!*	سد ـ سدي ـ سدوا
yiguṣṣ			*he cuts*	يقص
guṣṣ	guṣṣii	guṣṣuu	*cut!*	قص ـ قصي ـ قصوا
yimšii			*he walks*	يمشي
ʔimšii	ʔimšii	ʔimšuu	*walk!*	امشي ـ امشي ـ امشوا

yinṭii			*he gives*	ينطي
ʔinṭii	ʔinṭii	ʔinṭuu	*give!*	انطي - انطي - انطوا
yištirii			*he buys*	يشتري
štirii	štirii	štiruu	*buy!*	اشتري - اشتري - اشتروا
yixallii			*he puts*	يخلّي
xallii	xallii	xalluu	*put!*	خلّي - خلّي - خلّوا
yiraawii			*he shows*	يراوي
raawii	raawii	raawuu	*show!*	راوي - راوي - راووا
yinsa			*he forgets*	ينسى
ʔinsa	ʔinsii	ʔinsuu	*forget!*	انسى - انسي - انسوا
yibḳa			*he stays*	يبقى
ʔibḳa	ʔibḳii	ʔibḳuu	*stay!*	ابقى - ابقي - ابقوا
yitmašša			*he takes a walk*	يتمشّى
ʔitmašša	ʔitmaššii	ʔitmaššuu	*take a walk!*	اتمشّى - اتمشّي - اتمشّوا
IIIa				
yiktib			*he writes*	يكتب
ʔiktib	kitbii	kitbuu	*write!*	اكتب - كتبي - كتبوا
yiškur			*he thanks*	يشكر
ʔiškur	šikrii	šikruu	*thank!*	اشكر - شكري - شكروا
yig9ud			*he sits; he wakes up*	يقعد
ʔig9ud	gi9dii	gi9duu	*sit down!; wake up!*	اقعد - قعدي - قعدوا
yilbas			*he wears*	يلبس
ʔilbas	libsii	libsuu	*put on, wear!*	البس - لبسي - لبسوا
yirja9			*he goes (comes) back*	يرجع
ʔirja9	rij9ii	rij9uu	*return!*	ارجع - رجعي - رجعوا
yisʔal			*he asks*	يسائل
ʔisʔal	siʔlii	siʔluu	*ask!*	اسائل - سئلي - سئلوا
yišrab			*he drinks*	يشرب
ʔišrab	širbii	širbuu	*drink!*	اشرب - شربي - شربوا
IIIb				
yikallim			*he speaks with, calls*	يكلّم
kallim	kalmii	kalmuu	*speak with, call!*	كلّم - كلّمي - كلّموا
yiga99id			*he wakes (someone) up*	يقعّد
ga99id	ga9dii	ga9duu	*wake (someone) up!*	قعّد - قعّدي - قعّدوا

yidawwir 9ala			*he looks for*	يدوّر على
dawwir 9ala	dawrii 9ala	dawruu 9ala	*look for!*	دوّر على ـ دوّري ـ دوّروا
yidaayin			*he lends*	يداين
daayin	daaynii	daaynuu	*lend!*	داين ـ دايني ـ داينوا
yitδakkar			*he remembers*	يتذكّر
ʔitδakkar	ʔitδakrii	ʔitδakruu	*remember!*	اتذكّر ـ اتذكّري ـ اتذكّروا

IV Commands of the following verbs are somewhat *irregular:*

yijii			*he comes*	يجي
ta9aal	ta9aalii	ta9aaluu	*come!*	تعال ـ تعالي ـ تعالوا
yaakul			*he eats*	ياكل
ʔukul	ʔuklii	ʔukluu	*eat!*	اكل ـ اكلي ـ اكلوا
yaaxuδ			*he takes*	ياخذ
ʔuxuδ *or* xuδ	ʔuxδii	ʔuxδuu	*take!*	اخذ ـ خذ ـ اخذي ـ اخذوا
yuugaf *or* yoogaf			*he stops; he stands up*	يوقف
ʔoogaf	ʔoogfii	ʔoogfuu	*stop!* or *stand up!*	اوقف ـ اوقفي ـ اوقفوا

6. Negative Commands.

ʔimšii	*walk!*	امشي
štirii	*buy!*	اشتري
guṣṣ	*cut!*	قص
laa timšii	*don't walk!*	لا تمشي
laa tištirii	*don't buy!*	لا تشتري
laa tguṣṣ	*don't cut!*	لا تقص

Above are commands to 'do-so-and-so'. Beneath them are the corresponding *negative commands* 'don't do so-and-so'. You will note that the negative commands consist of laa plus a *you* incompleted action form. The feminine and plural forms are as follows:

laa timšii (f)	*don't walk!*	لا تمشي
laa tištirii	*don't buy!*	لا تشتري
laa tguṣṣii	*don't cut!*	لا تقصي
laa timšuu (pl)		لا تمشوا
laa tištiruu		لا تشتروا
laa tguṣṣuu		لا تقصوا

Note that they are incompleted action forms, but without the final –n.

Following are a few more typical examples of negative commands. The feminine and plural forms are included only where they present some variation from the masculine.

laa truuḥ	*don't go!*	لا تروح
laa tjiib	*don't bring!*	لا تجيب
laa tnaam	*don't go to sleep!*	لا تنام
laa txaaf	*don't fear!*	لا تخاف

laa tsidd	*don't close!*	لا تسد
laa tinsa	*don't forget!*	لا تنسى
laa tibḳa	*don't stay!*	لا تبقى
laa tsawwii	*don't do; don't make!*	لا تسوّي
laa txallii	*don't put!*	لا تخلّي
laa traawii	*don't show!*	لا تراوي
laa titmašša	*don't take a walk!*	لا تتمشّى
laa tiktib laa tkitbii laa tkitbuu	*don't write!*	لا تكتب لا تكتبي - لا تكتبوا
laa tig9ud laa tigi9dii laa tgi9duu	*don't sit down; don't wake up!*	لا تقعد لا تقعدي - لا تقعدوا
laa tiftaḥ laa tfitḥii laa tfitḥuu	*don't open!*	لا تفتح لا تفتحي - لا تفتحوا
laa tidxul laa tdixlii laa tdixluu	*don't enter!*	لا تدخل لا تدخلي - لا تدخلوا
laa tirja9 laa trij9ii laa trij9uu	*don't return!*	لا ترجع لا ترجعي - لا ترجعوا
laa tijii laa tijii laa tijuu	*don't come!*	لا تجي لا تجي - لا تجوا
laa taakul laa taaklii laa taakluu	*don't eat!*	لا تاكل لا تاكلي - لا تاكلوا
laa taaxuδ laa taaxδii laa taaxδuu	*don't take!*	لا تاخذ لا تاخذي - لا تاخذوا
laa toogaf laa toogfii laa toogfuu	*don't stop; don't stand!*	لا توقف لا توقفي - لا توقفوا

7. yixallii.

Here are several sentences you have met.

xalliihum hinaak!	*Put them there!*	خلّيهم هناك !
wayn xallayt ilmuus?	*Where did you put the razor?*	وين خلّيت الموز ؟
xallii nitmašša!	*Let's take a walk!*	خلّي نتمشّى !
xallii nšuuf ilḳaayma!	*Let us see the list!*	خلّي نشوف القائمة !
xalliiha timṭur!	*Let 'er rain!*	خلّيها تمطر !
xal'lii yidxul!	*Have him come in!*	خلّيه يدخل !
xal'lii yijii 9indii!	*Have him come to me!*	خلّيه يجي عندي !

The verb yixallii, as you know, means *he put, he places.* You see from the above that it also means *he has someone do something*, or *he causes someone to do something.* You see both meanings in the above sentences, where the command xallii *put!*, and *let, cause, have!* is found. You will observe that the pronoun endings do not have to be used with xallii because the other verb form shows who is to do the action: xallii nšuuf is sufficient, but you can say the full form xalliina nšuuf for *Let us see!*

The negative forms are as follows:

xallii maa nsawwii haaδa!	*Let's not do this!*	خلّي ما نسوّي هذا !
xallii hassa maa nruuḥ!	*Let's not go now!*	خلّي هسّه ما نروح !
laa txal'lii yiruuḥ!	*Don't let him go!*	لا تخلّيه يروح !
laa txalliiha tijii!	*Don't let her come!* or *Don't have her come!*	لا تخلّيها تجي !

EXERCISES

A. *Supply* ba9ad *with pronoun endings.*

1. ʔariid ʔaakul ba9ad; (ba9ad) joo9aan.
2. maa yiriiduun yištagluun liʔann (ba9ad) ti9baaniin.
3. ʔiḥna tfarrajna 9ala bagdaad, bass (ba9ad) maa šifna kulha.
4. sa9iid, (ba9ad) laazim tištugul?
5. jamiila, (ba9ad) mariiḍa?
6. ʔaxuuya gaal raaḥ yikallimnii bittalafoon, bass (ba9ad) maa kallamnii.
7. triid ba9ad šii? na9am, (ba9ad) maa ʔa'kalit kaafii.
8. laa tga99idnii minn waḳit; (ba9ad) ni9saan.

B. Pronoun Endings with Forms Ending in –a or –aw. *Select the correct verb forms.*

1. ilmudiir (*gave me*) miftaaḥ-ilgurfa.	nṭa, nṭaanii, nṭaytnii
2. ʔuxtii maa (*gave me*) halifluus.	nṭat, nṭatna, nṭatnii
3. ʔaftikir (*they saw me*) ʔadxul bil9arabaana.	šaafaw, šaafoona, šaafoonii
4. (*He put them*) bisiiyaarta.	xalla, xallaahum, xallaana
5. (*They made them*) minn xašab.	sawwaw, sawwoohum, sawwooha
6. wayn (*did they put her*)?	xallaw, xalloohum, xallooha
7. wayn raaḥat jamiila? laa (*forget her*)!	tinsa, tinsaaha, tin'saa
8. ṣaar kaθiir minn (*they wrote to me*).	kitbaw, kitboolii, kitboolak.
9. halmaktuub maktuub bil9arabii; maa ʔagdar (*I read it*).	ʔaḳra, ʔaḳraaha, ʔaḳ'raa

10. θinaynhum gaalaw (*they saw you*) lamma kaanaw fii šaari9-irrašiid. — šaafaw, šaafook, šaafoonii

11. ʔijaw likay yišuufuun sa9iid, bass maa (*they saw him*). — šaafaw, šaa'foo, šaafoona

C. PRONOUN ENDINGS WITH VERB FORMS. *Replace the noun in parentheses by a pronoun ending added to the preceding verb, with whatever changes are necessary. The first sentence is an example.*

1a. šifna (sa9iid wuḥasan) yitmaššuun ibδaak iṣṣoob.

1b. šifnaahum yitmaššuun ibδaak iṣṣoob.

2. ilboy xalla (jinaṭna) giddaam ilmayz.

3. samma (ʔibna) muṣṭafa.

4. binaw (ʔarba9-jisuur) 9ala nahar-dijla.

5. maa ʔagdar ʔaḳra (halḳaayma).

6. sa9iid nisa (siiyaarta).

7. jaabaw (binthum) wiiyaahum.

8. xallayna (siiyaaraatna) wara lbayt.

9. falšaw (ijjisuur) wubinaw jisuur jadiida.

10. sim9aw (ilbint) tiḥčii wiiya ʔuxutha.

D. COMMANDS. *Select the masculine, feminine, or plural command called for.*

1. sa9iid, (*go bring*) issiiyaara! — ruuḥ jiib, ruuḥii jiibii, ruuḥuu jiibuu.
2. jamiila, (*go to bed*)! — ruuḥ naam, ruuḥii naamii, ruuḥuu naamuu
3. ʔarjuukum (*close*) ilbaab! — sidd, siddii, sidduu
4. boy, (*give me*) lbill! — nṭiinii, nṭiinii, nṭuunii
5. ʔarjuukum (*show us*) lḥadaayiḳ! — raawiina, raawiina, raawuuna
6. ʔarjuuk (*read*) haaδa! — ʔiḳra, ʔiḳrii, ʔiḳruu
7. ʔarjuuč (*come in*)! — ʔidxul, dixlii, dixluu
8. (*Thank*) 9amkum 9alifluus! — ʔuškur, šikrii, šikruu
9. ruuḥ (*put on*) badla θaaniya! — ʔilbas, libsii, libsuu
10. (*Listen*)! ʔakuu rijjaal yimšii waraana. — ʔisma9, sim9ii, sim9uu
11. ʔummii, (*sew*) haaδa! — xayyuṭ, xayṭii, xayṭuu
12. jamiila, (*remember*) laazim trij9iin lilbayt minn waḳit! — ʔitδakkar, ʔitδakrii, ʔitδakruu

E. MORE COMMANDS. *The sentences are spoken to a man. What would you say to a girl? To more than one person? The first sentence is an example.*

1a. ʔarjuuk zuurnii bilbayt!

1b. ʔarjuuč zuuriinii bilbayt!

1c. ʔarjuukum zuuruunii bilbayt!

2. štiriilii waaḥid minhum!

3. ʔigsil ʔiidayk!

4. ʔig9ud hinaa!

5. kallim sa9iid bittalafoon!

6. xaḷḷuṣ haššuġul!

7. ʔukul haaδa!

8. xuδna lilḥadiiḳa!

9. ʔoogaf ibmakaanak!

F. *Incompleted action verbs are given in parentheses. Replace them by the corresponding masculine command.*

1. (yiktib) haaδa biddaftar.

2. (yiguṣṣ) ša9arii.

3. ʔarjuuk (yibii9lii) siiyaartak.

4. (yibḳa) wiiyaay.

5. (yidris) zayn.

6. (yišrab) haaδa.

7. maa ʔa9ruf wayn ilmasbaḥ; (yisʔal) šaxuṣ θaanii.

8. (yizayyin) liḥaytii.

9. (yaakul) halʔakil.

G. NEGATIVE COMMANDS. *Give the feminine and plural forms.*

1. laa tsidd ilbaab!

2. laa tnaam mitʔaxxir!

3. laa tkallim sa9iid bittalafoon!

4. laa tišrab haaδa!

5. laa tištuġul liδaak irrijjaal!

H. *Replace the incompleted action forms in parentheses by negative commands. The first is an example.*

1a. (yiguṣṣ) ša9arii kaθiir. 1b. laa tguṣṣ ša9arii kaθiir!

2. (yisawwii) haaδa.
3. (yijii) mit?axxir ?iδa triid taakul šii.
4. (yixallii) siiyaartak hinaak.
5. (yinsa) laazim tištugul 9indii.
6. (yig9ud) ibδaak ilmakaan.
7. (yiruuḥ) biduun fluusak.
8. (yaaxuδ) issiiyaara.
9. (yaakul) halportaḳaala; ?aḍinn hiiya ḥaamḍa.
10. (yisidd) ilbaab.

I. *Give the feminine and plural forms of the negative commands in sentences 6 to 10 above.*

J. *Select the correct form called for by the sentence. The verbs are chiefly those introduced in the Basic Sentences of this Unit. Both completed and incompleted action forms are found and some have pronoun endings.*

1. sa9iid, ilbaarḥa gilitlii ?inta raaḥ (yikallimnii, itkallimnii, itkalmuunii).
2. na9am, ridit (yikalmak, ?akalmak, nkalmak), bass maa gi'darit.
3. hal ?intum (sima9, si'ma9it, sima9tum) 9ann jisir-mood?
4. laa, ba9adna maa (sima9, sima9tii, sima9na) 9anna.
5. ḥasan, (ya9nii, ta9nii, ?a9nii) štguul?
6. gilit raaḥ ?aruuḥ, bass maa kunit (ya9'nii, ta9'nii, ?a9'nii).
7. yigluun raaḥ (yifalliš, yifalšuun, itfalšuun) ijjisir il9atiig ?illii mabnii minn xašab.
8. na9am, sima9na ?ilḥukuuma raaḥ (yibnii, tibnii, ?abnii) jisir jadiid fii makaan-ijjisir il9atiig.
9. hassa ?inta zirit bagdaad wilbaṣra; ?ay wiḥda ?inta (ḥabb, ḥabbayt, ḥabbaytii) ?akθar?
10. ?ana (ḥabb, ḥabbayt, ḥabbayna) ilbaṣra ?akθar minn bagdaad, bass bagdaad (yi9jibnii, ti9jibnii) kaθiir.

WHAT WOULD YOU SAY?

1. *You want to see the city.*
   - *a.* layš maa tijii wiiyaay? — ١ ـ ليش ما تجي ويّاي ؟
   - *b.* ilyoom xooš yoom; laazim inruuḥ nitmašša. — ٢ ـ اليوم خوش يوم ، لازم نروح نتمشى •
   - *c.* xallii lyoom inruuḥ nitfarraj 9ala bagdaad. — ٣ ـ خلّي اليوم نروح نتفرّج على بغداد •

2. *Let's take Said — but where is he?*
   - *a.* wayn huuwa? — ١ ـ وين هو ؟
   - *b.* tiftikir huuwa raaḥ yijii? — ٢ ـ تفتكر هو راح يجي ؟
   - *c.* maa ʔaḍinn huuwa mawjuud hinaa. — ٣ ـ ما اظن هو موجود هنا •

3. *At his office.*
   - *a.* ʔaḍinn nuujda bidaayirta. — ١ ـ اظن نوجده بدائرته •
   - *b.* minuu gaallak huuwa hinaak? — ٢ ـ منو قال لك هو هناك ؟
   - *c.* yimkin maa yikuun biddaayra. — ٣ ـ يمكن ما يكون بالدائرة •

4. *Later you ask Said if he would like to come along.*
   - *a.* xallii naaxuδ sa9iid wiiyaana. — ١ ـ خلّي ناخذ سعيد ويّانا •
   - *b.* tḥibb tijii wiiyaana nitfarraj fii bagdaad? — ٢ ـ تحب تجي ويّانا نتفرّج في بغداد ؟
   - *c.* ilyoom xooš yoom; nigdar inšuuf kulšii. — ٣ ـ اليوم خوش يوم ، نقدر نشوف كل شي •

5. *He asks where you are going.*
   - *a.* šraaḥ taakluun? — ١ ـ شراح تاكلون ؟
   - *b.* šitguuluun? — ٢ ـ شتقولون ؟
   - *c.* šitriiduun itšuufuun? — ٣ ـ شتريدون تشوفون ؟

6. *To see everything.*
   - *a.* kull ilbalda, ʔiδa nigdar. — ١ ـ كل البلدة اذا نقدر •
   - *b.* maa ʔaḍinn nigdar inšuuf šaari9-irrašiid. — ٢ ـ ما اظن نقدر نشوف شارع الرشيد •
   - *c.* ʔaḥibb ʔaraawiikum kulšii. — ٣ ـ احب راويكم كل شي •

7. *Said isn't too busy.*
   - *a.* laazim ʔarja9 liddaayra minn wakit. — ١ ـ لازم اروح للدائرة من وقت •
   - *b.* maa ʔagdar ʔajii wiiyaakum minn sabab ʔana mariiḍ. — ٢ ـ ما اقدر اجي ويّاكم من سبب انا مريظ •
   - *c.* ʔana faarug ilyoom; ʔagdar ʔajii wiiyaakum. — ٣ ـ انا فارغ اليوم ، اقدر اجي ويّاكم •

8. *There are two ways to get to the park.*
   - *a.* ilḥadaayiḳ ibδaak iṣṣoob. — ١ ـ الحدائق بي ذاك الصوب •
   - *b.* nigdar nimšii hinaak. — ٢ ـ نقدر نمشي هناك •
   - *c.* nigdar inruuḥ bilbaaṣṣ ʔaw bilbalam. — ٣ ـ نقدر نروح بالباص او بالبلم •

9. *Going by boat has a drawback.*

a. haaδa ṭṭariiḳ muu zayn lilmašii.
b. tiftikir nigdar naaxuδ ilbalam lilḥadiiḳa?
c. ʔiδa naaxuδ ilbalam, laazim nimšii baaḳii ṭṭariiḳ.

١ ـ هذا الطريق مو زين للمشي •
٢ ـ تفتكر نقدر ناخذ البلم للحديقة ؟
٣ ـ اذا ناخذ البلم لازم نمشي باقي الطريق •

10. *You wonder how many bridges there are over the river.*

a. nahar-dijla kabiir ʔaw ṣagiir?
b. wayn tiftikir nahar-dijla — huuwa bil9iraaḳ ʔaw bamriika?
c. kam jisir ʔakuu 9ala nahar-dijla?

١ ـ نهر الدجلة كبير او صغير ؟
٢ ـ وين تفتكر نهر دجلة هو، بالعراق او بامريكا ؟
٣ ـ كم جسر اكو على نهر دجلة ؟

11. *Four; two are recent.*

a. ʔarba9-jisuur; ʔilḥukuuma binat θinayn minhum gabul sabi9-siniin.
b. xamsa, bass kulhum 9ala gayr nahar.
c. maa ʔaḍinn ʔakuu jisuur 9ala nahar-dijla.

١ ـ اربع جسور ، الحكومة بنت اثنين منهم قبل سبع سنين •
٢ ـ خمسة ، بس كلهم على غير نهر •
٣ ـ ما اظن اكو جسور على نهر دجلة •

12. *You've heard about the Maude Bridge.*

a. yigluun jisir-mood filbaṣra; haaδa saḥiiḥ?
b. sima9na kaθiir 9ann jisir-mood; wayn huuwa?
c. sima9na bagdaad balda 9ala nahar-dijla.

١ ـ يقولون جسر مود في البصرة ، هذا صحيح ؟
٢ ـ سمعنا كثير عن جسر مود ، وين هو ؟
٣ ـ سمعنا بغداد بلدة على نهر دجلة •

13. *He points it out.*

a. hajjisir kulliš jadiid.
b. jisir-mood huuwa jjisir ijjadiid ʔillii 9ala yamiinna.
c. maa ʔašuuf jisir-mood.

١ ـ هذا الجسر كلّش جديد •
٢ ـ جسر مود هو الجسر الجديد اللي على يميننا •
٣ ـ ما اشوف جسر مود •

14. *There was an old bridge on the same site.*

a. tiftikir haaδa jisir jamiil?
b. laazim nimšii fooga.
c. kaan ʔakuu waaḥid 9atiig mabnii minn xašab.

١ ـ تفتكر هذا جسر جميل ؟
٢ ـ لازم نمشي فوقه •
٣ ـ كان اكو واحد عتيق مبني من خشب •

15. *What became of the old one?*

a. hal fal'šoo lamma binaw hajjisir?
b. hal ḥaw'loo ʔila makaan θaanii?
c. hal xal'loo hinaa lišaan issayyaaraat?

١ ـ هل فلّشوه لما بنوا ها الجسر ؟
٢ ـ هل حوّلوه الى مكان ثاني ؟
٣ ـ هل خلّوا هنا لشان السيّارات ؟

16. *And where did it get its name?*

a. layš sam'moo jisir-mood?
b. ʔakuu gayr jisir-mood bil9iraaḳ?
c. layš bi'noo?

١ ـ ليش سمّوه جسر مود ؟
٢ ـ اكو غير جسر مود بالعراق ؟
٣ ـ ليش بنوه ؟

17. *It was named after a general.*

a. minn sabab General Maude ḥabb bagdaad hawaaya. — ١ ـ من سبب جنرال مود حب بغداد هوايه •

b. minn sabab General Maude xaḷḷaṣ bagdaad minn ilʔatraak. — ٢ ـ من سبب جنرال مود خلّص بغداد من الاتراك •

c. minn sabab General Maude sikan fii bagdaad. — ٣ ـ من سبب جنرال مود سكن في بغداد •

18. *That was during the first World War.*

a. haaδa kaan fii lḥarb iθθaaniya. — ١ ـ هذا كان في الحرب الثانية •

b. haaδa kaan filḥarb il9aalamiiya. — ٢ ـ هذا كان في الحرب العالمية •

c. haaδa kaan lamma bagdaad kaanat balda ṣagiira. — ٣ ـ هذا كان لما بغداد كانت بلدة صغيرة •

19. *You see an island. It is popular as a summer resort.*

a. biššita ijjazra tkuun faarga liʔann maakuu biiha naas. — ١ ـ بالشتاء الجزيرة تكون فارغة لان ماكو بيها ناس •

b. bass biṣṣayf itkuun malyaana liʔann ʔakuu biiha masaabiḥ wugahaawii. — ٢ ـ بس بالصيف اتكون مليانة لان اكو بيها مسابح وقهاوي •

c. kull ilgahaawii biiha yi9jibuunii. — ٣ ـ كل القهاوي بيها يعجبوني •

20. *You are undecided about Baghdad.*

a. maa ʔaḍinn ti9jibnii. — ١ ـ ما اظن تعجبني •

b. hiiya balda ḳadiima wuba9ad maa šifit kaθiir minha. — ٢ ـ هي بلدة قديمة وبعد ما شفت كثير منها •

c. ʔagdar ʔagullak ba9ad kam yoom. — ٣ ـ اقدر اقول لك بعد كم يوم •

LISTENING IN

John and Bill plan to see more of Baghdad.

Concluding RECORD 19B

BILL John, xallii lyoom inruuḥ nitfarraj 9ala bagdaad. — بل ـ جان ، خلّي اليوم نروح نتفرّج على بغداد •

JOHN 9aal. triid naaxuδ sa9iid wiiyaana? — جان ـ عال ، تريد ناخذ سعيد ويّانا ؟

BILL zayn. wayn hassa huuwa? — بل ـ زين ، وين هو هسّه ؟

JOHN yumkin biddaayra. — جان ـ يمكن بالدائرة •

BILL kallima bittalafoon. — بل ـ كلّمه بالتلفون •

JOHN muu laazim; daayirta ḳariiba minn hinaa. — جان ـ مو لازم ، دائرته قريبة من هنا •

BILL tamaam, ʔatδakkar fii šaari9-irrašiid. — بل ـ تمام ، افتكّر في شارع الرشيد •

Beginning RECORD 20A

(*At Said's Office.*)	
JOHN sa9iid, triid tijii wiiyaana nitfarraj fii bagdaad?	جان ـ سعيد ، تريد تجي ويـّانا نتفرّج في بغداد ؟
SAID šinuu triiduun itšuufuun?	سعيد ـ شنو تريدون تشوفون ؟
JOHN kull ilbalad ʔiδa nigdar. baʔadna maa šifna kaθiir.	جان ـ كل البلدة اذا قدر • بعدنا ما شفنا كثير •
SAID na9am, ʔana faarug ilyoom. ʔagdar hassa ʔajii wiiyaakum.	سعيد ـ نعم ، انا فارغ اليوم ، اقدر هسـّه اجي ويـّاكم •
BILL bilʔawwal xallii nruuḥ lilḥadaayik. ba9adna maa šifnaahum.	بل ـ بالاوّل خلـّي نروح للحدائق ! بعدنا ما شفناهم •
JOHN nigdar nimšii lihinaak?	جان ـ تقدر نمشي لهناك ؟
SAID laa, humma bδaak iṣṣoob. nigdar nruuḥ bilbaaṣṣ ʔaw bilbalam. ʔay waaḥid triiduun?	سعيد ـ لا ، همـّا بذاك الصوب • نقدر نروح بالباص او بالبلم • اي واحد تريدون ؟
JOHN bilbalam.	جان ـ بالبلم •
SAID ʔiδa naaxuδ ilbalam, laazim nimšii baak̇ii ṭṭariik̇.	سعيد ـ اذا ناخذ البلم ، لازم نمشي باقي الطريق •
JOHN maa yixaalif.	جان ـ ما يخالف •
(*They walk to the river and hire a boat.*)	
BILL kam jisir ʔakuu 9ala nahar-dijla?	بل ـ كم جسر اكو على نهر دجلة ؟
SAID ʔarba9-jisuur.	سعيد ـ اربع جسور •
BILL šgad 9umurhum?	بل ـ شقد عمرهم ؟
SAID maa ṣaar hawaaya minn ḃinoohum. ilḥukuuma binat θinayn minhum gabul sabi9-siniin.	سعيد ـ ما صار هواية من بنوهم • الحكومة بنت ثنين منهم قبل سبع سنين •
BILL si'ma9it kaθiir 9ann jisir-mood; wayn huuwa?	بل ـ سمعت كثير عن جسر مود ، وين هو ؟
SAID ijjisir ilaδii 9ala yamiinna.	سعيد ـ الجسر الذي على يميننا •
JOHN haaδa jjisir kulliš jadiid. kaan ʔakuu jisir gabul maa binaw haaδa?	جان ـ هذا الجسر كلـّش جديد • كان اكو جسر قبل ما بنوا هذا ؟
SAID na9am, kaan ʔakuu waaḥid 9atiig mibnii minn xišab.	سعيد ـ نعم ، كان اكو واحد عتيق مبني من خشب •
BILL hal fal'šoo lamma binaw hajjisir?	بل ـ هل فلـّشوه لما بنوا ها الجسر ؟
SAID laa, ḥaw'loo ʔila makaan θaanii.*	سعيد ـ لا ، حوّلوه الى مكان ثاني •
JOHN layš sam'moo jisir-mood?	جان ـ ليش سمـّوه جسر مود ؟
SAID minn sabab General Maude, ʔillii xaḷḷaṣ bagdaad minn ʔatraak.	سعيد ـ من سبب جنرال مود اللي خلـّص بغداد من الاتراك •
JOHN yamta?	جان ـ يمتى ؟
SAID haaδa kaan fii lḥarb il9aalamii, ʔa9nii ʔilḥarb ilʔawwal. tšuufuun ijjazra ʔilaδii lbalam waaguf yamha?	سعيد ـ هـذا كان في الحرب العـالمي ، اعني الحرب الاوّل • تشوفون الجزرة الذي البلم واقف يمها ؟

* The record has makaan taanii. θ has become *t* after a preceding *n*.

BILL na9am.

SAID hajjazra kulliš jamiila; bişşayf kunna daayman inruuḥ lihinaak.

BILL ?akuu hassa naas biiha?

SAID laa, bass bişşayf itkuun milyaana li?ann ?akuu biiha masbaḥ wugahaawii.

BILL ?aḍinn bagdaad ti9jibnii.
John, štiftikir biiha?

JOHN hassa maa ?agdar ?aguul. hiiya madiina ķadiima wuba9ad maa šifit kaθiir.
?agdar ?agullak ba9ad kam yoom.

بل ـ نعم •

سعيد ـ هاي الجزيرة كلّش جميلة • بالصيف كنّا دائما
نروح لهناك •

بل ـ اكو هسّه نامس بيها ؟

سعيد ـ لا ، بس بالصيف تكون مليانة لأن اكو بيها
مسبح وقهاوي •

بل ـ اظن بغداد تعجبني •
جان ،شتفتكر بيها ؟

جان ـ هسّه ما اقدر اقول • هي مدينة قديمة وبعد ما
شفت كثير • اقدر اقول لك بعد كم يوم •

VOCABULARY

baagii (same as baaḳii)	
baaḳii, baaḳiya (f)	remaining, staying
ilbaaḳii	the remainder, the rest
baaḳii-ṭṭariiḳ	the rest of the way
baaṣṣ (baṣṣaat)	bus (pl)
balam (ʔablaam)	rowboat (pl)
yibna (bina)	he builds (he built)
binaw	they built
bi'noo	they built him
daayra *or* daaʔira (f)	office
daayratna	our office
daayirtii	my office
faarug, faarga (f)	empty; unoccupied, free
yifalliš (fallaš)	he tears down (he tore down)
falšaw	they tore down
fal'šoo	they tore him down
gabul	before; ago
gabul sabi9-siniin	seven years ago
gabul maa	before (with verbs)
gabul maa binaw hajjisir	before they built this bridge
gahwa (gahaawii)	coffee shop (pl)
gayr	other, different; non-
gayr muslim	non-Moslem
ḥadiiḳa (ḥadaayiḳ)	park (pl)
yiḥawwil (ḥawwal)	he moves, he takes (to another place)
ḥawlaw	they moved
ḥaw'loo	they moved him
ilḥukuuma	the government
jadiid, –a	new
jazra (f)	island (small)
jisir (jisuur)	bridge (pl)
kam *or* čam	some; several; how many?
ba9ad kam yoom	after a few days
yikallim (kallam)	he talks, he calls
ilkaraada	the Karada (a section of Baghdad)
yikuun (kaan)	he will be
ḳadiim, –a	old, ancient (of things)
ḳariib, –a (minn)	near (to)
liʔann	because
mabnii *or* mibnii (minn) mabniiya (f)	built of
madiina (f)	city
malyaan *or* milyaan, –a (minn)	full (of)
masbaḥ (masaabiiḥ)	swimming place (pl)
nahar (nhuur)	river (pl)
nahar-dijla (m)	the Tigris River
yisammii (samma)	he names, he calls (he named, called)
sammaw	they named
sam'moo	they named him
yisma9 (sima9) 9ann	he hears (heard) about
sina (siniin)	year (pl)
ṣoob	side (of the river)
δaak iṣṣoob	the other side (of the river)
šaari9 (šawaari9)	street (pl)
šaari9-irrašiid	Rashid Street
taḳriiban	about, almost
tamaam	perfect, right
yitfarraj (tfarraj) 9ala *or* bii	he looks around
yitδakkar (tδakkar)	he remembers
ṭariiḳ	way, road
waaguf, waagfa	standing; stopped
yixaḷḷuṣ (xaḷḷaṣ)	he completes; he frees (he completed; he freed)

xašab *or* xišab	wood	ya9nii (9ina)	he (it) means (he meant)
?atraak (turkii)	Turks (Turkish; a Turk)	?a9nii	I mean
		yi9jib (9ijab)	he pleases
		ti9jibnii	she pleases me, I like her
9aalam	world (noun)		
9aalamii, 9aalamiiya (f)	world (adjective)	ti9ijbak	she pleases you, you like her
9atiig, –a	old (of things)		

UNIT 11

Seeing the Sights (continued)

BASIC SENTENCES

Continuing RECORD 20A

ENGLISH EQUIVALENTS	AIDS TO LISTENING	ARABIC SPELLING
Said	*Said*	سعيد
(the) walking	ilmašii	المشي
I'm tired of walking.	ʔaanii ti9baan minn ilmašii.	اني تعبان من المشي ٠
carriage	9arabaana	عربانة
Let's take a carriage.	xallii naaxuδ 9arabaana.	خلّي ناخذ عربانة ٠
John	*John*	جان
lazy	kislaan *or* kaslaan*	كسلان
You're both [just] lazy.	θinaynkum kislaaniin.	ثنينكم كسلانين ٠
Bill	*Bill*	بل
we ride	nirkab	نركب
(you) alone	waḥdak	وحدك
We're going to ride; you can walk by yourself.	ʔiḥna raaḥ nirkab; tigdar timšii waḥdak.	احنا راح نركب، تقدر تمشي وحدك ٠
John	*John*	جان
coming	jaay	جاي
No, I'm coming with you.	laa, ʔaanii jaay wiiyaakum.	لا ، آني جاي ويّاكم ٠
Said	*Said*	سعيد
carriage driver	9arabančii	عربنچي

Beginning RECORD 20B

ENGLISH EQUIVALENTS	AIDS TO LISTENING	ARABIC SPELLING
take us!	waddiina	ودّينا
park *or* garden	ḥadiiḳa	حديقة
the King Ghazi Park	ḥadiiḳat-ilmalik-gaazii	حديقة الملك غازي
Driver, take us to the King Ghazi Park.	9arabančii, waddiina liḥadiiḳat-ilmalik-gaazii.	عربنشي،ودّينا لحديقة الملك غازي.
Bill	*Bill*	بل
building	binaaya	بناية
What's this building?	šinuu halbinaaya?	شنو هاي البناية ؟
Said	*Said*	سعيد
mosque	jaami9	جامع
This is a mosque.	haaδa jaami9.	هذا جامع .
prayer	ṣaḷaat	صلاة
place of prayer	maḥall-iṣṣaḷaat	محل الصلاة
a Moslem	muslim	مسلم
church	kaniisa	كنيسة
Christians	naṣaara	نصارى
The mosque (he) is the place of prayer for Moslems like a church for Christians.	ijjaami9 huuwa maḥall-iṣṣaḷaat lilmuslimiin miθil ilkaniisa linnaṣaara.	الجامع هو محل الصلاة للمسلمين مثل الكنيسة للنصارى .
Bill	*Bill*	بل
long *or* tall	ṭawiil	طويل
What's that tall building?	šinuu halbinaaya ṭṭawiila?	شنو هاي البناية الطويلة ؟
Said	*Said*	سعيد
minaret	minaara	منارة
That's a minaret.	haaδii minaara.	هذي منارة .
Bill	*Bill*	بل
use *or* purpose	faayda	فائدة
What's the purpose of the minaret?	šinuu faaydat-ilminaara?	شنو فائدة المنارة ؟
Said	*Said*	سعيد
muezzin	muʔaδδin	موءذّن
he calls	yid9uu	يدعو
The muezzin calls the people to prayer from it.	minha ʔilmuʔaδδin yid9uu nnaas liṣṣaḷaat.	منها الموءذّن يدعو الناس للصلاة .
John	*John*	جان
Can we go into the mosque?	nigdar nidxul bijjaami9?	نقدر ندخل بالجامع ؟

ENGLISH EQUIVALENTS	AIDS TO LISTENING	ARABIC SPELLING
Said	*Said*	سعيد
(you) alone (pl)	waḥidkum	وحدكم
You can't go in alone because you aren't Moslems.	maa tgidruun tidxuluun waḥidkum minn sabab ʔintum muu muslimiin.	ما تقدرون تدخلون وحدكم من سبب انتم مو مسلمين •
John	*John*	جان
Can you take us with you?	tigdar taaxuδna wiiyaak?	تقدر تاخذنا ويّاك ؟
inside	daaxil	داخل
I'd like to see the inside of the building.	ʔaḥibb ʔašuuf daaxil-ilbinaaya.	احب اشوف داخل البناية •
Said	*Said*	سعيد
to here	ʔila hinaa	الى هنا
I'll see you tomorrow and we'll come back here.	ʔašuufkum baačir wunirja9 ʔila hinaa.	اشوفكم باكر و نرجع الى هنا •
Driver	*Driver*	عرباشي
which you want (her)	litriiduunha	لتريدونها
This is the park you want.	haay lḥadiiķa litriiduunha.	هاي الحديقة لتريدونها •
you want me	triiduunii	تريدوني
I wait for you	ʔanṭiḍirkum	انتظركم
Do you want me to wait for you?	triiduunii ʔanṭiḍirkum?	تريدوني انتظركم ؟
(*The next day at the hotel.*)		
Said	*Said*	سعيد
ready	ḥaaḍir	حاضر
Are you ready to go?	ʔinta ḥaaḍir itruuḥ?	انت حاضر تروح ؟
Where's John?	wayn John?	وين جان ؟
I told him	gilitla	قلت له
he waits for me	yinṭiḍirnii	ينتظرني

Beginning RECORD 21A

ENGLISH EQUIVALENTS	AIDS TO LISTENING	ARABIC SPELLING
I told him to wait for me here.	gilitla yinṭiḍirnii hinaa.	قلت له ينتظرني هنا •
Bill	*Bill*	بل
we find him	nuujda *or* noojda	نوجده
He told me we'd find him in the lobby.	gaallii nuujda biṣṣaaloon.	قال لي نوجده بالصالون •
camera	kaamira	كامرة
Can I take the camera with me?	ʔagdar ʔaaxuδ ilkaamira wiiyaay?	اقدر آخذ الكامرة ويّاي ؟

ENGLISH EQUIVALENTS	AIDS TO LISTENING	ARABIC SPELLING
films	ʔaflaam	افلام
I brought a lot of films from America.	jibit ʔaflaam kaθiira minn ʔamayrika.	جبت افلام كثيرة من امريكا •
fearing *or* afraid	xaayif	خايف
I was afraid I couldn't buy them (from) here.	kunit xaayif maa ʔagdar ʔaštiriihum minn hinaa.	كنت خايف ما اقدر اشتريهم من هنا•
Said	*Said*	سعيد
take her!	xuδha	خذها
Yes, take it with you.	na9am, xuδha wiiyaak.	نعم ، خذها ويّاك •
forbidden	mamnuu9	ممنوع
taking (noun)	ʔaxuδ	اخذ
pictures	ṣuwar	صور
[the] taking of pictures	ʔaxuδ-ṣuwar	اخذ صور
(from) outside	minn barra	من برّة
Taking pictures in the mosque is forbidden, but you can take them outside.	mamnuu9 ʔaxuδ-ṣuwar fijjaami9, bass tigdar taaxuδha minn barra.	ممنوع اخذ صور في الجامع بس تقدر تاخذها من برّة •
(*In the lobby.*)		
Said	*Said*	سعيد
appointment	maw9id	موعد
What, have you forgotten our appointment?	šinuu, ʔinta nisayt maw9idna?	شنو ، انت نسيت موعدنا ؟
John	*John*	جان
No, I haven't forgotten it.	laa, maa nisayta.	لا ، ما نسيته •
Are we going to walk or take a taxi?	raaḥ nimšii ʔaw naaxuδ taaksii?	راح نمشي او ناخذ تاكسي ؟
Said	*Said*	سعيد
is needed *or* is necessary	yiḥtaaj	يحتاج
We don't need a taxi.	maa yiḥtaaj taaksii.	ما يحتاج تاكسي •
My car's waiting at the door.	siiyaartii waagfa bilbaab.	سيّارتي واقفة بالباب •
(*At the mosque.*)		
Said	*Said*	سعيد
We have to go in by the big door.	laazim nidxul minn ilbaab ilkabiir.	لازم ندخل من الباب الكبير •
(*They go into the courtyard, and Said points to the main building.*)		
they pray	yiṣalluun	يصلّون
The people pray inside that building.	fii daaxil-halbinaaya ʔinnaas yiṣalluun.	في داخل ها البناية الناس يصلّون •

ENGLISH EQUIVALENTS	AIDS TO LISTENING	ARABIC SPELLING
chairs	karaasii	كراسي
benches	txuut	تخوت
prayer-rugs	sijaajiid	سجاجيد
Notice there aren't [any] chairs and benches in it, only prayer-rugs.	šuufuu maakuu fiiha karaasii wutxuut, bass sijaajiid.	شوفوا ماكو فيها كراسي وتخوت ، بس سجاجيد .
John	*John*	جان
statues	timaaθiil	تماثيل
mosques	jawaami9	جوامع
pulpits	manaabir	منابر
Are there [any] statues or pictures in the mosques?	hal ?akuu timaaθiil ?aw ṣuwar bijjawaami9?*	هل اكو تماثيل او صور بالجوامع ؟
Said	*Said*	سعيد
he finds *or* there is found	yuujad	يوجد
No, there are only pulpits.	laa, bass yuujad manaabir.	لا ، بس يوجد منابر .
pulpit	mambar	منبر
This is the pulpit.	haaδa lmambar.	هذا المنبر .
Bill	*Bill*	بل
the time of prayer	waḳt-iṣṣaḷaat	وقت الصلاة
When is the time of prayer?	yamta waḳt-iṣṣaḷaat?	يمتى وقت الصلاة ؟

Beginning RECORD 21B

ENGLISH EQUIVALENTS	AIDS TO LISTENING	ARABIC SPELLING
Said	*Said*	سعيد
dinner	9iša	عشى
After (the) dinner.	ba9ad il9iša.	بعد العشى .
We have to go before the people come.	laazim inruuḥ gabul maa tijii nnaas.	لازم نروح قبل ما تجي الناس .
I take you	?aaxuδkum	آخذكم
Do you want me to take you to the hotel?	triiduunii ?aaxuδkum lil?uutayl?	تريدوني آخذكم للاوتيل ؟
John	*John*	جان
take us!	xuδna	خذنا
No, just take us to the King Ghazi Bridge.	laa, bass xuδna ?ila jisir-ilmalik-gaazii.	لا ، بس خذنا الى جسر الملك غازي .

ANALYSIS

1. *'Alone', 'by one's self'.*

tigdar timšii waḥdak.	*You can walk alone.*	تقدر تمشي وحدك .
maa tgidruun itduxluun waḥidkum.	*You can't go in alone.*	ما تقدرون تدخلون وحدكم .

From the above you see that waḥid, with the respective pronoun endings, is equivalent to *alone, by one's self.*

2. *A note on* naas *people.*

fii daaxil-halbinaaya nnaas yiṣalluun.	*Inside this building, the people pray.*	في داخل ها البناية الناس يصلّون.
laazim inruuḥ ba9ad maa tijii nnaas.	*We have to go before the people come.*	لازم نروح بعد ما تجي الناس .

You will observe in the above sentences that naas *people* can be with either a plural verb form (as yiṣalluun *they pray*), or with a feminine singular verb form (as tijii *she (it) comes*).

3. Pronoun Endings with Verbs, Summary.

sidd	*close!*	سد
sidda	*close him (it)!*	سده
šifit	*I saw*	شفت
šifta	*I saw him*	شفته
šifna	*we saw*	شفنا
šifnaahum	*we saw them*	شفناهم
šaafaw	*they saw*	شافوا
šaafoonii	*they saw me*	شافوني

Above, simple verb forms are followed by the corresponding verb forms with pronoun endings. Once again you will observe that when pronoun endings are added to verb forms (just as you learned about nouns and prepositions), it is not always a process of simple addition to an unchanged form. That is, the form with the pronoun ending is not always the same as the form without the ending. In this section you will see the verb forms with the pronoun endings. You will recall that some of the pronoun endings begin with a consonant. These are –ha *her*, –nii *me*, –na *us*, –kum *you* (pl), and –hum *them*. The other endings begin with a vowel. These are –a *him*, –ak *you* (m), and –ič *you* (f). In the examples given hereafter, remember that –ha *her* is used to represent all the consonant-initial endings. Similarly, the ending –a *him* is used to represent all the vowel-initial endings.

I

sadd	*he closed*	سد
sadda	*he closed him (it)*	سده
sadha	*he closed her (it)*	سدها

As you have observed before, a double consonant remains before vowel endings, but it is simplified before consonant endings.

II

yixallii	*he puts*	يخلّي
yixalliiha	*he puts her (it)*	يخلّيها
yixal'lii	*he puts him (it)*	يخلّيه
yixalliik	*he puts you* (m)	يخلّيك

The above pattern is followed by verb forms whose combining form ends in a vowel. Note –k instead of –ak for *you* (m) and –č instead of –ič *you* (f). Below are the other verb forms which follow this pattern. You will note that the combining form is slightly different from the free form.

šaafaw	*they saw*	شافوا
šaafooha		شافوها
šaa'foo		شافوه
šifna	*we saw*	شفنا
šifnaaha		شفناها
šif'naa		شفناه
šiftum	*you saw* (pl)	شفتم
šiftuuha		شفتوها
šif'tuu		شفتوه
yišuufuun	*they see*	يشوفون
yišuufuuha		يشوفوها
yišuu'fuu		يشوفوه
tšuufuun	*you see* (pl)	تشوفون
tšuufuuha		تشوفوها
tšuu'fuu		تشوفوه
tšuufiin	*you see* (f)	تشوفين
tšuufiiha		تشوفيها
tšuu'fii		تشوفيه

In the above verbs you will observe that the combining forms differ from the free forms in the following ways:

1. –aw is replaced by –oo– in the combining form.
2. Verbs ending in –a have –aa– in the combining form.
3. –tum is replaced by –tuu– in the combining form.
4. –uun and –iin usually lose the –n in the combining form. Some speakers, however, keep the –n, and say yišuufuunha *they saw her* and yišuufuuna *they saw him*, and so on.

III And now, free forms having a single vowel before a single final consonant.

a

šifit	*I saw*	شفت
ki'tabit	*I wrote*	كتبت
xaḷ'ḷaṣit	*I finished*	خلّصت
šifitha		شفتها
kitabitha		كتبتها
xaḷḷaṣitha		خلّصتها

šifta شفته
kitabta كتبته
xaḷḷaṣta خلّصته

b

kallim	*talk with!*	كلّم
xaḷḷuṣ	*finish!*	خلّص

kallimha كلّمها
xaḷḷuṣha خلّصها

kalma كلّمه
xaḷṣa خلّصه

c

ya9ruf	*he knows*	يعرف
yiktib	*he writes*	يكتب
?iktib	*write!*	اكتب
?uḍrub	*hit!*	اضرب
?iftaḥ	*open!*	افتح

ya9rufha يعرفوها
yiktibha يكتبها
?iktibha اكتبها
?uḍrubha اضربها
?iftaḥha افتحها

yi9arfa يعرفه
yikitba يكتبه
?ikitba اكتبه
?uḍurba اضربه
?ifitḥa افتحه

You will note that the first of each series above is a free verb form having a single vowel before a single final consonant. The second forms are these verbs with consonant endings added. You will note that there is *no* change *before the consonant endings* (except for the regular stress shift). It is the third member of each series which you will note especially. Here the verb is with vowel endings, and you will note that there are a few differences. In summary, you will observe that:

1. The vowels i and u (before t of the agent affixes) remain before consonant endings, but they drop out before vowel endings (examples under *a*).
2. If i or u is preceded by a doubled consonant, the doubled consonant is simplified when i or u drops (examples under *b*).
3. But if i or u is preceded by two unlike consonants, then there is rearrangement within the word (examples under *c*). (This last arrangement of yiktibha beside yikitba will remind you of the pattern of yiskin beside yisiknuun and yis?al beside yisi?luun, and so on.)

IV *Position of stress.*

Finally we come to the question of the position of stress. In all the forms above (with the exception of forms like yixal'lii *he puts him*, šaa'foo *they saw him*, etc.) the stress has followed the mechanical pattern. (If you have forgotten what this is, see Note Two in Unit Two.) There are, however, two other forms where the stress is not according to the mechanical pattern.

Note the following:

a		
ḍirab	*he hit*	ضرب
ḍi'raba	*he hit him*	ضربه
xaḷḷaṣ	*he finished*	خلّص
xaḷ'ḷaṣa	*he finished him*	خلّصه
b		
šaafat	*she saw*	شافت
šaa'fata	*she saw him*	شافته
saddat	*she closed*	سدت
sad'data	*she closed him*	سدته
ḍirbat	*she hit*	ضربت
ḍir'bata	*she hit him*	ضربته
nisat	*she forgot*	نست
ni'sata	*she forgot him*	نسته
xaḷṣat	*she finished*	خلّصت
xaḷ'ṣata	*she finished him*	خلّصته

You will observe that the forms in the last column have the stress on the vowel preceding the vowel-initial pronoun ending, even though this is contrary to the mechanical habit. You will also note that it is the *completed action he* and *she* forms which happen to fit this pattern. All others follow the mechanical habit.

In conclusion, if you look over all the verb forms having pronoun endings, you will arrive at this general rule for the position of stress:

In verb forms having pronoun endings added, the stress always falls on the vowel preceding the pronoun ending.

EXERCISES

A. *Supply with* waḥid *with pronoun endings.*

1. maa gidarna nidxul ___ bijjaami9.
2. layš ʔinta riḥit ___? ridit ʔaruuḥ wiiyaak.
3. layš itriiduun itruuḥuun ___?
4. šifna θilaaθ-banaat gaa9diin ___.
5. maa xaḷḷaṣut iššugul; maa gi'darit ʔasaw'wii ___.
6. risal binta ___ lissuug lamma huuwa kaan billayl.
7. il9arabančii kaan gaa9id ___ bil9arabaana.

B. Add –ha *she (it)*, then –a *him (it)* to the correct forms of the following verbs:

I

jaabaw	*they brought*
raadaw	*they wanted*
zaaraw	*they visited*
kitbaw	*they wrote*
ḍirbaw	*they hit*
xaḷṣaw	*they finished*
xallaw	*they put*
sawwaw	*they made*

II

jibna	*we brought*
laa tinsa	*don't forget!*
ʔiḳra	*read!*
xalla	*he put*
sawwa	*he made*
nisa	*he forgot*
nisayna	*we forgot*
xallayna	*we put*

III

šiftum	*you saw*
jibtum	*you brought*
kitabtum	*you wrote*
risaltum	*you sent*
xallaytum	*you put*
sawwaytum	*you made*
šaggaytum	*you tore*
širabtum	*you drank*

IV

yiriiduun	*they want*
yišiiluun	*they pick up, they carry*
yikitbuun	*they write*
yiḍirbuun	*they hit*
yigluun	*they say*
yaakluun	*they eat*
yaaxδuun	*they take*
yixalluun	*they put*
yixaḷṣuun	*they finish*

V

jibit	*I brought; you brought*
ridit	*I wanted; you wanted*
ki'tabit	*I wrote; you wrote*
ḍi'rabit	*I hit; you hit*
xaḷ'ḷaṣut	*I finished; you finished*
kal'lamit	*I talked with, I called*
ʔiktib	*write!*
ʔuḍrub	*hit!*
ʔiftaḥ	*open!*

VI

kitab	*he wrote*
ḍirab	*he hit*
fitaḥ	*he opened*
xaḷḷaṣ	*he finished*
kallam	*he talked with, he called*
tδakkar	*he remembered*

VII

šaafat	*she saw*
jaabat	*she brought*
kitbat	*she wrote*
ḍirbat	*she hit*
nisat	*she forgot*
sawwat	*she made*
xallat	*she put*
xaḷṣat	*she finished*
kalmat	*she talked with, she called*
tδakrat	*she remembered*

C. Add –ak (–k) *you* (m), then –kum *you* (pl) to the verbs in parentheses. Make whatever changes are necessary in the form of the verb.

1. ḍannayt (šifit) lamma ʔana kunit jaay minn iššugul.
2. ʔuxuutii gaaloolii humma (šaafaw) yoom ilxamiis.
3. baačir raaḥ (ʔakallim) bittalafoon.
4. jamiila maa (kalmat).
5. minuu (ḍirab)?
6. (yiriiduun tijii) wiiyaahum.

D. Replace the nouns in parentheses by pronoun endings added to the preceding verb. Make whatever changes are necessary in the verb form. The first sentence is an example.

1a. nigdar inšuuf (ilgurfa)?
1b. nigdar inšuufha?

2. ʔarjuuk sidd (ilbaab) lamma titḷa9.
3. ilwalad gaṣṣ (ʔiida).
4. wayn raaḥ itxallii (siiyaartak)?
5. maa jibit (siiyaartii).
6. ḍannayt šifit (sa9iid) yirkab bilbalam.
7. laa, sa9iid maa kaan bilbalam; ʔiḥna šifna (sa9iid) yitmašša bδaak iṣṣoob.
8. gulluulii, layš maa jibtum (ilmaywa)?
9. yigluun yiriiduun yišuufuun (ʔaxuuk).
10. minuu kitab (halmaktuub)?
11. ʔana maa ki'tabit (haaδa).
12. laa tinsa (halmaktuub)!
13. yamta raaḥ itxaḷḷuṣ (šuglak)?
14. ʔiktib (haaδa) biddaftar!
15. ʔarjuuk ʔuḍrub (badiltii) ʔuutii!
16. maa ʔagdar ʔaftaḥ (ilbaab).
17. kallim (sa9iid) bittalafoon!
18. maa ʔa9ruf (ḥasan).
19. yigluun yi9arfuun (ʔaxuuya).
20. minuu sawwa haaδa? ʔaḍinn ʔuxtii hiiya sawwat (haaδạ).

WHAT WOULD YOU SAY?

1. *You are tired of walking.*
   a. ʔana 9iṭšaan wuʔariid ʔašrab maay. ١ ـ انا عطشان واريد اشرب ماي •
   b. laazim naaxuδ 9arabaana. ٢ ـ لازم ناخذ عربانة •
   c. ʔana ti9baan minn ilmašii; ʔariid ʔaaxuδ 9arabaana. ٣ ـ انت تعبان من المشي ، اريد اخذ عربانة •

2. *Your friend says to hurry, he has a carriage.*
   a. tigdar timšii waḥdak ʔiδa triid. ١ ـ تقدر تمشي وحدك اذا تريد •

b. ruuḥ ʔila wayn maa triid; ʔana ʔariid ʔanaam.
٢ ـ روح الى وين ما تريد ، انا اريد انام •

c. laa titʔaxxar kaθiir; il9arabaana waagfa.
٣ ـ لا تتأخّر كثير ، العربانة واقفة •

3. *You compare a mosque to a church.*

a. yigluun ʔakuu jaami9 fii New York.
١ ـ يقولون اكو جامع في نيويورك •

b. ijjaami9 lilmuslimiin miθil ilkaniisa linnaṣaara.
٢ ـ الجامع للمسلمين مثل الكنيسة للنصارى •

c. kam jaami9 ʔakuu bil9iraaḳ?
٣ ـ كم جامع اكو بالعراق ؟

4. *What about the minaret?*

a. halbalam iṭṭawiil maa 9inda ṣaaḥib.
١ ـ هلبلم الطويل ما عبده صاحب •

b. šinuu δiič ilbinaaya ṭṭawiila wušinuu faaydatha?
٢ ـ شنو ذيك البناية الطويلة وشنو فائدتها ؟

c. nigdar nidxul ibδiič ilbinaaya ṭṭawiila?
٣ ـ نقدر ندخل بذيك البناية الطويلة ؟

5. *The muezzin calls the people to prayer from it.*

a. ilmuʔaδδin yiḥmil ḥimil kabiir 9ala δahra.
١ ـ الموءذّن يحمل حمل كبير على ظهره •

b. δiič minaara, wuminha ilmuʔaδδin yid9uu nnaas liṣṣalaat.
٢ ـ ذيك المنارة ، ومنها الموءذن يدعو الناس للصلاة •

c. sima9it fadd muʔaδδin yiriid yiruuḥ ʔila jaami9na.
٣ ـ سمعت فد موءذّن يريد يروح الى جامعنا •

6. *You are told you can't go inside the mosque alone.*

a. maa tgidruun tijuun wiiyaay.
١ ـ ما تقدرون تجون وياي •

b. triiduunii ʔadris fii baytna ʔaw fijjaami9?
٢ ـ تريدون ادرس في بيتنا او في الجامع ؟

c. maa tgidruun itduxluun waḥidkum liʔann ʔintum muu muslimiin.
٣ ـ ما تقدرون تدخلون وحدكم لان انتم مو مسلمين •

7. *Your friend can take you with him sometime.*

a. fadd yoom ʔariid ʔatmašša ʔila makaan muu ḳariib.
١ ـ فد يوم اريد اتمشّى الى مكان مو قريب •

b. yimkin fadd yoom ʔaruuḥ ʔila šuglii.
٢ ـ يمكن فد يوم اروح الى شغلي •

c. yimkin fadd yoom ʔagdar ʔaaxuδkum.
٣ ـ يمكن فد يوم اقدر آخذكم •

8. *You would like to see the inside of the building.*

a. ʔaḥibb ʔašuuf daaxil-ilbinaaya.
١ ـ احب اشوف داخل البناية •

b. ʔaḥibb ʔašuuf ilbinaaya minn barra.
٢ ـ احب اشوف البناية من برّه •

c. laa traawiina halbinaaya.
٣ ـ لا تراوينا هاي البناية •

9. *At your destination the carriage driver asks if you want him.*

a. triiduunii ʔaakul wiiyaakum?
١ ـ تريدوني آكل وياكم ؟

b. ʔinṭiḍirnii yamm il9arabaana.
٢ ـ انتظرني يم العربانة •

c. triiduunii ʔanṭiḍirkum?
٣ ـ تريدوني انتظركم ؟

10. *He tells you how much you owe.*

a. ʔarjuuk daayinnii diinaar ʔaw diinaarayn.
b. layš maa tinṭiinii miiya wxamsiin-filis?
c. ʔarjuuk, ʔariid xamsiin-filis.

١ ـ ارجوك دايني دينار او دينارين •
٢ ـ ليش ما تنطيني مية وخمسين فلس •
٣ ـ ارجوك ، اريد خمسين فلس •

11. *You can't take pictures in the mosque.*

a. maa ʔaḍinn tigdar taaxuδ ṣuwar.
b. mayxaalif, bass laazim tilbas θoobak.
c. mamnuu9 ʔaxuδ-ṣuwar fijjaami9.

١ ـ ما اظن تقدر تاخذ صور •
٢ ـ ما يخالف بس لازم تلبس ثوبك •
٣ ـ ممنوع اخذ الصور في الجامع •

12. *Can you take them outside?*

a. ilḥukuuma 9indha ṣuwar hawaaya.
b. ʔaḥibb ʔaaxuδ ṣuwar minn kulšii.
c. ʔagdar ʔaaxuδ ṣuwar minn barra?

١ ـ الحكومة عندها صور هواية •
٢ ـ احب آخذ صور من كل شيء •
٣ ـ اقدر آخذ صور من برّه ؟

13. *Anyway, your friend says you can't find films in Baghdad.*

a. yisawwuun ʔaflaam fii bagdaad.
b. maa tigdar tuujad ʔaflaam ibbagdaad.
c. muu laazim tištirii ʔaflaam minn ʔamriika.

١ ـ يسوّون افلام في بغداد •
٢ ـ ما تقدر توجد افلام ببغداد •
٣ ـ مو لازم تشتري افلام من امريكا •

14. *You had thought of that.*

a. štiraythum minn ʔamriika gabul maa jiit ʔila hinaa.
b. xallii ništirii kam filim minn ʔamriika.
c. halʔaflaam 9atiiga.

١ ـ اشتريتهم من امريكا قبل ما جيت الى هنا •
٢ ـ خلّي نشتري كم فلم من امريكا •
٣ ـ هاي الافلام عتيقة •

15. *Later your friend thinks you forgot your appointment with him.*

a. laa tinsa ddaftar bišṣaaloon.
b. šinuu ʔinta nisayt maw9idna?
c. gullii, yamta lmaw9id?

١ ـ لا تنسى الدفتر بالصالون •
٢ ـ شنو انت نسيت موعدنا ؟
٣ ـ قل لي يمتى الموعد ؟

16. *He has his automobile.*

a. siiyaartii muu mawjuuda hinaa.
b. maa ʔaḍinn niḥtaaj ʔila siiyaara.
c. maa yiḥtaaj; siiyaartii waagfa yamm ilbaab.

١ ـ سيّارتي مو موجودة هنا •
٢ ـ ما اظن نحتاج الى سيّارة •
٣ ـ ما يحتاج ، سيارتي واقفة يم الباب •

17. *At the mosque your friend again explains its purpose.*

a. layš maa tduxluun fii halbinaaya?
b. xallii nruuḥ inṣallii.
c. fii daaxil-halbinaaya nnaas yiṣalluun.

١ ـ ليش ما تدخلون الى هلبناية ؟
٢ ـ خلّي نروح نصلّي •
٣ ـ في داخل هاي البناية الناس يصلّون •

18. *He points out that there aren't any chairs or benches, only prayer-rugs.*

a. maakuu biiha timaaθiil ʔaw ṣuwar, bass sijaajiid.

١ ـ ماكو بيها تماثيل وصور ، بس سجاجيد •

b. maakuu biiha karaasii wutxuut, bass sijaajiid.

٢ ـ ماكو بيها كراسي وتخوت ، بس سجاجيد •

c. ʔayḍan biljawaami9 yuujad manaabir.

٣ ـ ايضا بالجوامع يوجد منابر •

LISTENING IN

John, Bill and Said have reached the other side of the river and are walking in the direction of one of the parks.

Continuing RECORD 21B

SAID ʔaanii ti9baan minn ilmašii; xallii naaxuδ 9arabaana.

سعيد ـ آني تعبان من المشي ، خلّي ناخذ عرباتة •

JOHN ʔaḍinn θinaynkum kislaaniin.

جان ـ اظن ثنينكم كسلانين •

BILL ʔiḥna raaḥ nirkab; tigdar timšii waḥdak ʔiδa triid.

بل ـ احنا راح نركب ، تقدر تمشي وحدك اذا تريد •

JOHN laa, ʔaanii jaay wiiyaakum.

جان ـ لا آني جاي ويّاكم •

SAID (*To the carriage driver*) 9arabančii, waddiina liḥadiiḳat-ilmalik-gaazii.

سعيد ـ عربنشي ، ودّينا لحديقة الملك غازي •

DRIVER mamnuun.

عربنشي ـ ممنون •

BILL sa9iid, šinuu halbinaaya?

بل ـ سعيد ، شنو هاي البناية ؟

SAID jaami9. ta9ruf šinuu jaami9?

سعيد ـ جامع ، تعرف شنو جامع ؟

BILL ʔaḍinn ijjaami9 miθil ilkaniisa linnaṣaara.

بل ـ اظن الجامع مثل الكنيسة للنصارى •

SAID tamaam; ijjaami9 maḥall-iṣṣalaat lilmuslimiin.

سعيد ـ تمام ، الجامع محل الصلاة للمسلمين •

BILL wušinuu halbinaaya ṭṭawiila yamm ijjaami9?

بل ـ وشنو هاي البناية الطويلة يم الجامع ؟

SAID haaδii minaara.

سعيد ـ هذي منارة •

BILL šinuu faaʔidat-ilminaara?

بل ـ شنو فائدة المنارة ؟

SAID minha ʔilmuʔaδδin yid9uu nnaas liṣṣalaat.

سعيد ـ منها الموءذّن يدعو الناس للصلاة •

JOHN sa9iid, nigdar nidxul bijjaami9?

جان ـ سعيد ، نقدر ندخل بالجامع ؟

SAID maa tigdaruun itduxluun waḥidkum liʔann ʔintum muu muslimiin.

سعيد ـ ما تقدرون تدخلون وحدكم لان انتم مو مسلمين •

JOHN tigdar fadd yoom taaxuδna wiiyaak? ʔaḥibb ʔašuuf daaxil-ilbinaaya.

جان ـ تقدر فد يوم تاخذنا ويّاك ؟
احب اشوف داخل البناية •

SAID zayn, ʔašuufkum bilʔuutayl yoom-ilʔaḥad ba9ad iḍḍuhur, wuba9dayn nirja9 ʔila hinaa.

سعيد ـ زين ، اشوفكم بالاوتيل يوم الاحد بعد الظهر ،
وبعدين نرجع الى هنا •

DRIVER haay ilḥadiiḳa litriiduunha.
triiduunii ʔanṭiḍirkum?

SAID laa. šgad itriid?

DRIVER xamsiin-fils.

(*Next day at the hotel.*)

SAID ʔinta ḥaaḍir itruuḥ?

BILL na9am.

SAID wayn John?
ʔaḍinn gilitla yinṭiḍirnii hinaa.

BILL huuwa yinṭiḍirna biṣṣaaloon.
gaallii nuujda hinaak.
sa9iid, ʔagdar ʔaaxuð ilkaamira wiiyaay?

SAID na9am, xuðha wiiyaak.
mannuu9 ʔaxuð-ṣuwar fijjaami9, bass tigdar taaxuðha minn barra.

BILL jibit ʔaflaam kaθiira minn ʔamriika, liʔann kinit xaayif maa ʔagdar ʔaštiriihum minn hinaa.

(*They go to the lobby.*)

JOHN wayn raayḥiin?

BILL šinuu ʔinta nisayt maw9idna wiiya sa9iid?

JOHN laa, maa nisayta.
raaḥ nimšii ʔaw naaxuð taaksii?

SAID laa, maa yiḥtaaj. siiyaartii waagfa bilbaab.

(*At the mosque.*)

SAID laazim nidxul minn ilbaab ilkabiir.
fii daaxil-halbinaaya innaas yiṣalluun.
tḥibbuun nidxul biiha?

JOHN balii, ʔiða nigdar.

BILL šuuf, John, maakuu fiiha karaasii wutxuut, bass sijaajiid.

JOHN ʔayḍan maakuu timaaθiil ʔaw ṣuwar.

SAID bijjawaami9 yuujad manaabir.
haaða huuwa lmambar.

(*Remaining conversation not recorded.*)

BILL yamta waḳit-iṣṣaḷaat?

SAID ba9ad il9iša.
laazim inruuḥ gabul maa tijii nnaas.
triiduunii ʔaaxuðkum lilʔuutayl?

JOHN laa, bass xuðna ʔila jisir-ilmalik-gaazii.

SAID zayn.

عربنشي ـ هاي الحديقة اللي تريدونها •
تريدوني انتظركم ؟
سعيد ـ لا ، شقد تريد ؟
عربنشي ـ خمسين فلس •

سعيد ـ انت حاضر تروح ؟
بل ـ نعم •
سعيد ـ وين جان ؟
اظن قلت له ينتظرني هنا •
بل ـ هو ينتظرنا بالصالون •
قال لي نوجده هناك •
سعيد ، اقدر آخذ الكامرة ويّاي ؟
سعيد ـ نعم ، خذها ويّاك •
ممنوع اخذ صور في الجامع ، بس تقدر تاخذها
من برّة •
بل ـ جبت افلام كثيرة من امريكا ، لان كنت خايف ما
اقدر اشتريهم من هنا •

جان ـ وين رايحين ؟
بل ـ شنو انت نسيت موعدنا ويّا سعيد ؟
جان ـ لا ، ما نسيته •
راح نمشي او ناخذ تاكسي ؟
سعيد ـ لا ، ما يحتاج ، سيّارتي واقفة بالباب •

سعيد ـ لازم ندخل من الباب الكبير •
في داخل ها البناية الناس يصلّون •
تحبون ندخل بيها ؟
جان ـ بلي ، اذا نقدر •
بل ـ شوف ، جان ، ماكو فيها كراسي وتخوت ، بس
سجاجيد •
جان ـ ايضا ماكو تماثيل او صور •
سعيد ـ بالجوامع يوجد منابر •
هذا هو المنبر •

بل ـ يمتى وقت الصلاة ؟
سعيد ـ بعد العشى •
لازم نروح قبل ما تجي الناس •
تريدوني آخذكم للاوتيل ؟
جان ـ لا ، بس خذنا الى جسر الملك غازي •
سعيد ـ زين •

VOCABULARY

barra (*or* xaarij)	outside
minn barra	from [the] outside
binaaya (f) (binaayaat)	building (pl)
daaxil	inside
fii daaxil-ilbinaaya	inside the building
yid9uu (di9a)	he calls, he invites
faayda (f)	use, purpose
filim (ˀaflaam)	film (pl)
yiguul (gaal)	he says, he tells (he said)
gilitla	I told him
yiḥtaaj	he needs, it's necessary,
maa yiḥtaaj	it isn't necessary
ḥaaḍir, ḥaaḍra	ready
ḥadiiḳa (ḥadaayiḳ)	park, garden (pl)
ḥadiiḳat-ilmalik gaazii	the King Ghazi Park
jaami9 (jawaami9)	mosque (pl)
kaamira (kaamiraat)	camera (pl)
kaniisa (kanaayis)	church (pl)
kursii (karaasii)	chair (pl)
kislaan, –a	lazy
mamnuu9	forbidden, not allowed
mambar (manaabir)	pulpit (pl)
mašii	(act of) walking
maw9id	appointment, date
minaara	minaret
muslim, muslimiin	Moslem (pl)
muˀaδδin	muezzin

nuṣraanii (naṣaara)	Christian, a Christian (pl)
yinṭiḍir (nṭiḍar)	he waits for
yirkab (rikab)	he rides (he rode)
sijjaada (sijaajiid)	prayer rug (pl)
yiṣallii (ṣalla)	he prays (he prayed)
ṣaḷaat *or* ṣaḷa	prayer
ṣuura (ṣuwar)	picture (pl)
taaksii	taxi
taxit (txuut)	bench (pl)
timθaal (timaaθiil)	statue (pl)
ṭawiil, –a	long; tall
yiwaddii (wadda)	he takes (from one place to another)
waḥid (with pronoun endings)	alone, by one's self
waḥidkum	you alone (pl)
waḥdii	alone, by myself
yuujad (wujad)	he finds; there is, there are
nuujda	we find him
xaayif, waayfa (minn)	afraid (of)
ˀaflaam (filim)	films (singular)
ˀaxuδ	(act of) taking
ˀaxuδ-ṣuwar	taking of pictures, picture taking
9arabaana (9arabaayin)	carriage (pl)
9arabančii (9arabančiiya)	carriage driver (pl)
9iša	dinner
9iṭšaan, –a	thirsty

UNIT 12

Second Review

A. True–False Test.

Beginning RECORD 22A

Here are 35 statements. Each statement will be read twice by your Guide, or else will be found given twice on the records. Which statements are true (in general), and which are false (in general)?

For the Guide, the True-False statements are in Arabic below.

١ ـ البلم مو معمول من الخشب •
٢ ـ مو لازم افلام لشان تاخذ صور •
٣ ـ ماكو حدائق في نهر دجلة •
٤ ـ ما تقدر تشتري جكاير بالليل •
٥ ـ يوجد رياجيل بالقهاوي •
٦ ـ ممنوع المشي بدون قنادر •
٧ ـ بعد العشى دائما لازم تشرب بيرا •
٨ ـ اكو مسلمين وايضا نصارى في بغداد •
٩ ـ الجوامع للمسلمين والكنائس للنصارى •
١٠ ـ كل العرب يسكنون في المدينة •
١١ ـ الناس ما يقدرون يدخلون في البنايات •
١٢ ـ قبل هالاسبوع انت ما كنت جوعان •
١٣ ـ الناس الكسلانين يحبون يشتغلون •
١٤ ـ كل البيوت مبنية من خشب •
١٥ ـ بالعراق يوجد بناية طويلة يسمّوها منارة •
١٦ ـ فائدة الكامرة هي اخذ صور •
١٧ البنات خايفين من الولد •
١٩ ـ اكو يوم الاثنين من كل اسبوع •
٢٠ ـ الناس ما يحملون المفاتيح بجيوبهم •
٢١ ـ اكثر الجيش لازم يقعد من وقت •
٢٢ ـ الامريكان ما عندهم لحية طويلة هسّه •
٢٣ ـ نلبس بدلاتنا تقريبا كل يوم •
٣٤ ـ كل واحد عنده فلوس كافية لكل شيء •
٢٥ ـ في كل مطعم في نغداد قائمة الاكل مكتوبة بالانكليزي •
٢٦ ـ كل امريكاني يقدر يحكي عربي •
٢٧ ـ الشكر مو دائما حلو •
٢٨ ـ كل واحد يحب بنت حلوة •
٢٩ ـ لازم يكون عندك فلوس حتّى تشتري تفاح او برتقال مستوي •
٣٠ ـ يوم الاحد كل الناس تقعد بالشارع وتحكي •
٣١ ـ بغداد بلدة قديمة ، لكن نيويورك بلدة جديدة •
٣٢ ـ الحرب العالمية الثانية اجت بعد الحرب العالمية الاولى !
٣٣ ـ لازم تركب بلبلم حتى تروح الى ذاك الصوب •
٣٤ ـ الامريكاني يحكي انكليزي وهو صغير •
٣٥ ـ الحكومة العراقية بنت جسور على نهر دجلة •

B. Conversations and Questions.

Continuing RECORD 22B, through RECORD 23A, and Beginning RECORD 23B

Listen to each of the four conversations, and answer in Arabic the few questions following each conversation. The Conversations and Questions are given below in Arabic for the Guide.

Conversation I.

جان ـ اليوم الصبح دوّرت النا على غرفة •
بل ـ وجدت شيء ؟
جان ـ نعم ، في اوتيل صغير في شارع الرشيد •
بل ـ شسوّيت ؟

جان - لما دخلت المدير اجا عندي وقال لي شيقدر يسوّي لي •
بل - قدرت تفهم شقال لك ؟
جان - افتهمت كل شيء بعد ما قلت له يحكي بواش •
بل - زين شقلت له ؟
جان - قلت له اريد اشوف غرفة لشان نفرين •
تعرف (بل) هو سائلني اذا هاي الغرفة الي والى مرتي •
بل - وشكان جوابك ؟
جان - طبعا قلت له ، الغرفة الي والى صديقي • بعد ما قلت له عنك اخذني الى فوق وتفرجت عليها •
بل - شفكرت بيها ؟
جان - الغرفة كبيرة وبيها حمّام خصوصي وايضا هي تبين باردة •
بل - شقد كانت الاجرة ؟
جان - دينار ونص باليوم اخذتها لمدة اسبوعين ودفعت الفلوس لقدّام • نقدر نروح لهناك في اي وقت اللي تريده •
بل - طيّب ، خلّي ناخذ جنطنا ونروح هسّه لاني اريد آخذ حمّام حار • وبعدين اريد انام •
جان - عال •

(الاسئلة)

١ - في اي شارع جان وجد غرفة ؟
٢ - قدر يفهم جان شقال له مدير الاوتيل ؟
٣ - شقال جان للمدير لكي يفهم ؟
٤ - ويّا من حكى جان لياخذ غرفة ؟
٥ - شجاوب جان ؟
٦ - شلون كانت الغرفة ، وشكان بيها ؟
٧ - الى يمتى جان دفع للغرفة ؟

Conversation 2.

حسن - اظن هذا المطعم فارغ ، تريدون ندخل بيه ؟
علي - خوش فكرة ، آني هواية جوعان •
حسن - في هذا المطعم نقدر ناكل كل شيء • من هالسبب دائما احب آكل هنا •
بل - افتكر هذا المطعم اللي انا وجان اكلنا بيه يوم الاحد •
علي - شاكلتم ؟
جان - بل اكل دجاج وانا اكلت لحم مشوي •
علي - شلون عجبكم الاكل ؟
جان - عجبني كثير لحم المشوي •
بل - بس الدجاج ما كان مطبوخ كثير •
علي - بعض المطاعم عندهم اكل احسن من غيرهم •
جان - تمام ، قبل يومين كنّا في مطعم واكلنا اكل لذيذ •
علي - بس دفعتم فلوس كثيرة •
بل - هسّه شراح تاكلون ؟
حسن - خلّي كلنا ناكل شيء واحد •
جان - شنو هو ؟
حسن - دجاج وتمن وبعدين نروح للجزرة وناكل الميوا هناك •

(الاسئلة)

١ - في اي مكان اكلوا ؟
٢ - هل عجبهم الاكل ؟
٣ - شكان الاكل على الميز ؟
٤ - هل كان المطعم فارغ لما دخلوا ؟
٥ - هل اكلوا الميوا في المطعم ؟

Conversation 3.

بل - شراح تسوّون بعد ما تاكلون ؟
علي - ظنيت اروح للمسبح •
حسن - انا يمكن بالبيت •
بل - افتكرت اذا ماكو عندكم شيء ، ليش ما تجون ويّانا نتفرّج على بغداد •
علي - فكرتك تبيّن زينة • حسن ، شتقول عنها ؟
حسن - عال •
بل - قبل كم يوم احنا وسعيد رحنا الى فد جامع •
حسن - شفتم الناس يصلّون ؟
بل - لا ، ما بقينا هواية • سعيد قال لنا لازم نروح قبل ما تجي الناس •
جان - طبعا شفنا المنارة وسمعنا الموءذّن يدعو الناس للصلاة •
بل - اذا عندنا وقت ، احب نروح الى ذاك الصوب لكي نتمشّى بالحدائق •
جان - لا تهتمون الى بل • هو اجى من تكسس ، الحدائق دائما تذكّره بيها •
حسن - مو هاليوم • انتظر الى باكر لكي اجيب سيّارتي وآخذكم الى كل محل •

(الاسئلة)

١ - الى اي مكان راحوا ذاك اليوم ؟
٢ - شقال جان اكو بتاكسس ؟
٣ - منو عنده سيّارة ؟
٤ - ليش لازم يطلعون من الجامع من وقت ؟
٥ - منو يحب يروح الى ذاك الصوب ؟

Conversation 4.

توم ـ سلام عليكم •
حلاّق ـ وعليكم السلام •
شتريدني اسوّي لك ؟
توم ـ اريد اقص لحيتي وازيّن شعري •
حلاّق ـ افتكر انت تريدني اقص شعرك وازيّن لحيتك•
توم ـ ما يخالف ، قص اللي تريده• ماكو عندي وقت كثير •
ما قصيت شعري من وقت اللي جيت الى بغداد •
حلاّق ـ هسّه شعرك مو طويل •
شقد صار لك هنا ؟
توم ـ تنين يوم •
حلاّق ـ انت تعني يومين • جيت من يوم الثلاثاء •
وين كنت قبل ما جيت الى هنا ؟
توم ـ كنت في البصرة لمدة اسبوع •
ارجوك لا تقص كثير ، لان ماكو عندي شعر هوايه •
حلاّق ـ شلون هذا ؟
توم ـ يبيّن زين •
حلاّق ـ تريد ماء على شعرك او لا ؟
توم ـ لا •
حلاّق ـ زين ، خلّصت كل شيء• نعيما •

(الاسئلة)

١ ـ الويش راح (توم) للحلاّق ؟
٢ ـ من اي بلد اجي توم الى بغداد ؟
٣ ـ كم يوم كان توم في بغداد قبل ما راح للحلاّق ؟
٤ ـ شقص ، شعره او لحيته ؟
٥ ـ هل الحلاّق خلّى ماء على شعره ؟

C. *Give the form of* ba9ad *or* waḥid *with the pronoun endings called for.*

1. hal kal'lamit sa9iid? laa, (ba9ad) maa kallamta.
   ١ ـ هل كلمت سعيد ؟ لا ، بعدني ما كلمته •
2. ṣaarilna kaθiir fii bagdaad, laakin (ba9ad) maa šifna lḥadaayiḳ.
   ٢ ـ صار لنا كثير في بغداد ، لكن بعدنا ما شفنا الحدائق•
3. il?amriikaan raaḥaw (waḥid) lijjaami9, bass maa gidraw yidixluun bii.
   ٣ ـ الامريكان راحوا وحدهم للجامع ، بس ما قدروا يدخلون به •
4. ri'kabit (waḥid) bilbalam liδaak iṣṣoob, wuba9dayn mišayt baaḳii-ṭṭariiḳ lilḥadiiḳa.
   ٤ ـ ركبت وحدي بلبلم لذاك الصوب وبعدين مشيت باقي الطريق للحديقة•
5. (ba9ad) maa sti'lamit maktuub minn ḥabiibtii.
   ٥ ـ بعدني ما استلمت مكتوب من حبيبتي •
6. mišayna kaθiir bass (ba9ad) muu ti9baaniin.
   ٦ ـ مشينا كثير بس بعدنا مو تعبانين •
7. (ba9ad) maa šiftum kull madiinat-bagdaad?
   ٧ ـ بعدكم ما شفتم كل مدينة بغداد ؟
8. ?aškurak, ?aftikir ?agdar ?axaḷḷuṣ iššugul (waḥid).
   ٨ ـ اشكرك ، افتكر اقدر اخلص الشغل وحدي •
9. John maa raad yiruuḥ (waḥid).
   ٩ ـ جان ما راد يروح وحده •

D. *Select the* Completed Action Verb *form required by each sentence.*

1. sa9iid maa (ḍirab, ḍirbat, ḍi'rabit) ?a'xuu.
   ١ ـ سعيد ما (ضرب ـ ضربت ـ ضربت) اخوه •
2. jamiila (šikar, šikrat, šikraw) ?umha 9alportaḳaala.
   ٢ ـ جميلة (شكر ـ شكرت ـ شكروا) امها على البرتقالة•
3. (fiham, fi'hamit, fihamtum) šinuu gilitlak?
   ٣ ـ (فهم ـ فهمت ـ فهمتم) شنو قالت لك ؟
4. ṣadiiḳii (gi9ad, gi9dat, gi9daw) minn waḳit wuraaḥ wiiyaay.
   ٤ ـ صديقي (قعد ـ قعدت ـ قعدوا) من وقت وراح ويّلي •

5. John (ga99adnii, ga99aditnii, ga9doonii) lamma gi9ad waław ʔana gilitla ridit ʔanaam mitʔaxxir.

٥ ـ جان (قعّدني ـ قعّدتني ـ قعّدوني) لما قعد ولو انا قلت له ردت انام متأخرة ٠

6. ʔiḥna (rija9, ri'ja9it, rija9na) minn wakit liʔann (kaan, kunit, kinna) ti9baaniin minn ilmašii.

٦ ـ احنا (رجع ـ رجعت ـ رجعنا) من وقت لان (كان ـ كنت ـ كنا) تعبانين من المشي ٠

7. ta9ruf šinuu John (iftikar, ifti'karit, iftikraw) bii haay ilgurfa?

٧ ـ تعرف شنو جان (افتكر ـ افتكرت ـ افتكروا) بي هاي الغرفة ؟

8. Bill maa (stilam, stilmat, stilmaw) maktuub minn ḥabiibta, laakin waaḥid minn ʔahla ʔija 9inda.

٨ ـ بل ما (استلم ـ استلمت ـ استلموا) مكتوب من حبيبته ، لكن واحد من اهله اجا عنده ٠

9. na9am, (štigal, šti'galit, štigalna) fii bagdaad wuhamm filbaṣra; ḥabbayt bagdaad ʔakθar minn ilbaṣra.

٩ ـ نعم ، (اشتغل ـ اشتغلت ـ اشتغلنا) في بغداد وهم في البصرة ، حبيت بغداد اكثر من البصرة ٠

10. riḥna ništirii siiyaara, bass ilmudiir (gaalinna, gaaloonna) huuwa baa9ha lišaxuṣ θaanii.

١٠ ـ رحنا نشتري سيّارة ، بس المدير (قال لنا ـ قالوا لنا) هو باعها لشخص ثاني ٠

11. minuu (sadd, saddayt, saddaw) ilbaab?

١١ ـ منو (سد ـ سديت ـ سدوا) الباب ؟

12. ilbint (ʔaxaδ, ʔixδat, ʔixδaw) 9arabaana ʔila bayt-9ammatha.

١٢ ـ البنت (اخذ ـ اخذت ـ اخذوا) عربانة الى بيت عمتها ٠

13. maa (nṭa, nṭayt, nṭayna) bakšiiš lilboy, laakin xallayna fluus 9almayz.

١٣ ـ ما (نطى نطيت ـ نطينـــا) بقشيش للبوي لـكن خلّينا فلوس على الميز ٠

14. (buka, bukayt, bukayna) yoomayn fii ʔuutayl ṣagiir, wuba9dayn riḥna ʔila ʔuutayl θaanii fii šaari9-irrašiid.

١٤ ـ (بقى ـ بقيت ـ بقينــــا) يومين في اوتيل صغير ، وبعدين رحنا الى اوتيل ثاني في شارع الرشيد ٠

15. ʔana (siʔal, si'ʔalit, siʔlaw) fadd rijjaal 9ann kaniisa, wuhuuwa (raawaanii, raawatnii) kaniistayn.

١٥ ـ انا (سائل ـ سائلت ـ سائلوا) فد رجّال عن كنيسة، وهو (راواني ـ راوتني) كنيستين ٠

16. ilbaarḥa sti'lamit maktuub, bass maa (gidar, gi'darit, gidraw) ʔak'raa liʔann huuwa maktuub bil9arabii.

١٦ ـ البارحة استلمت مكتوب بس ما (قدر ـ قدرت ـ قدروا) اقراه لان هو مكتوب بالعربي ٠

17. lamma kunit ṣagiir, kunit ʔagdar (yiḥkii, tiḥkii, ʔaḥkii) fransaawii.

١٧ ـ لما كنت صغير كنت اقدر (يحكي ـ تحكي ـ احكي) فرنساوي ٠

18. minuu (sawwa, sawwat, sawwayt) haaδa?

١٨ ـ منو (سوّى ـ سوّت ـ سوّيت) هذا ؟

19. ḥasan (wugaf, wugfat, wu'gafit) biššaari9 wu(ḥiča, ḥičat, ḥičayt) wiiya muṣṭafa.

١٩ ـ حسن (وقف ـ وقفت ـ وقفت) بالشارع و (حكى ـ حكت ـ حكيت) ويّا مصطفى ٠

20. šwakit ʔinta wṣadiikak (dixal, di'xalit, dixaltum) fijjaami9?

٢٠ ـ شوقت انت وصديقك (دخل ـ دخلت ـ دخلتم) في الجامع ؟

E. MORE COMPLETED ACTION VERB FORMS. *Read through the following sentences, replacing the* HE *form by the* THEY *form. Then say the* I *form and the* WE *form.*

1. (sikan) fii bagdaad θilaaθ-isniin.

١ ـ سكن في بغداد ثلاث سنين ٠

2. (dixal) bijjaami9.

٢ ـ دخل بالجامع ٠

3. (ʔaxaδ) ṣuurat-bagdaad. — ٣ – اخذ صورة بغداد .
4. (sadd) ilbaab. — ٤ – سد الباب .
5. (ḍann) huuwa kaan ḳawii. — ٥ – ظن هو كان قوي .

6. (baa9) siiyaarta. — ٦ – باع سيّارته .
7. (xalla) ssiiyaara bilbayt. — ٧ – خلّى السيارة بالبيت .
8. (štira) tiffaaḥa ḥilwa. — ٨ – اشترى تفاحة حلوة .
9. (naam) kull illayl. — ٩ – نام كل الليل .
10. (nisa yaaxuδ) ilkaamra. — ١٠ – نسى ياخذ الكاميرة .

F. Incompleted and Completed Action Forms. *Replace the incompleted action forms in parentheses by the corresponding completed action forms. The first sentence is an example.*

1a. (ʔariid) ʔaruuḥ bilbalam. — ١ – اريد اروح بالبلم .
1b. ridit ʔaruuḥ bilbalam. — ردت اروح بالبلم .

2. (yiriid) yisuufnii 9ala ššugul. — ٢ – يريد يشوفني على الشغل .
3. (raaḥ injiib) ṣadiiḳna wiiyaana. — ٣ – راح نجيب صديقنا ويّانا .
4. layš (itguul) ʔinta ti9baan? — ٤ – لیش تقول انت تعبان ؟
5. (yiruuḥuun) yisim9uun ilmuʔaδδin yid9uu nnaas liṣṣaḷaat. — ٥ – يروحون يسمعون المؤذن يدعو الناس للصلاة .

6. hiiya (tguul) giddaamna ṭariiḳ-bagdaad. — ٦ – هي تقول قدّمنا طريق بغداد .
7. (yinaam) kull ilyoom. — ٧ – ينام كل اليوم .
8. (yilbas) badla jadiida. — ٨ – يلبس بدلة جديدة .
9. ʔuxtii (tig9ud) minn waḳit likay tištugul bilbayt. — ٩ – اختي تقعد من وقت لكي تشتغل بالبيت .
10. (raaḥ ʔaakul) hawaaya. — ١٠ – راح آكل هواية .

11. (nišrab) čaay ḥaliib. — ١١ – نشرب شاي حليب .
12. ilwulid (yisiʔluun) 9ann ṣadiiḳhum. — ١٢ – الولد يسائلون عن صديقهم .
13. yamta (raaḥ tirij9uun)? — ١٣ – يمتى راح ترجعون ؟
14. (raaḥ yibḳa) 9idna. — ١٤ – راح يبقى عندنا .
15. ʔuxtii (tiḳra) lmaktuub. — ١٥ – اختي تقرأ المكتوب .

16. minayn (raaḥ tištirii) θoob jadiid? — ١٦ – منين راح تشتري ثوب جديد ؟
17. mitʔassif, ʔana (ʔansa) ʔismak. — ١٧ – متأسف ، انا انسى اسمك .
18. (raaḥ yinṭuun) fluus kaθiira lilwalad. — ١٨ – راح ينطون فلوس كثيرة للولد .
19. š(itsawwuun) hinaa? — ١٩ – شتسوّون هنا ؟
20. (raaḥ txallii) ssiiyaara wara lbayt. — ٢٠ – راح تخلّي السيّارة وراء البيت .

G. Commands. *The following sentences are spoken to a man. Make the necessary changes to speak them to a girl, then to more than one person.*

1. ruuḥ naam! — ١ – روح نام !
2. gullii šitriid! — ٢ – قول لي شتريد !
3. ʔibḳa wiiyaay! — ٣ – ابقى ويّاي !
4. ʔištirii lportaḳaal ʔiδa humma ḥiluu. — ٤ – اشتري البرتقال اذا هما حلو !
5. ʔigsil ʔiidayk! — ٥ – اغسل ايديك !
6. ʔudxul hinaa! — ٦ – ادخل هنا !

7. ʔig9ud ḳariib minnii! ٧ ـ اقعد قريب مني !
8. ʔisʔal šaxuṣ θaanii! ٨ ـ اسائل شخص ثاني !
9. kallim sa9iid lamma tig9ud! ٩ ـ كلّم سعيد لما تقعد !
10. naḍḍuf badiltii! ١٠ ـ نظّف بدلتي !
11. xaḷḷuṣ šuġlak gabul maa itruuḥ! ١١ ـ خلّص شغلك قبل ما تروح !
12. ʔoogaf ibmakaanak! ١٢ ـ اوقف بمكانك !

H. MORE COMMANDS. *Give the masculine singular command form of the words in parentheses.*

1. (yibii9) kull ilmaywa. ١ ـ يبيع كل الميوا •
2. (yiguṣṣ) illaḥam. ٢ ـ يقص اللحم •
3. (yinṭii) baḳšiiš lilḥammaal. ٣ ـ ينطي بقشيش للحمّال •
4. (yisawwii) haaδa. ٤ ـ يسوّي هذا •
5. (yiḍrub) badiltii ʔuutii. ٥ ـ يضرب بدلتي اوتي •
6. (yiftaḥ) ilmaktuub. ٦ ـ يفتح المكتوب •
7. (yisma9) šinuu ʔana ʔaguullak. ٧ ـ يسمع شنو انا اقول لك •
8. (yiga99id) ʔaxuuk lamma tig9ud. ٨ ـ يقعّد اخوك لمّا تقعد •
9. halyoom (yištugul) zayn. ٩ ـ هليوم يشتغل زين •

I. *What are the corresponding* NEGATIVE COMMANDS, *masculine form, for the above?*

J. MORE NEGATIVE COMMANDS. *Give the corresponding feminine and plural forms.*

1. laa timšii lihinaak! ١ ـ لا تمشي الى هناك •
2. laa tšigg ilwaraḳ! ٢ ـ لا تشق الورق •
3. laa truuḥ waḥdak! ٣ ـ لا تروح وحدك •
4. laa tsawwii haaδa! ٤ ـ لا تسوّي هذا •
5. laa taaxuδ siiyaartii! ٥ ـ لا تأخذ سيّارتي •
6. laa tinsa tijii minn waḳit! ٦ ـ لا تنسى تجي من وقت •
7. laa tiktib 9alwaraḳ! ٧ ـ لا تكتب على الورق •
8. laa tig9ud 9almayz! ٨ ـ لا تقعد على الميز •
9. laa taakul hawaaya! ٩ ـ لا تاكل هواية •
10. laa toogaf bilbaab! ١٠ ـ لا توقف بالباب •
11. laa txaḷḷuṣ iššugul! ١١ ـ لا تخلص الشغل •
12. laa tkallimnii! ١٢ ـ لا تكلّمني •
13. laa tga99idnii! ١٣ ـ لا تقعّدني •
14. laa tirja9 lihinaak! ١٤ ـ لا ترجع الى هناك •
15. laa tnaam hinaak! ١٥ ـ لا تنام هناك •

K. VERBS WITH PRONOUN ENDINGS. *Replace the words in parentheses by the proper form of the verb plus ending at the right.*

1. nriid (naaxuδ halgurfa). naaxδa, naaxuδha ١ ـ نريد ناخذ هل غرفة • (ناخذه ـ ناخذها)
2. laa (taaxuδ iddaftar)! taaxδa, taaxuδha ٢ ـ لا تاخذ الدفتر • (ناخذه ـ تاخذها)
3. (xallayna jinaṭna) bissiiyaara ٣ ـ خلّينا جنطنا بالسيارة • (خلّينا ـ خلّيناهم)
 xallaynaaha, xallaynaahum
4. ʔana (nisayt ilmiftaaḥ) jawwa 9almayz. ٤ ـ انا نسيت المفتاح جوّه على الميز • (نسيته ـ نسيتها)
 nisayta, nisaytha

5. ilḥammaal (ṭaḷḷa9 jinaṭna) ʔila gurfatna. ṭaḷḷa9ha, ṭaḷḷa9hum

٥ ـ الحمّال طلّع جنطنا الى غرفتنا • (طلّعها طلّعهم)

6. minuu (dagg ijjaraṣ)? dagga, dagha

٦ ـ منو دق الجرس ؟ (دقّه ـ دقّها)

7. tigdar (tuujad ilḥibir) ʔiδa tdawwir 9a'lay. tuujda, tuujadha

٧ ـ تقدر توجد الحبر اذا تدوّر عليه • (توجده ـ توجدها)

8. ilʔuutačii (naḍḍaf badiltii). naḍḍafa, naḍḍafha

٨ ـ الاوتشي نظّف بدلتي • (نظّفه ـ نظّفها)

9. ʔana (libasit θoobii ljadiid). libasta, libasitha

٩ ـ انا لبست ثوبي الجديد • (لبسته ـ لبستها)

10. šloon (gaṣṣayt wajhak)? gaṣṣayta, gaṣṣaytha

١٠ ـ شلون قصيت وجهك ؟ (قصيته ـ قصيتها)

11. (gisalit ʔiidayya) bilmaay ilbaarid. (gisalta, gisalithum)

١١ ـ غسلت ايديّ بالماء البارد • (غسلته ـ غسلتهم)

12. ilmudiir (kitab ilḳaayma). kitaba, kitabha.

١٢ ـ المدير كتب القائمة • (كتبه ـ كتبها)

13. (ʔiktib haaδa)! kitba, ʔiktibha

١٣ ـ اكتب هذا • (اكتبه ـ اكتبها)

14. huuwa maa (ya9ruf δaak). yi9arfa, ya9rufha

١٤ ـ هو ما يعرف ذاك • (يعرفه ـ يعرفها)

L. More Verb Forms with Pronoun Endings. *Replace the verbs with the ending* –ha HER *by the corresponding form with the ending* –a HIM. *The first is an example.*

1a. yamta raaḥ (itšuufuuha)?

١ ـ يمتى راح تشوفوها ؟

1b. yamta raaḥ itšuu'fuu?

يمتى راح تشوفوه ؟

2. (šifnaaha) lamma kinna nirkab ibsiiyaartii.

٢ ـ شفناها لما كنا نركب بسيّارتي •

3. ʔana ḍannayt humma (jaabooha) lamma ʔijaw 9indak.

٣ ـ انا ظنيت هما جابوها لما اجوا عندك •

4. laa, gaaloolii raaḥ (yijiibuuha) fiššahar ijjaay.

٤ ـ لا قالوا لي راح يجيبوها في الشهر الجاي •

5. layš maa (jibtuuha)?

٥ ـ ليش ما جبتوها ؟

6. minayn raaḥ (tištiriiha)?

٦ ـ منين راح تشتريها ؟

7. ʔarjuuk (xalliiha) hinaak.

٧ ـ ارجوك خلّيها هناك •

8. ba9adnii maa (šifitha).

٨ ـ بعدني ما شفتها •

9. ʔana maa (kitabitha).

٩ ـ انا ما كتبتها •

10. yiriid (yikallimha).

١٠ ـ يريد يكلمها •

11. ʔariid (ʔaxaḷḷuṣha), ʔiδa ʔagdar.

١١ ـ اريد اخلصها اذا اقدر •

12. minuu (ḍirabha)?

١٢ ـ منو ضربها ؟

13. ʔuxtii maa (šaafatha)?

١٣ ـ اختي ما شافتها ؟

14. laa (taaxuδha) wiiyaak.

١٤ ـ لا تاخذها ويّاك •

15. ʔaftikir ʔinta (tuujadha) fii maḥall θaanii.

١٥ ـ افتكر انت توجدها في محل ثاني •

M. More Pronoun Endings. *Replace the verb form with the ending* –ak YOU (m) *with the corresponding form with the ending* –kum YOU (pl).

1. layš laazim (ʔaš'kurak)?

١ ـ ليش لازم اشكرك ؟

2. muṣṭafa wusa9iid gaaloolii humma (šaafook).

٢ ـ مصطفى وسعيد قالوا لي هما شافوك •

3. minuu (nṭaak) ilbaķšiiš? — ٣ ـ منو نطاك البقشيش ؟
4. layš sa9iid (ḍi'rabak)? — ٤ ـ ليش سعيد ضربك ؟
5. ðiič ilbint gaalat hiiya (šaa'fatak). — ٥ ـ ديك البنت قالت هي شافتك ٠
6. ʔakuu ḍaabuṭ yiriid (yišuufak). — ٦ ـ اكو ضابط يريد يشوفك ٠
7. šagdar (ʔasawwiilak)? — ٧ ـ شقدر اسوّي لك ؟
8. halyoom maa (šiftak). — ٨ ـ هليوم ما شفتك ٠
9. minuu (kal'lamak)? — ٩ ـ منو كلّمك ؟
10. minuu (si'ma9ak)? — ١٠ ـ منو سمعك ؟

ADDITIONAL AIDS

Numbers — Counting — Time

NUMBERS

Ending RECORD 2A (1 to 10)
Ending RECORD 23B (11 to 2,000)

ONE TO TEN

waaḥid	١ - واحد
θinayn	٢ - ثنتين
θilaaθa	٣ - ثلاثة
ʔarba9a	٤ - اربعة
xamsa	٥ - خمسة
sitta	٦ - ستة
sab9a	٧ - سبعة
θimaanya	٨ - ثمانية
tis9a	٩ - تسعة
9ašra	١٠ - عشرة

ELEVEN TO TWENTY

ʔiida9aš	١١ - ايدعش
θina9aš	١٢ - اثنعش
θilaṭṭa9aš	١٣ - ثلطعش
ʔarbaaṭa9aš	١٤ - ارباطعش
xamiṣṭa9aš	١٥ - خمصطعش
ṣiṭṭa9aš	١٦ - صطعش
sba9ṭa9aš	١٧ - سبعطعش
θimunṭa9aš	١٨ - ثمنطعش
tsa9ṭa9aš	١٩ - تسعطعش
9išriin	٢٠ - عشرين

TEN TO A HUNDRED

9ašra	١٠ - عشرة
9išriin	٢٠ - عشرين
θilaaθiin	٣٠ - ثلاثين
ʔarba9iin	٤٠ - اربعين
xamsiin	٥٠ - خمسين
sittiin	٦٠ - ستين
sab9iin	٧٠ - سبعين
θimaaniin	٨٠ - ثمانين
tis9iin	٩٠ - تسعين
miiya	١٠٠ - مية

A HUNDRED TO A THOUSAND

miiya	١٠٠ - مية
miitayn	٢٠٠ - ميتين
θilaaθ-miiya	٣٠٠ - ثلاث مية
ʔarba9-miiya	٤٠٠ - اربع مية
xamis-miiya	٥٠٠ - خمس مية
sit-miiya	٦٠٠ - ست مية
sabi9-miiya	٧٠٠ سبع مية
θiman-miiya	٨٠٠ - ثمان مية
tisi9-miiya	٩٠٠ - تسع مية
ʔalif	١٠٠٠ - الف

A THOUSAND TO TEN THOUSAND

ʔalif	١٠٠٠ - الف
ʔalfayn	٢٠٠٠ - الفين
θilaat-taalaaf	٣٠٠٠ - ثلاثة آلاف
ʔarbaʔ-taalaaf	٤٠٠٠ - اربعة آلاف
xamis-taalaaf	٥٠٠٠ - خمسة آلاف
sit-taalaaf	٦٠٠٠ - ستة آلاف
sabi9-taalaaf	٧٠٠٠ - سبعة آلاف
θiman-taalaaf	٨٠٠٠ - ثمانية آلاف
tisi9-taalaaf	٩٠٠٠ - تسعة آلاف
9ašir-taalaaf	١٠،٠٠٠ - عشرة آلاف

HUNDRED-THOUSANDS

miit-ʔalif	١٠٠،٠٠٠ - مية الف
miitayn-ʔalif	٢٠٠،٠٠٠ - ميتين الف
θilaaθ-miit-ʔalif	٣٠٠،٠٠٠ - ثلاث مية الف
ʔarba9-miit-ʔalif	٤٠٠،٠٠٠ - اربع مية الف
xamis-miit-ʔalif	٥٠٠،٠٠٠ خمس مية الف
sit-miit-ʔalif	٦٠٠،٠٠٠ - ست مية الف
sabi9-miit-ʔalif	٧٠٠،٠٠٠ - سبع مية الف
θiman-miit-ʔalif	٨٠٠،٠٠٠ - ثمن مية الف
tisi9-miit-ʔalif	٩٠٠،٠٠٠ - تسع مية الف
malyoon	١،٠٠٠،٠٠٠ - مليون

You will notice that the set from eleven to twenty has more emphatic consonants (as ṭ and ṣ) and will probably require more practice than the others.

Most of the words for hundreds and thousands are compounds. Before miiya *hundred* the numbers are in their combining form, which have no final –a, in addition to other changes.

As first member of a compound, miiya itself has the form miit- (miit-ʔalif *hundred thousand*).

As second member of a compound, ʔaalaaf *thousands* has the form -taalaaf. Before this, the numbers have forms ending in t (θilat-taalaaf *three thousand*).

Practice the numbers given above. Go through them several times. Then take turns counting.

COUNTING ABOVE TWENTY is *one and twenty*, *two and twenty*, and so on up to a hundred:

9išriin	*twenty*	عشرين
waaḥid wu9išriin	*one and twenty*	واحد وعشرين
θinayn wu9išriin	*two and twenty*	ثنين وعشرين
θilaaθa w9išriin	*three and twenty*	ثلاثة وعشرين
waaḥid wuθilaaθiin	*one and thirty*	واحد وثلاثين
xamsa wθilaaθiin	*five and thirty*	خمسة وثلاثين

Two or more numbers are always joined together by *and*. Between consonants this is spoken as wu– or uu– (waaḥid wu9išriin or waaḥid uu9išriin; after –a it is usually w and the two are pronounced together as aw (xamsa wθilaaθiin); and it is usually just w– before ʔarba9a (warba9a, warbaṭa9aš, warba9iin).

HUNDREDS are named first:

miiya	*a hundred*	مية
miiya wwaaḥid	*a hundred and one*	مية وواحد
miiya wxamsa	*a hundred and five*	مية وخمسة
miiya wxamsa w9išriin	*a hundred and five and twenty*	مية وخمسة وعشرين

NUMBERS OVER A THOUSAND always begin with *thousand*, as *a thousand and two hundred;* you *never* say *twelve hundred.*

ʔalif wumiiya	*a thousand and a hundred*	الف ومية
ʔalif wumiitayn	*a thousand and two hundred*	الف وميتين
ʔalif wutisi9-miiya wxamsa wʔarba9iin	*nineteen hundred and forty-five*	الف وتسع مية وخمسة واربعين
fii sanat-ʔalif wutisi9-miiya wsitta wʔarba9iin	*in the year nineteen forty-six*	في سنة الف وتسع مية وستة واربعين

SIMPLE ARITHMETIC

he adds	yijma9	يجمع
Add one and one.	ʔijma9 waaḥid uuwaaḥid.	اجمع واحد وواحد .
it makes, it amounts to	yisaawii	يساوي
plus	zaayid	زائد
One and one makes two.	waaḥid uuwaaḥid yisaawii θinayn.	واحد وواحد يساوي ثنين .
Two and two makes four.	θinayn wuθinayn yisaawii ʔarba9a.	ثنين وثنين يساوي اربعة .
he subtracts from	yiṭraḥ minn	يطرح من
Subtract six from ten.	ʔiṭraḥ sitta minn 9ašra.	اطرح ستة من عشرة .
minus	naakuṣ	ناقص
Ten minus six makes four.	9ašra naakuṣ sitta yisaawii ʔarba9a.	عشرة ناقص ستة يساوي اربعة .

he multiplies by	yiḍrub fii	يضرب في
Multiply five by two.	ʔiḍrub xamsa fii θinayn.	اضرب خمسة في ثنين •
in, times	fii	في
Five times two is ten.	xamsa fii θinayn yisaawii 9ašra.	خمسة في ثنين يساوي عشرة •
he divides by	yiķassim 9ala	يقسّم على
Divide ten by five.	ķassim 9ašra 9ala xamsa.	قسّم عشرة على خمسة •
divided by	taķsiim	تقسيم
Ten divided by five makes two.	9ašra taķsiim xamsa yisaawii θinayn.	عشرة تقسيم خمسة يساوي ثنين •

Note that waaḥid always takes the masculine yisaawii. The remaining numbers can freely take the feminine tsaawii as well.

Exercise.

Go through the material above several times. All the material given there is not of the greatest importance, but it is given together for your convenience.

Afterwards, close your books and *add* the numbers as 'one and one makes two', 'two and two makes four'. Thereafter *multiply* the numbers as 'two times two makes four' and so on. If desired you can use the other simple arithmetic expressions for further practice.

Finally, check the following problems. In these simple problems check the answer as true or false. Supply the correct answer for those you find are false.

T	F	1. θinayn wuθinayn yisaawii ʔarba9a.	١ — ٢ + ٢ = ٤
T	F	2. θinayn naaķuṣ waaḥid yisaawii θilaaθa.	٢ — ٢ — ١ = ٣
T	F	3. sitta wsitta yisaawii θina9aš.	٣ — ٦ + ٦ = ١٢
T	F	4. θilaaθa wsab9a yisaawii 9ašra.	٤ — ٣ + ٧ = ١٠
T	F	5. xamsa fii xamsa yisaawii xamsa w9išriin.	٥ — ٥ × ٥ = ٢٥
T	F	6. tis9a naaķuṣ θilaaθa yisaawii sitta.	٦ — ٩ — ٣ = ٦
T	F	7. ʔarba9a fii θinayn yisaawii θimaanya.	٧ — ٤ × ٢ = ٨
T	F	8. θimaanya taķsiim θilaaθa yisaawii xamsa.	٨ — ٨ ÷ ٣ = ٥
T	F	9. sab9a naaķuṣ θilaaθa yisaawii xamsa.	٩ — ٧ — ٣ = ٥
T	F	10. θina9aš naaķuṣ θilaaθa yisaawii tis9a.	١٠ — ١٢ — ٣ = ٩
T	F	11. 9išriin wu9išriin yisaawii ʔarba9iin.	١١ — ٢٠ + ٢٠ — ٤٠
T	F	12. tis9a fii θinayn yisaawii tisi9ṭa9aš.	١٢ — ٩ × ٢ = ١٩
T	F	13. tis9a fii θilaaθa yisaawii sab9a w9išriin.	١٣ — ٩ × ٣ = ٢٧
T	F	14. θilaaθiin naaķuṣ 9išriin yisaawii ʔarba9iin.	١٤ — ٣٠ — ٢٠ = ٤٠
T	F	15. sittiin fii θinayn yisaawii miiya wʔarba9iin.	١٥ — ٦٠ × ٢ = ١٤٠
T	F	16. sab9a fii sab9a yisaawii tis9a warba9iin.	١٦ — ٧ × ٧ = ٤٩
T	F	17. θimaanya taķsiim ʔarba9a yisaawii θinayn.	١٧ — ٨ ÷ ٤ = ٢
T	F	18. xamsa fii 9ašra yisaawii xamsiin.	١٨ — ٥ × ١٠ = ٥٠
T	F	19. θimaanya naaķuṣ ʔarba9a yisaawii θinayn.	١٩ — ٨ — ٤ = ٢
T	F	20. tis9iin naaķuṣ sittiin yisaawii θilaaθiin.	٢٠ — ٩٠ — ٦٠ = ٣٠

T	F	21. waaḥid uuwaaḥid uusitta yisaawii sab9a.	٧ =٦+١+١ —٢١
T	F	22. θilaaθa wxamsa yisaawii xamiṣṭa9aš.	١٥ = ٥ + ٣ —٢٢
T	F	23. ʔarba9a wxamsa yisaawii tis9a.	٩ = ٥ + ٤ —٢٣
T	F	24. θilaaθa fii 9ašra yisaawii θilaaθiin.	٣٠ = ١٠ × ٣ —٢٤
T	F	25. xamsa fii sitta yisaawii ʔiida9aš.	١١ = ٦ × ٥ —٢٥
T	F	26. 9ašra w9ašra yisaawii 9išriin.	٢٠ = ١٠ + ١٠ —٢٦
T	F	27. θilaaθiin naaḳuṣ xamsa yisaawii xamsa w9išriin.	٢٥ = ٥ —٣٠ —٢٧
T	F	28. sab9a taḳsiim θinayn yisaawii θilaaθa wnuṣṣ.	٣ ١/٢ = ٢ ÷ ٧ —٢٨
T	F	29. miiya wmiitayn yisaawii θilaaθ-miiya.	٣٠٠=٢٠٠+١٠٠—٢٩
T	F	30. sit-miiya naaḳuṣ miiya yisaawii xamis-miiya.	٥٠٠=١٠٠—٦٠٠—٣٠
T	F	31. tisi9ṭa9aš naaḳuṣ tis9a yisaawii 9ašra.	١٠ = ٩ — ١٩—٣١
T	F	32. ʔarbaaṭa9aš taḳsiim sab9a yisaawii θinayn.	٢ = ٧ ÷ ١٤—٣٢
T	F	33. xamsa fii sab9a yisaawii xamsa wθilaaθiin.	٣٥ = ٧ × ٥ —٣٣
T	F	34. waaḥid wuθina9aš wusitta yisaawii θimunṭa9aš.	١٨=٦+١٢ + ١ —٣٤
T	F	35. sitta wθina9aš yisaawii θimunṭa9aš.	١٨ = ١٢ + ٦ —٣٥
T	F	36. sittiin taḳsiim θinayn yisaawii θilaaθiin.	٣٠ = ٢ ÷٦٠—٣٦
T	F	37. θimaaniin naaḳuṣ waaḥid wuxamsiin yisaawii sab9a w9išriin.	٢٧=٥١—٨٠—٣٧
T	F	38. ʔarba9-miiya wsabi9-miiya yisaawii ʔalif wumiitayn.	١٢٠٠=٧٠٠+٤٠٠—٣٨
T	F	39. θina9aš fii θina9aš yisaawii miiya wʔarba9a wʔarba9iin.	١٤٤=١٢ × ١٢—٣٩
T	F	40. 9ašra fii 9išriin yisaawii miitayn.	٢٠٠=٢٠ × ١٠—٤٠

What is the Iraqi for these problems?

1. One and two makes three.
2. Two times two is four.
3. Five times five is twenty-five.
4. Eight minus four makes four.
5. Eight divided by two makes four.
6. Ten times ten makes a hundred.
7. Thirty and thirty makes sixty.
8. Twelve divided by two makes six.
9. Eighteen minus ten makes eight.
10. Four and four makes eight.
11. Six and three makes nine.
12. Six minus three makes three.
13. Fourteen divided by seven makes two.
14. Thirteen minus six makes seven.
15. Three and four makes seven.
16. Five times twenty makes a hundred.
17. Seven times six makes forty-two.
18. Nine and six makes fifteen.
19. Four and seven makes eleven.
20. Eleven and twelve makes twenty-three.

COUNTING THINGS

When it comes to *counting things*, there are several points to be noted. First, waaḥid (waaḥda *or* wiḥda) is an adjective and follows its noun. Since the singular noun by itself indicates only one item, it isn't necessary to say waaḥid with it.

walad waaḥid	*one boy*	ولد واحد
bint waaḥda *or* wiḥda	*one girl*	بنت واحدة

Second, *two* is expressed by the ending –ayn added to the noun.

waladayn	*two boys*	ولدين
bintayn	*two girls*	بنتين

Third, from three on the number forms a *noun-compound with the thing counted.* However, only nine numbers have two forms, the one free and the other as first member of a compound (θilaaθa, θilaaθ- *or* θilaθ-; ˀarba9a, ˀarba9-; xamsa, xamis-; sitta, sit-; sab9a, sabi9-; θimaanya, θimaan- *or* θiman-; tis9a, tisi9-; 9ašra, 9ašir-; and miiya, miit-).

θilaaθ-wulid	*three boys*	ثلاث ولد
ˀarba9-wulid	*four boys*	اربع ولد
xamis-wulid	*five boys*	خمس ولد
sit-wulid	*six boys*	ست ولد
sabi9-wulid	*seven boys*	سبع ولد
θiman-wulid	*eight boys*	ثمن ولد
tisi9-wulid	*nine boys*	تسع ولد
9ašir-wulid	*ten boys*	عشر ولد
ˀiida9aš-walad	*eleven boys*	ايدعش ولد
θina9aš-walad	*twelve boys*	اثنعش ولد
9išriin-walad	*twenty boys*	عشرين ولد
miit-walad	*a hundred boys*	مية ولد
θilaaθ-miit-walad	*three hundred boys*	ثلاث مية ولد

From three to ten, the *plural form* of a noun is used with the number (three boys). From eleven on, the *singular* is used (eleven boy, a hundred boy, etc.). It is the *last number just before the noun* which determines whether the singular or plural of the noun is used:

a hundred boys	miit-walad	مية ولد
a hundred and five boys	miiya wxamis-wulid	مية وخمس ولد
a hundred and one boys	miit-walad uuwaaḥid	مية ولد وواحد

Exercise.

Count the things which are listed below. Count them from one to fifteen, and then by tens to a hundred. The first three numbers are given; from them you can give the others.

boy	walad waaḥid	waladayn	θilaaθ-wulid
man	rijjaal waaḥid	rijjaalayn	θilaaθ-riyaajiil
soldier	jundii waaḥid	jundiyayn	θilaaθ-jinuud
mile	miil waaḥid	miilayn	θilaaθ-miiyaal

dinar	diinaar waaḥid	diinaarayn	θilaaθ-dinaaniir
fils	filis waaḥid	filsayn	θilaaθ-ifluus
day	yoom waaḥid	yoomayn	θilaaθ-ʔayyaam
million	malyoon waaḥid	malyoonayn	θilaaθ-milaayiin
girl	bint waaḥda	bintayn	θilaaθ-banaat
year	sana waaḥda	santayn	θilaaθ-isniin
clock	saa9a waaḥda	saa9atayn	θilaaθ-saa9aat
minute	daḳiiḳa waaḥda	daḳiiḳtayn	θilaaθ-daḳaayiḳ
second	θaaniya waaḥda	θaaniitayn	θilaaθ-θawaanii

TIME

a quarter	rubu9	ربع
a third	θiliθ	ثلث
a half	nuṣṣ *or* nuṣuf	نص (ايضا) نصف
a minute	daḳiiḳa (daḳaayiḳ, *pl*)	دقيقة ـ دقايق
a second	θaaniya (θawaanii, *pl*)	ثانية ـ ثواني
except; less	ʔilla	الاّ
hour; watch	saa9a (saa9aat, *pl*)	ساعة ـ ساعات
how much?	bayš	بيش
What time is it?	issaa9a bayš *or* bayš issaa9a?	بيش الساعة ؟
It's one o'clock.	issaa9a bilwiḥda.	الساعة بالوحدة .
It's two o'clock.	issaa9a biθθintayn.	الساعة بالثنتين .
Three o'clock.	biθθilaaθa.	بالثلاثة .
The watch is running.	issaa9a timšii.	الساعة تمشي .
The watch is stopped.	issaa9a waagfa.	الساعة واقفة .

Notice that bil– *in the* corresponds roughly to English *o'clock.* It is almost always used with the numbers in answer to the question issaa9a bayš? The answer can be:

issaa9a biθθilaaθa.	الساعة بالثلاثة .
biθθilaaθa.	بالثلاثة .
θilaaθa.	ثلاثة .

One o'clock is bilwiḥda and *two o'clock* is biθθintayn (*not* θinayn). Thereafter, the hours are just the numbers preceded by bil–, as bilxamsa *five o'clock*, biθθi'na9aš *twelve o'clock*, and so on.

PARTS OF AN HOUR

It runs *three and a minute, three and two minutes*, and so on up to the half-hour mark. The minutes can be counted.

(3:01) θilaaθa wdaḳiiḳa	*three and a minute*	٣:١ ـ ثلاثة ودقيقة
(3:02) θilaaθa wdaḳiiḳtayn	*three and two minutes*	٣:٢ ـ ثلاثة ودقيقتين
(3:03) θilaaθa wθilaaθa	*three and three minutes*	٣:٣ ـ ثلاثة وثلاثة

(3:05) θilaaθa wxamsa	*three and five minutes*	٣:٥ ـ ثلاثة وخمسة
(3:10) θilaaθa w9ašra	*three and ten minutes*	٣:١٠ ـ ثلاثة وعشرة

In addition, the hour is divided into *quarters, thirds,* and *halves:*

(3:15) θilaaθa wrubu9	*three and a quarter*	٣:١٥ ـ ثلاثة وربع
(3:20) θilaaθa wθiliθ	*three and a third*	٣:٢٠ ـ ثلاثة وثلث
(3:30) θilaaθa wnuṣṣ	*three and a half*	٣:٣٠ ـ ثلاثة ونص

Now, after the half-hour mark, the point of view changes:

(3:40) ʔarba9a ʔilla θiliθ	*four less a third*	٣:٤٠ ـ اربعة الا ثلث
(3:45) ʔarba9a ʔilla rubu9	*four less a fourth*	٣:٤٥ ـ اربعة الا ربع
(3:50) ʔarba9a ʔilla 9ašra	*four less ten*	٣:٥٠ ـ اربعة الا عشرة
(3:55) ʔarba9a ʔilla xamsa	*four less five*	٣:٥٥ ـ اربعة الا خمسة
(3:59) ʔarba9a ʔilla daḳiiḳa	*four less a minute*	٣:٥٩ ـ اربعة الا دقيقة

Notice especially these two times:

(3:25) θilaaθa wnuṣṣ ʔilla xamsa	*three and a half less five*	٣:٢٥ ـ ثلاثة ونص الا خمسة
(3:35) θilaaθa wnuṣṣ wuxamsa	*three and a half and five*	٣:٣٥ ـ ثلاثة ونص وخمسة

TIME EXPRESSIONS

bil– is *at*

ʔašuufak bilwiḥda.	*I'll see you at one.*	اشوفك بالوحدة .
ʔija biθθilaaθa.	*He came at three.*	اجا بالثلاثة .

gabl il– is *before*

ta9aal gabl iθθintayn!	*Come before two!*	تعال قبل الثنتين .
raaḥ gabl issitta.	*He went before six.*	داح قبل الستة .

ba9ad il– is *after*

raaḥ nruuḥ ba9ad ilwiḥda.	*We are going to go after one.*	راح نروح بعد الوحدة .
jiit ba9ad ilʔarba9a.	*I came after four.*	جيت بعد الاربعة .

lil– is *until*

gilit raaḥ ʔaštuġul lilwiḥda, laakin štiġalit liθθintayn.	*I said I was going to work until one, but I worked until two.*	قلت راح اشتغل للوحدة لكن اشتغلت للثنتين .

WHAT TIME IS IT?

Select the right time:

(1) 3:20

θilaaθa wnuṣṣ	١ ـ ٣:٣٠ ـ ثلاثة ونص
θilaaθa ʔilla θiliθ	٣:٤٠ ـ ثلاثة الا ثلث
θilaaθa wθiliθ	٣:٢٠ ـ ثلاثة وثلث

(2) 1:00	
issaa9a bilwiḥda	٢ ـ ١:٠٠ ـ الساعة بالوحدة
issaa9a biθθintayn	٢:٠٠ ـ الساعة بالثنتين
θimaanya ʔilla θiliθ	٧:٤٠ ـ ثمانية الا ثلث
(3) 6:02	
sitta wdaḳiiḳtayn	٣ ـ ٦:٢ ـ ستة ودقيقتين
sab9a ʔilla daḳiiḳtayn	٦:٥٨ ـ سبعة الا دقيقتين
tis9a w9ašra	٩:١٠ ـ تسعة وعشرة
(4) 8:45	
tis9a wrubu9	٤ ـ ٩:١٥ ـ تسعة وربع
tis9a ʔilla rubu9	٨:٤٥ ـ تسعة الا ربع
θimaanya wrubu9	٨:١٥ ـ ثمانية وربع
(5) 3:25	
θilaaθa wxamsa	٥ ـ ٣:٥ ـ ثلاثة وخمسة
θilaaθa wnuṣṣ ʔilla xamsa	٣:٢٥ ـ ثلاثة ونص الا خمسة
θilaaθa wnuṣṣ wuxamsa	٣:٣٥ ـ ثلاثة ونص وخمسة
(6) 4:15	
xamsa ʔilla rubu9	٦ ـ ٤:٤٥ ـ خمسة الا ربع
ʔarba9a wrubu9	٤:١٥ ـ اربعة وربع
ʔarba9a wsab9a	٤:٠٧ ـ اربعة وسبعة
(7) 5:10	
sab9a ʔilla xamsa	٧ ـ ٦:٥٥ ـ سبعة الا خمسة
xamsa ʔilla sab9a	٤:٥٣ ـ خمسة الا سبعة
xamsa w9ašra	٥:١٠ ـ خمسة وعشرة
(8) 2:30	
θilaaθa ʔilla xamsa	٨ ـ ٢:٥٥ ـ ثلاثة الا خمسة
θintayn wunuṣṣ	٢:٣٠ ـ ثنين ونص
θintayn wunuṣṣ wuxamsa	٢:٣٥ ـ ثنتين ونص وخمسة
(9) 7:40	
sab9a wθiliθ	٩ ـ ٧:٢٠ ـ سبعة وثلث
θimaanya ʔilla rubu9	٧:٤٥ ـ ثمانية الا ربع
θimaanya ʔilla θiliθ	٧:٤٠ ـ ثمانية الا ثلث
(10) 3:35	
θilaaθa ʔilla xamsa	١٠ ـ ٢:٥٥ ـ ثلاثة الا خمسة
ʔarba9a ʔilla xamsa	٣:٥٥ ـ اربعة الا خمسة
θilaaθa wnuṣṣ wuxamsa	٣:٣٥ ـ ثلاثة ونص وخمسة

(11) 5:58

sitta ʔilla daḳiiḳtayn	١١ ـ ٥:٥٨ ـ ستة الا" دقيقتين
sitta wdaḳiiḳtayn	٦:٠٢ ـ ستة ودقيقتين
xamsa wdaḳiiḳtayn	٥:٠٢ ـ خمسة ودقيقتين

(12) 11:50

ʔiida9aš ʔilla 9ašra	١٢ ـ ١٠:٥٠ ـ ايدعش الا" عشرة
θina9aš wu9ašra	١٢:١٠ ـ ثنعش وعشرة
θina9aš ʔilla 9ašra	١١:٥٠ ـ ثنعش الا" عشرة

Give the Iraqi for the time indicated below:

4:00	3:45	4:40
4:30	9:40	6:10
5:30	5:40	8:15
2:10	5:50 '	At six o'clock.
2:15	6:45	
2:20	8:58	Before one.
8:00	1:00	After five-thirty.
1:05	1:25	
7:15	1:35	Until three.

DISTANCE

the distance	ilmasaafa	المسافة
between	bayn	بين
in the train	bilḳiṭaar	بالقطار
in the plane	biṭṭayyaara	بالطيّارة
How far is Basra from Baghdad?	šgad ilmasaafa bayn ilbaṣra wubagdaad?	شقد المسافة بين البصرة وبغداد ؟
About thirteen hours by train, or three or four hours by plane.	taḳriiban θilaṭ'ṭa9aš-saa9a bilḳiṭaar, ʔaw θilaaθa ʔaw ʔarba9-saa9aat biṭṭayyaara.	تقريبا ١٣ ساعة بالقطار او ٣ او ٤ ساعات بالطيّارة •

In Iraq, distance between two points is usually given in terms of the time necessary to get there via the prevailing means of transportation.

AGE

your age	9umrak	عمرك
How old are you?	šgad 9umrak?	شقد عمرك ؟
my age	9umrii	عمري
I am twenty-one.	9umrii waaḥid wu9išriin.	عمري واحد وعشرين •

older than	ʔakbar minn	اكبر من
One of my brothers is three years older than me.	waaḥid minn ʔuxuutii θilaaθ-isniin ʔakbar minnii.	واحد من اخوتي ثلاث سنين اكبر مني •
younger than	ʔaṣgar minn	اصغر من
two years	santayn	سنتين
The other is two years younger than me.	iθθaanii santayn ʔaṣgar minnii.	الثاني سنتين اصغر مني •
together	sawa	سوى
We are the same age.	9umurna sawa.	عمرنا سوى •
His age is the same as mine.	9umra miθil 9umrii.	عمره مثل عمري •

DAYS

What is today?	šinuu lyoom?	شنو اليوم ؟
Sunday	yoom ilʔaḥad	يوم الاحد
Monday	yoom iθθinayn	يوم الاثنين
Tuesday	yoom iθθilaaθaaʔ	يوم الثلاثاء
Wednesday	yoom ilʔarba9aaʔ	يوم الاربعاء
Thursday	yoom ilxamiis	يوم الخميس
Friday	yoom ijjim9a	يوم الجمعة
Saturday	yoom issabit	يوم السبت
the days of the week	ʔayyaam-ilʔisbuu9	ايّام الاسبوع

The names of the days of the week are related to the numbers, with the exception of Friday. Sunday is the first day, Monday the second day, and so on to Friday. Friday is the appointed day for Moslems to meet together for religious services. Hence the name for Friday, yoom ijjim9a, which means the day of gathering together. Since Friday is the religious day of rest, it corresponds to our Sunday.

MONTHS

month	šahar	شهر
What month are you going to leave Baghdad?	fii ʔay šahar raaḥ titruk bagdaad?	في اي شهر راح تترك بغداد ؟
intending	naawii	ناوي
I intend to go to Basra in April.	naawii ʔaruuḥ lilbaṣra fii niisaan.	ناوي اروح للبصرة في نيسان •
three months	θilaat-ʔišhuur	ثلاث اشهور
I will stay there three months.	raaḥ ʔabḳa θilaat-ʔišhuur biiha.	راح ابقى ثلاث اشهور بيها •

the months of the year	ʔišhuur-issana	اشهور السنة
January	kaanuun iθθaanii	كانون الثاني
February	šibaaṭ	شباط
March	ʔaaδaar	آذار
April	niisaan	نيسان
May	ʔayyaar	أيار
June	ḥizayraan	حزيران
July	tammuuz	تموز
August	ʔaab	آب
September	ʔayluul	ايلول
October	tašriin ilʔawwal	تشرين الاول
November	tašriin iθθaanii	تشرين الثاني
December	kaanuun ilʔawwal	كانون الاول

NUMBER ADJECTIVES

On the sixth day we looked for work.	bilyoom issaadis dawwarna 9ala šugul.	باليوم السادس دوّرنا على شغل •
Have the fourth man come to see me.	xallii yijii 9indii rrijjaal irraabi9.	خلّي يجي عندي الرجّال الرابع •

The *number adjectives* follow a common adjective pattern, namely that of saakin (saakna). Below they are given in both masculine and feminine form. Note that only *the first* and *the sixth* have markedly different forms from the corresponding numbers, waaḥid and sitta.

the first	ilʔawwal (m)	ilʔuula (f)	الاول - الاولى
the second	iθθaanii	iθθaaniya	الثاني - الثانية
the third	iθθaaliθ	iθθaalθa	الثالث - الثالثة
the fourth	irraabi9	irraab9a	الرابع - الرابعة
the fifth	ilxaamis	ilxaamsa	الخامس - الخامسة
the sixth	issaadis	issaadsa	السادس - السادسة
the seventh	issaabi9	issaab9a	السابع - السابعة
the eighth	iθθaamin	iθθaamna	الثامن - الثامنة
the ninth	ittaasi9	ittaas9a	التاسع - التاسعة
the tenth	il9aašir	il9aašra	العاشر - العاشرة
the eleventh	ilʔiida9aš (m, f)		الايدعش
the twentieth	il9išriin		العشرين
the hundredth	ilmiiya		المية
the thousandth	ilʔalif		الالف

You will note that from the eleventh on, the number adjective has no special form, but instead consists of the number itself with the article prefix (ilʔiida9aš). This is both masculine and feminine.

APPENDICES

I. Key to Aids to Listening

In the AIDS TO LISTENING, each symbol stands for *one sound only*. A single symbol is used even for sounds that are written with two or more symbols in English. It follows that every symbol written stands for a sound that must be pronounced. The approximate values of the symbols are as follows:

a	A sound ranging from *e* in *get* through *a* in *about* to *o* in *got.*	salla *basket* ʔinta *you* (m) ṭabiib *doctor*
aa	A sound ranging from *a* in *bad* to *a* in *father.*	maa *not* yawaaš *slowly*
aw	A vowel combination of the *a* in *about* followed by *u* in *rude.* Note especially that the *a* of this combination is the *a* of *about* and NOT the *a* of *father.*	ʔaw *or* sawwa *he made* šaafaw *they saw*
ay	A sound like *ay* in *say*, but with less of the final gliding effect.	wayn *where* bayt *house*
ayy	When followed by another y, *ay* is a vowel combination of an a-sound followed by an e-sound (*e* as in *meet*). Note especially that the *a* of this combination is the *a* of *about* and NOT the *a* of *father.*	šwayya *a little* zayyin *shave!*
aay	A sound like *ai* in *aisle.*	jigaayir *cigarettes* haay *this* (f)
b	Is *b*, as in *back.*	bayt *house*
č	Is *ch* in *chin.*	simač *fish*
d	Is *d*, as in *dim.*	ʔariid *I want*
ḍ	Like *th* in *that*, but with the tongue stiffer.	ḍuhur *noon*
f	Is *f*, as in *fish.*	šaaf *he saw*
g	Is *g*, as in *go.*	gubaḷ *ahead*
ġ	Is a gargle-like sound.	ġayr *different*
h	Is *h*, as in *how.*	hamm *too, also*
ḥ	Is a strong h-sound, for which the throat muscles are tensed.	laḥam *meat*
i	Like *i* in *kid.*	sitta *six*
ii	Like *ee* in *see.*	ʔaanii *I*

j	Is *j*, as in *judge*.	jisir *bridge*
k	Is *k*, as in *kick*.	kull *all, every*
ḳ	A k-like sound made with the farthest back part of the tongue.	ḳariib *near*
l	An l-sound made with the tip of the tongue touching back of the upper front teeth.	balii *yes* jabal *mountain*
ḷ	Like l, but with the back of the tongue raised.	gubaḷ *straight ahead*
m	Is *m*, as in *meet*.	maa *not*
n	Is *n*, as in *no*.	zayn *well*
oo	Like *o* in *go*, but without the final gliding effect. The lips must be rounded.	šloon *how*
p	Is *p*, as in *put*.	puutayta *potatoes*
r	A trilled r-sound. The tip of the tongue trills just back of the upper front teeth.	ʔariid *I want* irrijjaal *the man*
s	Is *s*, as in *see*.	siinama *movie*
ṣ	A thicker s-sound, with the tongue farther back and stiffer.	ṣaar *he became* ṣirit *I became*
š	Like *sh* in *ship*.	šinuu *what*
t	Is *t*, as in *tin*.	tiin *figs*
ṭ	Is made farther back than the *t* in *talk*. The tongue is stiffer.	ṭaar *he flew*
u	Like *u* in *put*, but with the lips rounded.	xubuz *bread* ʔaškurak *I thank you.*
uu	Like *u* in *rude*.	šuuf *see!*
w	Is *w*, as in *want*.	wayn *where*
x	A sound like you make in scraping your throat.	xubuz *bread* šixaaṭa *a match*
y	Is *y*, as in *yet*.	yamiin *right side*
z	Is *z*, as in *maze*.	zayn *good, well*
ʔ	Is a sharp break before, between, or after vowels.	masaaʔ ilxayr *Good evening.*
9	A sharp sound made by tightening the throat muscles.	9arabii *Arabic* na9am *yes*
θ	Like *th* in *think*.	θinayn *two*
δ	Like *th* in *that*.	δaak *that* (m)

II. Index to Pronunciation Practices

III. Reading Arabic

1. Arabic is written and printed from *right* to *left.*

2. Consonants are written, but single vowels (except –a at the end of words) are not written (*as* whr r y gng? *for* Where are you going?).

3. There are no capital letters.

4. There are 6 consonant characters which *do not join* a following character. They are the characters for d δ r z ʔ and w. On the other hand, any character can join with a preceding joining character.

5. Some characters have slightly differing forms depending on whether or not they (1) follow one of the non-joining characters, or (2) stand at the end of the word or alone. The form of character at the end of a word usually varies the most.

6. One speech sound (ḍ) is represented by two different characters. For this reason, words containing these characters will have to be distinguished.

7. Doubling of consonants is marked by a small w-like character placed over the consonant character. Usually, however, this mark is omitted.

8. Punctuation marks have been borrowed from the West. In keeping with the direction of writing, they have been reversed.

9. *Consonant characters.* There are, then, four possible situations for any consonant character: (1) non-final but not joined to a preceding character, (2) non-final, joined to a preceding character, (3) final, joined to a preceding character, and (4) final but not joined to a preceding character. The last named form is also used when the character stands entirely alone, not in a word. Character forms are given in that order at the right, with illustrative words at the left. Remember that the Arabic is to be read from right to left.

---

b — بـ ـبـ ـب ب

bint	بنت
liban	لبن
ʔab	اب

č (*same as for* k) — كـ ـكـ ـك ك

čabiir	كبير
yiḥčii	يحكي
ʔaškurič	اشكرك

---

d	د ـد ـد
daras	درس
tidris	تدرس
sidd	سد
raad	راد

The two characters for ḍ must be distinguished.

ḍ	ضـ ـضـ ـض ض
ḍa9iif	ضعيف
ʔayḍan	ايضا
maraaḥiiḍ	مراحيض
	ظـ ـظـ ـظ ظ
ḍuhur	ظهر
yiḍinn	يظن
tfaḍḍul	تفضّل

f	فـ ـفـ ـف ف
filfil	فلفل
šaaf	شاف

g (*same as for* ḳ; *or* k *in newer words*)	قـ ـقـ ـق ق
gabul	قبل
rugba	رقبة
suug	سوق
glaaṣ	كلاس
jigaayir	جكاير

g	غـ ـغـ ـغ غ
gayr	غير
šugul	شغل
faarug	فارغ

h		هـ ـهـ ـه ه
	huuwa	هو
	sahil	سهل
	wajih	وجه
ḥ		حـ ـحـ ـح ح
	ḥibir	حبر
	laḥam	لحم
	raaḥ	راح
j		جـ ـجـ ـج ج
	jibin	جبن
	sajjil	سجّل
	dijaaj	دجاج
k		كـ ـكـ ـك ك
	kull	كل
	makaan	مكان
	ʔilak	الك
ḳ		قـ ـقـ ـق ق
	ḳalam	قلم
	baḳar	بقر
	ḥallaaḳ	حلاق
l		لـ ـلـ ـل ل
	laḥam	لحم
	kulliš	كلّش
	kull	كل

ḷ (*same as for* l)			ل ـل ـلـ لـ
	ḷaṭiif	لطيف	
	?aḷḷa	الله	
	xaaḷ	خال	

m			م ـم ـمـ مـ
	minn	من	
	simač	سمك	
	?umm	ام	

n			ن ـن ـنـ نـ
	niktib	نكتب	
	minnak	منُّك	
	titin	تتن	

p (*same as for* b)			بـ
	pooṣṭa	بوصطة	

r			ر ـر ـر ر
	raas	راس	
	jaras	جرس	
	ṭaar	طار	

s			س ـس ـسـ سـ
	sabab	سبب	
	jisir	جسر	
	bass	بس	

ṣ			ص ـص ـصـ صـ
	ṣaar	صار	
	yiṣiir	يصير	
	gaṣṣ	قص	

š	ﺷ ﺸ ﺶ ﺵ
šugul	شغل
tišrab	تشرب
baķšiiš	بقشيش

t	ﺗ ﺘ ﺖ ﺕ
tiktib	تكتب
titin	تتن
banaat	بنات

ṭ	ﻃ ﻄ ﻂ ﻁ
ṭaar	طار
muṭar	مطر
šixaaṭ	شخاط

w	ﻭ ﻮ ﻭ
walad	ولد
yisawwii	يسوّي
waļaw	ولو

x	ﺧ ﺨ ﺦ ﺥ
xubuz	خبز
maxzan	مخزن
ʔax	اخ

y	ﻳ ﻴ ﻲ ﻱ
yišrab	يشرب
ṭayyib	طيب
wiiyaay	ويّاي

z	ز ز ز
zirit	زرت
yizuur	يزور
xubuz	خبز

The consonant sound indicated by our symbol ʔ is written in Arabic with the character known as hamza. It is a small hook-like character *accompanying* one of *three* other characters (namely for y w and the character named ʔalif), and is written in varying positions. At the beginning of a word, it is ordinarily omitted, leaving the ʔalif alone. In other positions, it is retained.

ʔ	أ ا اء ئـ ئى وء ؤ
ʔašrab	اشرب
siʔal	ساءل
masaaʔ	مساء
muʔmin	مؤمن
daayman *or* daaʔiman	دائما

9	ع ـعـ ع ع
9arab	عرب
na9am	نعم
baa9	باع

θ	ث ثـ ث ث
θiliθ	ثلث
miθil	مثل
θiliθ	ثلث

δ	ذ ذ ذ
δaak	ذاك
kaδδaab	كذّاب
taaxuδ	تاخذ

10. *Vowels:* Single vowels are not indicated. (In dictionaries and complete texts they are marked above or below the line of writing.) Double vowels, however, are associated with the characters for y and w and the character ʔalif. Note the following spellings.

(a) The character for y is found in ay and ii.

bayt	بيت
tiin	تين

(b) The character for w is found in aw, uu and oo.

ʔaw	او
muu	مو
šloon	شلون

(c) Various markings are associated with a and aa in certain positions in various words. First remember that ʔalif at the *beginning* of a word can be read as ʔ plus any single vowel.

ʔakil	اكل
ʔišrab	اشرب
ʔudxul	ادحل

ʔaa–: At the *beginning* of a word, ʔaa– is written with a curved bar over ʔalif.

ʔaakul	آكل

–aa–: Double aa *within* a word is always represented by ʔalif.

banaat	بنات
jigaayir	جكاير

–aa: Double aa at the *end* of a word is represented by ʔalif alone.

maa	ما
laa	لا

–a: Single –a at the end of some words (chiefly ʔana, ʔiḥna, the agent affix –na as in šifna, and the pronoun endings –na *us, our* and –ha *her*) is represented by ʔalif alone.

ʔana	انا
ʔiḥna	احنا
šifna	شفنا
šaafna	شافنا
baytna	بيتنا
ʔabuuha	ابوها

–a: Single –a at the end of (1) verb forms of the pattern of yitmašša, tmašša, yinsa, nisa, and miša, and (2) 9ala and ʔila is represented by a character (known as ʔalif maksuura) like that for y, but without the two dots below.

tmašša	تمشّى
yitmašša	يتمشّى
nisa	نسى
yinsa	ينسى
miša	مشى
9ala	على
ʔila	الى

–a: Single –a at the end of *feminine* nouns and adjectives is represented by a character (known as taʔ marbuuṭa) like that for final –h, but topped by two dots:

madrasa	مدرسة
siiyaara	سيّارة
zayna	زينة

11. *Spellings.* For the most part, Arabic spellings represent directly Arabic speech sounds. A small number of spellings do not correspond to the current spoken form. Such traditional spellings in the following systems will be noted where they deviate from direct representation of the speech sounds.

11.1 *The Article Prefix.*

ilbayt	البيت
ilmuus	الموس
ijjayš	الجيش
innaas	الناس

The article prefix is always written as ʔalif plus l. Remember that the doubling is spoken but not written.

11.2 *The separate Pronouns.*

huuwa	هو
hiiya	هي
ʔinta	انت
ʔintii	انتي
ʔana	انا
or ʔaanii	آني

humma	همّا

ʔintum	انتم

ʔiḥna	احنا

11.3 *Pronoun Endings.*

baytii	بيتي

baytak	بيتك

baytič	بيتك

bayta	بيته

baytha	بيتها

baytna	بيتنا

baytkum	بيتكم

baythum	بيتهم

Note that –ak and –ič are both spelled with –k, while –a *his, him* is spelled with an –h. The final ʔalif of –ha *her* and –na *our, us* has been mentioned above (9, c).

11.4 *Feminine nouns and adjectives.*

ilmadrasa kabiira.	المدرسة كبيرة ٠

madrasat-ṣadiiḳii kabiira.	مدرسة صديقي كبيرة ٠

madrastii kabiira.	مدرستي كبيرة ٠

Feminine nouns and adjectives ending in –a are written with the character shown above (called taʔ marbuuṭa). It is replaced by the character for t (called taʔ ṭawiila) only when *pronoun endings* are added. Note that the members of a noun compound are written as separate words.

The plurals of feminine nouns and adjectives are spelled with ʔalif and t as expected.

ilbanaat ḥilwaat.	البنات حلوات ٠

ilbanaat maa waagfaat.	البنات ما واقفات ٠

11.5 *Masculine nouns ending in –a* have their spelling with ʔalif and hamza retained.

hawa	هواء

šita	شتاء

wara	وراء

11.6 *Agent Affixes.*

šuuf	شوف

šuufii	شوفي

šuufuu	شوفوا

yišuuf	يشوف
tšuuf	تشوف
tšuuf	تشوف
tšuufiin	تشوفين
ʔašuuf	اشوف
yišuufuun	يشوفون
tšuufuun	تشوفون
nšuuf	نشوف
šaaf	شاف
šaafat	شافت
šifit	شفت
šiftii	شفتي
šifit	شفت
šaafaw	شافوا
šiftum	شفتم
šifna	شفنا

Note that the final ʔalif traditionally added to the plural command form and to the completed action third person plural ('they' form) has been retained in the spellings of this text.

IV. Instructions to Guide

yisual
luaul
luul

ارشادات الى الدليل

المطلوب منك مساعدة جماعة من الامريكيين على فهم
وتكلم اللغة العربية العامية المستعملة في العراق٠ كل ما
هنالك هو ان تتكلم هذه اللغة معهم لفرض تعليمهم كيفية
تقليد الطريقة التي تتكلمها والتي يفهمها اي شخص من
بلادك ٠ كذلك يطلب منك الانتباه الكلي الى لفظهم
وتصحيح ما هو مغلوط والطلب اليهم باعادة ما تصححه لهم
عدة مرات حتى يتم اللفظ على الوجه الاكمل وكلما
استطاعوا لفظ الكلمات او العبارات مثلك نكون قد حصلنا
على الغاية المتوخاة ٠

بجانبك شخص آخر يدعى مدرب الطلبة ووظيفته
مكالمة الطلبة باللغة الانكليزية وهو المسوءول الوحيد
عن طريقة التدريس وفي الوقت نفسه يكون كطالب معهم
يصغي الى القائك ٠ ان جميع الطلبة ومدربهم مزودون بكتب
تحتوي على المواد التي تقرأها في الصف ٠ وستجد مقابل
هذه المواد تهجئتها باللغة الانكليزية التي ستسهل على
الطلبة لفظها بالعربية ٠

وظيفتك هي تعليم الطلبة وتعودهم على الكلام ولست
توضيح اللغـة لهم ٠ مدرب الطلبـة سوف يوضح لهم
بالانكليزية ما يراه مناسبا ويجب عليك عدم التوضيح لهم
لان هذا هو من اختصاص مدرب الطلبة ٠ لفرض تعليم
الطلبة اللهجة العراقية ينبغي عليك ان تتكلم معهم بنفس
الطريقة التي تتكلمها في بيتك ومع اخوانك وان يكون
كلامك طبيعي لا سريع ولا بطيء وبدون تصنع او تكلف ٠
كذلك تكلم الطريقة التي مارستها واعتبر نفسك عند قراءة
المواد كأنك تخاطب صديقا لك ٠ واذا كان كلامك

بطيء جدا ربما يتعذر على الطلبة تعلم اللغة الطبعية لذلك
حاول ان تكون معتدلا في كلامك لانهم يحاولون بقـدر
المستطاع ان يتكلموا العربية حسبما تلقنها لهم وتذكر
ايضا بان الطلبة يريدون فهم الكلام الذي يسمعونه في
الشارع ٠

خطة هذا الكتاب

هذا الكتاب يحتوي على محادثة باللهجة العراقية التي
سوف تتكلمها مع الطلبة في اللغتين العربية والانكليزية
وعليك تحضير الفصل المختص قبل دخولك الصف ليتيسر
لك قراءته على الطلبة بسهولة في كل اجتماع ٠

كيفية قراءة هذا الكتاب

مدرب الطلبة سوف يقرأ بالانكليزية الكلمة او العبارة
المقابلة لها بالعربية وعندما ينتهي منها عليك بقراءة العربية٠
عليك ان تقرأ الكلمة او العبارة امام الطلاب مرتين
او اكثر على الاقل وان تدع الطلاب ليكرروا لفظها بعدك
في كل مرة حتى يستطيعوا لفظها جيدا ٠ ثم يوجد
اسطوانات تتضمن دروسا في هذا الموضوع فاذا تصغي
لها تفهم الطريقة المطلوبة لمتابعة العمل ٠

ملاحظات على التهجئة

تذكر دائما بان الغاية من وضع هذا الكتاب هو تعليم
الطلبة اللهجة او اللغة الدارجة في العراق دون الاهتمام
او التقيد باللغة العربية الفصحى لذلك وجدنا من الضروري
استعمال اسهل طريقة لتهجئة بعض الكلمات باللغة الدارجة
بدلا من الفصحى للوصول الى المعنى المقصود فمثلا
نكتب «منين انت» عوضا عن «من اين انت» واحنا بدلا
من نحن وهكذا الى اخره ٠

Vocabularies

EXPLANATION

In the two vocabularies, arrangement is according to the English alphabet, with other symbols last, as follows:

a b č d ḍ f g g h ḥ i j k ḳ l ḷ m n o p r s ṣ š t ṭ u w x
y z ʔ 9 θ δ.

Further illustrative sentences are included in the English-Arabic vocabulary. In verbs, the English stem is given, with the completed action form preceding the incomplete action form of the Iraqi. Plurals of nouns and most adjectives are given in parentheses.

ARABIC–ENGLISH VOCABULARY

baab (ʔabwaab) *door*
baačir *tomorrow;* baačir billayl *tomorrow night;* baačir iṣṣubuḥ *tomorrow morning*
baadinjaan *eggplant*
baaḳii, baaḳiya, baaḳiyiin (adjective) *remaining*
baaḳii *remainder*
ilbaarḥa OR imbaarḥa *yesterday;* ilbaarḥa billayl *last night;* ʔawwalt-ilbaarḥa *the day before yesterday*
baarid, baarda *cold* (of things)
baaṣṣ (baaṣṣaat) *bus*
baa9, yibii9 *sell;* bayyaa9 *clerk*
baa9is, baa9sa, baa9siin *miserable*
baddal, yibaddil *change* (something) (SAME AS gayyar)
badla (f) (badlaat) *suit;* badiltii *my suit*
bagdaad (f) *Baghdad;* bagdaadii, bagdaadiiya, bagdaadiyiin *Baghdadi, of Baghdad*
baḳar *cattle*
baḳšiiš *tip* (money)
balad (bilaad) *city, community*
balad (bilaad OR buldaan) *country* (state)
balam (blaam) *rowboat*
balii *yes* (familiar)
bardaan, –a, –iin *cold* (of persons)
barmiil (baraamiil) *barrel*
barra *outside*
basiiṭ *simple, easy*
bass *only, but*
bašara (f) *skin*
baṣra: ilbaṣra (f) (*the*) *Basra;* baṣrii, baṣriiya *of Basra*
baṭṭal, yibaṭṭil *stop, cease*
bayn *between*
bayš *how much*
bayt (byuut) *house*
bayyan, yibayyin *appear, look, seem*
bayyan, yibayyin *show, represent*
bayyaa9 *clerk*
bayḍ *eggs;* bayḍa *an egg*
bayḍa (f), ʔabyaḍ (m), biiḍ (pl) *white*
ba9ad *still, yet; more, in addition, else*
ba9ad *after;* ba9ad ilḥarb *after the war;* ba9ad baačir *day after tomorrow;* ba9ad maa *after* (with verbs)
ba9dayn *afterwards*
ba9iid, –a, –iin *distant, far;* ba9iid minn *far from*
biduun *without;* biduunii *without me;* biduun maa (before verbs) *without*
bii, bi–, b– *in; for* (of cost)
biiḍ (pl) *white*
biira (f) *beer*
bika, yibkii *weep*
biḳa, yibḳa *stay, remain;* baaḳii (m) *remaining*
bil– *o'clock;* bilxamsa *five o'clock*
bilaad (pl) *countries;* bilaad il9arab *the Arab countries*
bilḥaḳiiḳa *actually*
bina, yibnii *build;* mabnii (minn) *built of*
binaaya (f) (binaayaat) *a building*
bint (f) (banaat) *girl; daughter;* bint-ʔibnii *my son's daughter*
bismaar (bisaamiir) *nail*
booṣṭa OR pooṣṭa (f) (booṣṭaat) *postoffice*
boy *waiter*
buṣal *onions;* buṣla (f) *an onion*
buṭul (bṭoola) *bottle;* buṭul maal ḥaliib *milk bottle*

čaadir *canvas*
čaakuuč (čawaakiič) *hammer*
čaan, yikuun *was; will be*
čaay *tea;* čaay-ḥaliib *tea with milk*
čabiir, –a (kbaar) *big; old* (of persons)

daar, yidiir *manage, direct;* mudiir *manager*
daar, yidiir *turn* (something); daar baala *he paid attention,* diir baalak *pay attention!*
daar, yidiir 9ala *look for*
daara, yidaarii *take care of*
daaxil *inside; domestic*
daayan, yidaayin *lend*
daayman *always*
daayra (f) (daayraat) *office;* daayratna *our office;* daayirtii *my office*
dabbar, yidabbir *arrange*
daftar (difaatir) *notebook*
dagg, yidigg *knock, ring*
daḳiiḳa (f) (daḳaayiḳ) *minute*
damm *blood*
darras, yidarris *teach;* mudarris *teacher*
darsa (f) *lesson;* darsatna *our lesson;* daristii *my lesson*
daxxan, yidaxxin *smoke*
days (dyuus) *breast*
difan, yidfan *bury;* madfuun, –a (adjective) *buried*
difa9, yidfa9 *pay;* madfuu9, –a (adjective) *paid*
difa9, yidfa9 *push;* madfuu9 (adjective) *pushed*
diinaar (dinaaniir) *dinar* (1000 fils)
dijaaj *chicken;* dijaaja (f) *a chicken*
dinya (f) *world;* iddinya baarda *it's cold*
diraasa (f) *education;* diraasa 9aaliya *broad education*
diras, yidris *study;* daaris, daarsa (adjective) *studying*
dirzan *dozen*
dixal, yidxul *enter, go in;* madxal *entrance;* duxuul *entering, entrance*
di9a, yid9uu *invite, call*
dukkaan (dikaakiin) *shop*
duunii, dunniiya *bad, spoiled*
duwa (m) *medicine*
duxtoor *doctor*

ḍaabuṭ (ḍubbaaṭ) *officer*
ḍaayiḳ, ḍaayḳa *narrow*
ḍahar *back;* ḍahrii *my back*
ḍaḳin *chin;* ḍaḳnii *my chin*
ḍall, yiḍill *keep on, continue*
ḍann, yiḍinn *think, suppose*
ḍa9iif, ḍa9iifa (ḍ9aaf) *weak; thin, slender*
ḍa99af, yiḍa99if *make thin*
ḍirab, yiḍrub *strike, hit;* yiḍrub . . . ?uutii *press* (clothes)
ḍudd *against, opposed to*
ḍuhur *noon;* ba9ad iḍḍuhur *afternoon;* gabul iḍḍuhur *before noon;* biḍḍuhur *at noon*
ḍu9uf *weakness*

faar, yifuur *boil, be boiling;* fawwar, yifawwir *make boil*
faarug, faarga *empty; unoccupied; free, not busy*
faayda (f) *purpose;* faaydat-halbinaaya *the purpose of this building*
fadd OR farid *some, a certain;* fadd yoom *someday*
faḳiir, –a (fuḳra) *poor*
fallaš, yifalliš *tear down*
farḥaan, –a, –iin *happy*
farid OR fadd *some, a certain*
fawwar, yifawwir *boil* (something)
fiham, yifham *understand;* mafhuum, –a (adjective) *understood*
fii *in,* fil– *in the*
fiimaanilaah *Goodbye.*
fikir *mind, idea;* fikrii *my mind*
filfil *pepper*
filim (?aflaam) *film; movie*
fils (fluus) *fils* (a coin)
finjaan (finaajiin) *cup*
fitaḥ, yiftaḥ *open* (something); maftuuḥ, –a (adjective) *opened*
fluus (pl) *fils; money;* fluus kaθiira *a lot of money*
foog *above; up; upstairs*
fraaš (fruuš) *bed*
fransaawii, fransaawiiya, fransaawiiyiin *French; Frenchman*
ftiham, yiftihim *understand*
ftikar, yiftikir *think*
fuḍḍa (f) *silver*
fusḥa *classical*
fuṭuur *breakfast*

gaal, yiguul *say, tell;* gullii *tell me!*
gaam, yiguum *begin* (to do something)
gaa9id, gaa9da, gaa9diin *sitting; awake*
gabul *before;* gabul ilḥarb *before the war; ago,* gabul sabi9-siniin *seven years ago;* gabul maa (preceding verbs) *before*
gahwa (f) *coffee; coffee shop;* gahaawii *coffee shops*
gaḥḥ, yiguḥḥ *cough*
gaṣṣ, yiguṣṣ *cut;* magṣuuṣ (adjective) *cut*
gaṣṣaab (gaṣaaṣiib) *butcher*
ga99ad, yiga99id *wake* (someone) *up*
gidar, yigdar *is able to, can*
giddaam *ahead, in front of;* giddaamak *ahead of you* (m)
gi9ad, yig9ud *sit down; wake up;* gaa9id *sitting; awake*
glaaṣ (glaaṣaat) *glass* (tumbler)
gubaḷ *straight ahead*

gaadii *beyond*
gaafil *careless*
gaalii, gaaliya *expensive;* ʔagla (minn) *more expensive (than)*
gaayib, gaayba *absent*
galab, yiglab *beat, win;* gaalib *winner*
gaḷṭaan, –a *wrong, in error*
ganii, ganiiya, ganiyiin *rich;* ʔagna (minn) *richer (than)*
garb *west;* garbii, garbiiya *western, of the west*
gariib, –a (gurba) *strange; a stranger*
gašš, yigišš *cheat* (someone); gaššaaš *cheater*
gayr *other, different; non-;* gayrii *someone besides me;* gayr muslim *non-moslem*
gayyar, yigayyir *change* (something); tagyiir *a change*
gazaal (gizḷaan) *gazelle*
gisal, yigsil *wash*
gurfa (f) (guraf) *a room;* gurfatna *our room;* guruftii *my room*

haak, haakii (f), haakuu (pl) *take!*
haay (f) *this*
haaδa (m), haaδii (f) *this*
haaδaak (m), haaδiič (f) *that*
haaδool OR haaδoolii OR δool *these*
habb, yihibb *blow*
hal (question asking particle; can be omitted)
hal– *this; these;* halbayt *this house;* halyoom *today;* halʔayyaam *nowadays;* hajjigaayir *these cigarettes;* hallayla *tonight*
halgad *so*
hamm *also, too*
handasa (f) *engineering*
hanna, yihannii *congratulate*
hassa *now; just* (with completed action verb form)
hawa (m) *air, wind, weather;* hawa baarid *cold air*
hawaaya *much, a lot*
hiiya *she*
hina OR hinaa OR hinaaya *here*
hinaak *there*
htamm, yihtumm *be important to*
humma *they*
huuwa *he*

ḥaadiθa (f) *accident*
ḥaaḍir, ḥaaḍra, ḥaaḍriin *ready, ready to* (do something)
ḥaafii *barefooted*
ḥaalan *at once, immediately*
ḥaalig *mouth;* ʔiftaḥ ḥaalgak *open your mouth!*
ḥaamuḍ, ḥaamḍa *sour*
ḥaarr, ḥaarra *hot*
ḥaayiz, ḥaayza, ḥaayziin *nervous, exciteable*
ḥaaywaan (ḥaaywaanaat) *animal*
ḥabb, yiḥibb *love; like; like to;* maḥbuub, –a (adjective) *loved*
ḥabiib, –a *sweetheart*
ḥaddaad *blacksmith*
ḥadiid *iron*
ḥadiiḳa (f) (ḥadaayiḳ) *park, garden*
ḥafla (f) *party*
ḥaḳiiḳa: bilḥaḳiiḳa *actually*
ḥaliib *milk*
ḥallaaḳ *barber*
ḥamdillaa: ilḥamdillaa *praise be to God; thank goodness*

ḥammaal (ḥammaaliin) *porter*
ḥammaam *bath; bathroom*
ḥamra (f) *red;* ʔaḥmar (m); ḥumur (pl)
ḥarb (m and f) *war;* ḥarbii, ḥarbiiya *military*
ḥariiḳa (f) *fire* (destructive)
ḥasan *Hassan* (man's name)
ḥašiiš *grass*
ḥatta *in order to*
ḥaṭṭ, yiḥuṭṭ *put, place;* maḥṭuuṭ, –a (adjective) *put, placed*
ḥawaalii *about, almost*
ḥawwal, yiḥawwil *move* (something)
ḥayy, ḥayya *alive, living*
ḥika, yiḥkii OR ḥiča, yiḥčii *speak;* ḥačii (noun) *talking, speech*
ḥiluu, ḥilwa, ḥilwiin *sweet;* ʔaḥla (minn) *sweeter (than)*
ḥimal, yiḥmil *carry, transport;* ḥimil *load, cargo;* ḥammaal *porter;* maḥmuul, –a (adjective) *carried*
ḥitaaj, yiḥtaaj *need;* maa yiḥtaaj *it isn't necessary*
ḥizayraan *June*
ḥooš (ḥawaaš) *house*
ḥukuuma (f) (ḥukuumaat) *government*
ḥumur (pl) *red*
ḥurriiya (f) *freedom*

jaab, yijiib *bring;* jaayib, jaayba (adjective) *bringing;* jaabat, tjiib *give birth to*
jaami9 (jawaami9) *mosque*
jaami9a (f) *university;* jaami9at-Columbia *Columbia University*
jaanib *side;* bii jaanib *beside*
jaawab, yijaawib *answer;* juwaab (noun) *answer*
jaay, jaaya, jaayiin (adjective) *coming*
jabal (jibaal) *mountain*
jadiid, –a, (jdaad) *new*
jamaal *beauty*
jamal (jimaal) *camel*
jamiil, –a (jmaal) *pretty; handsome*
jammaal (jammaaliin) *camel-driver*
jaras (ʔajraas) *bell*
jariida (f) (jaraayid) *newspaper*
jarr, yijirr *pull;* mjarr *drawer*
jarrab, yijarrub *try;* tajriba (f) *attempt*
jasuur, –a, –iin *brave*
jawwa *below; under; downstairs*
jayb (jyuub) *pocket*
jayš (jyuuš) *army*
jazra (f) *island* (small)
jibin *cheese*
jigaara (f) (jigaayir) *cigarette*
jima9, yijma9 *add*
jinṭa (f) (jinaṭ) *bag, suitcase;* jinṭatha *her bag;* jinuṭtii *my bag*
jinuub *south;* jinuubii *southern, of the south*
jisim (jisuum) *body*
jisir (jisuur) *bridge;* jisir-mood *the Maude Bridge*
jiδab, yijδab *attract*
joo9aan, –a, –iin *hungry*
jumla (f) *sentence*
jundii (jinuud) *soldier*
juwaab *an answer;* juwaaba *his answer*

kaafii, kaafiya *enough*
kaamira (f) *camera*
kaan OR čaan *was, were;* kaan yištugul *he was working; he used to work;* kaan laazim yiktib *he should have written*
kaanuun ilʔawwal *December*
kaanuun iθθaanii *January*
kaatib, kaatba, kaatbiin (adjective) *writing*
kabaab *cutlet*
kabiir, –a (kbaar) *big; old* (of people)
kalaam *speech*
kalb (kluub); kalba (f) *dog*
kallaf, yikallif *cost*
kallam, yikallim *talk to, call;* kallimnii bittalafoon *call me on the phone!*
kamm OR čamm *several; how many;* (always with singular noun) kamm ʔax *how many brothers?*
kaniisa (f) (kanaayis) *church*
kariim, –a *generous*
karwaan (karaawiin) *caravan*
kaθiir, –a (kθaar) *many; much; a lot*
kaδδaab *liar*
kibar, yikbar *grow, get big*

kiis (ʔakyaas) *bag*
kisar, yiksir *break (something)*
kislaan, –a, –iin *lazy;* ʔaksal minn *lazier than*
kišaf, yikšif *examine; uncover*
kitaab (kutub) *book*
kitaaba (f) (noun) *writing*
kubur *bigness, size*
kull *all; every;* kulha *all of her;* kulla *all of him;* kull yoom *everyday;* kull šii *everything;* kull waaḥid *everyone*
kulliiya (f) (kulliiyaat) *college;* kulliiyat-bag̣daad *College of Baghdad*
kulliš *very; too*
kursii (karaasii) *chair*
kuθur *amount*

ḳaaṭ (ḳuuṭ) *suit*
ḳaayma (f) (ḳaaymaat) *list;* ḳaaymat-ilʔakil *menu*
ḳabiiḥ, –a (ḳbaaḥ) *ugly*
ḳadiim, –a *old, ancient*
ḳalam *pencil, pen;* ḳalam-rṣaaṣ *lead pencil;* ḳalam-ḥibir *pen*
ḳalb *heart*
ḳaliil, –a (ḳlaal) *little, few*
ḳamiiṣ (ḳumṣaan) *shirt*
ḳariib, –a, –iin *near*
ḳariya (f) *village*
ḳarrar, yiḳarrir *decide*
ḳaṣiir, –a (ḳṣaar) *short*
ḳawii OR guwii, ḳawiiya OR guwiiya (ḳwaay) *strong; hard* (of materials)
ḳibal, yiḳbal *accept;* maḳbuul, –a *accepted*
ḳifil (ʔaḳfaal) *lock*
ḳiima (f) *price;* ḳiimatha *her price;* ḳiimta *his price*
ḳira, yiḳra *read*
ḳiṣim *part;* ḳiṣim minn *part of*
ḳiṭaar *train*
ḳundara (f) (ḳanaadir) *shoe*
ḳundarčii *shoemaker*

laam, yiluum *blame;* loom (noun) *blame*
laban OR liban *buttermilk* (cultured)
laff, yiliff *wrap, bind;* malfuuf, –a (adjective) *bound, wrapped*
laffaafa (f) *bandage*
laḥam *meat;* laḥam-xanziir *pork;* laḥam-xurfaan *mutton;* ʔabuu-laḥam *meat-seller*
lamma *when, while*
law *if*
layš *why*
layl *nighttime;* layla (f) (lyuul) *a night;* billayl *during the night;* ilbaarḥa billayl *last night;* bukra billayl *tomorrow night*
layyin, layna (lyaan) *soft;* layyin wiiya *easy on*
laa OR laaʔ *no;* laa . . . wulaa *neither . . . nor;* laa truuḥ *don't go!*
laabis, laabsa, laabsiin *wearing*
laakin OR wulaakin *but*
laazim *necessary;* laazim ʔaruuḥ *I have to go;* kint laazim ʔaruuḥ *I should have gone*
laδiiδ, –a *tasty*
libas, yilbas *wear;* laabis, laabsa *wearing;* malbuus, –a (adjective) *worn*
libin *brick;* libna (f) *a brick*
libnaan *Lebanon;* libnaanii, libnaaniiya *Lebanese, of Lebanon*
ligiddaam *in advance*
liḥja (f) *dialect*
liḥya (f) *beard;* liḥyatna *our beard;* liḥaytii *my beard*
likay *in order to*
lima9, yilma9 *shines, is shining*
lišaan *in order to, for*
liyamta *until when*
lizam, yilzam *catch; hold*
liʔann *because* (liʔannii ʔaxaδt kitaaba *because I took his book*)
li9ab, yil9ab *play;* li9ib (noun) *playing;* laa9ib, laa9ba, laa9biin (adjective) *playing*
loom *blame*
loon (ʔalwaan) *color*
luga (f) (lugaat) *language*
luuluu *pearl; Pearl* (girl's name)

ḷaṭiif, –a (ḷṭaaf) *nice, pleasant;* ʔaḷṭaf (minn) *nicer (than)*

maa (with verbs and prepositions) *not* (maa ʔafham *I don't understand*); (huuwa maa hinaa *he isn't here*); maa yixaalif *it doesn't matter*
maaḥad *nobody*
maakuu *there isn't, there aren't*
maal *belonging to; for;* maala, maalta *his;* maalak, maaltak *yours* (m); maalič, maaltič *yours* (f); maalha, maalatha *hers;* maalhum, maalathum *theirs;* maalkum, maalatkum *yours* (pl); maalna, maalatna *ours*
maay *water*
maa9uun (mawaa9iin) *dish;* maa9uun-timman *dish of rice*
maaḍii, maaḍiya *last;* sant-ilmaaḍiya *last year*
mabnii OR mibnii (minn) *built* (*of*)
madanii, madaniiya *civilian*
madfuun, –a (adjective) *buried*
madiina (f) (mudun) *city;* madiinat-bagdaad *the city of Baghdad*
madrasa (f) (madaaris) *school*
maftuuḥ, –a (adjective) *open*
maglii, magliiya *fried*
maḥall (maḥallaat) *place; establishment*
maḥaṭṭa (f) *railroad station*
maḥbas (maḥaabis) *ring* (finger)
maḥbuub, –a (adjective) *loved, beloved*
maḥṭuuṭ, –a (adjective) *placed, put*
makaan (makaanaat) *place; space, room*
makšuuf, –a (adjective) *uncovered; examined*
maktuub, –a (adjective) *written*
maktuub (mikaatiib) *letter*
maḳbuul, –a *acceptable*
malaabis (pl) *clothing*
malbuus, –a (adjective) *worn*
malfuuf, –a (adjective) *wrapped*
malik (maluuk) *king*
malyaan, –a (minn) *full* (*of*)
malyoon (malaayiin) *million*
mambar (manaabir) *pulpit*
mamlaka (f) *kingdom;* ilmamlaka l9arabiiya issa9uudiiya *the kingdom of Saudi Arabia*
mamnuun, –a, –iin *obliged, appreciative*
mamnuu9, –a *forbidden*
manaax *weather*
manaaḍir (pl) (*eye*) *glasses*
mansii, mansiiya (adjective) *forgotten*
manšuul (*head*) *cold*
mara (f) *wife;* martii *my wife;* marat-9ammii *wife of my father's brother*
maraaḥiiḍ (pl) *toilet*
maraḍ *disease;* maraḍ-ilḳalib *heart disease*
mariiḍ, –a (murḍa) *sick*
markab (maraakib) *ship*
marra (f) *a single time, once;* marratayn *twice, two times;* θilaaθ-marraat *three times*
masaaʔ *evening;* masaaʔ ilxayr *Good evening!*
masaafa (f) *distance*
masbaḥ (masaabiḥ) *swimming place*
masjuun (masaajiin) *prisoner*
maskiin, –a (masaakiin) *poor; unfortunate*
masʔuul, –a *responsible*
mašguug, –a *torn*
mašguul, –a, –iin *busy*
mašhuur, –a, –iin *famous*
mašii (noun) *walking*
mašruub *drink, beverage*
maṭbuux, –a (adjective) *cooked*
maṭ9am (maṭaa9im) *restaurant*
mawaašii *livestock*
mawjuud OR moojuud, –a, –iin *found; present*
mawluud, –a *born*
maw9id *appointment, engagement*
maywa OR miiwa (f) *fruit*
mayz (myuuz) *table*
mazra9a (f) (mazaari9) *farm*
ma9a *with;* ma9aay *with me;* ma9aak *with you* (m); ma9a ssalaama *Goodbye.*
ma9aaš *wages*
ma9iiša (f) *livelihood*
ma9mal (ma9aamil) *factory;* ma9mal-siiyaaraat *automobile factory*
mgaddii *beggar*
mgaym *clouds;* mgayma *cloudy*
miflis *broke* (financially)
miftaaḥ (mifaatiiḥ) *key*
miil (miiyaal) *mile*
miiwa (f) OR maywa (f) *fruit*
miiya (f) *hundred;* miit-filis *one hundred fils;* ilmiiya *the hundredth;* bilmiiya *percent*
miizaan *scales* (weighing)
miliḥ *salt*

minaara (f) (minaaraat) *minaret*
minaa? *port*
minayn *where from*
minn *from; since; than;* minn faḍlak *if you* (m) *please;* minn sabab *because;* minn waḳit *early*
minuu *who?*
misak, yimsak *hold; catch*
mistaḥii *ashamed*
mitzawwij, mitzawja, mitzawjiin *married*
mit?akkid, mit?akda, mit?akdiin *sure, certain*
mit?assif, mit?asfa, mit?asfiin *sorry*
mit?axxir, mit?axra, mit?axriin *late*
miša, yimšii *walk;* maašii, maašiya, maašiyiin (adjective) *walking;* mašii (noun) *walking*
miša, yimšii *go, run* (of machinery)
mišmiš *apricots;* mišmiša (f) *an apricot*
mišwii *stewed*
mi9taad, –a, –iin *accustomed*
miθil *like, resembling; as . . . as;* miθil maa (before verbs) *like, the way*
moṣul: ilmoṣul (f) *Mosul*
msawwas *decayed*
mudarris, mudarrisa *teacher*
mudda (f) *period of time;* muddat-šahar *a month's time*
mudiir (mudaraa?) *manager*
mufiid, –a *beneficial*
muhandis (muhandisiin) *engineer*
muhimm, –a *important;* ?ahamm *more important*
muḳaawil *contractor*
muḳtadir *capable*
muluk (?amlaak) *property*
mumarriḍa (f) *nurse*
mumkin *possible, likely, perhaps*
murr, –a *bitter;* ?amarr (minn) *bitterer (than)*
muslim, –a, –iin *Moslem*
mustaḳbil *future;* bilmustaḳbil *in the future*
mustašfa (f) (mustašfayaat) *hospital*
maṭar OR muṭar *rain*
muṭrat, tumṭur (f) *it rains*
muu (not used with verbs) *not*
muus (mwaas) *razor*
mu?allif *author*
mu?aδδin *muezzin*
mu?min, –a, –iin *faithful, pious*

mu9aḍḍaf, –a, –iin *employee*
mu9allim, –a, –iin *teacher*
mzayyin *barber*
m9ayyan, –a (adjective) *appointed*

naaḳuṣ *minus*
naam, yinaam *sleep; go to bed;* naayim *sleeping*
naar (niiraan) *fire* (useful)
naas (pl) *people*
naasii, naasiya (adjective) *forgetting, forgetful*
naaš, yinuuš *reach*
naawaš, yinaawuš *hand over*
naawii, naawiya, naawiyiin *intend to*
naayim, naayma, –iin *sleeping*
nadii, nadiiya *wet;* ?anda (minn) *wetter (than)*
nafar (nafaraat) *person*
nafis *breath; self;* nafsii *myself;* nafsa *himself*
nafuṭ *oil;* šarikat-innafuṭ *the oil company*
nahaar *daytime;* binnahaar *during the day*
nahar (?anhur) *river;* nahar-dijla (m) *Tigris river*
najjaar (najjaariin) *carpenter*
naḳdan *cash;* yidfa9 ilḳiima naḳdan *he pays cash*
naṣaara *Christians*
našiiṭ *active*
našla (f) *(head)cold*
nayšan, yinayšin *aim* (a gun)
na9am *yes* (polite)
na9iiman (said to one who has just had a haircut or has just dressed up)
naḍiif, –a (nḍaaf) *clean*
naḍḍaf, yinaḍḍuf *clean, make clean*
niisaan *April*
niišan, yiniišan *aim* (a gun)
nija, yinja *succeed*
nisa, yinsa *forget;* mansii *forgotten*
nizal, yinzil *go down, light*
ni9saan, –a, –iin *sleepy*
nkisar, yinkisar *break* (self)
noom (noun) *sleep*
noo9 *kind, sort;* ?ay noo9 *what kind?*
nuḳta (f) *period* (in punctuation)
nuṣraanii (naṣaara) *Christian*

nuṣṣ OR nuṣuf *half;* nuṣṣ-dirzan *a half dozen;* nuṣṣ-illayl *midnight*
nuurii *Nouri* (man's name)
nṭa, yinṭii *give;* nṭiinii waaḥid *give me one!*
nṭiḍar, yinṭiḍir *wait for;* minṭiḍir *waiting*

paakayt *package;* paakayt-jigaayir *a package of cigarettes*
portaḳaal *oranges;* portaḳaala (f) *an orange*
puutayta *potatoes*

raabi9, raab9a (adjective) *fourth*
raad, yiriid *want, want to*
raaḥ, yiruuḥ *go;* raayiḥ, raayḥa, raayḥiin *going*
raaḥ *going to;* raayiḥ ʔaktib *I'm going to write.*
raas (ruus) *head*
raawa, yiraawii *show*
raayiḥ, raayḥa, –iin (adjective) *going*
raaʔii *opinion;* raaʔya *his opinion;* raaʔyii *my opinion*
rafii9, –a (rfaa9) *thin, slender*
raggii *watermelon;* raggiiya (f) *a watermelon*
rajil *husband;* rajilha *her husband*
rajja9, yirajji9 *return* (something), *take back*
raṣaaṣa (f) (raṣaaṣ) *bullet*
raxiiṣ, –a (rxaaṣ) *cheap*
raʔiis OR rayyis (ruʔasaaʔ) *chief, head, boss;* raʔiis-ilma9mal *the head of the factory*
riiyaal (ʔaryaal) *riyal* (200 fils)
rija9, yirja9 *return, go back, come back*
rijil *leg;* rijlayn (two) *legs;* rijlayya *my legs*
rijjaal (riyaajiil) *man*
rikab, yirkab *ride*
risal, yirsil *send*
riss *rice*
rubu9 *a quarter, a fourth*

saabi9, saab9a (adjective) *seventh*
saadis (f) saadsa (adjective) *sixth*
saag, yisuug *drive*
saakin, saakna, –iin (adjective) *living, staying*
saakin, saakna *quiet, calm*
saalim, saalma *safe*
saawa, yisaawii *make, amount to*
saa9a (f) (saa9aat) *hour; clock;* issaa9a bayš? *What time is it?;* bissaa9a *at once*
saa9ad, yisaa9id *help*
sabab *cause, reason;* minn ʔay sabab *why?, for what reason?;* minn sabab *because;* minn hassabab *for this reason*
sab9a *seven;* sabi9-siniin *seven years*
sab9iin *seventy*
sadd, yisidd *close, shut;* masduud, –a (adjective) *closed*
safiina (f) (sufun) *sailboat*
sahil, sahla (shaal) *easy*
sahhal, yisahhil *make easy*
sajjal, yisajjil *register*
salaam *peace;* bissalaam *during peace;* salaam 9alaykum *Peace be upon you;* wu9alaykum issalaam *And upon you be peace* (customary greeting and response)
saliim, –a *sound, whole*
salla (f) (sallaat) *basket*
sallam, yisallim *greet;* sallam 9ala, yisallim 9ala *say hello to*
samiin, –a (smaan) *fat*
samma, yisammii *name, call*
samra (f), ʔasmar (m); sumur (pl) *brown*
sana (f) (siniin) *year;* sant-ijjaaya *the coming year, next year*
sanawii, sanawiiya *yearly*
sawa *together*
sawwa, yisawwii *do, make;* msawwa, msawwaaya (adjective) *made*
saxiif, –a (sxaaf) *stupid*
sayyidii *sir*
sa9iid, –a, –iin *happy; Said* (man's name)
sbaaṭa9aš *seventeenth*
siinama (f) (siinamaat) *movie theater*
siiyaara (f) (siiyaaraat) *automobile*
simač *fish;* simča (f) *a fish*
simaḥ, yismaḥ *allow; excuse*
sijin (sijuun) *prison*
sijjaada (f) (sijaajiid) *prayer-rug*
sikan, yiskin *live, stay*
sima9, yisma9 (9ann) *hear* (about)
sinn (sinaan) *tooth*
sitra (f) *hat*

sitta *six;* sitt-miiya *six hundred*
sittiin *sixty*
siyaaḳa (f) (noun) *driving*
si?al, yis?al *ask*
skamlii (skamliiyaat) *chair*
sooda (f); ?aswad (m); suud (pl) *black*
stanga, yistangii *pick out*
sta9mal, yista9mil *use*
stilam, yistilim *get, receive*
sumur (pl); ?asmar (m); sumur (pl) *brown*
suud (pl); ?aswad (m); sooda (f) *black*
suug (?aswaag) *market*

ṣaabuun *soap;* ṣaabuuna (f) *a cake of soap*
ṣaada *plain;* čaay ṣaada *plain tea*
ṣaaḥib, ṣaaḥba (?aṣḥaab) *owner, master; friend*
ṣaaloon *lobby*
ṣaar, yiṣiir *become, get; happen, take place; pass* (of time)
ṣabaaḥ ilxayr *Good morning.*
ṣaddaḳ, yiṣaddiḳ *believe* (something)
ṣadiiḳ, –a (ṣudḳaan) *friend*
ṣaff *line, row; class*
ṣafra (f); ?aṣfar (m); ṣufur (pl) *yellow*
ṣagiir, –a (ṣgaar) OR ṣgayr, ṣgayra (ṣgaar) *small; young* (of people)
ṣaḥiiḥ, –a (ṣḥaaḥ) *true*
ṣaḥra (f) (ṣaḥaarii) *desert*
ṣalaat *prayer*
ṣalla, yiṣallii *pray*
ṣammuun *bread* (loaves, rolls); ṣammuuna (f) *a loaf of bread*
ṣanduug (ṣanaadiig) *box, case, chest*
ṣarii9, –a *fast, quick*
ṣaṭaḥ (ṣuṭuuḥ) *roof*
ṣayf *summer;* biṣṣayf *during the summer*
ṣa9ib, ṣa9ba (ṣ9aab) *hard, difficult*
ṣifir *zero*
ṣiin: iṣṣiin (f) *China;* ṣiinii, ṣiiniiya, ṣiiniiyiin *Chinese, of China*
ṣiraf, yiṣraf *spend;* maṣruuf, –a (adjective) *spent*
ṣiṭṭa9aš *sixteenth*
ṣi9ad, yiṣ9ad *climb*
ṣoob *riverbank;* δaak iṣṣoob *the other bank*
ṣooda (f) *soda*
ṣubuḥ *morning;* biṣṣubuḥ *during the morning;* haṣṣubuḥ *this morning;* baačir iṣṣubuh *tomorrow morning*
ṣufur (pl) *yellow*
ṣur9a (f) *speed*
ṣuuf *wool*
ṣuura (f) (ṣuwar) *picture*

šaaf, yišuuf *see; look*
šaakir (man's name) *Shakir*
šaal, yišiil *pick up, carry;* šaayil, šaayla *carrying*
šaari9 (šawaari9) *street;* šaari9-irrašiid *Rashid Street*
šaaṭir, šaaṭra *smart;* ?ašṭar *smarter*
šaayib *old man*
šagg, yišigg *tear;* mašguug (adjective) *torn*
šahar (?ishuur) *month;* šahar ijjaay OR šahar ilyijii *next month*
šajar *trees;* šajara (f) *a tree*
šakar *sugar*
šakil *way, manner;* bihaššakil *in this way*
šakuu *what is there, what are there?*
šams (f) *sun*
šaraab *wine*
šariif, –a *honest*
šarika (f) (šarikaat) *company;* šarikat-innafuṭ *the oil company*
šarḳ *east;* biššarḳ *in the east;* šarḳii, šarḳiiya *eastern*
šaxuṣ (?ašxaaṣ) *person*
šayx (šyuux) *sheik*
ša9ar *hair*
šbii *what is in?;* šbiik? *What is the matter with you* (m)*?*
šgad *how far*
šibaaṭ *February*
šib9aan, –a *full* (of food)
šii (?ašyaa?) *thing, something, anything*
šika, yiškii (9ala) *complain* (*about*)
šikar, yiškur *thank;* ?aškurak *I thank you*
šimaal *north;* šimaalii, šimaaliya *northern*
šinuu OR š(i)– *what, what thing*
širab, yišrab *drink;* mašruub, –a (adjective)

drunk, drunk up; yišrab jigaayir *he smokes cigarettes*
šita (m) *winter;* biššita *during the winter*
šixaaṭ *matches;* šixaaṭa (f) *a match*
šloon *how;* šloonak? *How are you?*
šoorba (f) *soup*
štigal, yištugul *work;* mašguul, –a (adjective) *busy*
štira, yištirii (minn) *buy (from)*
šugul *work;* šuglii *my work*
(šugul) ˀašgaal (pl) *business*
šwayya *a little, some*

taaksii *taxi*
taajir (tujjaar) *merchant*
taasi9, taas9a (adjective) *ninth*
tabdiil (noun) *change*
tadriis (noun) *teaching*
taḥsiin *improvement*
tagyiir (noun) *change*
tajriba (f) (noun) *attempt*
taḳriiban *about, almost*
talafoon *telephone*
tamaam *perfect, complete*
tamm, yitimm *complete*
tamm baala, yitimm baala *worry about*
tammuuz *July*
tamur *dates;* tamra (f) *a date*
tašriin ilˀawwal *October*
tašriin iθθaanii *November*
taˀmiir (noun) *building*
taxat (txuut) *bench*
taxx, yituxx *bump*
tayl *wire*
tazdiir (noun) *exporting*
ta9aal, –ii, –uu (command) *come!*
ta9yiin *appointment*
tbaddal, yitbaddal *change* (self)
tdaayan, yitdaayan *borrow*
tfarraj, yitfarraj (9ala OR bii) *look around*
tfaḍḍal, –ii, –uu *if you please; be good enough to*
tgadda, yitgadda *have noon meal*
tiffaaḥ *apples;* tiffaaḥa (f) *an apple*
tiin *figs;* tiina (f) *a fig*
tijaar (f) *commerce;* tijaarii, tijaariya *commercial*
tilmiiδ (tilaamiiδ) *student*
timman *rice*
timθaal (timaaθiil) *statue*
tiraḥ, yitraḥ (minn) *subtract*
tirak, yitruk *leave (a place)*
tis9a *nine;* tisi9-wulid *nine boys*
tis9iin *ninety*
titin *tobacco;* yišrab titin *smoke*
ti9baan, –a, –iin *tired*
tiθlij (f) *it snows*
tkallam, yitkallam *talk, carry on conversation*
tmašša, yitmašša *take a walk*
tnaffas, yitnaffas *breathe*
tsaaṭa9aš *nineteenth*
tšarraf, yitšarraf *be honored;* ˀatšarraf *I'm honored* (said on being introduced to someone)
turkii, turkiiya *Turkish;* turkii (ˀatraak) *a Turk*
twannas, yitwannas *amuse (one's self)*
tˀammal, yitˀammal *hope*
tˀassaf, yitˀassaf *be sorry;* mitˀassif, mitˀasfa, –iin *sorry*
t9allam, yit9allam *learn*
t9ašša, yit9ašša *have evening meal*
tδakkar, yitδakkar *remember*

ṭaar, yiṭiir *fly;* ṭaayir, ṭaayra (adjective) *flying;* ṭayyar, yiṭayyir *make (something) fly*
ṭabiib (ˀaṭibaaˀ) *doctor*
ṭab9an *of course*
ṭaḷḷa9, yiṭaḷḷi9 *bring out, bring up*
ṭariiḳ (ṭuruḳ) *road, way*
ṭariiḳa (f) *custom*
ṭawiil, –a (ṭwaal) *long; tall*
ṭayr (ṭyuur) *bird*
ṭayyaar (ṭayyaariin) *aviator*
ṭayyaara (f) (ṭayyaaraat) *airplane*
ṭayyar, yiṭayyir *fly (something)*
ṭayyib, ṭayba, ṭaybiin *good;* ˀaṭyab (minn) *better (than)*
ṭa9aam *food*
ṭiin *mud*
ṭila9, yiṭla9 *go out; go up, rise*

ṭiḷab, yiṭḷub *demand (something)*
ṭoopa (f) (ṭoopaat) *ball*
ṭuul *height, length*

waada9, yiwaadi9 *say goodbye to*
waafaḳ, yiwaafiḳ *agree*
waaguf, waagfa, –iin *standing; stopped*
waaḥid, wiḥda *one;* ilwaaḥid, ilwiḥda *apiece*
waaṣi9, waaṣ9a *extensive*
wadda, yiwaddii *take* (transport); waddiinii *take me!*
waggaf, yiwagguf *stop (something)*
waḥid *alone;* waḥdii *I alone;* waḥdak *you* (m) *alone*
waja9, yuuja9 *ache, pain (someone)*; raasii yuuja9nii *my head aches (me)*
wajih (wujuh) *face*
wakiil (wukalaaʔ) *agent*
wakit OR waḳit *time;* šwaḳit *at what time, when?;* kull waḳit *always*
walad (wulid) *boy*
waḷaw *although*
wannas, yiwannis *entertain (someone)*
wara *behind;* waraay *behind me;* waraak *behind you* (m); ʔila wara *backwards*
waraḳ (ʔawraaḳ) *paper;* warḳa (f) *a sheet of paper*
waṣṣa, yiwaṣṣii *order*
waṣux, waṣxa (wṣaax) *dirty*
waziir (wuzaraaʔ) *minister* (governmental)
wayn *where;* wayna? *where is he?;* wayn maa (with verbs) *wherever*
wazin *weight;* wazna *his weight*
wiḥda (f) *one;* waaḥid (m) *one*
wiiya *with;* wiiyaaya *with me;* wiiyaa *with him*
wilaaya (f) *state;* ilwilaayaat ilmuttaḥida *the United States*
wu–, w–, uu– *and*
wugaf, yuugaf OR yoogaf *stop (self); stop doing*
wuga9, yuuga9 *fall*
wujad, yuujad *find*
wuji9 *ache, pain;* wuji9-raas *headache*
wulad, yuulad *give birth to*
wuṣal, yuuṣal *arrive at, get to;* wuṣuul *arrival*
wuṣla (f) *piece;* wuṣlat-ḥadiid *a piece of iron*

xaaḷ *mother's brother, uncle* (maternal); xaaḷa (f) *mother's sister, aunt* (maternal)
xaamis, xaamsa *fifth*
xaawlii (xawaalii) *towel*
xaayif, xaayfa, xaayfiin (minn) *afraid (of)*
xabbaaz (xibaabiiz) *baker*
xabbar, yixabbir *announce, give news to*
xadd (xduud) *cheek*
xafiif, –a (xfaaf) *light* (weight); *thin*
xaliij *bay*
xalla, yixallii *put, place; cause, let, have (someone do something)*
xaḷḷ *vinegar*
xaḷḷaṣ, yixaḷḷiṣ *finish, get through;* xaḷṣaan, –a *finished, (all) gone*
xamiṣṭa9aš *fifteenth*
xamsa *five;* xamis-ʔayyaam *five days*
xamsiin *fifty*
xanziir (xanaaziir) *pig;* laḥam-xanziir *pork*
xaṣṣ *lettuce;* raas-xaṣṣ *head of lettuce*
xaṣṣ, yixuṣṣ *belong to*
xašab OR xišab *wood*
xašim *nose*
xašin, xašna (xšaan) *hard, tough*
xaṭar *danger*
xawaat (pl) *sisters*
xayyaaṭ *tailor*
xayṭ *thread*
xayyam, yixayyim *camp, pitch camp*
xayyar, yixayyir *choose*
xayyaṭ, yixayyiṭ *sew*
xibaz, yixbuz *bake;* xabbaaz *baker;* maxbaz *bakery*
xooš (always precedes noun) *good;* xooš walad *good boy*
xtinaḳ, yixtaniḳ (bii) *choke (on)*
xubuz *bread*
xurfaan (xuruuf) *sheep;* laḥam-xurfaan *mutton*
xuṣuuṣii, xuṣuuṣiiya *special, private*
xuḍra (f); ʔaxḍar (m); xuḍur (pl) *green; vegetables*

yaabis, yaabsa *dry*
yaakul, ʔakal *eat*
yaaxuδ, ʔaxaδ *take*

yamin, yamna *right;* 9aynii lyamna *my right eye*
yamm *beside, near;* yammii *beside me*
yamta *when?*
yamiin *rightside;* 9ala yamiinak *on your* (m) *right*
yasaar *leftside;* 9ala yasaarak *on your* (m) *left*
yawaaš *slowly*
yihuudii, yihuudiiya (yihuud) *Jewish*
yikuun *be, am, will be*
yimkin *perhaps*
yimnaawii *righthanded*
yisir, yisra *left;* 9aynii lyisra *my left eye*
yisraawii *lefthanded*
yoom (ʔayyaam) *day;* ilyoom OR halyoom *today;* bilyoom *perday;* yoom ijjum9a *Friday* yoom issabit *Saturday;* yoom ilxamiis *Thursday;* yoom ilʔaḥad *Sunday;* yoom ilʔarba9aaʔ *Wednesday;* yoom iθθilaaθaaʔ *Tuesday;* yoom iθθinayn *Monday;* yoom-ilmiilaad *birthday;* halʔayyaam *nowadays*
yuujad *there is* (*found*), *there are*

zaar, yizuur *visit*
zaawiya (f) (zawaaya) *angle, corner*
zaḷaaṭa (f) *salad*
zanjiil (zanaajiil) *chain*
zarga (f); ʔazrag (m); zurug (pl) *blue*
zayn, –a, –iin *good, well; then, in that case;* muu zayn *bad*
zayt *oil*
zaytuun *olives;* zaytuuna (f) *an olive;* zaytizzaytuun *olive oil*
zayyan, yizayyin *shave; beautify*
zi9al, yiz9al *make* (*someone*) *angry;* zi9laan, –a, –iin *angry*
zooj *husband;* zooja (f) *wife*
zubud *butter*
zurug (pl) *blue*

ʔaab *August*
ʔaanii *I*
ʔaaxar *another*
ʔaaxir *last*
ʔaaδaar *March*

ʔab *father;* ʔabuuya *my father;* ʔabuu-laḥam *meatseller;* ʔabuu-jigaayir *cigarette seller*
ʔabrad (minn) *colder* (*than*)
ʔabyaḍ (m); bayḍa (f); biiḍ (pl) *white*
ʔab9as (minn) *more miserable*
ʔadwan (minn) *worse* (*than*)
ʔaḍ9af (minn) *thinner* (*than*); *weaker* (*than*)
ʔafḳar (minn) *poorer* (*than*)
ʔagla (minn) *more expensive* (*than*)
ʔagna (minn) *richer* (*than*)
ʔahamm (minn) *more important*
ʔahanniik *Congratulations!* (literally, *I congratulate you*)
ʔahil *family;* ʔahlii *my family;* ʔahilha *her family*
ʔahlan wusahlan *Welcome!; Glad to know you!*
ʔaḥad *anybody*
ʔaḥla (minn) *sweeter* (*than*)
ʔaḥmar (m); ḥamra (f); ḥumur (pl) *red*
ʔaḥsan (minn) *better* (*than*); ilʔaḥsan *the best*
ʔajmal (minn) *prettier* (*than*)
ʔajnabii, ʔajnabiiya (ʔajaanib) *foreign*
ʔajwa9 (minn) OR joo9aan ʔakθar (minn) *hungrier* (*than*)
ʔakal, yaakul *eat*
ʔakiid, –a *sure*
ʔakil (ʔaklaat) *food*
ʔakla (f) *a meal*
ʔaksal (minn) *lazier* (*than*)
ʔakuu *there is, there are*
ʔakθar (minn) *more* (*than*)
ʔaḳall (minn) *less* (*than*); ʔaḳallan *at least*
ʔaḳbaḥ (minn) *uglier* (*than*)
ʔaḳrab (minn) *nearer* (*than*)
ʔaḳṣar (minn) *shorter* (*than*)
ʔaḳwa (minn) *stronger* (*than*)
ʔalif (ʔaalaaf) *thousand*
ʔalmaanya (f) *Germany*
ʔalyan (minn) *softer* (*than*)
ʔalṭaf (minn) *nicer* (*than*)
ʔaḷḷaa *Allah;* ʔaḷḷaa bilxayr *Good day.*
ʔamarr (minn) *more bitter* (*than*)
ʔamiin, –a *faithful, honest*
ʔamriika OR ʔamayrika *America;* ʔamriikaanii, ʔamriikaaniiya (ʔamriikaan) *American*
ʔana *I*

ʔanda (minn) *wetter* (*than*)

ʔarbaaṭa9aš *fourteen*

ʔarba9a *four;* ʔarba9-ʔayyaam *four days;* ʔarba9iin *forty*

ʔarfa9 (minn) *thinner* (*than*)

ʔarjuuk, ʔarjuuč, ʔarjuukum *Please!*

ʔarḳaam *numbers*

ʔaruḍ (ʔaraaḍii) *land; earth; floor*

ʔarxaṣ (minn) *cheaper* (*than*)

ʔasaf *regret;* ma9a lʔasaf *I'm sorry.*

ʔashal (minn) *easier* (*than*)

ʔaslam (minn) *safer* (*than*)

ʔasman (minn) *fatter* (*than*)

ʔasmar (m); samra (f); sumur (pl) *brown*

ʔassas, yiʔassis *establish*

ʔaswad (m); sooda (f); suud (pl) *black*

ʔas9ad (minn) *happier* (*than*)

ʔaṣaḥḥ (minn) *truer* (*than*)

ʔaṣfar (m); ṣafra (f); ṣufur (pl) *yellow*

ʔaṣgar (minn) *smaller* (*than*)

ʔaṣ9ab (minn) *harder* (*than*)

ʔašgal (minn) *busier* (*than*)

ʔašhar (minn) *more famous* (*than*)

ʔašyaaʔ *things*

ʔaṭwal (minn) *longer* (*than*)

ʔaṭyab (minn) *better* (*than*)

ʔaw *or*

ʔawwal *first;* bilʔawwal *first of all, at first;* ʔawwalii (adjective) *first*

ʔax *brother;* ʔaxuuya *my brother;* ʔaxuu-ṣadiiḳii *my friend's brother;* ʔuxwaan *brothers;* ʔuxwaanii *my brothers* OR ʔuxwa *brothers;* ʔuxuutii *my brothers*

ʔaxaff (minn) *lighter* (*than*)

ʔaxaδ, yaaxuδ *take;* xuδ (command) *take;* ʔaxuδ (noun) *taking*

ʔaxiiran *at last*

ʔaxšan (minn) *harder* (*than*)

ʔaxḍar (m); xaḍra (f); xuḍur (pl) *green*

ʔay *which?*

ʔaybas (minn) *drier* (*than*)

ʔayluul *September*

ʔayyaar *May*

ʔayḍan *moreover*

ʔazrag (m); zarga (f); zurug (pl) *blue*

ʔa9ḳal (minn) *smarter* (*than*)

ʔa9tag (minn) *older* (*of things*)

ʔaθgal (minn) *heavier* (*than*)

ʔaθxan (minn) *thicker* (*than*)

ʔibin *son;* ʔibinha *her son;* ʔibnii *my son;* ʔibin-ʔaxuuya *my brother's son;* ʔibin-9ammii *son of my father's brother*

ʔiḥna OR ʔaḥna *we*

ʔii *yes* (familiar)

ʔiida9aš *eleven;* ilʔiida9aš *the eleventh*

ʔiiṭaaḷii, ʔiiṭaaḷiiya *Italian*

ʔija, yijii *come*

ʔila, ʔil–, li– *to, for; until;* ʔilii *for me;* ʔilak *for you* (m)

ʔilaah *God*

ʔilla *except; less*

ʔillii OR ʔilaδii *who, whom, what, which*

ʔilwayš *why*

ʔingliizii, ʔingliiziiya (ʔingliiz) *English*

ʔinj (ʔinjaat) *inch*

ʔinšaḷḷa *God willing . . .* (said whenever planning to do something, OR when referring to intended action)

ʔinta OR ʔanta (m) *you;* ʔintii (f) *you;* ʔintum (pl) *you*

ʔisbuu9 (ʔasaabii9) *week*

ʔisim (ʔasaamii) *name;* ʔismii *my name;* ʔisimha *her name;* ʔisim-ṣadiiḳii *my friend's name;* šismak? *What is your* (m) *name?*

ʔiδa *if; whether*

ʔoofiis *office*

ʔubra (f) *needle*

ʔujra (f) *price* (rental)

ʔumm (f) (ʔumahaat) *mother;* ʔummii *my mother*

ʔuutačii *clothes presser*

ʔuutayl (ʔuutaylaat) *hotel*

ʔuutii *pressing iron*

ʔuxut (xawaat) *sister;* ʔuxtii *my sister;* ʔuxutha *her sister*

ʔuxwaan *brothers*

9aadatan *usually*

9aaḳil, 9aaḳla *smart*

9aal *good, excellent*

9aalam *world*

9aalamii, 9aalamiiya (adjective) *world, of the world*
9aalii, 9aaliya *high*
9aamil (9ummaal) *workman*
9aaṣima (f) *capital*
9aaš, yi9iiš *make a living*
9aašir, 9aašra (adjective) *tenth*
9abaal– *thought that;* ʔana 9abaalii . . . *I thought that . . .*
9ajjab, yi9ajjib *surprise, astonish*
9ajuuz (f) *old woman*
9ala, 9al– *on, upon, concerning;* 9alayna *upon us;* 9alayya *upon me*
9albarraka *You have been blessed* (said to someone who has just acquired something new or achieved something)
9alii (man's name) *Ali*
9allam, yi9allim *teach;* mu9allim *teacher*
9amm *father's brother, uncle* (paternal); 9amma (f) *father's sister*
9anab *grapes;* 9amba (f) *a grape*
9ann *about, concerning; from*
9anwaan *address*
9arabaana (f) (9arabaayin) *carriage*
9arabii, 9arabiiya (9arab) *Arabic, Arab;* il9arab *the Arabs*
9arag *arak* (a beverage)
9ariiḍ, –a *wide;* ʔa9raḍ *wider*
9arraf, yi9arrif (9ala) *introduce (to)*
9ašiira (f) (9išaayir) *tribe*
9ašra *ten;* 9ašir-doolaaraat *ten dollars*
9atiig, –a *old* (of things); ʔa9tag *older*
9awwaj, yi9awwij *bend (something)*
9ayn (9iyuun) *eye*
9ayyan, yi9ayyin *appoint*
9aḍḍ, yi9aḍḍ *bite*
9iḍar, yi9ḍir *excuse;* ʔi9ḍirnii *Excuse me!*
9ijab, yi9jib *please (someone),* ʔana yi9jibnii 9arag *I like arag*
9ilas, yi9lis *chew*
9ina, ya9nii *mean*
9ind *have, has, for;* 9indii *I have,* 9inda ʔaxuuya *my brother has;* yištugul 9indii *he works for me*
il9iraaḳ *Iraq;* 9iraaḳii, 9iraaḳiiya, 9iraaḳiiyiin *Iraqi, of Iraq*
9iraf, ya9ruf *know;* ma9ruuf, –a (adjective) *known*
9iša *evening meal*
9išriin *twenty;* il9išriin *twentieth*
9izam, ya9zim (9ala) *invite (to)*
9ooda (f) *stick*
9umur *life; age;* šgad 9umra? *How old is he?*

θaaliθ, θaalθa (adjective) *third*
θaamin, θaamna (adjective) *eighth*
θaanii, θaaniya (adjective) *second; other;* marra θaaniya *a second time*
θaaniya (f) (θawaanii) (noun) *a second* (of time)
θagiil, –a (θgaal) *heavy*
θaxiin, –a (θxaan) *thick*
θilaaṭṭa9aš *thirteen*
θilaaθa *three;* θilaaθ-banaat *three girls;* θilaaθiin *thirty*
θiliθ (noun) *a third*
θimaanya *eight;* θimaan-siniin *eight years;* θimaaniin *eighty*
θinayn *two; both;* θinayn minhum *two of them;* θinaynhum *both of them*
θina9aš *twelve*
θintayn: biθθintayn *two o'clock*
θmunṭa9aš *eighteenth*
θoob (θawaab) *shirt*

δaaka OR δaak OR haaδaaka, haaδaak (m) *that;* δaak ilwalad *that boy*
δahab *gold;* δahabii *golden, of gold*
δayl *tail*
δiič OR haaδiič (f) *that;* δiič ilbint *that girl*

ENGLISH–ARABIC VOCABULARY

able: is able to: gidar, yigdar (maa gidar yitnaffas. *He wasn't able to breathe.*)
about, almost: hawaalii, taķriiban
about, concerning: 9ann (maa ˀa9ruf šii 9anna. *I don't know anything about him.*)
above: foog
absent: gaayib, gaayba, gaaybiin
accept: ķibal, yiķbal (ķibal naṣiiḥtii. *He accepted my advice.*)
acceptable: maķbuul, –a
accident: ḥaadiθa (f) (ṣaarat ḥaadiθa biššaari9. *There was an accident in the street.*)
accustomed: mi9taad, –a, –iin (ˀana ˀašrab biira mi9taad bass biṣṣayf. *I'm accustomed to drink beer only during the summer.*)
ache: wuja9, yuuja9: (raasii yuuja9nii. *My head aches.*)
active: našiiṭ, –a (kaan našiiṭ bilmadrasa. *He was active in school.*)
actually, really: bilḥaķiiķa (bilḥaķiiķa huuwa rijjaal ˀamiin. *Really he is an honest man.*)
add: jima9, yijma9 (ˀijma9 waaḥid uuwaaḥid! *Add one and one!*)
addition: in addition: ba9ad
address: 9anwaan (šinuu 9anwaanak? *What is your address?*)
advance: in advance: ligiddaam
afraid (of): xaayif, xaayfa, –iin (minn) (ˀaxuuya kaan xaayif yiruuḥ lilmustašfa. *My brother was afraid to go to the hospital.*)
after: ba9ad; **after** (with verbs): ba9ad maa; **afterwards:** ba9dayn
again: marra θaaniya (ˀarjuuk sawwii nafsilwaajib marra θaaniya. *Please do the same assignment again.*)
against, opposed to: ḍudd (huuwa ḍuddii bkull šii. *He is against me in everything.*)
agent: wakiil (wukalaaˀ) (huuwa wakiil maal šarikat-bayt-illinč bilbaṣra. *He is an agent for the House of Linch company in Basra.*)
ago: gabul (gabul sabi9-siniin *seven years ago*)
agree: waafaķ, yiwaafiķ (ˀana maa ˀagdar ˀawaafķak ibraaˀyak. *I can't agree with your opinion.*)
ahead: giddaam; **ahead of you:** giddaamak; **straight ahead:** gubaḷ
aim (a gun): nayšan, yinayšin OR niišan, yiniišin (nayšin wuba9dayn ˀuḍrub! *Aim, then shoot!*)
air, wind: hawa (m); **cold air:** hawa baarid
airplane: ṭayyaara (f) (ṭayyaaraat)
Ali (man's name): 9alii
alight, land: nizal, yinzil (iṭṭayyaara maa gidrat tinzil bilmaṭaar liˀann kann ˀakuu ḍabaab. *The airplane couldn't land at the airport because there was a fog.*)
alive: ḥayy, ḥayya (iljundii ba9ada ḥayy; maa maat. *The soldier is still alive; he hasn't died.*)
all: kull; **all of us:** kulna; **all day:** kull ilyoom
all gone: xaḷṣaan, –a (illiban xaḷṣaan. *The buttermilk is all gone.*)
Allah: ˀaḷḷaa
allow: simaḥ, yismaḥ (ilmudarris simaḥlii ˀadxul liṣṣaff. *The teacher allowed me to enter the class.*)
almost: hawaalii, taķriiban
alone: waḥid; **you alone:** waḥdak; **she alone:** waḥidha
also, too: hamm
although: waḷaw (baačir raaḥ ˀaštugul waḷaw ˀana ṭi9baan. *I'm going to work tomorrow although I'm tired.*)
always: daayman; kull waķit (kull waķit ˀinta titšakka minn šuglak. *You are always complaining about your work.*)

America: ʔamriika OR ʔamayrika; **American:** ʔamriikaanii, ʔamriikaaniiya (ʔamriikaan)

amount: kuθur; **amount to, make:** saawa, yisaawii (θilaaθa wθilaaθa yisaawii sitta. *Three and three makes six.*)

amuse (self): twannas, yitwannas (twannas! *Have a good time!*)

and: wu–, w–, uu–

angle, corner: zaawiya (zawaaya)

angry: zi9laan, –a, –iin (čaanat zi9laana minna. *She was angry at him.*)

angry: make angry: zi9al, yiz9al (huuwa zi9alnii. *He made me angry.*)

animal: ḥaaywaan (ḥaaywaanaat)

announce, give news: xabbar, yixabbir bii (xabbarnii bzawwaj-ʔaxuu. *He told me about the marriage of his brother.*)

another: ʔaaxar (jiiblii waaḥid ʔaaxar. *Bring me another one.*)

answer: jaawab, yijaawib (layš maa tjaawibnii? *Why don't you answer me?*); **answer** (noun): juwaab (šinuu juwaabak? *What is your answer?*)

anybody: ʔaḥad (maa šifit ʔaḥad yitmašša ba9ad nuṣṣ-illayl. *I didn't see anybody walking after midnight.*)

anything: šii (maa ʔa9ruf šii 9ann šuglak. *I don't know anything about your work.*)

apiece: ilwaaḥid, ilwiḥda

appear, look, seem: bayyan, yibayyin

apples: tiffaaḥ; **an apple:** tiffaaḥa (f)

appoint: 9ayyan, yi9ayyin (9ayyannii kaatib fii daayirta. *He appointed me clerk in his office.*)

appointed (adjective): m9ayyan (ʔana m9ayyan mnilwuzaara raaʔisan. *I am appointed directly through the ministry.*)

appointment (noun): ta9yiin (waafaḳ ilmudiir 9ala ta9yiinii. *The director approved my appointment.*)

appointment, engagement (noun): maw9id (nisayt maw9idna. *I forgot our appointment.*)

apricot: mišmiš; **an apricot:** mišmiša

April: niisaan

Arabic: 9arabii, 9arabiiya (9arab); **Arab countries:** bilaad il9arab (il9iraaḳ huuwa ḳisim minn bilaad il9arab. *Iraq is part of the Arab world.*)

arak: 9arag

army: jayš (jyuuš) (huuwa raaḥ yidxul bijjayš. *He is going to enter the army.*)

arrange: dabbar, yidabbir (dabbar ʔamursaafarii ʔila ʔamriika. *He arranged my trip to America.*)

arrival: wuṣuul

arrive at, reach: wuṣal, yuuṣal (wuṣalna lgahwa. *We reached the coffee shop.*)

as . . . as: miθil, preceded by adjective (halkitaab ṭayyib miθil δaak. *This book is as good as that.*)

ashamed: mistaḥii (ʔana mistaḥii minnak. *I'm ashamed of you.*)

ask: siʔal, yisʔal (minuu siʔalak haaδa? *Who asked you this?*)

asleep: naayim, naayma, –iin

attempt (noun): tajriba (f)

attract: jiδab, yijδab

August: ʔaab

aunt (father's sister): xaaḷa (f); (mother's sister) 9amma (f)

author: muʔallif

automobile: siiyaara (siiyaaraat); **my automobile:** siiyaartii; **our automobile:** siiyaaratna; **a Ford:** siiyaarat-Ford; **automobile factory:** ma9mal-siiyaaraat

aviator: ṭayyaar, –iin

awake (adjective): gaa9id, gaa9da, –iin

back: ḍahar; **my back:** ḍahrii

backwards: ʔila wara

bad: duunii, duuniiya; muu zayn

bag: kiis (ʔakyaas) (9indii kiisayn-timman. *I have two bags of rice.*)

bag, suitcase: jinṭa (f) (jinaṭ); **her bag:** jinṭatha; **my bag:** jinuṭtii

Baghdad: bagdaad (f); **Baghdadi:** bagdaadii, bagdaadiiya, bagdaadiyiin

bake: xibaz, yixbuz; **baker:** xabbaaz (xibaabiiz)

ball: ṭoopa (f) (ṭoopaat)

bandage: laffaafa (f)

barber: ḥallaaḳ; mzayyin

barefooted: ḥaafii, ḥaafiya
barrel: barmiil (baraamiil)
basket: salla (f) (sallaat)
Basra: ilbaṣra (f); of Baṣra: baṣrii, baṣriiya
bath: ḥammaam (ʔaxaδit ḥammaam. *I took a bath.*)
bathroom: ḥammaam (ʔakuu fiiha ḥammaam xuṣuuṣii? *Does it have a private bathroom?*)
bay: xaliij
be; will be: yikuun (ʔakuun hinaa. *I will be here.*)
beard: liḥya (f); **my beard,** liḥaytii
beat, win: galab, yiglab (galabnii billi9ib. *He beat me in the game.*)
beautify: zayyan, yizayyin
beauty: jamaal (hiiya mašhuura bjamaalha. *She is famous for her beauty.*)
because: liʔann (huuwa zi9laan liʔannii ʔaxaδit kitaaba. *He is angry because I took his book*); minn sabab
become, get: ṣaar, yiṣiir (yiriid yiṣiir ṭabiib. *He wants to become a doctor.*)
bed: fraaš (fruuš)
beer: biira (f)
before: gabul (*before the war:* gabul ilḥarb); **before** (with verb): gabul maa (ʔana šifta gabul maa riḥit. *I saw him before I went.*)
beggar: mgaddii
begin: btida, yibtidii (btidayt ʔaktib maktuub. *I began to write a letter.*)
begin (to do something): btida, yibtidii; gaam, yiguum
behind: wara (waraay *behind me*)
believe (something): ṣaddaḳ, yiṣaddiḳ
bell: jaras (ʔajraas) (sima9it ijjaras yidigg. *I heard the bell ringing.*)
belong to: xaṣṣ, yixuṣṣ; **belongs to:** maal, maala (f) (halbayt maalii. *This house is mine.*)
below: jawwa
bench: taxat (txuut)
bend (something): 9awwaj, yi9awwij
beneficial: mufiid, mufiida (hadduwa mufiid limaraḍak. *This medicine is good for your illness.*)
beside, near: yamm (ʔig9ud yammii! *Sit beside me!*); bii jaanib (ṣadiiḳtii čaanat gaa9da bjaanbii bissiinama. *My girl friend was sitting beside me in the movie.*)
best: ilʔaḥsan
better (than): ʔaḥsan (minn) OR ʔaṭyab (minn)
between: bayn (čaan waaguf binnuṣṣ, bayn ʔabuu wumma. *He was standing in the middle, between his father and his mother.*; baynii wubayna ʔakuu 9adaawa. *There is bad feeling between me and him.*)
beyond: gaadii
big; old (of people): kabiir, kabiira (kbaar) OR čabiir, čabiira (kbaar)
bird: ṭayr (ṭyuur)
birth; give birth to: wulad, yuulad; **birthday:** yoom-ilmiilaad
bite: 9aḍḍ, yi9aḍḍ
bitter: murr, –a (halmaay murr. *This water is bitter.*); **more bitter:** ʔamarr (minn) (halgahwa ʔamarr minn δiič. *This coffee is bitterer than that.*)
black: ʔaswad (m), sooda (f), suud (pl)
blacksmith: ḥaddaad
blame: laam, yiluum; **blame** (noun): loom
blood: damm
blow: habb, yihibb
blue: ʔazrag (m), zarga (f), zurug (pl) (hiiya šagra wu9iyuunha zurug. *She is blond and her eyes are blue.*)
body: jisim (jsuum)
boil: faar, yifuur (ilmaay yifuur. *The water is boiling.*); **boil** (something): fawwar, yifawwir (huuwa fawwar ilmaay. *He boiled the water.*)
book: kitaab (kutub)
born: mawluud, –a, –iin (ʔaxuuya čaan mawluud bamriika. *My brother was born in America.*)
borrow: tdaayan, yitdaayan (tdaayanta minnii. *You borrowed it from me.*)
both: θinayn (θinaynna *both of us*)
bottle: buṭul (bṭoola) (haaδa buṭul maal ḥaliib. *This is a milk bottle.*)
box: ṣanduug (ṣanaadiig)
boy: walad (wulid OR ʔawlaad)
brave: jasuur, –a, –iin

bread (flat): xubuz; **loaves, rolls:** ṣammuun; **a loaf of bread:** ṣammuuna (f)

break (something): kisar, yiksir (kisar rijla. *He broke his leg.*); **break** (self): nkisar, yinkisar (nkisar ilbuṭul. *The bottle broke.*)

breakfast: fuṭuur (fuṭuurak ḥaaḍir. *Your breakfast is ready.*)

breast: days (dyuus) (dyuusha ṭaal9a. *Her breasts protrude.*)

breath: nafis; **breathe:** tnaffas, yitnaffas (maa ʔagdar ʔatnaffas. *I can't breathe.*)

brick: libin (halbayt mabnii minn libin. *This house is made of brick.*)

bridge: jisir (jisuur)

bring: jaab, yijiib; **bringing:** jaayib, jaayba, –iin

bring out: ṭalla9, yiṭalli9 (ṭalla9 jinaṭii mnilʔuutayl. *He brought my bags out of the hotel.*)

bring up: ṭalla9, yiṭalli9 (ṭalli9 jinaṭna foog! *Bring our bags upstairs!*)

broke (financially): miflis (ʔana miflis. *I'm broke.*)

brother: ʔax; **brothers:** ʔuxwaan OR ʔuxwa **my brothers:** ʔuxwaanii OR ʔuxuutii

brown: ʔasmar (m), samra (f), sumur (pl)

build: bina, yibnii (ʔariid ʔabniilii bayt. *I want to build me a house.*); (act of) **building:** taʔmiir (ʔana mašguul ibtaʔmiir ḥoošii. *I'm busy building my house.*)

building: binaaya (f) (binaayaat) (ilminaara binaaya 9aaliya. *The minaret is a high building.*)

built (of): mabnii, mabniiya (minn) (hajjisir mabnii minn xišab. *This bridge is built of wood.*)

bullet: raṣaaṣa (f) (raṣaaṣ)

bump: taxx, yituxx (laa ttuxx xašmak! *Don't bump your nose!*)

bury: difan, yidfan; **buried** (adjective): madfuun, –a (huuwa madfuun fii maḳbaratilʔingliiz fii bagdaad. *He is buried in the English cemetery in Baghdad.*)

bus: baaṣṣ (baaṣṣaat)

business: ʔašgaal (pl of šugul) (ilʔašgaal waagfa hassa. *Business is slow now.*)

business: tijaara (f) (humma bittijaara. *They are in business.*)

busy: mašguul, –a (ʔana mašguul ibtaʔmiirḥoošii. *I'm busy building my house.*); **busier** (than): ʔašgal (minn) (maa ʔaftikir ʔinta ʔašgal minnii. *I don't think you are busier than me.*)

but: laakin OR wulaakin

butcher: gaṣṣaab (gaṣaaṣiib)

butter: zubud (ʔakuu 9indak zubud taaža? *Have you any fresh butter?*)

buttermilk (cultured): laban OR liban

buy (from): štira, yištirii (minn) (štirayta minn dukkaan ṣagiir. *I bought it from a small shop.*)

call, talk to: kallam, yikallim (kallama bittalafoon. *He called him on the phone.*)

calm: saakin, saakna, –iin (ilhawa saakin. *The air is calm.*)

camel: jamal (jimaal); **camel-driver:** jammaal (jammaaliin)

camera: kaamira (f)

camp (somewhere): xayyam, yixayyim (xayyamna biččool. *We camped in the country.*)

can: gidar, yigdar (maa gidar yiruuh. *He couldn't go.*)

canvas: čaadir (ilxayma msawwaaya minn čaadir. *The tent is made of canvas.*)

capable: muḳtadir (huuwa mudiir muḳtadir. *He is a capable manager.*)

capital: 9aaṣima (f) (bagdaad hiiya 9aaṣimatil9iraaḳ. *Baghdad is the capital of Iraq.*)

caravan: karwaan (karaawiin)

careless: gaafil, gaafla (kaan gaafil 9ann halmasʔala. *He was careless in this matter.*)

carpenter: najjaar (najjaariin)

carriage: 9arabaana (f) (9arabaayin); **carriage-driver:** 9arabančii

carry, pick up: šaal, yišiil (šiil iṣṣanduug! *Carry the box!*); **carrying:** šaayil, šaayla, –iin (kaan šaayil kitaaba. *He was carrying his book.*)

carry, transport: ḥimal, yiḥmil

cash (in cash): naḳdan (laazim tidfa9 ilkiima naḳdan. *You have to pay cash.*)

catch: lizam, yilzam (lizam ṭayr kabiir. *He caught a big bird.*)

catch: misak, yimsak (misak ṭoopa biida. *He caught the ball in his hand.*)

cattle: baḳar

cause, let, have: xalla, yixallii (xalliiha tidxul! *Have her come in!*)

cause, reason: sabab (šinuu ssabab? *What's the reason?*)

certain OR **some**: fadd OR farid (ʔasawwii haaδa fadd yoom. *I'll do this someday.*)

chain: zanjiil (zanaajiil) (kalbii 9inda zanjiil ibrugubta. *My dog has a chain on his neck.*)

chair: skamlii (skamliiyaat); kursii (karaasii)

change (something): baddal, yibaddil (baddal θooba ilwaṣux wulibas waaḥid naḍiif. *He changed his dirty shirt and put on a clean one.*; laa tbaddil fikrak! *Don't change your mind!*) OR gayyar, yigayyir (ruuḥ gayyir malaabsak! *Go change your clothes!*)

change (noun): tagyiir OR tabdiil (ʔakuu tabdiil fii minhaaj-ilmadrasa. *There is a change in the schedule of the school.*)

change (self): tgayyar, yitgayyar OR tbaddal, yitbaddal (ilmanaax yitbaddal minn yoom ʔila yoom. *The weather changes from day to day.*)

cheap: raxiiṣ, –a (rxaaṣ); **cheaper** (than): ʔarxaṣ (minn)

cheat: gašš, yigišš (gašnii bilḳiima. *He cheated me on the price.*); **cheater**: gaššaaš

cheek: xadd (xduud) (xaddak ʔaḥmar. *Your cheek is red.*)

cheese: jibin

chew: 9ilas, yi9lis (laazim ti9lis hadduwa. *You have to chew this medicine.*)

chicken: dijaaj; **a chicken**: dijaaja (f)

chief, head, boss: rayyis OR raʔiis (ruʔasaaʔ) (kaan rayyis-ilma9mal. *He was head of the factory.*)

chin: ḍaḳin (xayyanit ḍaḳnii. *I shaved my chin.*)

China: iṣṣiin (f) (iṣṣiin hiiya bilaad ḳadiima. *China is an ancient country.*)

Chinese: ṣiinii, ṣiiniiya, ṣiiniyiin

choke: xtinaḳ, yixtaniḳ (huuwa xtinaḳ ib9aḍm maal simač. *He choked on a fish bone.*)

choose: xayyar, yixayyir (xayyir ʔiδa triid truuḥ lilbaṣra bilḳiṭaar ʔaw bilmarkab. *Choose whether you want to go to Basra by train or by boat.*)

Christian: nuṣraanii (naṣaara)

church: kaniisa (f) (kanaayis)

cigarette: jigaara (f) (jigaayir); **cigarette seller**: ʔabuu-jigaayir

city: balad (bilaad) OR madiina (f) (mudun)

civilian: madanii, madaniiya (filbaṣra ʔakuu maṭaar madanii. *There is a civilian airport in Basra.*)

class: ṣaff

classical: fusḥa (haaδa maktuub bil9arabii lfusḥa. *This is written in classical Arabic.*)

clean: naḍiif, –a (nḍaaf); **make clean**: naḍḍaf, yinaḍḍuf (naḍḍaf sinaana. *He cleaned his teeth.*)

clerk: bayaa9, –a

climb: ṣi9ad, yiṣ9ad (ṣi9ad ijjabal. *He climbed the mountain.*)

clock: saa9a (f) (saa9aat); **five o'clock**: bilxamsa

close, shut: sadd, yisidd (sidd ilbaab! *Close the door!*); **closed**: masduud, –a (ilbaab masduud. *The door is closed.*)

clothes presser: ʔuutačii

clothing: malaabis (čint laabis malaabis 9arabiiya. *I was wearing Arabic clothing.*)

clouds: mgaym; **cloudy**: mgayma (iddinya mgayma. *It is cloudy.*)

coffee: gahwa (f); **coffee shop**: gahwa (f) (gahaawii)

cold: baarid, baarda; **cold** (of persons): bardaan, –a, –iin; **(head)cold**: našla (f) (9indii našla ḳawiiya. *I have a bad cold.*) **(head)cold**: manšuul (ʔana manšuul. *I have a cold.*); **colder** (than): ʔabrad (minn)

college: kulliiya (f) (kulliiyaat) (yisammuuha kulliiyat-bagdaad. *They call it the College of Baghdad.*)

color: loon (ʔalwaan) (ʔay loon 9iyuunak? *What color are your eyes?*)

come: ʔija, yijii (minayn jiit? *Where did you come from?*); **come** (command): ta9aal, –ii, –uu (ta9aal hinaa ! *Come here!*); **coming** (adjective): jaay, jaaya, jaayiin (šifitha jaaya mnilmadrasa. *I saw her coming from school.*)

come back: rija9, yirja9 (laazim tirja9 minn waḳit. *You have to come back early.*)

commerce: tijaara (f) (huuwa yištugul bittijaara. *He is a businessman.*); **commercial:** tijaarii (huuwa yidiir maḥall tijaarii kabiir. *He manages a large firm.*)

company: šarika (f) (ʔana ʔaštugul fii šarikat-innafuṭ. *I work for the oil company.*)

complain (about): šika, yiškii (9ala) (šika 9alayya 9ind ilmudiir. *He complained about me to the manager.*)

complete: tamm, yitimm (kull šii tamm 9ala kayfak; ba9ad šitriid? *Everything is done as you wish; what more do you want?*)

congratulate: hanna, yihannii (ʔahanniik! *Congratulations!*)

contractor: muḳaawil

cook: ṭibax, yiṭbux; **cooked** (adjective): maṭbuux, –a (hattimman laayin; huuwa muu maṭbuux zayn. *This rice is soft; it isn't cooked good.*); **cook:** ṭabbaax

cost: kallaf, yikallif (yikallif diinaarayn. *It costs two dinars.*); **cost, price:** ḳiima (f); cost, rental: ʔujra (f)

cough: gaḥḥ, yiguḥḥ (imbaarḥa billayl gaḥḥayt kaθiir. *I coughed a lot last night.*)

could: SEE **can**

country (state): balad (bilaad) (il9iraaḳ balad mustaḳill. *Iraq is an independent country.*); **the Arab countries:** bilaad il9arab

course: of course: ṭab9an (ṭab9an yiriid yiḥčii 9arabii lamma yikuun bil9iraaḳ. *Of course he wants to speak Arabic when he is in Iraq.*)

cousin: (son of father's brother) ʔibin-9ammii; (daughter of father's brother) bint-9ammii; (son of mother's brother) ʔibin-xaaḷii; (daughter of mother's brother) bint-xaaḷii

cup: finjaan (finaajiin) (širabit finjaan-gahwa ʔamriikaaniiya. *I drank a cup of American coffee.*)

custom: ṭariiḳa (f) (haaðii ṭariiḳa 9arabiiya. *This is an Arabic custom.*)

cut: gaṣṣ, yiguṣṣ (laa tguṣṣ ša9arii ! *Don't cut my hair!*)

cutlet: kabaab

danger: xaṭar (ʔakuu xaṭar. *It's dangerous.*)

dates: tamur; **a date:** tamra (f)

daughter: bint (banaat)

day: yoom (ʔayyaam); **day after tomorrow:** ba9ad baačir; **per day:** bilyoom; **daytime:** nahaar; **during the day:** binnahaar

decayed: msawwas (9indii fadd sinn msawwas. *I have a decayed tooth.*)

December: kaanuun ilʔawwal

decide: ḳarrar, yiḳarrir (ḳarrarit ʔaštiriilii siiyaara šahar ijjaay. *I've decided to buy me an automobile next year.*)

demand: ṭilab, yiṭlub (yiṭlub minnii ʔaruuḥ wiiyaa. *He demanded me to go with him.*)

desert: ṣaḥra (ṣaḥaarii)

dialect: liḥja (f) (yiḥčii 9arabii billiḥja llibnaaniiya. *He speaks Arabic in the Lebanese dialect.*)

different: gayr (precedes noun) (nṭiinii gayr badla! *Give me a different suit!*)

dinar (1000 fils): diinaar (dinaaniir)

dinner (evening meal): 9iša (ta9aal waḳt-il9iša ! *Come at dinner time!*)

direct, manage: daar, yidiir (huuwa yidiir maḥall tijaarii kabiir. *He manages a large firm.*)

dirty: waṣux, waṣxa (wṣaax) (ʔiidayya waṣxa. *My hands are dirty.*)

disease: maraḍ; **heart disease:** maraḍ-ilḳalib

dish: maa9uun (mawaa9iin); **dish of rice:** maa9uun-timman

distance: masaafa (f) (šgad ilmasaafa bayn bagdaad wilbaṣra? *What is the distance between Baghdad and Basra?*)

do; make: sawwa, yisawwii (šloon itsawwii haaða? *How do you do this?* minuu sawwa halmiftaaḥ? *Who made this key?*)

doctor: duxtoor OR ṭabiib

dog: kalb (m) (kluub); kalba (f) (kalbaat)

domestic: daaxil

don't: laa with incompleted action verb form (laa txalliinii waḥdii! *Don't leave me alone!*)

door: baab (ʔabwaab) (sidd ilbaab! *Close the door!*)

down: jawwa; **downstairs:** jawwa

dozen: dirzan

drink: širab, yišrab; **drink, beverage:** mašruub

drive: saag, yisuug (tigdar itsuug issiiyaara? *Can you drive the automobile?*); **driving** (noun): siyaaḳa (f) (ʔana ʔat9allam siyaaḳa. *I'm learning how to drive.*)

dry: yaabis, yaabsa; **drier** (than): ʔaybas (minn)

early: minn waḳit (gi9adit minn waḳit. *I woke up early.*)

east: šarḳ; **in the east:** biššarḳ; **eastern:** šarḳii, šarḳiiya

easy: sahil, sahla (shaal); **easier** (than) ʔashal (minn)

easy (on someone): layyin (wiiya) (ṣiir layyin wiiyaaya! *Be easy on me!*)

eat: ʔakal, yaakul (laa taakul kulliš! *Don't eat too much!*)

education: diraasa (f) (9inda diraasa 9aaliya. *He has a broad education.*)

eggplant: baadinjaan

eggs: bayḍ; **an egg:** bayḍa

eight: θimaanya; **eight days:** θimaan-ʔayyaam; **eighth** (adj) θaamin, θaamna; **eighty:** θimaaniin

eighteenth: θmunṭa9aš

eleven: ʔiida9aš; **eleventh** (adjective): ilʔiida9aš

else, more: ba9ad (maa ʔariid šii ba9ad. *I don't want anything else.*)

employee: mu9aḍḍaf (mu9aḍḍafiin)

empty: faarug, faarga

engineer: muhandis (muhandisiin); **engineering:** handasa (f)

English: ʔingliizii, ʔingliiziiya (ʔingliiz) (ʔaḥčii ʔingliizii. *I speak English.*)

enough: kaafii, kaafiya (9indak fluus kaafiya? *Do you have enough money?*)

enter, go in, come in: dixal, yidxul (bii) (laazim yidxul bijjayš. *He has to enter the army.*)

entertain (someone): wannas, yiwannis (wannasnii lamma zirit mazra9ta. *He entertained me when I visited his farm.*)

establish: ʔassas, yiʔassis (iššarika raaḥ itʔassis madrasa. *The company is going to establish a school.*)

establishment: maḥall (maḥallaat)

evening: masaaʔ; masaaʔ ilxayr: **Good evening**)

every: kull; **every day:** kull yoom; **everyone:** kull waaḥid; **everything:** kull šii; **everything, whatever:** kull maa (kull maa ḥičayt, huuwa tamaam. *Everything you said is correct.*)

examine: kišaf, yikšif (ʔariid ʔakšif ʔawraaḳak. *I want to examine your papers.*)

excellent: 9aal

except: ʔilla

excuse: simaḥ, yismaḥ; (ʔismaḥlii! *Excuse me!*) OR 9iḍar, yi9ḍir (ʔi9ḍirnii! *Excuse me!*)

expensive: gaalii, gaaliya; **more expensive** (than): ʔagla (minn)

exporting (noun): tazdiir (il9iraaḳ saadisdaawla bil9aalam ibtazdiir-innafuṭ. *Iraq is the sixth country in the world in exporting oil.*)

extensive: waaṣi9, waaṣ9a (9inda ʔiraaḍii waaṣ9a yamm bagdaad. *He has extensive lands near Baghdad.*)

eye: 9ayn (9iyuun) (šinuu loon-9iyuunak? *What is the color of your eyes?*)

face: wajih (wujuh)

factory: ma9mal (ma9aamil)

faithful, honest: ʔamiin, –a

fall: wuga9, yuuga9

family: ʔahil; **her family:** ʔahilha; **my family:** ʔahlii

famous: mašhuur, –a, –iin; **more famous:** ʔašhar (minn)

far (from): ba9iid, –a, –iin (minn)

farm: mazra9a (f) (mazaari9)

fat: samiin, –a (smaan) (huuwa kulliš samiin. *He is very fat.*)
father: ʔab; **my father:** ʔabuuya; **my friend's father:** ʔabuu-ṣadiiḳii
February: šibaaṭ
few: ḳaliil, –a (ḳlaal) (tiinaatii ḳlaal. *I have few figs.*)
fifteenth: xamiṣṭa9aš
fifth (adjective): xaamis, xaamsa
fifty: xamsiin
figs: tiin; **a fig:** tiina (f)
film: filim (ʔaflaam)
fils (a coin): fils (fluus)
find: wujad, yuujad
fine: 9aal
finish, get through: xaḷḷaṣ, yixaḷḷiṣ (lamma xaḷḷaṣiṭ, ta9aaal 9indii. *When you get through, come to me.*)
finished, all gone: xaḷṣaan, –a
fire (destructive): ḥariiḳa (f); **fire** (useful): naar (niiraan)
first (adjective) ʔawwal (haaδii ʔawwal jigaara ʔadaxxinha lyoom. *This is the first cigarette I've smoked today.*); **first of all, at first:** bilʔawwal
fish: simač; **a fish:** simča (f)
five: xamsa; **five days:** xamis-ʔayyaam
floor: ʔaruḍ
fly: ṭaar, yiṭiir (iṭṭayyaara ṭaarat minn New York ʔila bagdaad. *The plane flew from New York to Baghdad.*); **flying** (adjective): ṭaayir, ṭaayra (iṭṭayyaar ṭaayir foog bagdaad. *The pilot is flying over Baghdad.*)
fly (something): ṭayyar, yiṭayyir (ʔana maa ʔagdar ʔaṭayyir ṭayyaara. *I can't fly an airplane.*)
for: ʔila, ʔil–; li– (štirayt θoob ʔila ʔaxuuya. *I bought a shirt for my brother.*); 9ind (yištugul 9indii. *He works for me.*); lišaan (nriid gurfa liṣaan nafarayn. *We want a room for two.*); **for** (cost): bii (yibii9uuhum θinayn ibmiit-filis. *They sell them two for a hundred fils.*); maal (haaδa kiis maal timman. *This is a bag for rice.*)
forbidden: mamnuu9, –a
foreign: ʔajnabii, ʔajnabiiya (ʔajaanib)
forget: nisa, yinsa; **forgetting** (adjective) naasii, naasiya (činit naasii lmiftaaḥ. *I used to forget the key.*)
forgotten (adjective): mansii, mansiiya
food: ṭa9aam; ʔakil (ʔaklaat)
forty: ʔarba9iin
found, present: mawjuud *or* moojuud, –a, –iin (huuwa mawjuud bilbayt. *He is at home.*)
four: ʔarba9a; **four days:** ʔarba9-ʔayyaam; **fourteen:** ʔarbaaṭa9aš; **fourth** (adjective) raabi9, raab9a
free (something): xaḷḷaṣ, yixaḷḷuṣ
freedom: ḥurriiya (f) (maakuu ḥurriiya hinaak. *There is no freedom there.*)
French: fransaawii, fransaawiiya (fransaawiiyiin)
Friday: yoom ijjum9a
fried: maglii, magliiya
friend: ṣadiiḳ, –a (ṣudḳaan); ṣaaḥib, ṣaaḥba (ʔaṣḥaab)
from: minn
fruit: maywa (f) *or* miiwa (f)
full (of): malyaan, –a (minn); **full** (of food): šib9aan, šib9aana
future: mustaḳbil (ʔatʔammal yikuun mustaḳbil ṭayyib lilmadrasa. *I hope there will be a good future for the school.*)

gazelle: gazaal (gizlaan)
generous: kariim, –a
Germany: ʔalmaanya (f)
get, become: ṣaar, yiṣiir (laa tṣiir zi9laan minnii! *Don't get angry with me!*)
get, receive: stilam, yistilim (maa stilamit maktuub. *I didn't get a letter.*)
get, take: ʔaxaδ, yaaxuδ (naaxuδ diinaarayn bilyoom. *We get two dinars a day.*)
get up, wake up: gi9ad, yig9ud; **awake:** gaa9id, gaa9da
girl: bint (f) (banaat)
give: nṭa, yinṭii (nṭiinii waaḥid! *Give me one!*)
give back: rajja9, yirajji9
gave birth to: jaabat, tjiib (jaabat walad. *She gave birth to a boy.*)

glass (tumbler): glaaṣ (glaaṣaat)
(eye)glasses: manaaḍir (pl) (laazim ʔalbas manaaḍir. *I have to wear glasses.*)
go: raaḥ, yiruuḥ (raaḥ libagdaad. *He went to Baghdad.*); **going:** raayiḥ, raayḥa, –iin (ʔiḥna raayḥiin lissiinama. *We are going to the movie.*); **going to** (do something): raaḥ (ʔana raaḥ ʔadris 9arabii. *I'm going to study Arabic.*)
go out: ṭiḷa9, yiṭḷa9 (maa raaḥ ʔaṭḷa9 barra. *I'm not going to go outside.*)
go up, rise: ṭiḷa9, yiṭḷa9 (hassa ṭiḷ9at iššams. *The sun just rose.*)
God: ʔilaah; **God willing . . .:** ʔinšaḷḷa (raaḥ ʔaruuḥ lilbaṣra ʔinšaḷḷa. *I'm going to go to Basra, I hope.*)
gold: δahab (halmaḥbas minn δahab. *This ring is of gold.*)
good: zayn, –a, –iin; ṭayyib, ṭayba, ṭaybiin; xooš (precedes noun) (huuwa xooš walad wuhumma xooš banaat. *He is a good boy and they are good girls.*)
good, excellent: 9aal
Good day: ʔaḷḷaa bilxayr: **good morning:** ṣabaaḥ ilxayr.
goodbye: fiimaanilaa OR ma9a ssalaama.
goodbye: say goodbye to: waada9, yiwaada9 (waada9nii lamma saafarit ʔila ṣuuriya. *He said goodbye to me when I left for Syria.*)
government: ḥukuuma (f) (ḥukuumaat)
grapes: 9anab; **a grape:** 9amba (f)
grass: ḥašiiš
green: ʔaxḍar (m), xaḍra (f), xuḍur (pl)
greet: sallam, yisallim (sallamit 9alayha. *I greeted her.*)
grow, get big: kibar, yikbar (maa yikbar kaθiir. *He isn't growing much.*)

had to: kaan laazim (kaan laazim ʔaruuḥ. *I had to go.*)
hair: ša9ar (ša9arii ʔaswad. *My hair is black.*)
haircut: (ʔariid ʔaguṣṣ ša9arii. *I want a haircut.*)
half: nuṣuf OR nuṣṣ; **half a dozen:** nuṣṣ-dirzan
hammer: čaakuuč (čawaakiič)
hand over, hand to: naawaš, yinaawuš (naawušnii lkitaab. *Hand me the book.*)
handsome: jamiil, jamiila (jmaal)
happy: farḥaan, –a; sa9iid, –a; **happier** (than): ʔas9ad (minn)
hard, difficult: ṣa9ib, ṣa9ba (ṣ9aab); **harder** (than) ʔaṣ9ab (minn)
hard, tough: xašin, xašna (xšaan) (hallaḥam xašin. *This meat is tough.*); **harder** (than) ʔaxšan (minn)
Hassan (man's name): ḥasan (ʔisma ḥasan. *His name is Hassan.*)
hat: sitra (f)
have, has: 9ind (9indii siiyaara. *I have an automobile.* 9ind ʔabuuya mazra9a. *My father has a farm.*)
have to, must: laazim (laazim nirja9 lilʔuutayl. *We have to go back to the hotel.*); **should have:** kaan laazim (kint laazim ʔaktib. *I should have written.*)
he: huuwa
head: raas (ruus); **headache:** wuji9-raas (9indii wuji9-raas. *I have a headache.*)
hear (about): sima9, yisma9 (9ann) (maa sima9tak: *I didn't hear you.*); (maa sima9it 9anha. *I haven't heard about her.*)
heart: ḳalb
heavy: θagiil, –a (θgaal); **heavier** (than): ʔaθgal (minn)
height: ṭuul (ṭuula xamis ʔaḳdaam wusitt-ʔinjaat. *He is five feet, six inches tall.*)
hello: say hello to: sallam, yisallim (sallimnii 9alayha *Say 'hello' to her for me!*)
help: saa9ad, yisaa9id (tigdar tsaa9idnii ibḳaaḍiiṭ tawḍiifii bilmiinaa? *Can you help me get a job in the port?*)
her: –ha (šifitha fii baytha. *I saw her in her house.*)
here: hina, hinaa, hinaaya; **to this place:** lihinaa; **from this place:** minn hinaa OR minnaa
here's OR **take!:** haak, –ii, –uu (haak ilifluus! *Here's the money!*)
hers: maalha (m), maalatha (f) (halmalaabis maalatha. *These clothes are hers.*)

high: 9aalii, 9aaliya (haṣṣuura 9aaliya. *This picture is high.*)

him: –a (riḥt wiiyaa. *I went with him.*; šifta fii siiyaarta. *I saw him in his car.*)

his: maala (m), maalta (f) (hassiiyaara maalta. *This automobile is his.*)

hold: misak, yimsak (ʔimsak tufuktii! *Hold my gun!*); **holding:** maasik, maaska

honest: šariif, –a

honored: be honored: tšarraf, yitšarraf (ʔana ʔatšarraf. *I'm honored.*)

hope: tʔammal, yitʔammal (ʔatʔammal ʔašuufak. *I hope I see you.*)

hospital: mustašfa (f) (mustašfayaat)

hot: ḥaarr, ḥaarra (iddinya ḥaarra lyoom. *It is hot today.*)

hotel: ʔuutayl (ʔuutaylaat)

hour: saa9a (saa9aat)

house: bayt (byuut) OR ḥooš (ḥawaaš)

how: šloon (šloonak? *How are you* (m)?) (šloona? *How is he?*) (šloon ta9ruf haaδa? *How do you know this?*)

how far: šgad (baytak šgad ba9iid minn hinaa? *How far is your house from here?*)

how many: kamm OR čamm with singular noun (kamm ʔax 9indak? *How many brothers do you have?*)

how much: bayš (bayš haaδa yikallif? *How much does this cost?*)

hundred: miiya (f) (maa kaan 9indii miit-doolaar. *I didn't have a hundred dollars.*); **hundredth** (adjective): ilmiiya; **per cent:** bilmiiya

hungry: joo9aan, –a, –iin; **hungrier** (than): ʔajwa9 (minn) OR joo9aan ʔakθar (minn)

husband: rajil OR zooj (ʔijat wiiya rajilha. *She came with her husband.*)

I: ʔana OR ʔaanii

idea: fikir (haaδa xooš fikir. *This is a good idea.*)

if (when): ʔiδa (ʔiδa huuwa yijii, ʔana ʔaruuḥ wiiyaa. *If he comes, I will go with him.*)

if (such were the case): **law** (law ʔana bmakaanak, ʔasawwii haaδa. *If I were in your place, I'd do this.*)

important: muhimm, –a (haaδa muu muhimm ʔilii. *This isn't important to me.*); **more important** (than): ʔahamm (minn) (huuwa ʔahamm minnak. *He is more important than you.*)

important: be important, be a concern to: htamm, yihtumm

improvement: taḥsiin (titin-il9iraaḳ kulliš zayn, laakin maa yihtammuun ibtaḥsiina. *The tobacco of Iraq is very good, but they don't care about improving it.*)

in: fii, bii, fi-, bi-, b- (fii bagdaad, *in Baghdad;* filbayt, *at home;* bbagdaad, *in Baghdad*)

inch: ʔinj (ʔinjaat)

inside: daaxil (šifta daaxil-halbinaaya. *I saw him inside this building.*)

intend: naawii, naawiya, naawiyiin (naawii ʔaruuḥ lilbaṣra fii niisaan. *I intend to go to Basra in April.*)

introduce (to): 9arraf, yi9arrif (9ala) (ʔariid ʔa9arfak 9ala ṣadiiḳii. *I want to introduce you to my friend.*)

invite, call: di9a, yid9uu (ilmuʔaδδin yid9uu nnaas liṣṣalaat. *The muezzin calls the people to prayer.*)

invite: 9izam, ya9zim (9izamnii lilgada. *He invited me to lunch.*)

Iraq: il9iraaḳ (m) (il9iraaḳ mamlaka. *Iraq is a kingdom.*); **Iraqi:** 9iraaḳii, 9iraakiiya, 9iraaḳiiyiin

iron: ḥadiid (halbismaar minn ḥadiid. *This nail is made of iron.*); **pressing iron:** ʔuutii (ʔiḍrub badiltii ʔuutii! *Press my suit!*)

island (small): jazra (f)

Italian: ʔiiṭaalii, ʔiiṭaaliiya (ʔakuu 9idna biira ʔiiṭaaliiya. *We have Italian beer.*)

January: kaanuun iθθaanii

Jewish: yihuudii, yihuudiiya (yihuud)

July: tammuuz

June: ḥizayraan

just: hassa (with completed action verb) (hassa 9irafit ʔinta ʔamriikaanii. *I just learned you are an American.*)

keep on: ḍall, yiḍill (ḍallayna nimšii. *We kept on walking.*)

key: miftaaḥ (mifaatiiḥ) (haaδa miftaaḥ-siiyaartii. *This is the key of my car.*)

kind, sort: noo9 (ʔay noo9 siiyaara triid? *What kind of car do you want?*)

king: malik (maluuk) (il9iraaḳ ḥikama θilaaθ-maluuk — fayṣal ilʔawwal, gaazii ʔilʔawwal, wufayṣal iθθaanii. *Three kings have ruled Iraq — Faisal the First, Ghazi the First, and Faisal the Second.*)

kingdom: mamlaka (f) (ilmamlaka l9arabiiya issa9uudiiya hiiya ḳisim muhimm minn ilbilaad il9arabiiya. *The kingdom of Saudi Arabia is an important part of the Arab countries.*)

knock: dagg, yidigg (daggayt 9albaab. *I knocked on the door.*)

know: 9iraf, ya9ruf (maa ʔa9ruf haaδa. *I don't know this.*); **know how:** 9iraf, ya9ruf (ya9ruf yiktib ʔingliizii. *He knows how to write English.*)

land: ʔaruḍ (ʔaraaḍii) (9indii ʔaraaḍii kaθiira yamm bagdaad. *I have a lot of land near Baghdad.*)

last: ʔaaxir (kaan gaa9id ibʔaaxir-iṣṣaff. *He was sitting last in the row.*) (ʔana činit ʔaaxir waaḥid bissibaaḳ. *I was the last one in the race.*)

last: at last: ʔaxiiran

last night: ilbaarḥa billayl; **last year:** sant-ilmaaḍiya (ʔijat sant-ilmaaḍiya. *She came last year.*)

late: mitʔaxxir, mitʔaxra, –iin (layš ʔintum mitʔaxriin? *Why are you late?*)

lazy: kislaan, –a, –iin; **lazier** (than): ʔaksal (minn) (yigluun huuwa ʔaksal minnii. *They say he is lazier than me.*)

learn: t9allam, yit9allam (ba9adnii maa t9allamit ʔasuug. *I haven't learned to drive yet.*)

least: at least: ʔaḳallan

leave: tirak, yitruk (maa ʔariid ʔatruk bagdaad. *I don't want to leave Baghdad.*); xalla, yixallii (xallayt ilkitaab 9almayz. *I left the book on the table.*)

Lebanon: libnaan; **Lebanese,** libnaanii, libnaaniiya

left: yisir, yisra (9aynii lyisra tooja9nii. *My left eye hurts me.*)

lefthanded: yisraawii (ʔana yisraawii. *I'm lefthanded.*)

leftside: yasaar; **on your left:** 9ala yasaarak

leg: rijil; **two legs:** rijlayn; **my legs:** rijlayya

lend: daayan, yidaayin (daayinnii θilaaθ-dinaaniir. *Lend me three dinars.*)

length: ṭuul (šgad ṭuula? *How long is it?* šgad ṭuulak? *How tall are you?*)

less (than): ʔaḳall (minn) (9indii fluus ʔaḳall minnak. *I have less money than you.*); ʔilla (bilʔarba9a ʔilla θiliθ. *At three forty.*)

lesson: darsa (f) (huuwa yidris darista. *He is studying his lesson.*)

letter: maktuub (mikaatiib) (maa stilamit maktuub minnak. *I didn't receive a letter from you.*)

lettuce: xaṣṣ

liar: kaδδaab

life; age: 9umur (ʔana b9umrii maa šifit miθil haaδa. *I have never seen anything like this before* (lit., *in my life.*)

light (weight): xafiif, –a (xfaaf) (halwaraḳ xafiif. *This paper is light.*) (humma xfaaf bilmašii. *They walk lightly.*); **lighter** (than): ʔaxaff (minn) (waznii ʔaxaff minnak. *I weigh less than you.*)

like: 9ijab, yi9jib (ʔana yi9jibnii 9arag. *I like arag.* bagdaad maa ti9jibnii. *I don't like Baghdad.*)

like, resembling: miθil (huuwa muu miθlak. *He isn't like you.*); **like, the way:** miθil maa (with verbs) (ʔana ʔasawwiiha miθil maa triid. *I will do it the way you want.*)

line, row: ṣaff

list: ḳaayma (f) (ḳaaymaat); **menu:** ḳaaymat-ilʔakil

little: a little, some: šwayya (9indii šwayya fluus. *I have a little money.*)

little, few: ḳaliil, –a (ḳlaal) (9indii waraḳ ḳaliil. *I have little paper.*)

live, stay: sikan, yiskin (sikanit fii bagdaad mudda ṭawiila. *I lived in Baghdad a long time.*); **living** (adjective): saakin, saakna, –iin (ʔiḥna saakniin bilʔuutayl. *We are living at the hotel.*)

livelihood: ma9iiša (f) (ilma9iiša bil9iraaḳ gaaliya. *Living in Iraq is expensive.*)

livestock: mawaašii (9idna mawaašii bilmazra9a. *We have cattle on the farm.*)

living: make a living: 9aaš, yi9iiš (maa ʔagdar ʔa9iiš fii halmadiina. *I can't make a living in this city.*)

load: ḥimil (ʔakuu ḥimil kaθiir bilmarkab. *There is a big load on the ship.*)

lobby: ṣaaloon

lock: ḳifil (ʔaḳfaal) (maakuu ḳifil bilbaab. *There is no lock on the door.*)

long: ṭawiil, –a (ṭwaal) (ṣaar mudda ṭawiila minn šiftak. *It has been a long time since I saw you.*); **longer** (than): ʔaṭwal (minn) (ʔinta muu ʔaṭwal minnii. *You aren't taller than me.*)

look, seem: bayyan, yibayyin (ʔinta tbayyan ti9baan. *You look tired.*)

look around: tfarraj, yitfarraj (9ala OR bii) (ʔariid ʔatfarraj ibbagdaad. *I want to look around Baghdad.*)

look for: daar 9ala, yidiir 9ala (ruuḥ diir 9alay! *Go look for him!*)

lot: a lot, much: hawaaya OR kaθiir (ʔakalit hawaaya. *I ate a lot.*) (ʔakuu siiyaaraat kaθiira bbagdaad. *There are lots of automobiles in Baghdad.*)

love: ḥabb, yiḥibb (ʔaktikir yiḥibbič. *I think he loves you* (f).) **loved** (adjective): maḥbuub, –a

lunch: have lunch (noon meal): tgadda, yitgadda (šwaḳit raaḥ nitgadda? *When are we going to have lunch?*)

make, do: sawwa, yisawwii (minuu sawwa halmiftaaḥ? *Who made this key?*) (šitsawwii hinaa? *What are you doing here?*)

make (someone do something): xalla, yixallii (huuwa xallaanii ʔaruuḥ wiiyaa. *He made me go with him.*)

make, amount to: saawa, yisaawii (waaḥid uuwaaḥid yisaawii θinayn. *One and one makes two.*)

man: rijjaal (riyaajiil)

manage, direct: daar, yidiir (huuwa raaḥ yidiir ilmadrasa. *He is going to direct the school.*); **manager:** mudiir (mudaraaʔ)

many: kaθiir, –a

March: ʔaaδaar

market: suug (ʔaswaag)

married (adjective): mitzawwij, mitzawja, –iin

match: šixaaṭa (f) (šixaaṭ)

matter: šbii- (šbiik? *What's the matter with you?*) **it doesn't matter:** maa yixaalif

Maude Bridge: jisir-mood

May: ʔayyaar

meal: ʔakla (f) (ridna yaakul ʔakla 9arabiiya. *We wanted him to eat an Arab meal.*)

mean: 9ina, ya9nii (šya9nii haada? *What does this mean?*)

meat: laḥam; **pork:** laḥam-xanziir; **mutton:** laḥam-xurfaan; **meat-seller:** ʔabuu-laḥam

medicine: duwa (m)

menu: ḳaaymat-ilʔakil (f)

merchant: taajir (tujjaar)

midnight: nuṣṣ-illayl

mile: miil (miiyaal)

military (adjective): ḥarbii, ḥarbiiya

milk: ḥaliib

million: malyoon (malaayiin)

minaret: minaara (f) (minaaraat)

mind, idea: fikir (laa tgayyir fikrak! *Don't change your mind!*)

mine: maalii (m), maaltii (f) (kull šii maalii, maalak. *Everything I have is yours.*)

minister (governmental): waziir (wuzaraaʔ)

minus: naaḳuṣ (9ašra naaḳuṣ sitta yisaawii ʔarba9a. *Ten minus six makes four.*)

minute: daḳiiḳa (f) (daḳaayiḳ)

miserable: baa9is, baa9sa; **more miserable** (than): ʔab9as (minn)

Monday: yoom iθθinayn

money: fluus (pl) (9indii fluus ḳaliila. *I have little money.*)

money of Iraq: a copper coin: filis (fluus); **silver coins:** ?arba9-fluus; 9ašir-fluus; 9išriin-filis; xamsiin-filis; riiyaal (200 fils); **paper:** rubu9-diinaar (250 fils); nuṣṣ-diinaar (500 fils); diinaar (1000 fils); xamis-diinaar, 9ašir-diinaar, xamsiin-diinaar, miit-diinaar, ?alif-diinaar

month: šahar (?išhur) (raaḥ ?atruk il9iraaḳ šahar ijjaay. *I'm going to leave Iraq next month.*)

more (than): ?akθar (minn)

more, in addition, else: ba9ad (maa ?ariid ba9ad. *I don't want anymore.*)

moreover: ?ayḍan (?akuu wulid wu?ayḍan banaat fii madrasatna. *There are boys and (even) girls in our school.*)

morning: ṣubuḥ (haṣṣubuḥ maa šiftak. *I didn't see you this morning.*); **during the morning:** biṣṣubuḥ; **tomorrow morning:** baačir iṣṣubuḥ

moslem: muslim, –iin; **non-moslem:** gayr muslim

mosque: jaami9 (jawaami9)

Mosul: ilmooṣul (f) (ilmooṣul hiiya madiina fii šimaal-il9iraaḳ. *Mosul is a city in the north of Iraq.*)

mother: ?umm (?umahaat)

mountain: jabal (jibaal) (hiimaalaaya hiiya ?a9la jibaal bil9aalam. *The Himalayas are the highest mountains in the world.*)

mouth: ḥaalig (?iftaḥ ḥaalgak! *Open your mouth!*)

move (something): ḥawwal, yiḥawwil (ḥawlaw ijjisir ?ila makaan θaanii. *They moved the bridge to another place.*)

movie (film): filim (?aflaam); **movie** (theater): siinama (f) (siinamaat)

much: hawaaya OR kaθiir (maa ?aḥibba kaθiir. *I don't like it much.*)

mud: ṭiin (wuga9 biṭṭiin. *He fell in the mud.*)

muezzin: mu?aδδin

mutton: laḥam-xurfaan

nail: bismaar (bisaamiir) (jiiblii bismaar ?abuu-θilaaθ-?injaat. *Bring me a three inch nail.*)

name: ?isim (?asaamii) (šismak? *What is your name?*)

name OR **call** (someone): (sammaw ilwalad šaakir. *They named the boy Shakir.*)

narrow: ḍaayiḳ, ḍaayḳa (hannahar ḍaayiḳ. *This river is narrow.*)

near: ḳariib (minn), ḳariiba, –iin (yiskin ḳariib minn hinaa. *He lives near here.*); **nearer** (than): ?aḳrab (minn)

necessary: laazim (haaδa muu laazim. *This isn't necessary.*)

need: ḥitaaj, yiḥtaaj (maa ?aḥtaaj siiyaara. *I don't need an automobile.*)

needle: ?ubra (f) (jiiblii ?ubra wuxayṭ! *Bring me a needle and thread!*)

neither . . . nor: laa . . . wulaa (laa ?ana wulaa ?inta minn ilbaṣra. *Neither you nor I am from Basra.*)

nephew: ?ibin-?axuuya OR ?ibin-?uxtii

nervous, exciteable: ḥaayiz, ḥaayza, –iin

new: jadiid, –a (haaδa jadiid ?ilii. *This is new to me.*)

newspaper: jariida (f) (jaraayid)

next: next month: šahar ijjaay OR šahar ilyijii

nice, pleasant: ḷaṭiif, –a (ḷṭaaf) (halmaḥall ḷaṭiif. *This place is nice.*); **nicer** (than): ?aḷṭaf (minn) (huuwa ?aḷṭaf minn ?axuu. *He is nicer than his brother.*)

night: nighttime: layl (maa tigdar tištugul billayl. *You can't work during the night.*); **a night:** layla (liyuul) (štigalit θilaaθ-liyuul. *I worked three nights.*); **tonight:** hallayla (šitriid nsawwii hallayla? *What shall we do tonight?*); **last night:** ilbaarḥa billayl; **tomorrow night:** baačir billayl

nine: tis9a; **nine days:** tisi9-?ayyaam; **nineteenth:** tsaaṭa9aš; **ninety:** tis9iin

no: laa OR laa?

nobody: maaḥad (maaḥad ?axaδhum. *No one took them.*)

non-: gayr; **non-moslem:** gayr muslim

noon: ḍuhur; **before noon:** gabul iḍḍuhur;

at noon: biḍḍuhur; **afternoon:** ba9ad iḍḍuhur
north: šimaal (yiskinuun bii šimaal-il9iraaḳ. *They live in the north of Iraq.*); **northern:** šimaalii
nose: xašim (taxxayt xašmii bilbaab. *I bumped my nose on the door.*)
not: (with verbs and prepositions) maa; (with adjectives and nouns) muu
notebook: daftar (difaatir)
Nouri (man's name): nuurii
November: tašriin *iθθaanii*
now: hassa; **nowadays** (hal?ayyaam) (šitsawwii hal?ayyaam? *What are you doing nowadays?*)
nurse: mumarriḍa (f)

obliged, appreciate: mamnuun, –a, –iin
o'clock: bil– (issaa9a bilxamsa. *It's five o'clock.*)
October: tašriin il?awwal
office: daayra (f) (daayraat); **our office:** daayratna; **my office:** daayirtii; ?oofiis
officer: ḍaabuṭ (ḍubbaaṭ) (waaḥid minn ?uxuutii ḍaabuṭ bijjayš. *One of my brothers is an officer in the army.*)
oil: nafuṭ (?aštugul fii šarikat-innafuṭ il?amriikaaniiya. *I work for the American oil company.*)
old (of persons): kabiir, –a (kbaar); (of things): 9atiig, –a (badiltii 9atiiga. *My suit is old.*); **older** (than) ?akbar (minn) OR ?a9tag (minn); **how old:** šgad 9umur– (šgad 9umrak? *How old are you?* 9umrii 9ašir-isniin. *I'm ten years old.*)
old, ancient: ḳadiim, –a (bagdaad hiiya balda ḳadiima. *Baghdad is an old city.*)
olives: zaytuun; **an olive:** zaytuuna (f); **olive oil:** zayt-izzaytuun
on, upon, concerning: 9ala; 9al– (with nouns); 9alay- (with pronoun endings); **concerning Baghdad:** 9ala bagdaad; **on the table:** 9almayz; **upon me:** 9alayya
one: waaḥid, wiḥda (f)
onions: buṣal; **an onion:** buṣla (f)
only: bass (?aḥčii 9arabii, bass muu kaθiir. *I speak Arabic, only not much.*)
open: fitaḥ, yiftaḥ; **open** (adjective): maftuuḥ, –a
opinion: raa?ii (raa?ya saxiif. *His opinion is stupid.*)
or: ?aw
oranges: portaḳaal; **an orange:** portaḳaala (f) (halportaḳaal ḥiluu. *These oranges are sweet.*)
order: in order to: ḥatta (laazim fluus ḥatta tištirii kull šii llitriida. *You have to have money in order to buy everything you want.*); likay (jiit lil9iraaḳ likay ?adris 9arabii. *I came to Iraq to study Arabic.*); lišaan (?ariid gurfa lišaan nafarayn. *I want a room for two people.*)
other, different: gayr (?ariid gayr halbadla. *I want another suit.*)
ours: maalna (m); maalatna (f) (halbayt muu maalna. *This house isn't ours.*)
outside: barra (huuwa waaguf barra. *He is standing outside.*)
owner: ṣaaḥib (?aṣḥaab) (ṣadiiḳii huuwa ṣaaḥib-halbayt. *My friend is the owner of this house.*)

package: paakayt; **package of cigarettes:** paakayt-jigaayir
paper: waraḳ (?awraaḳ); **a sheet of paper:** warḳa (f) (halwarḳa xafiifa. *This sheet of paper is thin.*)
park, garden: ḥadiiḳa (f) (ḥadaayiḳ)
party: ḥafla (f) (?akuu ḥafla fii baytii. *There is a party in my house.*)
pay: difa9, yidfa9 (kaan laazim ?adfa9la θilaaθ-dinaaniir. *I had to pay him three dinars.*)
pay attention: daar baala, yidiir baala (diir baalak! *Look out!*)
peace: salaam (il9iraaḳ 9aaš bissalaam waḳt-ilḥarb. *Iraq lived in peace during the war.*)
Pearl (girl's name): luuluu
pen: ḳalam-ḥibir OR ḳalam
pencil: ḳalam-rṣaaṣ OR ḳalam

people: naas (kull innaas gaa9diin biššaari9. *All the people are sitting in the street.*)
pepper: filfil
perfect, complete: tamaam (halmayz muu msawwa tamaam. *This table isn't made completely.*) (kull maa hičayt, huuwa tamaam. *Everything you said is perfectly right.*)
perhaps: yimkin OR mumkin
period (punctuation): nuḳta.
period of time: mudda (f) (štigalit mudda ṭawiila. *I worked a long time.*)
person: nafar (nafaraat) (ʔakuu makaan ʔila sitt-nafaraat fii siiyaartii. *There is room for six persons in my car.*)
person: saxuṣ (ʔašxaaṣ)
pick out: stanga, yistangii (stangii šii llitriida! *Pick out what you want!*)
picture: ṣuura (f) (ṣuwar) (ṣuurat-minn haaδa? *Whose picture is this?*)
piece: wuṣla (f) (jiiblii wuṣlat-ḥadiid! *Bring me a piece of iron.*)
pig: xanziir (xanaaziir)
place: maḥall (maḥallaat) (fii ʔay maḥall tištuġul? *What place do you work?*); makaan (makaanaat) (law ʔana bmakaanak, ʔaruuḥ. *If I were in your place, I'd go.*)
placed (adjective): maḥṭuuṭ, –a
plain: ṣaada (xaliifa daayman yišrab čaay ṣaada. *Khalifa always drinks plain tea.*)
play: li9ab, yil9ab; **player:** laa9ib, laa9ba, laa9biin; **playing** (noun): li9ib
please: ʔarjuuk (m); ʔarjuuč (f); ʔarjuukum (pl)
please (someone): 9ijab, yi9jib (baġdaad ti9ijbak? *Do you like Baghdad?*)
please: if you please: minn faḍlak, minn faḍilkum OR tfaḍḍal, tfaḍḍaluu
pleasant: ḷaṭiif, –a (ḷṭaaf)
pocket: jayb (jyuub)
poor: faḳiir, –a (fuḳra); **poor, wretched:** maskiin, –a (masaakiin); **poorer** (than): ʔafḳar (minn)
pork: laḥam-xanziir
port: minaaʔ (ilbaṣra minaaʔ muhimm bil9iraaḳ. *Basra is an important port in Iraq.*)
porter: ḥammaal (ḥammaaliin)
possible, likely: mumkin
postoffice: boosṭa OR poosṭa
potatoes: puutayta
praise be to God, thank goodness: ilḥamdillaah
pray: ṣalla, yiṣallii; **prayer:** ṣaḷaat
prayer-rug: sijjaada (sijaajiid)
press: ḍirab . . . ʔuutii, yiḍrub . . . ʔuutii (ʔiḍrub badiltii ʔuutii ! *Press my suit!*)
pretty; handsome: jamiil, –a, –iin; **prettier:** ʔajmal (minn) (hiiya ʔajmal minn ʔuxutha. *She is prettier than her sister.*)
price (sale): ḳiima (f); **her price:** ḳiimatha; **his price:** ḳiimta; (rental): ʔujra (ʔijaar) (šgad ʔujrat-halġurfa? *What is the rent for this room?*)
prison: sijin (sijuun); **prisoner:** masjuun (masaajiin)
private: xuṣuuṣii, xuṣuuṣiiya (fiiha maakuu ḥammaam xuṣuuṣii. *It doesn't have a private bath.*)
property: muluk (ʔamlaak) (halbayt mulkii. *This house is my property.*)
pull: jarr, yijirr
pulpit: mambar (manaabir)
purpose: faayda (f) (šinuu faaydat-halbinaaya? *What is the purpose of this building?*)
push: difa9, yidfa9 (maa difa9ta. *I didn't push him.*)
put, place: ḥaṭṭ, yiḥuṭṭ OR xalla, yixallii; **put** OR **placed** (adjective): maḥṭuuṭ, –a OR mxalla, mxallaaya

quarter, a fourth: rubu9
(question particle): hal
quiet: saakin, saakna (halwalad saakin wušaaṭir. *This boy is quiet and intelligent.*)

rain: maṭar OR muṭar; **it rains** (f): muṭrat, tumṭur
railroad station: maḥaṭṭa (f)
razor: muus (mwaas)
reach: naaš, yinuuš (maa ʔagdar ʔanuuš iṣṣuura. *I can't reach the picture.*)

read: ḳira, yiḳra (ʔiḳraaha ʔilii! *Read it to me!*)

ready: ḥaaḍir, ḥaaḍra (ʔana ḥaaḍir ʔaruuḥ. *I'm ready to go.*)

receive: stilam, yistilim (stilamit maktuubayn. *I received two letters.*)

receive, charge: ʔaxaδ, yaaxuδ (naaxuδ diinaarayn bilyoom. *We charge two dinars a day.*)

red: ʔaḥmar (m), ḥamra (f), ḥumur (pl)

register: sajjal, yisajjil (ʔarjuuk sajjil ʔismak! *Please register your name!*)

regret: ʔasaf (ma9a lʔasaf. *I'm sorry.*)

remain: biḳa, yibḳa (ʔibḳa hinaa! *Stay here!*); **remainder:** baaḳii (laazim nimšii baaḳii-ṭṭariiḳ. *We have to walk the rest of the way.*); **remaining** (adjective): baaḳii, baaḳiya, baaḳiyiin

remember: tδakkar, yitδakkar (maa ʔatδakkar ʔismak. *I don't remember your name.*)

rental fee: ʔujra (f) (ʔijaar); **her rental fee:** ʔujratha; **his rental fee:** ʔujurta

responsible: masʔuul, –a (huuwa lmasʔuul. *He is the one responsible.*)

restaurant: maṭ9am (maṭaa9im)

return, go back to, come back to: rija9, yirja9 (rija9it lilʔuutayl. *I returned to the hotel.*); **return** (something): rajja9, yirajji9 (huuwa maa rajja9 kitaabii. *He didn't return my book.*)

rice: timman, riss

rich: ganii, ganiiya, ganiyiin; **richer** (than): ʔagna (minn)

ride: rikab, yirkab

right: yamna (9aynii lyamna maa tooja9nii. *My right eye doesn't hurt me.*); **righthanded:** yimnaawii (ʔana yimnaawii. *I'm right-handed.*); **right side:** yamiin (baytii 9ala yamiinak. *My house is on your right.*)

ring: dagg, yidigg (ijjaras yidigg. *The bell is ringing.*) (digg ijjaras! *Ring the bell!*)

ring (finger): maḥbas (maḥaabis)

river: nahar (ʔanhur) (innahar muu waaṣi9. *The river isn't wide.*); **riverbank:** ṣoob (ilḥadiiḳa bδaak iṣṣoob. *The park is on the other bank.*)

riyal (200 fils): riiyaal (ʔaryaal)

road, way: ṭariiḳ (ṭuruḳ)

roof: ṣaṭaḥ (ṣuṭuuḥ)

room: gurfa (f) (guraf); **our room:** gurfatna; **my room:** guruftii; **room** OR **space:** makaan (maakuu makaan bissiiyaara. *There isn't room in the car.*)

rowboat: balam (blaam)

run (of machinery): miša, yimšii (saa9tii timšii zayn. *My watch runs good.*)

safe: saalim, saalma; **safer** (than): ʔaslam (minn)

Said (man's name): sa9iid

sailboat: safiina (f) (sufun)

salad: zaḷaaṭa (f)

salt: miliḥ (bil9iraaḳ maa yixalluun miliḥ bizzibid. *In Iraq, they don't put salt in the butter.*)

same: nafis (sawwii nafs-ilwaajib marra θaaniya! *Do the same assignment again!*)

Saturday: yoom issabit

say, tell: gaal, yiguul; **tell me!:** gullii, guuliilii, guuluulii!

say goodbye to: wadda9, yiwaddi9 (wadda9naaha. *We told her goodbye.*)

say hello to: sallam 9ala, yisallim 9ala (sallamit 9alayha. *I said hello to her.*)

scales (weighing): miizaan

school: madrasa (f) (madaaris)

second (adj): θaanii, θaaniya, θaaniyiin; **second** (noun): θaaniya (θawaanii) (nṭiḍarit xamis-θawaanii. *I waited five seconds.*)

see: šaaf, yišuuf

seem: bayyan, yibayyin

self: nafis (ʔana nafsii sawwayta. *I myself made it.*)

sell: baa9, yibii9 (yibii9hum raxiiṣ. *He sells them cheap.*)

send: risal, yirsil (risalnii maktuub mnilbaṣra. *He sent me a letter from Basra.*)

sentence: jumla (f) (ʔiḳra hajjumla! *Read this sentence!*)

September: ʔayluul

seven: sab9a; **seven days:** sabi9-ʔayyaam;

seventeen: sbaaṭa9aš; **seventh** (adjective): saabi9, saab9a; **seventy:** sab9iin

several: kamm OR čamm (kaan fii bagdaad kamm yoom. *He was in Baghdad several years.*)

sew: xayyaṭ, yixayyiṭ

Shakir (man's name): šaakir

shave: zayyan, yizayyin (ʔariid ʔazayyin. *I want a shave.*)

she: hiiya

sheep: xuruuf (xurfaan)

sheik: šayx (šyuux)

shine: lima9, yilma9 (siiyaartii tilma9. *My automobile is shiny.*)

ship: markab (maraakib)

shirt: ḳamiiṣ (ḳumṣaan) OR θoob (θawaab)

shoe: ḳundara (f) (ḳanaadir); **shoemaker:** kundarčii

shop: dukkaan (dikaakiin)

short: ḳaṣiir, –a (ḳṣaar); **shorter** (than): ʔaḳṣar (minn)

should have: kaan laazim (kint laazim ʔaktib. *I should have written.*)

show: raawa, yiraawii (raawiinii wayna! *Show me where he is!*)

show, represent: bayyan, yibayyin (haṣṣuura tbayyin siiyaara jadiida. *This picture shows a new automobile.*)

shut: sadd, yisidd (sidd ilbaab! *Close the door!*); **shut, closed** (adjective): masduud, –a (ilbaab masduud. *The door is closed.*)

sick: mariiḍ, –a (murḍa) (haaδa yixalliinii mariiḍ. *This makes me sick.*)

side (of the river): ṣoob

silver: fuḍḍa

simple, easy: basiiṭ, –a

since: minn (ṣaar mudda minn šiftak. *It has been a long time since I saw you.*)

sir: sayyidii

sister: ʔuxut (xawaat); **her sister:** ʔuxutha; **my sister:** ʔuxtii

sit down: gi9ad, yig9ad (ʔig9ad hinaa! *Sit here!*); **sitting** (adjective): gaa9id, gaa9da, gaa9diin

six: sitta; **six days:** sitt-ʔayyaam; **sixteenth;** ṣiṭṭa9aš; **sixth** (adjective): saadis, saadsa; **sixty:** sittiin

size (bigness): kubur (šgad kubra? *How big is it?*)

skin: bašara (f) (bašartak naa9ma. *Your skin is soft.*)

sleep: naam, yinaam (maa nimit kaafii. *I didn't sleep enough.*); **sleep** (noun): noom; **sleeping** (adjective): naayim, naayma, naaymiin (šifitkum naaymiin. *I saw you sleeping.*); **sleepy:** ni9saan, –a, –iin

slowly: yawaaš

small: ṣagiir, –a (ṣgaar); **smaller** (than): ʔaṣgar (minn)

smart: šaaṭir, –a OR 9aaḳil, 9aaḳla; **smarter** (than): ʔa9ḳal (minn)

smoke: daxxan, yidaxxin (ʔana maa ʔadaxxin. *I don't smoke.*); **smoke cigarettes:** širab jigaayir, yišrab jigaayir (ʔaxuuya maa yišrab jigaayir. *My brother doesn't smoke cigarettes.*)

snows: it snows: tiθlij (f)

so: halgad (ʔana halgad ti9baan, maa ʔagdar ʔaštugul. *I'm so tired, I can't work.*)

so far, yet: ba9ad (ba9adnii maa xaḷḷaṣta. *I haven't finished it yet.*)

soap: ṣaabuun; **a bar of soap:** ṣaabuuna (f)

soda: ṣooda

soft: layyin, layna (lyaan) (ittimman layyin. *The rice is soft.*); **softer** (than): ʔalyan (minn)

soldier: jundii (jinuud)

some, a certain: fadd; **some day:** fadd yoom; **a certain man:** fadd rajjaal

someone else: gayr; **someone else** (other than me): gayrii; **someone else** (other than him): gayra

son: ʔibin; **her son:** ʔibinha; **my son:** ʔibnii; **sons:** wulid OR ʔawlaad

sorry: mitʔassif, mitʔasfa, –iin (ʔana mitʔassif. *I'm sorry.*); **be sorry:** tʔassaf, yitʔassaf (tʔassafna liʔanna maa ʔija wiiyaana. *We were sorry he didn't come with us.*)

sound: saliim, –a (9inda jisim saliim. *He has a sound body.*)

soup: šoorba (f); **chicken soup:** šoorbat-dijaaj

sour: ḥaamuḍ, ḥaamḍa

south: jinuub; **southern:** jinuubii

speak: ḥika, yiḥkii; OR ḥiča, yiḥčii

special: xuṣuuṣii, xuṣuuṣiiya
speech: kalaam (ʔuuzin kalaamak! *Weigh your speech!*)
speed: ṣur9a (xaffif ṣur9at-issiiyaara! *Slow down!*)
spend: ṣiraf, yiṣraf (ṣirafit 9alayya doolaar. *You spent a dollar on me.*)
standing (adjective): waaguf, waagfa, –iin (layš ʔintum waagfiin hinaa? *Why are you standing here?*)
state: wilaaya (f)
statue: timθaal (timaaθiil)
stay: biḳa, yibḳa (biḳayt hinaak mudda ṭawiila. *I stayed there a long time.*); **staying** (adjective): saakin, saakna, –iin
stewed (adjective): mišwii (maa ʔaḥibb laḥam mišwii. *I don't like stewed meat.*)
stick: 9ooda (f)
still, yet: ba9ad (ba9adnii joo9aan. *I'm still hungry.*)
stop: wugaf, yoogaf (wugafit ʔaḥčii wiiyaaha. *I stopped and talked to her.*); **stopped** (adjective): waaguf, waagfa, –iin (issiiyaara waagfa biššaari9. *The car is stopped in the street.*)
stop, cease doing: baṭṭal, yibaṭṭil (baṭṭal mniššugul. *I stopped (from) the work.*)
stop (something): waggaf, yiwagguf (huuwa waggaf siiyaarta. *He stopped his car.*)
stranger: gariib, –a (gurba OR garbiin)
street: šaari9 (šawaari9); **Rashid Street:** šaari9-irrašiid
strong: ḳawii, ḳawiiya OR guwii, guwiiya; **stronger** (than): ʔaḳwa (minn)
student: tilmiiδ (tilaamiiδ)
study: diras, yidris
stupid: saxiif, –a, (sxaaf)
subtract: tiraḥ minn, yitraḥ minn (ʔitraḥ sitta minn 9ašra! *Subtract six from ten!*)
succeed: nija, yinja (ʔiδa tidris, tinja. *If you study, you will succeed.*)
sugar: šakar
suit: badla (f) (badlaat): **our suit:** badlatna; **my suit:** badiltii; OR ḳaaṭ (raaḥ ʔaštirii ḳaaṭ-hiduum. *I'm going to get a suit of clothing.*)
summer: ṣayf; **of the summer:** ṣayfii
sun: šams (f) (iššams kulliš ḥaarra. *The sun is very hot.*)
Sunday: yoom ilʔaḥad
have supper (evening meal): t9ašša, yit9ašša (tḥibb tit9ašša wiiyaana hallayla? *Would you like to have supper with us tonight?*)
suppose, think: ḍann, yiḍinn (ḍannayt ʔinta minn barra. *I thought you were from the country.*)
sure: mitʔakkid, mitʔakda, –iin (ʔinta mitʔakkid? *Are you sure?*); OR ʔakiid, –a ʔinta ʔakiid? *Are you sure?*)
surprise, astonish: 9ajjab, yi9ajjib
sweet: ḥiluu, ḥilwa, ḥilwiin (ilgahwa ḥilwa. *The coffee is sweet.* hiiya bint ḥilwa. *She is a sweet girl.*); **sweeter:** ʔaḥla (minn)
sweetheart: ḥabiib, ḥabiiba (ḥabiibtii maa kitbatlii maktuub. *My sweetheart didn't write me a letter.*)
swimming place: masbaḥ (masaabiḥ)

table: mayz (myuuz)
tail: δayl (δayla ṭawiil. *Its tail is long.*)
tailor: xayyaaṭ
take: ʔaxaδ, yaaxuδ; **take!:** xuδ!; **taking** (noun): ʔaxuδ (ʔaxuδ-ṣuwar mamnuu9. *Taking pictures is forbidden.*)
take (transport): wadda, yiwaddii (waddiina lilḥidaayiḳ! *Take us to the parks!*)
take back, return: rajja9, yirajji9 (maa rajja9it kitaaba. *I didn't take his book back.*)
take care of: daara, yidaarii (ilmumarriḍa tdaarii ilmariiḍ. *The nurse is caring for the sick person.*)
talk to, call: kallam, yikallim (kallima bittalafoon! *Call him on the telephone!*); **talk, carry on conversation:** tkallam, yitkallam (nitkallam kaθiir. *We talk a great deal.*)
tall: ṭawiil, –a (ṭwaal)
tasty: laδiiδ, –a (halʔakil kulliš laδiiδ. *This food is very tasty.*)
taxi: taaksii
tea: čaay
teach: 9allam, yi9allim (ṣadiiḳa 9allama

yisuug. *His friend taught him to drive.*); OR darras, yidarris (ʔadarris fii madrasa xuṣuuṣiiya. *I teach in a private school.*); **teaching** (noun): tadriis (tadriis-il9arabii muu kulliš ṣa9ib. *Teaching Arabic isn't too hard.*); **teacher:** mudarris, –a OR mu9allim, –a

tear: šagg, yišigg (laa tšigg ilwaraḳ! *Don't tear the paper!*)

tear down: fallaš, yifalliš (fallaš bayta. *He tore his house down.*)

telephone: talafoon (kallimnii bittalafoon! *Call me on the telephone!*)

tell: gaal, yiguul (minuu gaallak haaδa? *Who told you this?*)

ten: 9ašra; **ten days:** 9ašir-ʔayyaam; **tenth** (adjective): 9aašir, 9aašra

than: minn (haaδa ʔakbar minn δaak. *This is bigger than that.*)

thank: šikar, yiškur (ʔaškurak. *Thanks.* šikarnii. *He thanked me.*)

that, that one: δaaka OR δaak (m), δiič (f) (δaak irrijjaal ʔabuuya. *That man is my father.* δiič ilbint ʔuxtii. *That girl is my sister.*)

theirs: maalhum, maalathum (haššugul maalii, muu maalhum. *This work is mine, not theirs.*)

then, in that case: zayn

there: hinaak

there is, there are: ʔakuu; **there isn't, there aren't:** maakuu

there is (found): yuujad (yuujad sijaajiid bijjiwaami9. *There are prayer rugs in mosques.*)

these: haaδoolii OR haaδool OR δool; hal–

they: humma

thick: θaxiin, –a (θxaan); **thicker** (than): ʔaθxaan (minn)

thin: xafiif, –a (xfaaf) (halwaraḳ xafiif. *This paper is thin.*)

thin, slender: rafii9, –a (rfaa9) (huuwa rafii9 miθil 9ooda. *He is as thin as a stick.*); OR ḍa9iif, –a (ḍ9aaf); **thinner** (than): ʔarfa9 (minn) OR ʔaḍ9af (minn)

thin: make thin: ḍa99af, yiḍa99if (ʔariid ʔaḍa99af nafsii. *I want to reduce.*)

thing, something, anything: šii OR šay (ʔašyaaʔ); **things:** ʔašyaaʔ

think: ftikar, yiftikir (šitiftikir 9anna? *What do you think about it?*)

think, suppose: ḍann, yiḍinn

third (adjective): θaaliθ, θaalθa; **a third** (noun): θiliθ

thirteen: θilaaṭṭa9aš

thirty: θilaaθiin

this: haaδa (m), haaδii AND haay (f); hal– (m, f AND pl)

thought that: 9abaal— (ʔana 9abaalii ʔinta minn ilbaṣra. *I thought you were from Basra.*)

thousand: ʔalif (ʔaalaaf)

thread: xayṭ (ʔariid ʔubra wuxayṭ. *I need a needle and thread.*)

three: θilaaθa; **three days:** θilaaθ-ʔayyaam

Thursday: yoom ilxamiis

Tigris river: nahar-dijla

time: wakit OR waḳit (šwaḳit raaḥ nruuḥ? *At what time are we going to go?*); **period of time:** mudda (kint hinaak mudda ṭawiila. *I was there a long time.*); **a single time, once:** marra (f); **a second time, again:** marra θaaniya (maa nijahit bilmarra ʔuula, laakin nijahit bilmarra θaaniya. *I didn't succeed the first time, but I succeeded the second time.*); **what time is it?:** issaa9a bayš?

tip (money): baḳšiiš

tired: ti9baan, –a, –iin

to, for until: ʔila, ʔil–, li–

tobacco: titin

today: ilyoom OR halyoom

together: sawa (šifit ṣadiiḳii wumarta yitmaššuun sawa. *I saw my friend and his wife walking together.*)

toilets: maraaḥiiḍ

tomorrow: baačir; **tomorrow morning:** baačir iṣṣubuḥ; **tomorrow night:** baačir billayl

tonight: hallayla

too: kulliš (hiiya kulliš samiina. *She is too fat.*)

tooth: sinn (sinaan *or* sinuun) (hassinn yooja9nii. *This tooth is aching.*)

torn (adjective): mašguug, –a

towel: xaawlii (xawaalii)

train: ḳiṭaar (ʔija bilḳiṭaar. *He came by train.*)
trees: šajar; **a tree:** šajara (f)
tribe: 9ašiira (f) (9išaayir)
true: ṣaḥiiḥ, –a (ṣḥaaḥ); **truer** (than) ʔaṣaḥḥ (minn)
try: jarrab, yijarrub (jarrub itsawwii haaδa! *Try to do this!*)
Tuesday: yoom ilθilaaθaaʔ
Turk: turkii (ʔatraak); **Turkish:** turkii, turkiiya
twelve: θina9aš
twentieth (adjective): il9išriin; **twenty:** 9išriin
twice: marratayn
two: θinayn; **two of, a couple of:** –ayn (9inda ʔibnayn. *He has two sons.* ʔiidayya waṣxa. *My hands are dirty.*); **two o'clock:** biθθintayn

ugly: ḳabiiḥ, –a (ḳbaaḥ); **uglier** (than) ʔaḳbaḥ (minn)
uncle (mother's brother): xaaḷ; (father's brother): 9amm
uncover: kišaf, yikšif. (kišafit šii jadiid. *I uncovered something new.*); **uncovered** (adjective); makšuuf, –a (ruuskum makšuufa. *Your heads are bare.*)
understand: fiham, yifham OR ftiham, yiftihim
United States: ilwilaayaat ilmuttaḥida
university: jaami9a (f) (ʔaxuuya tilmiiδ fii jaami9at-Columbia. *My brother is a student at Columbia University.*)
unoccupied: faarug, faarga
until: ʔila, ʔil-, li-
up: foog; **upstairs:** foog
use: sta9mal, yista9mil (maa ʔasta9mil haaδa. *I don't use this.*)
usually: 9aadatan (9aadatan ʔašrab čaay. *I usually drink tea.*)

vegetables: xuḍra
very: kulliš
village: ḳariya
vinegar: xaḷḷ
visit: zaar, yizuur (layš maa tzuurnii? *Why don't you visit me?*)

wages: ma9aaš
wait for: nṭiḍar, yinṭiḍir (nṭiḍarnii yamm ilbaab. *He waited for me near the door.*)
waiter: boy
wake up: gi9ad, yig9ud; **wake (someone) up:** ga99ad, yiga99id (laa tga99idnii lamma tig9ud! *Don't wake me up when you wake up!*)
walk: miša, yimšii; **take a walk:** tmašša, yitmašša; **walking** (noun): mašii (ʔana ti9baan minn ilmašii. *I'm tired of walking.*); **walking** (adjective): maašii, maašiya, maašiyiin
want: raad, yiriid
war: ḥarb; **of war, military** (adjective): ḥarbii, ḥarbiiya
was, were: kaan OR čaan (kaan gaa9id yammii. *He was sitting near me.* kaanaw yimšuun lissuug. *They were walking to the market.*)
wash: gisal, yigsil (ruuḥ ʔigsil ʔiidayk! *Go wash your hands!*)
water: maay (ilmaay baarid. *The water is cold.*)
watermelon: raggii; **a watermelon:** raggiiya (f)
way: ṭariiḳ (ṭuruḳ) (bṭariiḳna šifna ṣaaḥibna. *On our way we saw our friend.*)
way, manner: šakil (ʔariidak itsawwii bihaššakil. *I want you to do it this way.*)
we: ʔiḥna OR ʔaḥna
weak: ḍa9iif, –a (ḍ9aaf); **weaker** (than): ʔaḍ9af (minn); **weakness:** ḍu9uf
wear: libas, yilbas; **wearing** (adjective): laabis, laabsa, –iin (ʔana laabis sitra. *I'm wearing a hat.*)
weather: manaax (šloon ilmanaax bamriika? *How is the weather in America?*)
Wednesday: yoom ilʔarba9aaʔ
week: ʔisbuu9 (9asaabii9) (maa šiftak halisbuu9. *I haven't seen you this week.*)
weep: bika, yibkii (ʔumma bikat lamma tirak bagdaad. *His mother wept when he left Baghdad.*)
weight: wazin (šgad waznak? *What is your weight?*)
welcome!: ʔahlan wusahlan!
west: garb (huuwa mnilgarb. *He's from the West.*); **western:** garbii, garbiiya
wet: nadii, nadiiya; **wetter** (than): ʔanda (minn)

what?: šinuu AND ši– (šinuu halbinaaya? *What is this building?*); (šitiftikir 9anha? *What do you think of it?*); **what is there?:** šakuu (šakuu 9indak? *What do you have?*)

when, while: lamma (lamma čint ṣagiir, sikanit ibbagdaad. *When I was little, I lived in Baghdad.*); **until when:** liyamta (liyamta lmaṭ9am yibḳa maftuuḥ? *How long does the restaurant stay open?*); **when?:** yamta (yamta raaḥ itruuḥ? *When are you going to go?*)

where: wayn (wayna? *Where is he?*); **wherever:** wayn maa (laazim ʔaruuḥ ʔila wayn maa yirsiluunnii. *I have to go wherever they send me.*); **where from:** minayn (minayn jiitum? *Where did you come from?*)

which?: ʔay (ʔay siiyaara triid tištirii? *Which automobile do you want to buy?*)

white: ʔabyaḍ (m), bayḍa (f), biiḍ (pl)

who?: minuu? (minuu šaafak? *Who saw you?*)

who, whom, which, what (relative): ʔillii OR llii (irrijjaal ʔillii ʔija huuwa ʔaxuuya. *The man who came is my brother.*) (issiiyaara ʔillii štiraytha hiiya miθil siiyaartii. *The car which you bought is like my car.*)

why: layš OR ʔilwayš

wide: 9ariiḍ, –a (hannahar 9ariiḍ. (*This river is wide.*)

wife: mara (f); **my uncle's wife:** marat-9ammii; **my wife:** martii OR zooja; **my wife:** zoojtii

wine: šaraab

winter: šita; **during the winter:** biššita

wire: tayl

with: wiiya OR ma9a; **with me:** wiiyaaya OR ma9aay

without: biduun: **without oil:** biduun zayt; **without me:** biduunii; **without** (before verb): biduun maa (raaḥ biduun maa šaafnii. *He went without seeing me.*)

wood: xašab OR xišab

wool: ṣuuf

work: šugul (šinuu šuglak? *What is your work?*); **work** (verb): štigal, yištugul (ʔariid ʔaštugul 9indak. *I want to work for you.*); **workman:** 9aamil (9ummaal)

world: 9aalam; **world** (adjective): 9aalamii, 9aalamiiya; **world** (as phenomenon of nature): dinya (iddinya baarda lyoom. *It's cold today.*)

worn (adjective): malbuus (halbadla čaanat malbuus gabul maa štiraytha. *This suit was worn before I bought it.*)

worry about: tamm baala, yitimm baala (ʔana tamm baalii 9indak. *I was worried about you.*) (laa ttimm baalak 9indii. *Don't worry about me!*)

worse (than): ʔadwan (minn) (huuwa ʔadwan minn ʔaxuu. *He is worse than his brother.*)

wrap, bind: laff, yiliff; **wrapped** (adjective): malfuuf, –a

write: kitab, yiktib (kitablii maktuub. *He wrote me a letter.*); **writing** (adjective): kaatib, kaatba, kaatbiin (šifta kaatib 9arabii. *I saw him writing Arabic.*); **writing** (noun) kitaaba (f) (halkitaaba ṣagiira. *This writing is small.*); **written** (adjective): maktuub, –a (halmaktuub maktuub bil9arabii. *This letter is written in Arabic.*)

wrong: gaḷṭaan, –a (ʔinta gaḷṭaan. *You're wrong.*)

year: sana (f) (siniin) (ʔariid ʔazuur libnaan sant-ijjaaya. *I want to visit Lebanon next year.*); **yearly:** sanawii (9indii taḳwiim sanawii. *I have a yearly calendar.*)

yellow: ʔaṣfar (m), ṣafra (f), ṣufur (pl)

yes: balii (familiar) na9am (polite), ʔii (familiar)

yesterday: ilbaarḥa OR imbaarḥa (f)

yet: ba9ad (ba9adnii maa šifta. *I haven't seen him yet.*)

you: ʔinta OR ʔanta (m); ʔintii (f); ʔintum (pl); **you** OR **your** (with verbs, prepositions, nouns): –ak (m), –ič (f), –kum (pl)

yours: maalak, maaltak (haaδa kitaab maalii; wayn maalak? *This book is mine; where's yours?*); **yours** (pl): maalkum, maalatkum (halifluus muu maalatkum. *This money isn't yours.*)

young (f people): ṣagiir, –a (ṣgaar)

zero: ṣifir